Modern Critical Interpretations

Modern Critical Interpretations

William Styron's
Sophie's Choice

Edited and with an introduction by
Harold Bloom
Sterling Professor of the Humanities
Yale University

CHELSEA HOUSE PUBLISHERS
Philadelphia

Printed and bound in the United States of America

10 9 8 7 6 5 4 3 2 1

∞ The paper used in this publication meets the minimum
requirements of the American National Standard for
Permanence of Paper for Printed Library Materials,
Z39.48-1984

Library of Congress Cataloging-in-Publication Data
William Styron's Sophie's choice / edited and with an introduction
by Harold Bloom.
        p. cm. — (Modern critical interpretations)
    Includes bibliographical references and index.
    ISBN 0-7910-6340-2 (alk. paper)
    1. Styron, William, 1925-   Sophie's choice. 2. World War,
1939–1945—Literature and the war. 3. Auschwitz
(Concentration camp—In literature. 4. Holocaust, Jewish
(1939–1945), in literature. I. Bloom, Harold. II. Series.

PS3569.T9 S6738 2001
813'.54—dc21   2001047546

Chelsea House Publishers
1974 Sproul Road, Suite 400
Broomall, PA 19008-0914

The Chelsea House World Wide Web address is
http://www.chelseahouse.com

Series Editor: Matt Uhler

Contributing Editor: Janyce Marson

Produced by Publisher's Services, Santa Barbara, California

Contents

Editor's Note

My Introduction judges *Sophie's Choice* to be a moral and imaginative effort too serious to be ignored, yet also too flawed to achieve permanence.

The critical essays begin with a useful note by Nancy Chinn, who identifies crucial strands in Styron's network of allusions in *Sophie's Choice*, after which Samuel Coale argues that Styron both exemplifies and transcends the limits of Southern Gothic romance.

Gavin Cologne-Brookes emphasizes Stingo as the center of *Sophie's Choice*, while Carolyn A. Durham traces the intricate references to Styron's own earlier novels.

Stingo's (and Styron's) human limitations suffer a caustic examination by William Heath, after which Elisabeth Herion-Sarafidis sees *Sophie's Choice* as the start of Styron's creative impasse, of which the monument is *Darkness Visible*, his meditation upon his own melancholies.

Michael Kreyling perceives that Styron boldly is reaching beyond his limits in confronting the Holocaust, while Richard G. Law argues that the book's narrative technique implicitly ratifies those limits.

The issue of involuntary parody is raised by Lars Ole Sauerberg, after which Rhoda Sirlin makes as strong a case for *Sophie's Choice* as possible, by focusing upon Stingo's supposed moral maturation.

Frederick N. Smith chronicles the role of both music and noise in Styron's novel, while Janet M. Stanford also addresses herself to the thematic function of music.

Styron, in conversation with Gideon Telpaz, takes issue with Elie Wiesel and defends his temerity in writing about the Holocaust.

Dawn Trouard sees Styron's descent into history as marking a turn to the Postmodern, after which Ralph Tutt concludes this volume by returning Styron to his origins in American Southern Gothic Romance.

Introduction

William Styron always seems to me an anomaly among the American novelists of his generation. His ambitious novels—*Lie Down in Darkness, Set This House on Fire, Confessions of Nat Turner,* and *Sophie's Choice*—are too serious, intelligent, and artful to be judged failures, and yet too weighed down by the sorrows of history, or the burdens of Styron's own consciousness, to sustain themselves as autonomous works of permanent eminence. The exception is a remarkable short novel, *The Long March,* that has carried me through a number of rereadings. Of Styron's gifts, there is little question: he is a powerful storyteller, a considerable stylist and rhetorician, and a writer of authentic moral and intellectual courage. It puzzles me that Styron should compare so sadly to Cormac McCarthy, who has something of the same relation to Faulkner and Robert Penn Warren that Styron has. *Blood Meridian,* McCarthy's astonishing masterpiece, is an unique miracle, but I reread *Suttree, Child of God,* and *All the Pretty Horses* with direct pleasure. Rereading Styron can be a difficult experience, because so much *materia poetica,* and so much aesthetic sensibility, seems to be voided by ambivalences set up within the novels themselves.

Sophie's Choice I find particularly difficult, because Holocaust fiction is, as everyone observes, an oxymoron. The only novel I know that partly surmounts this barrier is E. L. Doctorow's recent *City of God,* which shrewdly interweaves the German evil with a contemplation of New York City on the eve of the third millennium. Styron's vision is darker: the destructiveness, mutual and self, of Sophie and Nathan carries the shadow of the Holocaust. With his customary audacity, Styron weaves this together with the *bildungsroman* of his own aesthetic-coming-of-age as the young Stingo, a representation of the novelist as a young man that veers too frequently into self-parody.

It seems ignoble to fault Styron for reaching beyond his grasp, and yet that aspiration is what distresses me when I attempt to reread *Sophie's Choice.*

1

Distress of that sort destroys the art of reading. Styron, intent upon prompting a difficult pleasure, gives the reader an insurmountable difficulty, since Sophie, Nathan, and Stingo become less and less sympathetic as the novel proceeds. Sophie's tragedy is too large for her (or for almost anyone), Nathan's schizophrenia is too realistic to be borne, and Stingo's growing resemblance to the dreadful Thomas Wolfe is all too plausible. Styron so piles up difficulties, for himself and for his reader, that Faulkner, if summoned from the grave, would declare himself unable to write himself out of this labyrinth.

Faulkner's originality has always been Styron's misfortune, and I again invoke Cormac McCarthy as contrast. Faulkner hovers too close for McCarthy, until the breakout into the Texas-Mexico badlands in what is almost a Holocaust novel, *Blood Meridian*, where the Holocaust is of the Native Americans. In El Paso, McCarthy continues to maintain his hard-won emergence as a great shadow's last embellishment, Faulkner safely transposed to the Southwest border country. Styron, in his struggle to transcend influence, takes on historical matters that would daunt an amalgam of Faulkner, Kafka, and Tolstoy, could one exist. Nat Turner's rebellion is intractable stuff, but so is the Haitian rebellion that Alejo Carpentier depicts so superbly in *The Kingdom of This World*. Yet no one has been able to transmute the Nazi Holocaust into important narrative fiction, and perhaps no one ever will. In *Nat Turner* and even more in *Sophie's Choice*, Styron is doom-eager, intent upon greatness but breaking himself upon what William Blake called the stems of generation.

Styron's best book, except for *The Long March*, seems to me *Darkness Visible*, where an adequate stance and answering style is discovered to confront the abyss of a depressiveness epic in its proportions and intensity. A lifelong teacher, I have learned slowly and painfully that people I thought hopelessly given to self-destruction can return decades later, with something of their promise realized despite all their previous deadlocks and sorrows. *Sophie's Choice* is both Styron's greatest effort and his largest failure, but he may yet emerge into a finer phase, so ample are his resources, so fierce is his drive for literary immortality.

NANCY CHINN

Games and Tragedy: Unidentified Quotations in *William Styron's* Sophie's Choice

Playful is not a word used to describe William Styron or his youthful persona Stingo. But I remember feeling that he, Styron, not Stingo, was playing a game with me, the academic reader. He knew that I would want to know the source of all of the unidentified quotations in *Sophie's Choice*. For most of them the clues are sufficient for discovering the original source. One, however, was most difficult and the last I identified. Feeling a great sense of accomplishment at my success with the others, I began to ask colleagues, especially seventeenth and eighteenth century scholars, if they recognized this line. As academics will, many thought it was familiar but none could provide a source. I imagined that the familiarity resulted from my going over and over it. Eventually, it struck me that it might be familiar to me, less as a general reader than as a reader of Styron's work. With some excitement I went back to Styron's earlier novels and found the quotation as an epigraph to Styron's first novel, *Lie Down in Darkness*. I laughed with delight. At that moment I felt strongly that Styron had intended through this game to provide himself and me with some relief from his very serious study of evil.

The use of quotations, especially as epigraphs to a novel, is a technique that William Styron has employed throughout his career. His last novel, *Sophie's Choice*, published in 1979, contains twelve passages from fiction or poetry, including two epigraphs from Rilke's *Fourth Duino Elegy* and André

From *English Language Notes* 33, no. 3. © 1996 by the Regents of the University of Colorado.

Malraux's *Lazarus*. The range of these sources, from the Bible to *Lazarus* (published in 1974), is consistent with the scope of the literary allusions which permeate the novel. While historical passages distance the reader from the story by disrupting the narrative, the literary quotations not only are part of the fabric of the story but also suggest that the novel is as much about Stingo as it is about Sophie. Of the five unidentified quotations, only one concerns death; all five are references to Stingo's lack of experience and clearly show the necessity of experience to a writer. With experience, the older Stingo is able to tell both Sophie's story and his own, stories which become inextricable in the telling.

Inexperience concerns Stingo throughout the novel and is crucial to the first unidentified quotation that appears within the narrative. Dismissed from his position as junior editor, Stingo is saying farewell to a senior editor at McGraw Hill, Farrell, with whom he has had a good working relationship. Farrell tells Stingo about his son who, like Stingo, aspired to be a writer. The two share common experiences: both were Marines and sent their fathers letters "written with the same weird amalgam of passion, humor, despair and exquisite hope that can only be set down by very young men haunted by the imminent appearance of death." Edward Christian Farrell, twenty-two like Stingo, died at Okinawa. When Stingo arrived there later, however, he found "no enemy, no fear, no danger at all, but, through the grace of history, a wrecked yet peaceful Oriental landscape across which [he] would wander unscathed and unthreatened during the last few weeks before Hiroshima." While telling his son's story, Farrell begins weeping, and Stingo's response is influenced by his own experience, or as he says, "my lack of it—nothing ever pierced me so deeply as Farrell's brief, desolating story of his son Eddie, who seemed to me immolated on the earth of Okinawa that I might live—and write."

Styron sets this game up with a clear suggestion about the author but not the actual selection. The only hint of the source is two earlier descriptions of Farrell reading Yeats in his office, so the reader too must read Yeats to find the lines quoted. Before speaking his last words to Stingo, Farrell recites the last six lines of Yeats's "Two Songs from a Play." After disclosing the painful story of his son's death,

> Farrell's voice came from a distance, breathing a despair
> past telling:
> "Everything that man esteems
> Endures a moment or a day . . .
> The herald's cry, the soldier's tread
> Exhaust his glory and his might:
> Whatever flames upon the night

Man's own resinous heart has fed."

Then he turned to [Stingo] and said, "Son, *write your guts out.*"

In his commentary on Yeats's poems, A. Norman Jeffares states that "these lines praise man who goes on creating heroically despite the fact that all things pass away." Farrell is thinking of his son when he recites "the soldier's tread," but his final words to Stingo emphasize the message of Yeats's poem which Farrell translates into a command. In spite of the fragility of life and the fragility of the artist's creation, artists bravely continue to create. Stingo concludes this first chapter by reaffirming his desire to write and recognizing the inexperience which he calls "the large hollowness I carried within me . . . [M]y spirit had remained landlocked, unacquainted with love and all but a stranger to death."

Stingo's "landlocked" spirit and his loneliness are clearly established in the first two chapters of *Sophie's Choice*. Even when he becomes friends with Sophie and Nathan, his isolation continues. In contrast to the Yeats reference, the second unidentified quotation is easier to solve than the first because the author is clearly Thomas Wolfe and the source is logically *Look Homeward, Angel* since the young Stingo would identify with Wolfe's autobiographical Eugene Gant. While discussing Rudolph Höss, Stingo refers to Thomas Wolfe and interjects what appears to be a superfluous quotation. Höss was "[b]orn in 1900, in the same year and under the same sign as Thomas Wolfe ('Oh lost, and by the wind, grieved, Ghost . . .')." The importance of Wolfe to Stingo's development as a writer causes him to make this connection between the two men. The parenthetical quotation is an even more personal reference. This line, which appears in the opening to the first part of *Look Homeward, Angel* and is repeated or echoed throughout the novel, holds twofold significance for Stingo. First, he uses it as a lament for its author, who died at thirty-nine. Secondly, it is Stingo's own lament, for he, like Eugene Gant, is lost. Stingo has no repeated refrain to capture the innocence and loneliness of "Oh lost," but many times throughout *Sophie's Choice* he laments both when circumstances make him painfully aware of his inexperience and isolation. Both Eugene and Stingo are alone at the conclusion of their stories. At the end of *Look Homeward, Angel*, Gant "was like a man who stands upon a hill above the town he has left, yet does not say 'The town is near,' but turns his eyes upon the distant soaring ranges." At the end of *Sophie's Choice*, Stingo escapes to nature's other great comforter, the sea.

Yet two earlier attempts to escape, a bus ride to the sea and a train trip south, are not consoling. Sophie accompanies Stingo on both trips; each includes Stingo's recollection of a quotation. The first provides the source for the title of Stingo's first novel; the other is the source of the title of Styron's first novel. These quotations also link Sophie with the heroines of the two first novels. The elegy, "Requiescat" by Matthew Arnold, which Stingo cites as the source for the working title of his first novel, *Inheritance of Night*, emphasizes the similarities among Sophie; Peyton Loftis, the heroine of Styron's *Lie Down in Darkness*; and Maria Hunt, the heroine of Stingo's novel-in-progress. The night before the trip to Jones Beach, Stingo encounters Sophie, who has returned to Yetta Zimmerman's to remove the rest of her possessions from her room. She and Nathan have parted because he has accused her of infidelity and questioned the reasons for her survival in Auschwitz. Sophie agrees to spend the weekend at Yetta's before moving, and she and Stingo plan to spend Saturday at the beach. On Friday night Sophie has recounted the events of her weekend with Nathan in Connecticut during the fall after their first meeting. Having so recently relived the horrible events surrounding their suicide pact and recalling his most recent accusations and departure, Sophie denounces Nathan and transfers her anger to all Jews. Her bitter attack occurs on the way to the beach on a bus full of children from Beth Israel School for the Deaf. Sophie's tirade only increases the anxiety Stingo already feels. When they arrive at the beach, the atmosphere provides no consolation. Increasing Stingo's depression is worry about the theft of his money and his unfinished novel. Describing his anxiety, he thinks:

> My ears echoed with a delirious, inconsolable passage from the *St. Matthew Passion* which had wept out of Sophie's radio earlier that morning, and for no special reason yet in fitting antiphony I recalled some seventeenth-century lines I had read not long before: ". . . since Death must be the *Lucina* of life, and even Pagans could doubt, whether thus to live were to die. . . ."

While this line addresses Stingo's immediate angst and foreshadows Sophie's subsequent attempt to drown herself, it also provides a connection between *Sophie's Choice* and *Lie Down in Darkness*. This excerpt from Sir Thomas Browne's *Urn Burial* is also the epigraph to *Lie Down in Darkness* which provides the remainder of the sentence that Stingo quotes:

> since our longest sun sets at right descensions, and makes but winterarches, and therefore it cannot be long before we lie down in darkness, and have our light ashes; since the brother of death daily haunts us with dying mementos, and time that grows old in itself, bids us hope no long duration;—diuturnity is a dream and folly of expectation.

Urn Burial, written in response to the discovery at Old Walsingham of more than forty Roman funerary urns, concerns the problem of evil as well as death and immortality. In the essay "Permutations of Death: A Reading of *Lie Down in Darkness*," Jan B. Gordon, referring to the novel's epigraph, suggests that "Styron's novel really explores the same themes, notably the relationship between death-in-life and life-in-death in a civilization which is itself trapped between the two. . . ." Stingo's first novel, Styron's first novel, and Stingo/Styron's *Sophie's Choice* also examine these themes. Sophie Zawistowska, like Peyton Loftis and Maria Hunt, lies down in darkness.

Another unidentified quotation appears when Stingo and Sophie are on the train south and Stingo recalls their day at Jones Beach. Prior to her attempted suicide by drowning, Sophie tells Stingo about Jozef, her lover during the time she lived in Warsaw. Working for the underground, Jozef killed Poles who betrayed Jews. One of his victims was a friend of theirs, a woman who was a double agent and had been a teacher of American literature. Because Sophie mentions that this woman's expertise was in Hart Crane, Stingo thinks of the poet and "felt [himself] shiver to a gull's cry, the rhythmic wash and heave of sullen waves. *And you beside me, blessed now while sirens sing to us, stealthily weave us into day. . . .*" Sophie continues the story of Jozef, and Stingo does not cite Crane's *The Bridge* as the source of the quotation. *The Bridge* concerns a heroic quest for self renewal and a world which clarifies the difficulties of modern life. Among Crane's major symbols are "the sea . . . , the depths of the psyche, and the renewal of life through death; a woman, associated particularly with the earth and the American continent, and presented in such figures as the Virgin Mary and the legendary Indian princess Pocahontas. . . ." It is the latter with whom Crane associates the woman in his Manhattan apartment in "The Harbor Dawn," the first of five poems which compose the second section of *The Bridge* entitled "Powhatan's Daughter." In the lines which Stingo quotes, "[t]he poet retreats from the cold world . . . to his lover's embrace. . . ." Stingo wishes to escape the cold world of Sophie's experiences and is seeking a lover's embrace throughout *Sophie's Choice*. Although secretly in love with Sophie, Stingo has held no real hope that his dream would ever be fulfilled. However, only moments after Sophie completes her account of Jozef and his death, she proposes that they swim nude. Sophie runs naked into the ocean, but Stingo is unable to follow: "So much had happened so quickly that my senses were spinning and I stood rooted to the sand. The shift in mood— the grisly chronicle of Warsaw, followed in a flash by this wanton playfulness." Sophie's frolicsome behavior echoes the description of Pocahontas provided by the epigraph to "Powhatan's Daughter." This epigraph, from William Strachey's *History of Travaile into Virginia Britannica*, describes the naked princess as "a well-featured but wanton yong girle" who caused the boys to perform cartwheels which she then emulated. Stingo's feelings for Sophie are akin to those of the boys who followed Pocahontas. Though as an adult Pocahontas became a Christian, Sophie, formerly a devout Catholic, becomes like the young pagan Pocahontas.

The fulfillment of Stingo's dream of having Sophie as lover appears imminent, but a fear, resulting in a "nameless and diabolical paralysis," prevents this. The poet of "The Harbor Dawn" appears unhindered by fear, but his dream of blissful union is interrupted by the rising sun and also remains unrealized. Stingo must wait until his night with Sophie in the hotel in Washington before she becomes his lover. Nevertheless, Crane's "theme of possession and loss" follows Stingo throughout his relationship with Sophie. On the way to Virginia Stingo imagines marital bliss with Sophie on the peanut farm his father inherited. He imagines their children, but more importantly, he imagines that this union will be followed by years of success as a writer. Stingo's fantasy aligns him with Hart Crane whose experience of lust and loneliness produces a longing for "the miraculous spirit that has the power to transform the ugliness and torpor of the quotidian world and the unbearable solitude of his own experience into something whole, perfect, pure. This spirit is imagined in Crane's poetry as an elusive female figure. To possess her is to claim her gift of beauty, grace, vision, poetry." Stingo's knowledge of Crane's work, shown by his memorized lines of *The Bridge*, suggests that he found a kindred spirit in the poet. It is significant also that he remembers part of "Powhatan's Daughter" which R.W.B. Lewis finds "the very heart and center of the epic movement. . . . [It] is an astonishing achievement . . . in language and rhythms that articulate [its] shifting interior activity across an immense vista of history, myth, and the personal life." Lewis's description of "Powhatan's Daughter" could apply to *Sophie's Choice*, which employs this same kind of shifting within a combination of history, fiction, and the narrator's personal experience.

Stingo's penchant for memorization goes back to his childhood, when he learned verses from the Bible. He recites lines from an unidentified Psalm on the train returning to New York after Sophie has deserted him to return to Nathan. Stingo seeks consolation in the Bible he carries. At first determined to forget Sophie, Stingo begins a bus trip to southeast Virginia but has gone only a few miles when he decides he must follow her back to New York. He realizes that "something terrible was going to happen to her, and to Nathan, and that [his] desperate journey to Brooklyn could in no way alter the fate they had embraced." Believing that he might have prevented their deaths had he followed Sophie immediately, Stingo was "swept by anguish. To the guilt which was murdering her just as surely as her children were murdered must there now be added [his] own guilt for committing the sin of blind omission that might help seal her doom as certainly as Nathan's own hands?"

The result of Stingo's anguish is "a bizarre religious convulsion, brief in duration but intense." Stingo always carries the Bible, "a literary convenience," but believes that he is an "agnostic, emancipated enough from the shackles of belief and also brave enough to resist calling on any such questionable gaseous vertebrate as the Deity, even in times of travail and suffering." But this suffering causes him to seek and find comfort from the Scriptures. Joined by a large, benevolent black woman who produces her own Bible from a shopping bag, Stingo opens his Bible and reads the first and seventh verses of the Forty-second Psalm: "*As the hart panteth after the water brooks so panteth my soul after thee, O God. . . . Deep calleth unto deep at the noise of thy waterspouts: all thy waves and thy billows are gone over me.*" Stingo is unable to find consolation from the psalmist who "has experienced the nearness of death, and the agony of the feeling that he has been forgotten by God." Just as the water imagery in the seventh verse of the psalm suggests the destructive nature of his troubles, "[t]he whole verse implies that God is the ultimate source of his troubles, although the motive may well be punishment." The water image can also be seen as a response to the thirst suggested in the first verse and stated in the second. Stingo's relationship with Sophie has fulfilled his thirst for experience. The tragic irony is that the knowledge he has so eagerly sought has become a terrible reality. Because of Sophie, Stingo can no longer say that he is "unacquainted with love and all but a stranger to death." Immediately after reading these lines from the Forty-second Psalm, Stingo feels he must be alone and goes to the washroom where he writes in his notebook "last bulletins of a condemned man, or the ravings of one who, perishing on the earth's most remote and rotted strand, floats crazed jottings in bottles out upon the black indifferent bosom of eternity." Some of the "ravings" in his notebook will provide sources for his own writing. Sophie's death and the death of his innocence enable Stingo to become a writer.

Beginning with epigraphs from Rilke and Malraux and ending with Emily Dickinson's "Ample make this bed," Styron frames his story with selections which express the novel's central concern with death, evil, and brotherhood. Throughout the narrative, he has carefully chosen words of other writers to interweave Stingo's movement from innocence to experience with Sophie's headlong journey toward death. Choosing not to identify some of these, Styron sets up a "game of cooperative competition which occurs only within the play sphere of the text and which has as its purpose the social act of shared articulation and comprehension." At the end of the novel, the author and reader share some sense of accomplishment but not complete understanding. Stingo and Styron clearly suggest that absolute understanding is not possible, making the *attempt* to understand all the more important.

SAMUEL COALE

Styron's Disguises: A Provisional Rebel in Christian Masquerade

Many of William Styron's strengths as a writer come from those that we associate with Southern fiction. Baroque rhetoric powers his narratives; Faulkner's ghost lingers in his language. He evokes the kind of doomed, guilt-ridden landscapes we associate with the Southern vision of the world. The problem of evil haunts him at all levels—social, psychological, meta-physical—and spawns the moral quest, the search for values of his heroes amid the stark realities of pain and suffering. Manichean conflicts ravage his prose, his outlook, his characters, as if an ultimate nihilism or irrevocable Greek fate savaged the vestiges of his own Christian faith or background. Such a war-torn spirit leads to certain death, to spiritual paralysis. He stalks the "riddles of personality" like the best romancers and sets up voices of "normalcy," moderate spokesmen, as clear-eyed witnesses to extraordinary events and persons: Culver to Mannix, Peter Leverett to Cass Kinsolving, Stingo to Sophie Zawistowska and Nathan Landau. A kind of existential, finally unexorcized sense of guilt relentlessly hounds him.

Styron writes in the tradition of the Southern gothic romance, moving from revelation to revelation, surprise to surprise, pacing his fiction as a series of building climaxes, each more shattering than the preceding one. He has written in this manner from the very first, as in *Lie Down in Darkness:* "it finally occurred to me to use separate moments in time, four or five long

From *Critique: Studies in Modern Fiction* 26, no. 2 (Winter 1985). © 1985 by the Helen Dwight Reid Educational Foundation.

dramatic scenes revolving around the daughter, Peyton, at different stages in her life. The business of the progression of time seems to me one of the most difficult problems a novelist has to cope with." The secret remains "a sense of architecture—a symmetry, perhaps unobtrusive but always there, without which a novel sprawls, become a self-indulged octopus. It was a matter of form."

Styron's gothic architecture comes complete with its aura of damnation and doom, a dusky cathedral filled with omens and auguries, nightmares and demonic shadows. And at the end of labyrinthine corridors appear the inevitable horrors: Peyton's suicide, Cass's murder of Mason Flagg, Nat's murder of Margaret Whitehead, Sophie's surrendering her daughter Eva to the gas ovens of Birkenau. Sambuco, "aloof upon its precipice, remote and beautifully difficult of access," the enclosed white temple of Nat Turner's dreams, "those days" of the 1940s in *Sophie's Choice:* here are the removed, withdrawn settings for dark romances. Nathan Landau wonders, however, if such a structure for fiction could be "a worn-out tradition," and John Gardner, reviewing *Sophie's Choice*, considered the ambiguous relationship between the evil of Auschwitz and "the helpless groaning and self-flagellation of the Southern Gothic novel." The suggestion is raised by both Styron and Gardner whether or not this kind of romance has outlived its usefulness, however passionately and grippingly re-created.

The ambiguous nature of Styron's vision may serve to undermine his gothic structures. For one thing, he often relies too heavily upon psychological explanations, a kind of rational reductionism that reduces metaphysical speculations to Freudian solutions. In *Lie Down in Darkness*, Styron deals with what his character, Albert Berger, calls, "this South with its cancerous religiosity, its exhausting need to put manners before morals, to negate all ethos . . . a *husk* of culture," in the new suburban middle-class South, a world hung up on its own narcissistic corruptions. These may be the result of the Old South gone dead, but a stronger case can be made for Oedipal tensions and familial dislocations along a purely psychological grid: nostalgia and self-indulgence, however alcoholic, however wounding, seem almost disconnected from any Southern past, or for that matter any past at all.

The trouble with the elegantly rendered and moving *The Confessions of Nat Turner* is that the religious fanatic cum prophet tells his own tale. All explanations and suggestions—psychological, tragic, Christian, heroic—tend to look like mere self-justifications. Nat as both interpreter and actor may see himself moving from Old Testament vengeance to New Testament charity and contrition, but within his own psychological maneuverings and suggestions, even this broadly mythic and religious design dissolves. The tidy psychology of the case study threatens to undermine the realities of any political action, any historical commitment. Manichean conflict—black vs. white, good vs. evil, master vs. slave—produces a kind of paralysis, a deeply felt and exquisitely written blank like the smooth white sides of that dreamed windowless enclosure.

Styron once suggested "that all my work is predicated on revolt in one way or another. And of course there's something about Nat Turner that's the ultimate fulfillment of all, this. It's a strange revelation." As he once described himself, he remains a "provisional rebel": his sufferers are witnessed at a distance, Mannix's "revolt" by Culver, Cass's angst by Leverett, Sophie's choices by Stingo. It is as if he has his cake—the rebellion, the guilt—and eats it, too—the "resurrection" and increased awareness of his witnesses. If many of Styron's rebels participate in a kind of self-mutilation or self-flagellation, his witnesses experience this as well, but at a distance. As we shall see in both *Set This House on Fire* and *Sophie's Choice*—for me his most passionate and fierce romances—violence and revenge are just barely, if at all, transmuted into Christian symbols; at times, the Christian imagery seems itself "provisional," a literary laying on of uncertain hands. We get finally not tragedies but melodramas, exorcisms rendered "safe" by the remarkably unscathed witnesses.

The whole question of Styron's notion of evil remains ambiguous. In *Lie Down in Darkness* Styron writes: "Too powerful a consciousness of evil was often the result of infantile emotions. The cowardly Puritan . . . , unwilling to partake of free religious inquiry, uses the devil as a scapegoat to rid himself of the need for positive action." Evil becomes a dodge, an excuse for inaction, paralysis, as if Manichean polarities produced only stalemate, fashioned in a fierce baroque prose style. And Styron adds: "Perhaps the miseries of our century will be recalled only as the work of a race of strange and troublous children, by the wise old men in the aeons which come after us." Infantile emotions: troublous children: a hint of adolescent angst sounded in a void? Evil as howling self? Is there something to Mailer's indictment of *Set This House on Fire* as the "magnum opus of a fat spoiled rich boy who could write like an angel about landscape and like an adolescent about people"? Does gothic doom become, then, rhetorical, a literary attitude, a Faulknerian mannerism laced with a fatal Fitzgerald-like glamour, overwrought in a gothic style?

Jonathan Baumbach suggests that *Set This House on Fire* "attempts the improbable: the alchemical transformation of impotent rage into tragic experience. Styron's rage is the hell-fire heat of the idealist faced by an unredeemably corrupt world for which he as fallen man feels obsessively and hopelessly guilty." This suggests also Gardner's assessment of Styron's writing as "a piece of anguished Protestant soul-searching, an attempt to seize all the evil in the world—in his own heart first—crush it, and create a planet fit for God and man." The Manichean battles in this book reveal the passionate intensity of this alchemical urge.

The sacred and the profane, the prudish and the prurient, God and nothingness, being and nihilism, doom and nostalgia, Anglo-Saxon and Italian honesty battle it out in *Set This House on Fire*. Peter Leverett, the moderate realistic lawyer, confronts Cass Kinsolving, the guilt-ridden visionary artist. Each has been attracted and played sycophant to the "gorgeous silver fish . . . a creature so strange, so *new*" that is Mason Flagg. Flagg represents a Manichean vision in his "dual role of daytime squire and nighttime nihilist," a distinctively American Jekyll and Hyde, "able in a time of hideous surfeit, and Togetherness's lurid mist, to revolt from conventional values, to plunge into a chic vortex of sensation, dope, and fabricated sin, though all the while retaining a strong grip on his two million dollars." Is this Styron's "provisional rebel?" He celebrates the new frontier of sexual adventure as a gnostic libertine, corrupt in his faith, would and reveals "that slick, arrogant, sensual, impertinently youthful, American and vainglorious face": the spoiled, self-indulgent American child, filled with unfulfilled desire, itself desirous of further increase. He suggests Styron's America in the Fifties, "a general wasting away of quality, a kind of sleazy common prostration of the human spirit," in times "like these when men go whoring off after false gods" in a realm of "moral and spiritual anarchy." Is there any wonder that Peter Leverett's father cries out for "something ferocious and tragic, like what happened to Jericho or the cities of the plain," a promise to "bring back tragedy to the land of the Pespi-Cola?"

The Manichean vision acquires metaphysical proportions in Cass's mind. He "dreamed wild Manichean dreams, dreams that told him that God . . . was weaker even than the evil He created and allowed to reside in the soul of man." Dreams "of women with burdens, and dogs being beaten, and these somehow all seemed inextricably and mysteriously connected, and monstrously, intolerably so" haunt him, the dog beaten to death but refusing to die, "which suffered all the more because even He in His mighty belated compassion could not deliver His creatures from their living pain."

Peter Leverett suffers a recurring nightmare of a shadow beyond the window in the dark, a friend bent on betrayal and murder but for no apparent reason. It is Cass who suggests "that whosoever it is that rises in a dream with a look on his face of eternal damnation is just one's own self, wearing a mask, and that's the fact of the matter." Evil becomes the self trapped in itself, a spirit at war with itself, a narcissistic and ineradicable sense of guilt that despite Cass's explanations of exile, orphanhood, ignorance, the war, his wife's Catholicism, his own "puddle of self" at the base of his artistic nature, his Anglo-Saxon background, his terror, his Americanness, his actions toward blacks, will not be overcome. "To triumph over self is to triumph over Death," Cass declares. "It is to triumph over that beast which one's self interposes between one's soul and one's God." Between that soul and God lurks the beast of the self, the solipsistic psychological center around which Styron's metaphysical and socio-cultural explanations of Manicheism pale. At one point Cass discusses "the business about evil—what it is, where it is, whether it's a reality, or just a figment of the mind," a cancer in the body or something "to stomp on like you would a flea carrying bubonic plague." He decides that "both of these theories are as evil as the evil they are intended to destroy and cure." Evil thus remains either "the puddle of self," which Styron belabors in the book, or the mystery of endless pain that knows no justification, a cruel beating down of the human spirit that in the end, like that puddle, suggests a perpetual entrapment, an imprisonment both of mind and matter, a Manichean mystery that can know release only in the worship of a demonic God or the furtive celebration of sex and sensation.

Both Leverett and Kinsolving press on to make their personal nightmares make sense. "Passionately he tried to make the dream give up its meaning," Styron writes of Cass. He might just as well be writing about his use of the gothic romance to surrender up the significance of his own dark dreams of perpetual conflict and combat. "Each detail was as clear in his mind as something which happened only yesterday, yet when he tried to put them all together he ended up with blank ambiguous chaos." The details refuse to conjure up the overall design: we have reached a standstill, an impasse. "These various horrors and sweats you have when you're asleep add up to something," Cass maintains, "even if these horrors are masked and these sweats are symbols. What you've got to do is get behind the mask and the symbol" Kinsolving suggests Melville's Ahab who, in penetrating the mask, reduces ambiguity to palpable design and submits willfully to the Manichean fire-worshippers at his side. He becomes his own devil. Cass cannot.

Set This House on Fire cries out for tragedy to alleviate its pain. Styron instead settles for melodrama, the *deus ex machina*, the Fascist-humanist Luigi who will not allow Cass to wallow in any more of his guilt. Luigi to Cass plays the wise father to the angst-ridden American adolescent: Cass is "relieved" of his guilt.

Kinsolving and Leverett meet years later to talk in a fishing boat on the Southern river of their childhoods. If at first both seem like opposites, they in fact blend into one Southern sensibility: bewitched and entranced by Flagg, they succumb to a rampant unanchored nostalgia that swallows everything before it, an omniverous sentimentality, "the sad nostalgic glamor," the Southern mind's ravenous appetite for "a hundred gentle memories, purely summer, purely southern, which swarmed instantly through his mind, though one huge memory encompassed all." Nostalgia begets narcissism or vice-versa: intensity of feeling replaces knowledge as the keystone to aware- ness. This nostalgia is not seen as tragic, as a flight from adulthood: it survives "pure" in its sweeping intensities, its rhetorical sweep—and is the ominous flip-side of Cass's dread, of Styron's gothic plot and structure. Cata- strophe, doom, guilt, phantoms, and diabolical enchantment draw Leverett to Flagg, Cass to Flagg, Leverett to Cass, but a rampant childhood nostalgia surmounts and floods them all, feeding upon itself.

As Flannery O'Connor suggested, "When tenderness is detached from the source of tenderness, its logical outcome is terror." That nostalgic tenderness cancels spiritual stalemate. As Joyce Carol Oates suggests in reference to Norman Mailer, "he has constructed an entire body of work around a Manichean existentialism [with] a firm belief in the absolute exis- tence of Evil [and] a belief in a limited God, a God Who is a warring element in a divided universe. . . . his energetic Manichaeanism forbids a higher art. Initiation . . . brings the protagonist not to newer visions . . . but to a dead end, a full stop." Melodrama deflates tragedy and for all its passion and power leaves a world split between suffering and sentimentality, a dark design of untransmuted spiritual impotence, mesmerized by a Manichean reality but unable or unwilling to succumb to its fatal power and terrifyingly realized inevitability. Perhaps "ultimate" rebellion would insist on such a vision. "Provisional" rebellion can only disguise it in Christian images and psychological explanations. The void which surrounds Cass's tirades, that outer world which dissolves in the wake of his internal cries, may reflect only his own narcissism, suggesting that Styron is intent upon withdrawing from the very Manichean vision he's so fiercely created into a safer hollow.

The Manichean vision of *Sophie's Choice* is announced in Styron's opening quotation from André Malraux's *Lazare:* "I seek that essential region of the soul where absolute evil confronts brotherhood." Nathan is both Sophie's savior and destroyer; love battles death; Calvinist Southerners are mesmerized by New York Jews; North and South fight over virtue or the lack of it; black and white, slave and master become both victims and accomplices of one another; out of the adversity Poland has suffered comes not compas- sion and charity but sustained anti-Semitic cruelty; sex in Stingo's 1940s at the age of twenty-two breeds both liberation and guilt; Sophie "could not bear the contrast between the abstract yet immeasurable beauty of music and the almost touchable dimensions of her own aching despair"; every choice is fraught with disaster; survival itself produces the ineradicable "toxin of guilt." Poland reflects a defeated South with "her indwelling ravaged and melancholy heart," the sense of inestimable loss, a legacy of "cruelty and compassion." Opposites attract, become entangled, lead to suicide as ultimate paralysis. Steiner's "two orders of simultaneous experience are so different, so irreconcilable to any common norm of human values, their coexistence is so hideous a paradox" that they like "Gnostic speculation imply, different species of time in the same world." Evil itself becomes the banality of duty and obedience, the belief in the "absolute *expendability* of human life," the reality of Auschwitz that cannot be finally understood.

The most "common norm of human values," Styron undermines is Christianity, at the same time he uses Christian imagery, apparently without irony, to describe the scope and mythic archetypes of his material: "I mean it when I say that no chaste and famished grail-tormented Christian knight could have gazed with more slack-jawed admiration at the object of his quest that I did at my first glimpse of Sophie's bouncing behind." A good line, but the Christian quest motif sticks to the entire form of Styron's use of the gothic romance: it is supposed to lead, however disastrously, to understanding, significance in ultimately religious terms. Stingo's own "Protestant moderation" invests sex with guilt and his "residual Calvinism" sparks his imagination with visions of doom and desecration. On the train, however, with the "dark priestess" toward the end of the book, the black woman, he "went into a bizarre religious convulsion, brief in duration but intense" and reads the Bible aloud with her, not the Sermon on the Mount, but "the grand old Hebrew woe seemed more cathartic, so we went back to Job," the archetypal victim, but one of residual faith, a kind the agnostic Stingo does not share. He disguises himself as the Reverend Entwistle to get a room with Sophie and admits that "the Scriptures were always largely a literary convenience, supplying me with allusions and tag lines for the characters in my novel," but what are we to make of Stingo's impression of Dr. Jemand von Niemand, the man who forces on Sophie her most chilling choice? He must have done so, Stingo speculates, because he thirsted for faith, and to restore God he first must commit a great sin: "All of his depravity had been enacted in a vacuum of sinless and businesslike godlessness, while his soul thirsted for beatitude." The great sin will shadow forth a greater faith "to restore his belief in God."

At the conclusion of the book, Stingo reads lines from Dickinson at the graves of Sophie and Nathan: "Ample make this bed. / Make this bed with awe; / In it wait till judgment break / Excellent and fair." After a night on the beach of Poesque dreams, being buried alive and awaking to find himself buried in sand like "a living cadaver being prepared for burial in the sands of Egypt," he welcomes the morning, blesses "my resurrection," and explains: "This was not judgment day—only morning. Morning: excellent and fair." The ironies are apparent, but so is the stab at symbolic resurrection, waking from the gothic nightmare, returned to the land of the living. It is as if Stingo/Styron wants it both ways again, provisionally damned, provisionally saved. Auschwitz disregarded "Christian constraint"; Stingo will not, despite the revelations of Sophie. He clings to his genteel moderation despite the "Sophiemania" that engulfs him and "laid siege to my imagination."

Gothic romance usually demands the waking from the nightmare, a return to normalcy after the exorcism. But Stingo, like Peter Leverett and Cass Kinsolving before him, will not surrender to being exorcized; he clings to the very fallacious and out-moded Christian doctrines the narrative of the romance undermines. Perhaps the gothic romance cannot embrace absolute evil; the term itself curdles the narrator's will to embrace it. Others will die; they will survive because of the very harried faith they have been "taught" during the romance to outgrow. Stingo's attraction to a certain morbidity is not the same thing as being "called the 'tragic sense'." It is too guarded, too self-protected, too distanced from the real Manichean vision of things by splendid baroque rhetoric and vocabularies of doom and dark auguries. He loves the doom as he loves a nostalgic South; it is a feeling in his bones, shiveringly enjoyable, a *frisson* of the spirit. Within that emotional solipsism, absolute evil proves sheerest poppycock.

Yet *Sophie's Choice* works with its escalating confessions, its ominous rhetoric, its sheer dramatic scope and power, as we learn of the real nature of Sophie's father, the many lovers from the murderer Jozef to the lesbian Wanda, the incredible choice of surrendering her daughter to the ovens. Stingo's climax literally occurs in bed—at last—with the pale, radiant Sophie; hers occurs with her suicide pact with Nathan: sex and death, twin dark towers of Manichean castles: semen and cyanide brutally intermingled. "Everyone's a victim. The Jews are also the victims of victims, that's the main difference." There is the frightening core of *Sophie's Choice*, evaded or at least displaced by Stingo's awakening from premature burial to the possibility of morning and of resurrection. Sophie weaves tale after tale before her "patient confessor," each until the end "a fabrication, a wretched lie, another fantasy served up to provide a frail barrier, a hopeless and crumbly line of defense between those she cared for, like myself, and her smothering guilt." But the Christian fabrications, the literary allusions, are themselves frail barriers and should crumble completely before the overwhelming presence of guilt, even as "small" in comparison to Sophie's as is Stingo's in relation to his mother's death, his native region, the money he inherited from the slave sold down river, Artiste (appropriately named). Gothic romance, aligned to Christian images of demonic nightmare, the dark night of the soul, and resurrection, itself crumbles as it did in Hawthorne's *The Marble Faun*, undone by the pit of Rome, or in Hawthorne's *The Blithedale Romance*, overwhelmed by the harsh reality of power, of masters and slaves beneath the veils. In Stingo's narrative, it does seem a "worn-out tradition."

Perhaps Styron writes at the end of Southern romance, or perhaps he has stretched the form to include a vision of the world that it cannot contain, that murky spurious mixture of Christian archetype and Manichean vision. Rational psychological explanations and Christian archetypes cannot encompass such a fierce conjuring up of guilt; they can only reduce and confine it. Styron's guilt will not be confined in any rational, religious scheme or design: it overwhelms every attempt to comprehend it, existing as some great Manichean "black hole" that can result only in ultimate withdrawal—the aescetics of suicide—or in sexual revelry—the libertinism of Mason Flagg, of Stingo's starving lust. Rhetoric, however intense and poetic, cannot transmute it into anything finally significant other than its own dark irrevocable existence, men and women entombed for life. As Rilke suggests in Styron's opening quote, "death, the whole of earth,—even before life's begun . . . this is beyond description!"

In Styron's world, we are really in Poe country. Faulkner transcended it by his genius, the depth of his complexity of vision; Flannery O'Connor surmounted it through an ultimate religious faith garbed in grotesque disguises, in the grim visages of serious clowns. Carson McCullers and Styron seem trapped within it, McCullers more certain of the Manichean shadows of her vision, setting it up as dark fable, as inevitable as death itself. Styron cautiously moves around it, hanging on to Christian images, archetypes, symbols despite the splendid proofs that they do not apply. Perhaps this is where the Southern tradition in American fiction ends, grappling with absolute evil outside its borders, serving up horrors as it would serve up childhood fantasies. Styron excels at it. His fiction drives itself toward a revelation he cannot or will not accept. All the magnificent rhetoric in the world will not gloss over the provisional nature of his vision, not mere ambiguity but at last evasion. The line between paradox and paralysis is a thin one. Styron's marvelous conjurings up of the former leads finally to the latter, and perhaps this is the absolute evil in contemporary society that haunts him the most.

GAVIN COLOGNE-BROOKES

Dialogic Worlds: Sophie's Choice

> *That, surely, is the point: to discover the*
> *relations between those done to death and*
> *those alive then, and the relations of both of*
> *us; to locate, as exactly as record and imagi-*
> *nation are able, the measure of unknowing,*
> *indifference, complicity, commission which*
> *relates the contemporary or survivor to the*
> *slain.*
>
> —George Steiner,
> *Language and Silence*

Up to *Sophie's Choice*, Styron's work had shown a steadily increasing awareness that his early discourse toward harmony, stemming partly from the
notion of an artist's separation from society, became less adequate the more
he took on political and historical concerns. He shifted from a straightforward attempt to compose aesthetic, moral, and social harmony from chaotic
events toward a position that set other aims ahead of the achievement of
harmony. His subject matter necessitated that, since it was impossible to do
justice to the historical and political issues that had come to absorb him by
refining the centripetal activity of seeking social and aesthetic harmony. In
the two novels immediately prior to *Sophie's Choice*, the imposition of

From *The Novels of William Styron: From Harmony to History.* © 1995 by Louisiana State
University Press.

harmony—the kind that Peter imposes on events or that Gray and others try to impose on Nat—is seen merely to evade answers or to perpetuate an unjust political hegemony.

The key dialogue in Styron's career, between a belief in the power of art to order and a growing commitment to examining the political and historical world, might seem to connect with Lukács' theories on the novel. Lukács, after all, praised *Set This House on Fire*, and Styron cited him in defending *The Confessions*. But Styron's concern with history and his shift to experimentation in subject more than in technique were not a return to nineteenth-century realism. Rather they assimilated, and also perhaps instigated, recent explorations into historical textuality—into what Hayden White calls the "fictions of factual representation"—and into the problematics of language.

Styron's shift away from the discourse toward harmony in making room for other priorities reaches its culmination in *Sophie's Choice*. With the Holocaust, Styron was writing about something in which it would, arguably, approach the brutish to seek aesthetic harmony. George Steiner and Theodor Adorno, writing of Holocaust-related art, have asked whether aesthetic harmony and pleasure are not a "barbaric" injustice to the victims of events that must never be papered over with meaning or used, even indirectly, in a text that is entertaining.

Although a movement toward harmony remains in *Sophie's Choice*, it is radically decentered, that is, no longer the text's central movement but only present in one dialogized discourse among others. Everything before this novel includes a movement toward harmony at some level, but Styron has with each work stepped farther back from his narrators to examine the implications of the insistence on composing voices. In juxtaposing differing world views and experiences—a common practice in Holocaust literature—he extended that pattern in *Sophie's Choice*, not only scrutinizing but openly sidelining and satirizing the artistic vision with which he began his career.

Of the world views that compete in the story itself, the most basic, because they involve the narration, are those of Stingo and the narrator. The way they compete, within what critics have often seen as a single narrative voice, bears on the overall strategy of the novel. It bears also on how we read the friendships Stingo, overseen by the narrator, has with Sophie and Nathan. These relationships are at the novel's center, but others, like the lighter misunderstandings of Stingo with Morris Fink, Leslie Lapidus, and Mary Grimball, also have a "place in this narrative."

There are also dialogues in passages where the narrator moves beyond Stingo's discourse and in effect functions as Styron. The writers of Holocaust literature with whom Styron converses include not only Steiner but Bruno

Bettelheim, Elie Wiesel, Richard L. Rubenstein, Simone Weil, and Hannah Arendt, and among those not mentioned, almost certainly Adorno, Lawrence L. Langer, and Primo Levi. Arendt clearly influenced the depiction of Höss and Dürrfeld, exemplars of the "banality of evil." Nevertheless, my focus will at the very start be on Langer and Steiner. At the end, I will look again, and more closely, at Steiner, as well as at Rubenstein. All three seem to inform the novel's structure.

Styron also enters into dialogue with his earlier work. His mention of Jewish writers has the purpose of making his novel explicitly—rather than implicitly, like *The Confessions*—a dialogue between his "particularized" or "distorted" Wasp views and the views of those closer to events. The novel is clearly in dialogue with the criticism of Styron's earlier work. What seemed weaknesses to the critics are rectified. Peter and Cass give way to a more dynamic dialogue between Stingo and Sophie, and Mason to the more engaging, intelligent Nathan. In contrast to the direct narration of *The Confessions*, both the narrative and the external voices in *Sophie's Choice* create layers between the narrator and the historical events. The memories are filtered through Sophie's unreliable voice, in newly learned English, then through Stingo, and again through the narrator's recall; they fade further through the dialogues the narrator has with other writers on the Holocaust.

What most distinguishes *Sophie's Choice* from the work by Styron preceding it is a schizophrenic theme in which not just words and views clash but also worlds. That sort of theme typifies other Holocaust writing as well, not least Steiner's *Language and Silence* and Langer's *The Holocaust and the Literary Imagination*. Steiner is quoted in the novel, but Styron also let the schizophrenic theme influence the novel's form. In that he was responsive to Langer's study, a copy of which stands, like *Language and Silence*, on his bookshelves in Roxbury.

Langer deals with both the question of aesthetic harmony and the existence of a sense of dislocation in the "literature of atrocity." Attending most to the writings of those with firsthand experience of the events, he sees as one of their chief concerns the portrayal of disparate worlds. In his preface, he describes his book's genesis in three personal moments of dislocation: his seeing, in 1964, "Polish children playing beneath bright sunshine" only yards from the gates of Auschwitz; his recognizing his inability, at the trial of Himmler's adjutant, Karl Wolff, "to connect the appearance of the man with the war crimes he was accused of"; and his feeling "that uncanny sense of discontinuity, of a fact inaccessible to the imagination in any coherent or familiar form," when he stood before a pastoral painting entitled *Dachau*.

Langer's interest is in "disjunction." The moments of dislocation he underwent make him wonder if the "literary intelligence" can "ever devise" forms "adequate to convey what the concentration camp experience implied for the contemporary now." As he sees it, the problem is how the disparate worlds of everyday life and of the Holocaust can be portrayed together in art. If "the existence of Dachau and Auschwitz as historical phenomena has altered not only our conception of reality, but its very nature," Langer believes that "the challenge to the literary imagination is to find a way of making this fundamental truth accessible to the mind and emotions of the reader." Looking at Paul Celan's poem "Fugue of Death," Jerzy Kozinski's *The Painted Bird*, and Wiesel's *Night*, he argues that the authors try to dislocate the reader, to ensure an initial reaction of discomfort rather than of aesthetic pleasure, before attempting a reorientation toward a perspective more appropriate to a post-Holocaust world.

In *Sophie's Choice*, Styron is, overtly and not, in dialogue with other accounts of Auschwitz and with Langer's view of the kind of art necessary for representing the world after the Holocaust. In one sense, the novel adheres to Langer's view that the need is to place disparate worlds in a single, disjunctive frame. The direct references to schizophrenia, leading up to the news that Nathan is a "paranoid schizophrenic," are part of this. Styron himself has called the novel a "split book." Sophie has a "schizoid conscience"; Dürrfeld—echoing Hannah Arendt on self-pity—says that the Jewish problem gives them "all schizophrenia, especially me"; and Poland is "soul-split." But in another sense, *Sophie's Choice* departs from the course Langer identifies. It begins not by dislocating the reader but by soothing the reader with the humorous preamble of a young man's angst, then unleashes the disturbing events at its core. Yet the opening chapters are set with traps, mines of minutiae, to catch the reader lulled by its casual air and encourage a reevaluation of Stingo's attitude once the details are set against the context of Auschwitz and the novel's pivotal events.

The challenge of finding artistic means adequate to yoking the disjunction is recognized by several Holocaust commentators, and the goal is put most succinctly by Steiner in the present chapter's epigraph. Styron quotes Steiner, who muses that when some were being killed at Treblinka, most, near or far, were getting on with everyday life. Steiner reflects, "The two orders of simultaneous experience are so different, so irreconcilable to any common norm of human values, their coexistence is so hideous a paradox— Treblinka *is* both because some men have built it and almost all other men let it be—that I puzzle over time. Are there, as science fiction and Gnostic speculation imply, different species of time in the same world, 'good time' and enveloping folds of inhuman time, in which men fall into the slow hands of the living damnation?" Steiner differs from Langer on the proper reaction to the disjunction. He suggests either silence or else an attempt to write about it, because "the next best thing is to try to understand." Rejecting silence, Styron begins by portraying a familiar world, and he seeks, in line and perhaps in response to Steiner, to connect Stingo's world view with the other reality, of Auschwitz—precisely to discover, in Steiner's words, the "relations between those done to death and those alive then." He strives "to locate, as exactly as record and imagination are able, the measure of unknowing, indifference, complicity, commission which relates the contemporary or survivor to the slain." But spurning the idea that the worlds are separate, Styron seeks to bare the conjunctive in the seemingly disjunctive—to indicate, in a recurrent image of the novel's, the sediment of evil inherent in everyday life.

This objective of displaying how the Holocaust connects with the rest of human behavior is evident throughout *Sophie's Choice*. Nathan observes that hydrogen cyanide exists in "Mother Nature in smothering abundance in the form of glycosides," which are found in pears, almonds, and peach pits. Here Styron has a metaphor for the evil he sees "at the *core*" of Stingo and Sophie. The novel perceives the best in life—"fellowship, familiarity, sweet times among friends"—to be in intimacy with the worst, the "bitter bottom of things." In the apparent conflict of existences—Steiner's "good time" and "inhuman time"—the commonality between them is at the cusp of the novel's attempt to grasp the "appalling enigma of human existence."

The novel's epigraphs fit Styron's theme. Rilke's reference to a child's death as something left in the "round mouth, like the choking core of a sweet apple," sets evil, like cyanide in fruit, at the core of life and relates as well, perhaps, to little Eva's death—the worst moment of evil, at the novel's core. Höss's daughter, Emmi, also springs to mind, since Sophie sees her as a "fetus, yet fully grown," caught in the midst of absolute evil, in Rilke's phrase, "even before life's begun." In another epigraph, Malraux' reference to a search for "that essential region of the soul where absolute evil confronts brotherhood" captures Styron's idea of the proximity of the best and worst in mankind. Far from Auschwitz' being a separate world, *Sophie's Choice* suggests that the evil that allowed it is embedded in seemingly diverse but familiar realities, much as Styron's theme is embedded in the novel like a "choking core."

In tying Stingo's story to Sophie's, the novel follows Steiner's suggestion of seeking connections between seemingly disparate worlds rather than that of Langer, according to which the expression of dislocation is the goal. Stingo's discomfort at the start is in the course of the narrative made to stand against experiences that shed ironic light on his "suffering." His angst appears embarrassingly self-centered and trivial alongside the story Sophie tells him, but also connected to it. A somber disjunction thus succeeds the entertaining opening, as we realize that what we laugh at or identify with in Stingo is inseparable from the horrors that become the novel's focus.

But because the novel does not take the disjunction as final, a discourse toward harmony of a sort is still evident, if decentered. Although the novel at first seems to reverse the movement toward harmony in Styron's previous novels, which began by dramatizing discord and conflict, discord exists early on here too, at least for Stingo. It is he who is confused and unhappy in the opening pages, sweating with literary and sexual frustration as his ceiling vibrates from the unbridled coupling of Sophie and Nathan. The narrator, it turns out, also has an urge to connect—if not to reconcile—certain voices, but that arises from the later juxtaposition of Stingo's anxieties with the world of Auschwitz. Stingo's movement toward harmony is decentered by the double-voiced narration, in which the narrator constantly, often openly, contests the viewpoint of his younger self.

On one level, *Sophie's Choice* is about Stingo in 1947, his meeting with Sophie and Nathan and his attempts to write, get laid, and harmonize his world in light of his frustrations and conflicting interests. He is a central character struggling to make sense of the voices that compete around him, voices that include not only Sophie's and Nathan's but his father's (a voice, as Michael Kreyling suggests, from an older, stabler world, ever less available to Stingo), Leslie's and Mary Alice's (voices that, as Kreyling also observes, present a gross parody of the novel's language trope), Dr. Blackstock's (the voice of almost the "happiest man on earth" until his wife dies in a car crash, illustrating the caprice of the world), and Morris Fink's (the voice of the worst specimen of ignorance ["What's Owswitch?"] in all the unknowing, indifference, and complicity portrayed). But taking Stingo as central leads some critics, like Joan Smith and Georgiana M. M. Colville, to refer, misleadingly, to "Stingo the narrator." The unnamed narrator explicitly states that he is not Stingo, in name or nature. Stingo, he says, "evaporat[ed] like a wan ghost" as the narrator aged, although Stingo he "still was" in the summer of 1947. He thus lays stress on the gap that time has created between his present and former view of events, and varies his diction according to the viewpoint he adopts. Still, however remotely connected with his former self, the narrator tells the story because his past self—the "insufferable" Stingo—is, like the narrator's past self in Malraux' *Lazarus*, a moral "encumbrance." The cleavage between Stingo and the narrator is vital, for the trials of "suffering Stingo" are told precisely because they are incommensurable with the real pain at the novel's core.

If it is misleading to describe Stingo as the narrator, it also obscures matters to say, without qualification, that the narrator is Styron. Certainly we are encouraged to draw analogies between Styron's life and what we come to learn of Stingo and the narrator, but *Sophie's Choice* is not just an autobiographical novel. Stingo's predicaments and dubious behavior are described in the service of the novel's aims and are not, as Smith believes, simply Styron's therapeutic attempt to "excuse" himself for what he did in the fairly distant past. Among the other offices they serve in the novel, they depict by analogy the distance between Styron's earlier and later notions of art. The sleight of hand that makes the novel seem autobiography—a magic that appears to have worked too well—connects the disparate worlds of postwar America and Auschwitz, and gives a sense of immediacy to the novel as a meeting place for voices that did not meet but might have.

Like Styron's earlier novels, *Sophie's Choice* begins with scenes of discord and conflict. But by satirizing Stingo and his brand of suffering, it decenters the discourse toward harmony. In the opening sections, the narrator depicts Stingo—similarly to Culver, Peter, and Nat—in frustration and turmoil. Lonely, bored at work, then uneasy with freedom, he yearns for direction and encouragement. His untethered state is worsened by youthful mood swings; one moment he has the "faith of a child in the beauty" he feels "destined to bring forth," the next his future is "misty" and "obscure." The emphasis in this comically turbulent opening is on language and voices. Stingo, retreating into his "cubicle," assuages his loneliness by reading widely and plunging into "make believe," and he vents his frustrations on the unsolicited manuscripts that threaten to bury him. At first he is described as a "political neuter," so oblivious is he of anything outside his immediate sphere of literature, southern history, and sex. His views on art keep political involvement at bay and validate a retreat from a menacing world. But what he will learn is that he has a responsibility to harness his yearnings to positive action and to act on his impulses, sexual and literary, not in isolation but in the context of society, of others, and of history.

Stingo's move to a "place as strange as Brooklyn" adds to his turmoil. New voices invade his world, tumbling into his mind and lodgings. Through the summer he is beset not only by his father's advice, the words of the writers he would emulate, and the voices of his novel but by Nathan's insults, Sophie's confessions, and the lingual nonsense of Leslie Lapidus. He must sort out a din of competing interests and perspectives to find his own position in the world as a person and a writer. The experiences and opinions that Sophie and Nathan soon confront him with are at first like the "indistinct" sounds of their arguments through his ceiling: "voices rising in rage, uttering words" he is "only just able to comprehend." But soon they invade his baby pink room, shattering his apathetic, largely southern, and literary outlook.

At the heart of his story is the impact of Sophie and Nathan on his world view. He feels that something is "inexplicably wrong" in Yetta's house, but this has as much to do with his own standpoint as with Sophie and Nathan. His acquaintance with them will lead him to question his assumptions about life and the literary career he is set on. Closeted in his little room trying to create art, supposedly immured in his private space, he finds himself beset by a confusion of voices, noises, and moods that threaten to bring his ceiling down. His purist view of art is brought to curb by the events he becomes involved in.

The narrator's subject is not merely Stingo and Sophie but the connections between their lives, and between Brooklyn and Auschwitz. The distinction between the narrator and Stingo contributes a salutary schizophrenic dimension to a text that amasses a series of temporal, vocal, and spatial dislocations into a seemingly unbridgeable chasm between what Stingo and Sophie know. With irony, the narrator comments implicitly and explicitly on Stingo's reactions, raising questions about Stingo's voice through ironic juxtaposition and direct comment.

In Chapter 1, Stingo's and the narrator's voices—and their views about the world and language—mingle humorously. The narrator tells of Stingo's attitude to manuscript reading:

> But at my age, with a snootful of English Lit. that made me as savagely demanding as Matthew Arnold in my insistence that the written word exemplify only the highest seriousness and truth, I treated these forlorn offspring of a thousand strangers' lonely and fragile desire with the magisterial, abstract loathing of an ape plucking vermin from his pelt. I was adamant, cutting, remorseless, insufferable. High in my glassed-in cubbyhole on the twentieth floor of the McGraw-Hill Building—an architecturally impressive but spiritually enervating green tower on West Forty-second street—I levelled the scorn that could only be mustered by one who had just finished reading *Seven Types of Ambiguity* upon these sad outpourings piled high on my desk, all of them so freighted with hope and clubfooted syntax.

Stingo's voice here is put in its place by the ventriloquizing narrator. What Stingo considers his "savagely demanding" requirement that "the written word exemplify only the highest seriousness" is traced by the narrator to a "snootful of English Lit.," a flimsy basis for a sense of superiority. By falling in with Stingo's collegiate shorthand—"English Lit."—the narrator underlines the formulaic superficiality of Stingo's mind-set. He obliquely conveys his reaction to Stingo's viewpoint through details like the "spiritually ener-vating" tower, where Stingo has his "glassed-in cubbyhole." The tower bespeaks Stingo's ivory-tower mentality, which, if "architecturally impres-sive," offers little more than surface gloss. The diction is often Stingo's, but the details enable the narrator to undermine Stingo's position through ironic imagery.

Among the details is an indication of the kind of pure literary criticism Stingo has been exposed to, William Empson's *Seven Types of Ambiguity* being a classic of the New Criticism taught him in college. A conflict of viewpoints is evident here. For Stingo, Empson's text is a legitimate authority on which to base literary judgment. But for the narrator the text ironically reinforces the impression not only of Stingo's purist attitude toward art but of his limited receptivity to other things, for the disdain in which he holds unpub-lished work of others is inseparable from his later failure of sensitivity toward Sophie. As larded with humor as the conflict is, the passage prompts a wari-ness about Stingo's insight and dictum. When, later, the narrator refers to the "lyrical, muscular copy" that got Stingo his publishing job, he mimics the language Stingo might have used, turning it back on him. A few pages later, the narrator calls it a "snotty, freewheeling style."

Gradually the divergence between viewpoints comes to touch more serious subjects. When Stingo lectures Nathan, the narrator again, with little but telling comment, lets him betray himself. The topic this time, however, is racism, and it relates to Stingo's area of specialty, southern history.

> "You seem to have no sense of history at all," I went on rapidly, my voice scaling up an octave, "none at all! Could it be because you Jews, having so recently arrived here and living mostly in big Northern cities, are really *purblind*, and just have no interest in or awareness or any kind of comprehension whatever of the tragic concatenation of events that have produced the racial madness down there? You've read Faulkner, Nathan, and you still have this assy and intolerable attitude of superiority toward the place, and are unable to see how Bilbo is less a villain than a wretched offshoot of the whole benighted system?" I paused, drew a breath and said, "I pity your blindness."

The narrator allows Stingo to hang himself in his own linguistic noose. In defending his precious South, he slips into stereotypes of Jews as bad as Nathan's of the South—imagining all Jews to be recent-immigrant city dwellers without any sense of the "tragic concatenation of events" in southern history. He has the insensitivity to expect them to recognize

Governor Bilbo—and by extension, Eichmann, Höss, and their ilk—less as evil than as merely "wretched" by-products of the systems of which they are a part. Stingo's parochialism enables him to see southern history as both central and pardonable. It is not that his ideas are invalid—in another context, like the "college dissertation" rattling through his head, they might be defensible—but that his anger betrays the kind of shortcomings and hypocrisy of which he accuses Nathan.

Stingo, moreover, confuses high language with high sentiments; his pretentious diction is out of proportion with his childish indignation over Nathan's slighting of the South. Frederick R. Karl finds Stingo's use of the word *purblind* unlikely and so a narrative lapse, but his use of such a word is vivid testimony that he has the practical equipment to write—the verbal dexterity—but lacks the experience and judgment to put it to good use. His rhetoric is by turn collegiate, abstract, and clichéd. His indignation reveals his immaturity just when he most feels he must impress. Instead of scorching Nathan with words like *concatenation* and *purblind* and shibboleths of sophistication like *racial madness* and *benighted system*, he wins only scorn—at the same time that he gauchely bumps into Faulknerian discourse. Having arrived in New York with an *American Collegiate Dictionary* among his few books, he is unwittingly constricted by it. His phrases are lifted from the senior-year papers he has only recently completed, and they compete—as in "assy and intolerable attitude"—with the slang of the college quadrangle. The narrator squeezes a last drop of irony out of Stingo's closing retort: "I pity your blindness." Accusing Nathan of "having no sense of history," Stingo, in his ivory tower, is the one who must learn to see himself, and his southern heritage, in its historic context.

Stingo displays some historical knowledge, but that is restricted to the South and is of a subjectively apologist complexion. "Outside of 'creative writing' . . . the history of the American South" was his "only serious academic concern" in college. Until he meets Sophie and Nathan, he does not venture beyond the narrow domain immediately concerning him. As the narrator says, "I had traveled great distances for one so young, but my spirit had remained landlocked." Meeting Sophie, he discovers a far wider universe. With time and experience, this will let him see that, whether as victim or accomplice, he, like Sophie, is vulnerable to being caught up in political phenomena that, in the way of Auschwitz, seem "too abstract, too *foreign* . . . to register fully on the mind." At this stage his historical sense is one of nationalism, which Steiner calls the "venom of our age." Styron's humorous irony is, on another level, deadly serious, since Stingo manifests symptoms of the kind of bigotry and intolerance figuring in the historical context of the Holocaust. Because Styron seeks to understand, in Steiner's words, the "relations between those done to death and those alive then," revealing the proximity between Stingo's callowness and a disastrous bigotry is a major purpose of the meandering, humorous opening.

What is also apparent in these early stages is Stingo's conception of the role of art. Though the subject has switched from literature to politics and history, Stingo's field of reference, and even his diction, remain largely literary. Typically, he refers to a southern novelist, Faulkner, whom he lauds, in modernist fashion, as almost a redeemer of the region's culture. He is incredulous that someone could read Faulkner and still have an "intolerable attitude of superiority toward the place," as if art could by itself redeem its shortcomings. But Stingo's modernist faith in art as a way to order reality is dialogized as the narrator continually points out the distance between himself and Stingo. He has an irreverent cockroach wander across the page of Stingo's copy of Donne's poetry, and he offers explicit commentary on excerpts from Stingo's journal. In describing Stingo's evaluation of manu-scripts, the narrator calls him a "supercilious young man." All this is the broad counterpart of a much subtler dialogue. Stingo's determination to have language exemplify the "highest seriousness and truth" is set against the narrator's concern with a world in which the Nazis have cast doubt on the possibility of allying language with any seriousness and truth. Stingo's later agonizing over whether to live in the South is about more than finding the most agreeable setting in which to live and write; it is in dialogue with the narrator's cares.

It is clear that the narrator—and of course Styron—have very different concerns from their younger self. But, like Stingo, the narrator is seeking meanings in the young man's experiences, while, in a broader frame, also seeking connections between Brooklyn and Auschwitz. He is sorting out the aspects of Stingo's mentality that are "worth preserving." He finds "vivid and valuable" the journal passages relating to "thwarted manhood," such as those dealing with Stingo's "black despair" over Leslie and Mary Alice. "So much of the rest," he says, consisted "of callow musings, pseudo-gnomic preten-tiousness," and "silly excursions into philosophical seminars" that he consigned them years ago to a "backyard auto-da-fé" in a symbolic act of purgation that is correlative with the novel itself. The "valuable" aspects of Stingo's voice, the narrator suggests, relate to "passions" rather than opin-ions. Stingo's feelings have value because they are genuine. His ideas and arguments, in contrast, are borrowed, and so, to use Sophie's phrase, "unearned."

What, finally, the narrator finds "worth preserving" unsatirized are three sentences, "wrung like vital juices," that offer some connection between the younger and older man. "Artless as they now seem," they at least suggest the values he retains. However gauchely, they attest to the emotions Stingo has endured. *"Let your love flow over all things"* affirms the truism of "love," which Stingo must redefine. The three lines of poetry "'Neath cold sand I dreamed of death/but awoke at dawn to see/in glory, the bright, the morning star," which he must reevaluate, affirm art. *"Someday I will understand Auschwitz,"* although naïvely stated, affirms the beginning of historical awareness and signals the direction the narrator's career will eventually take.

Nostalgic though the narrator is about his days of "first novelhood," he is also examining Stingo's behavior. He is not merely, as Crane puts it, "criticizing, and even humiliating," Stingo but striving to understand his young self—to trace the path by which the intolerant, often intolerable, Stingo matured. The search for connections between the two conflicting voices in the apparently unitary narrative also marks a link between the narrator and Sophie, since, in a far more marked way, she too finds her past self an encumbrance.

Awareness of the double-voiced narration is vital to comprehending Stingo's relationship with Sophie and Nathan. Several critics have attacked the portrayal of Sophie after missing the distinction between voices. Colville calls the novel "one of the worst male chauvinist novels 'ever penned by man or beast'" because of the way "Stingo, the male narrator," treats Sophie. William Heath complains about the "problem of egotism" precisely because he sees no distinction. Judith Ruderman argues that Sophie's "sexual nature has many qualities of the postpubescent wish-fulfillment variety; Stingo's appropriately, Styron's less so," and Smith complains that Stingo's affection "manifests itself in a self-obsessed form which seems to have more to do with lust than affection." Smith conflates all three voices—Stingo's, Styron's, and the narrator's—when she says that it is hard "to read the book" without "cursing Styron/Stingo for his failure to give Sophie the help she needs; confronted with her despair and anguish, the narrator's main concern remains his now urgent sexual appetite." The failure to distinguish between voices leads to misreadings. Ruderman, right about the presence of "postpubescent" fantasy in Sophie's sexuality, is left troubled at having to ascribe such thoughts to the narrator. Smith is right about Stingo's—but not the narrator's—"self-obsessed . . . lust." Colville ends up tarring Styron with—besides leaning to voyeurism, homosexuality, and nazism—being an overgrown child.

Such criticism not only misses the gap between the narrator and Stingo but also fails to notice that the narrator, like Sophie, is involved in a confession. Heath deplores how Stingo's concerns "compete" with Sophie's story, when they should form an "understated ironic counterpoint." But in tune with Langer and Steiner, surely such disjunction is the point; the reader is meant to feel discomfort at Stingo's language against the backdrop of Auschwitz. Although Stingo's views plainly color the description of Sophie, the narrator is constantly ventriloquizing Stingo's diction and arguing with it, to emphasize Stingo's often ambivalent behavior. In retelling Sophie's confessions through Stingo, he must confess the behavior and attitudes of his younger self, Sophie's confessor, in a merging of roles that matches his concern with seemingly disparate worlds that are in fact linked.

In the triangular relationship between Stingo, Sophie, and Nathan, Stingo's world view is pointedly juxtaposed against Sophie's and against Auschwitz, and the relationship emerges through both Stingo's voice and the narrator's. Stingo's focus is on the narrow question of how, in different ways, he, Sophie, and Nathan can move toward personal and social harmony. In contrast, the narrator pays primary attention to the way Stingo's interest in Sophie leads her to recount her experiences at Auschwitz, which puts Stingo's behavior and attitudes during the Brooklyn summer in a different light. While Stingo struggles to make sense of his feelings, the narrator is making connections between the supposedly disparate worlds of Brooklyn and Auschwitz.

On one level, Stingo, Sophie, and Nathan are all striving for personal harmony. Sophie and Nathan, who are in large measure at the bottom of Stingo's distress, are themselves seeking coherence. Both their lives are fragmented. Nathan, says Larry, has "never got his mind in order," and Sophie is an "incomplete" person, struggling to come to terms with her past. The harmony the two of them at times seem to possess, like Cass's alcohol-based harmony, is a "precarious equilibrium." Nathan is on drugs, and Sophie's reclothing of "herself in self-assurance and sanity" drapes only a "thin outer layer" over inner disintegration. Her "chaotically" actuating love for Nathan and his "tormented underside" compete with whatever is positive in their intimacy. Nathan says that Sophie has taught him "about *everything*. Life!" she says that she has experienced "*rebirth*" through Nathan. He has brought her the "happiest days she had ever known," yet he is also partly her "destroyer." Unsurprisingly, then, Stingo's "elation," even at their best moments, is "mixed with apprehension." Their struggle is fundamental to the novel's bittersweet schizophrenia, and the connection between the best and worst of life.

Stingo's friendship with Sophie is dubious from the start. He befriends her for two reasons, both of which put in relief his limitations. In the first place, he, as a fledgling writer, is eager to hear about experiences he has not had himself; he has his own youthfully insensitive dose of the "ghoulish opportunism" writers are "prone to." Moreover, he thinks Sophie has a "resemblance to Maria Hunt," the girl whose suicide has given him a subject for his novel. In the second place, he wants to know her out of sexual motives. That makes him Nathan's rival as well as his friend. As, squirming "with mixed discomfort and delight," he listens to stories of her "past love life," it becomes plain that the portrayal of Sophie is filtered through the mind of a young man of "staggeringly puerile inexperience."

Here too Stingo's viewpoint is dialogized by the narrator, so that Stingo's and Sophie's differing uses of language are always conspicuous. At first, the play of voices is lighthearted. Stingo and Nathan literally have a word contest. Sophie is struck by the number of English words for the French word *vélocité*, and the two men compete with examples. Stingo, the budding writer, proves Nathan's equal, while Sophie looks on helpless. But as earlier, an amusing use of language takes on wider significance. Stingo may have a good command of English, whereas Sophie is new to it and far from adept, but because of the care she must take with her words and because of her experiences, she later shows a far greater awareness of the complexity and elusiveness of meaning. She has, after all, experienced a world where everyday language has been overturned, where a man like Höss can consign thousands a day to death but dismiss her attempt to get him "to contravene proper authority" as "disgusting." In more ways than one she knows more languages than Stingo.

We have hints of Stingo's misproportioned diction when the narrator describes the young man's view of Sophie's sexuality: "Despite past famine," he observes, "her behind was as perfectly formed as some fantastic prize-winning pear." The jarring caused by Stingo's reference to Sophie as a piece of fruit links with images elsewhere in the novel. If the epigraph from Rilke once more comes to mind, so does Nathan's observation that the seeds of evil exist at the core of everyday life. Stingo's view of Sophie as an edible object also places him uncomfortably close to the likes of Höss and Sophie's father, who both saw her as an object—an instrument for the achievement of their warped ends. Similarly, Stingo's sexual use of her continues a pattern: she has been raped twice, once at Auschwitz, by Wilhelmine—a lingual rape that, as Kreyling suggests, is appropriate to the novel's emphasis on lingual domination—and then in Brooklyn, when she is finger-raped in the subway. But she was also nearly used sexually by Höss, as she is finally used by Stingo. These last two events are hardly comparable in more specific terms, but in such parallels resides the connection between seemingly disparate worlds.

The narrator's implicit commentary on Stingo's perspective, through juxtaposition and images, shadows Stingo's entire relationship with Sophie. The jarring between the young man's diction of everyday life and the experiences she confronts him with propels the theme of disjunction. Stingo has the habit of describing minor events in high-blown language; he sees his first sexual encounter with Sophie as "cataclysmic." Unable to respond to Sophie's foreplay on their last night, he resolves "to commit suicide," and after a night spent with her, he tells her that he slept "like a corpse." Such discourse of collegiate angst becomes insensitive hyperbole in the context of Sophie's story.

Stingo's diction calls to mind the world of Auschwitz, emphasizing his naïve insensitivity, when he offers Sophie advice. On their trip south, he not only warns her that they must marry "to avoid ugly gossip" but tells her that Nathan "is *insane*" and must "be *institutionalized*." In both cases, his callow invocation of lawful institutions—his daring, even, to discuss morality and sanity—is out of bounds given the law Sophie has been subjected to, a kind that Höss dared not disobey, that governed the institution he ran. Stingo fails to make connections that are painfully obvious to Sophie and the narrator.

The narrator is ever reminding the reader that Stingo's activities are to be set against Auschwitz. Like the rotten core of the metaphorical apple, the language of atrocity is also at the center of Stingo's avowals of his determination to have his way with Leslie. In his journal, he describes how he finally manages to fondle a breast, which turns out to feel "like a soggy ball of dough beneath my hand, itself tightly imprisoned within the rim of a murderous brassiere made of wormwood and wire." The concentration-camp imagery connects his experiences with Sophie's even while the two worlds seem utterly distant.

During Stingo and Sophie's trip south, Sophie tries to coax him out of the narrow thoughtlessness his diction evinces. He is preoccupied by thoughts of home and marriage, unaware of the reverberations that the word *home* has for Sophie. She does not go along with his plans passively. "Where are we truly going? What home?" she asks. By "home," Stingo means not merely the peanut farm his father has offered him but an idealized vision of his youth that he would like to return to—a comfortable, enclosed life away from modernity but "with all the modern American conveniences." Quizzed by Sophie, Stingo begins to see that his vision is illusory, although he still does not understand that "home" might remind Sophie of her past—her father, her children—or that marriage might remind her of her just aborted engagement to Nathan.

Sophie asks Stingo to spell out his notion of their future, again turning his own words back on him: "'Once we get settled'? What's going to happen then? How do you mean 'get settled,' Stingo dear?" Previously, Sophie asked questions about the meanings of words because she was genuinely unsure. But now she does so because Stingo is insensible to his ill choice of words. Caught in his fantasies, he manages to become "thoughtlessly oblivious" to the effect her confession has had on her. The fissure between Sophie's discourse and Stingo's understanding of it remains. When Sophie calls him "Stingo dear," her words do not, as Stingo assumes, voice her love for him but bespeak a motherly affection that, typically, he misinterprets.

But there are signs that Stingo is learning. Words, he begins to realize, must be reexamined, and sometimes redefined, in light of what Sophie has told him. After one of Nathan's outbursts, the narrator says that he "would ever after define the word 'distraught' by the raw fear" in her face. Such is the disparity between Stingo's speech and Sophie's on that train ride south that, as he talks, he is aware that his words have the "exact timbre and quavering resonance of a proposal I had once seen and heard George Brent, of all the solemn assholes, make to Olivia de Havilland." His recognition that his vocal forms are borrowed at least signals a growing awareness, although linguistic inadequacy continues to dog him as the shaky eloquence of youth tumbles into cliché: "You'll always be my—well, my . . . ," he begins, groping for a "properly tender" phrase. But the best he can come up with is "Number One," which even to him sounds "hopelessly banal"; in fact it is the same phrase he used, at age eighteen, in a letter to his father about his college football team. How his college vocabulary hobbles him is symptomatic of how far he still is from discovering a more mature outlook. When he does finally say, "I love you," the narrator, in a Flaubertian undercutting, has Sophie go "to the bathroom."

There are, as can be expected in a novel of this length, some lapses in strategy. When the narrator tells us that he had "to torture" himself "by reading as much as I could find of the literature of *l'univers concentra-tionnaire*," Heath rightly bridles. The narrator rather than Stingo is speaking here, and his turn of phrase seems as exaggerated and arch and malformed as Stingo's. He also comes strikingly close to deploying the strategy he quotes Arendt as saying the Nazis adopted: the trick of turning sensibilities inward "so that instead of saying: what horrible things I did to people!, the murderers would be able to say: what horrible things I had to watch in the pursuance of my duties, how heavily the task weighed upon my shoulders!" There is not, of course, an exact equivalence in what Styron does, but, like Stingo and Sophie as Styron portrays them, he too is directing tender feelings inward, rather than outward to the victims he is reading about. When the narrator—and implicitly the author—fall into approximately the modes of thought they are opposing, however, this fortifies rather than undermines the novel's theme of complicity.

Stingo's brash naïveté is an effective device in the novel precisely because he has few qualms about prying into memories that Sophie more than once expresses a wish not to talk about and that Nathan is sensitive enough not to stir up. Stingo's thoughtlessness allows him to learn her secrets, and the tension the narrator creates between Stingo's voice and Sophie's story is conceptually fundamental. His voice comes to make its own confession: of the narrator's, Styron's, perhaps America's, perhaps most people's, ignorance, disengagement, and complicity through indifference or self-interest.

Although the viewpoints of Stingo and Sophie clash, however, the narrator also seeks connections, bringing out their similarities. They are physically united, of course, in the final sexual union but are more profoundly joined by the similarities of attitude toward people and events in what Stingo shows about himself in New York and in what Sophie reveals in her confessions.

A number of critics, including Smith, Alvin H. Rosenfeld, and Robert Alter, see their sexual union—and the general emphasis on Stingo's sexual strivings—as gratuitous or worse. But that aspect of the story has also been defended, not least by Rubenstein, who argues that "far from weakening the novel, Stingo's sexual struggles are integral to his unique voyage from innocence to experience." Certainly, they are consistent with, and vital to, the display of transactions between dialogic worlds. His sexual union with Sophie is not only a final reminder of the immense gap between them but also encapsulates a further development in his "voyage of discovery." His fantasy comes true, but ultimately it will have an unforeseen meaning for him, bringing his loss of political and historical as well as sexual innocence.

The scene is a natural culmination of the clashes on which the novel is built, since the sex act has utterly different meanings for the two characters. The narrator points out that Sophie's actions—as earlier, where Stingo is a "surrogate Josef"—have little to do with Stingo and are scarcely more than "a plunge into carnal oblivion and a flight from memory." Stingo himself appears less interested in Sophie than in practicing all that he has avidly read about. His discourse is at times more appropriate to a car enthusiast than to a passionate lover: "I was delighted that the 'female superior' posture was every bit as pleasurable as Dr. Ellis had claimed, not so much for its anatomical advantages . . . as for the view it afforded me of that wideboned Slavic face brooding above me, her eyes closed and her expression so beautifully tender and drowned and abandoned in her passion that I had to avert my gaze." In one sense, Sophie and Stingo could hardly be more separate as persons. Each is using the other, and experiencing the coupling in an unshared way. Stingo might as easily be musing over the merits of a stick shift with full-length front bench, while Sophie is privately "abandoned in her passion," letting carnal ecstasy shelter her from the consciousness on which her guilt feeds. For Sophie, sex, whether with Stingo or Nathan, allows her to escape her sense of self, by producing a transitory "inseparability of flesh" that prevents her from telling "whether she is lost in herself or in him." But if Sophie begins as an object for Stingo ("as for the view . . . of"), he cannot avoid seeing her as a person too. He switches from surface description of her body and face to a contemplation of her expression—and so of Sophie as subject not just object—until he has to avert his gaze. No longer the technical enthusiast, he shows some slight shame over the advantage he—or she?—is taking. Stingo's dawning recognition that he is using Sophie is part of his journey toward understanding. Our human capacity to help or abuse others, depending on whether we identify with or dehumanize them, is, after all, what much of the novel is about. If Sophie's sexual nature is what motivates Stingo to listen to her—he is, after all, as usurious as he fancies Jews to be, since he hopes desperately for a return on his invested time, either sexually or in a good story line—he gets much more than he was angling for, since she teaches him, directly and indirectly, about himself.

The sexual union between Sophie and Stingo amounts to a physical, not a mental, harmony. It is a union literally beyond language: a "kind of furious obsessed wordlessness finally—no Polish, no English, no language, only breath"—and a momentary escape from the problems of verbal miscommunication. A truer understanding of the connections between Stingo's behavior and Sophie's story, prefigured by Stingo's evanescent recognition of Sophie as subject, matures only years later, when the narrator can admit that "at the time" he was "unable to see" that Sophie's actions were an attempt "to beat back death." She may initiate him sexually, but his initiation into the complexities of life is vastly more important. Stingo and Sophie experience a "propinquity of flesh," but the narrator's focus is on the unbridgeable gap left despite that. What for Stingo is a harmony only slightly tarnished by a vague uneasiness is for the narrator a crucial point in moving away from the dubious preoccupations and actions of his young manhood. The scene marks both Stingo's sexual initiation and the beginning of his growth out of political innocence. It affords him his first glimpse of the implications of his actions, and so opens the way to a truer knowledge of his position in the world.

The narrator is interested in more subtle, far reaching connections than the mere coupling of two individuals. He suggests a deeper connection between Stingo and Sophie in one of the failings they share: prejudice. Most of the characters—Wanda perhaps being the exception—are prejudiced to a degree. Some, like Höss and Sophie's father, are obviously so, but, too, Nathan's view of Poles can match the prejudice of any anti-Semite, and even Stingo's upright, moral "Southern liberal" father yields to prejudice in reacting to New York's "barbarity." Both Stingo and Sophie are more than ready, in moments of irritation or anger, to bring out a kind of hip-flask anti-

Semitism. On their bus ride to the beach, Sophie complains about Nathan, and Stingo suspects Morris Fink of stealing. Earlier, what began as a possibly fair complaint by Sophie that Leslie and her friends were "picking their little scabs" soon shifted to invective against the Jewishness of their behavior. Here, similarly, Sophie's personal grievances against Nathan—legitimate or not—soon center on his being Jewish. Upset for different reasons, Sophie and Stingo each launch into an anti-Semitic tirade.

But what might have constituted merely a recognition by the novel of the prejudice inherent in human life, turns into something more. Sophie and Stingo find themselves surrounded by "little deaf mutes" who form an "eerie, soundless retinue" as they cross the beach. With Stingo considering bringing charges against "that fucking little hebe," Morris Fink, the silent children suddenly disperse, "as if responding to some soundless signal." The children call to mind the children of Auschwitz, including Sophie's own, and act as silent witnesses to the indulgence Sophie and Stingo allow themselves. The Holocaust, we are reminded, is with us still, and the conditions that led to it remain. The notion that Auschwitz is an aberration, of another world, is a dangerous fallacy.

Stingo and Sophie are also connected insofar as they share a fervent desire to remain uninvolved—a desire that the narrator consistently portrays as hopeless. Both try to avoid choices and the confrontation an issues, but both learn that apathy is complicity and that evasion may contribute to the disintegration of choice itself. Stingo considers himself "a writer, an artist," who by his definition has "more exalted goals" than to "play the hapless supernumerary in some tortured melodrama"; Sophie masquerades as "the stainless, the inaccessible, the uninvolved." Stingo sees himself as a "political neuter," and Wanda says Sophie has "no politics." But as Stingo is "fated to get ensnared" with Sophie and Nathan, so Sophie was "adventitiously ensnared" by a Nazi roundup of the resistance members she would not help. Throughout, the choice of political aloofness proves illusory or backfires: there is no sure escape. Suddenly, Sophie was plunged into the Auschwitz "selection" she had heard of, and suddenly Stingo's self-important selection and rejection of manuscripts—a source of humor early on—is seen to copy, if faintly, Von Niemand's doings. *Sophie's Choice* is partly about how Sophie and Stingo learn, like Rambert in Camus' *The Plague*, that such "business is everybody's business."

Sophie's and Stingo's escapist tendencies link with the novel's title, and with the "choice" Sophie had to make between her children, Eva and Jan, on the platform at Auschwitz. That "choice" was no choice at all. She and her children were trapped in machinery where the individual has almost no leeway, so that Von Niemand's gesture was a gross parody of conceding an opportunity to choose. Probably both her children were to die, so all she could do was delay the death of one or the other and inevitably be saddled with guilt over what she had done. But the novel is also concerned with the real choices that result from recognizing that the one choice we cannot make—but that Stingo and Sophie attempt—is to remain remote from political and historical forces. Both Sophie and Stingo are confronted by such choices. Sophie had to decide, among other things, whether to help the resistance, in and out of the camp, and whether to help her father by typing and distributing his racist tracts. Stingo, for his part, must decide whether to delay his novel by becoming involved with Sophie and Nathan—whether to stay, as Larry has asked him, to watch over Nathan or go up to New England and try to seduce Mary Alice Grimball. Given the kinds of decisions Sophie in Poland and Stingo in Brooklyn come to, the theme of choice raises questions of personal and social responsibility. Stingo begins to learn, in literary as well as personal terms, that nobody, let alone an artist, can be apart from society. Von Niemand's offer of a choice to Sophie reemphasizes how delusory is her belief in privileged detachment.

The friendship of Stingo and Sophie develops along lines similar to those of the novel as a whole. Starting with disjunction, it gradually yields connections. Stingo eventually recognizes an "intolerable distance" between them "preventing any real communion." But Stingo's recognition of the gap is an assurance of its narrowing as he begins moving toward understanding. It also drives home that the narrator has all along been aware of the jarring he has portrayed. The reading of the narrative as double voiced, reflecting the novel's dialogic conflicts, is confirmed.

The novel's chronotopic pattern, especially that involving Stingo and Sophie, helps bring Auschwitz and the quotidian together. There are traces of the idyllic chronotope in Sophie's early portrayal of her father's house in Cracow and in Stingo's recall of the peanut farm, but these are subordinate. The major time-space juxtaposition is of the Pink Palace in Brooklyn and Haus Höss at Auschwitz, both variations on the castle chronotope deriving from the gothic genre. The two houses, like Gothic castles but with a difference, are linked by their peculiar capacity to disturb. Both houses—similarly to Sambuco—give a sense of their being set apart. The Pink Palace radiates vibrations that suggest something is "inexplicably wrong." The Höss house, with its kitsch and its willfully oblivious family acting out a grim pastiche of normal family life, inspires horror precisely because of the banal normality of its fittings and of the behavior inside given the horrors surrounding it. Two planes of existence seem to intersect there: out of one window, a gallant stallion admired by Höss, and out of the other, the platform where Nazi selections take place. When the wind changes, the beauty of the woods is blanketed by "smoke from the ovens at Birkenau."

The contrast between the houses, especially with regard to the place Sophie has had in each, bears on the story. In the Pink Palace, at least when Nathan is sane, Sophie is queen. Living on the second floor, she is adored by Stingo below and celebrated by Nathan, and she dines on steak and burgundy. At Auschwitz, considered privileged just to be in Haus Höss, she was a "piece of Polish Dreck," "among the lowliest of the low," and she lived "deep in the ground" nibbling cold slops. Up in the attic was Rudolph Höss himself, on whose commonplace and indifferent mind she vainly rested her hopes. If individualism is celebrated in Brooklyn, in Auschwitz the individual was a cipher, clawing for survival. Because we see only the least brutal side of Auschwitz, as we saw the least brutal side of slavery in *The Confessions*—Sophie was a house slave—the real horror remains outside the novel's bounds. For the months in the main camp that Stingo is not told about, we must turn to Wiesel, Levi, or the countless documentary studies like Martin Gilbert's *The Holocaust* or Elie A. Cohen's *Human Behaviour in the Concentration Camp*.

Auschwitz and the quotidian also come together to batter each other in the chronotope of the train. The misunderstandings between Stingo and Sophie climax on the ride south. For both it is a journey home, even though the word *home* is a battleground of meaning. For both it is a journey into the past. But what for Stingo is nostalgic, is for Sophie horrific: "The train sped across New Jersey's satanic industrial barrens, the clickey-clack momentum hurling us past squalid slums, sheet-metal sheds, goofy drive-ins with whirling signs, warehouses, bowling alleys built like crematoriums, cremato- riums built like roller rinks, swamps of green chemical slime, parking lots, barbarous oil refineries with their spindly upright nozzles ejaculating flame and mustard-yellow fumes." Their escape by train becomes simultaneously her journey to Auschwitz. Discourse from that earlier world—*crematorium, fumes*—invades the description of the everyday world. Sophie's stumble to the end of the car is the physical correlate of her mental movement back- ward. She ends up slumped "on the floor" in a railroad car with a "padlocked glass door crisscrossed by wire mesh," as if in a train to Auschwitz. But in another interpenetration of Auschwitz and the ordinary, her actual journey to the camp was by elegant carriage. Again the idea that Auschwitz and everyday life can be segregated—that we can discount the Holocaust as an aberration—is subverted.

Nathan, the schizophrenic in whom the "attractive and compelling" seem in "equipoise with the subtly and indefinably sinister," personifies the novel's theme. If two conflicting forms of human experience are juxtaposed in

Sophie's Choice, Nathan's schizophrenia encapsulates the clash, since in him, to quote the novel's epigraph from Malraux, "evil confronts brotherhood." Through him, seemingly disparate worlds beyond him are set in dialogue. Nathan is both Sophie's "savior" and her "destroyer." A "golem" as far as Morris Fink is concerned, he is for Stingo alternately a "monstrous Caliban," a "mentor, pal, savior, sorcerer," and a "colossal prick." His nursing of Sophie back to health is the antithesis of the Nazi nihilism she has been subjected to. Yet in his violent moods his voice booms through Stingo's ceiling with the "measured cadence of booted footfalls," in an image that joins him to the world Sophie has escaped.

Stingo's initial attraction to Nathan is as selfish as his early friendship with Sophie. He is only too ready to lap up the praise Nathan offers, and to accept Nathan's handout. For him, Nathan is a resource along the road to literary success. Their friendship is shaped by a "puerile inexperience" that keeps him from wondering about Nathan's mental state, and a "guileless-ness" that stops him from distinguishing between insights and ravings. Won over by Nathan's praise, he is ready to believe Nathan's ludicrous stories, and to see his tale of having been the "only Jewish Albigensian monk . . . St. Nathan le Bon" as merely an "extravagant piece of waggery."

Stingo's friendship with Nathan is bound up with Sophie to such an extent that there are no conversations between them without Sophie present. But when Nathan and Stingo talk together, Nathan's schizo-phrenic personality invariably catches him off guard, thereby revealing aspects of his character. Nathan's gift for mimicry often amuses Stingo, but when Nathan gets venomous, he threatens "certain crucial underpinnings" of Stingo's outlook. Nathan's attacks on the South goad Stingo into showing how muddled his outlook is. And when Stingo refuses to toast the death of Governor Bilbo, of Mississippi, Nathan baits him into defending Bilbo, and then mimics him. As governor, argues Stingo, Bilbo's "important reforms" included establishing a "highway commission," a "board of pardons," and the "first tuberculosis sanatorium."

> "He added manual training and farm mechanics to the curriculum of the schools. And finally he introduced a program to combat ticks . . ." My voice trailed off.
>
> "He introduced a program to combat ticks," Nathan said.
>
> Startled, I realized that Nathan's gifted voice was in perfect mockery of my own—pedantic, pompous, insufferable. "There was a widespread outbreak of something called Texas fever among the Mississippi cows," I persisted uncontrollably. "Bilbo was instrumental—"

> "You fool," Nathan interrupted, "you silly klutz. Texas fever!
> You *clown!* You want me to point out that the glory of the Third
> Reich was a highway system unsurpassed in the world and that
> Mussolini made the trains run on time?"

Like Sophie, only more brutally, Nathan tests Stingo's complacent and narrowly southern viewpoint by turning his words back on him and setting them in a broader context. His questioning is integral to Stingo's growth in awareness. Sophie and Nathan not only invade the physical privacy of Stingo's room but also apply pressure to the narrow viewpoint he has on art and life in general. Nathan especially, with the encyclopedic knowledge of a brilliant obsessive, gets Stingo to realize how narrow his own interests have been but also challenges him on his own terms, making him reflect on everything from Nazism to what Nathan calls the "worn-out tradition" of southern writing.

For the novel, Nathan's Nazi obsessions enable further connections between the world of Auschwitz and American society. The upheaval Nathan visits on Stingo extends well beyond his initial foot-in-the-door insistence that Stingo leave his novel and enjoy their company. Nathan's madness also explodes Stingo's Sophie-like hope that he can remain uninvolved, solitary in his creativity. The revelation of Nathan's illness shows him that his rejection of the "raw dirty world" for the sanctuary of art cannot be sustained. Much as Sophie had heard of Nazi selections but "thrust them out of her mind" since they seemed so "unlikely to happen to her," Stingo has "heard of madness" but always "considered it an unspeakable condition . . . safely beyond [his] concern." Like Sophie, though, he finds that what seemed safely distanced from his life has become a part of it. The abstraction of madness is suddenly "squatting in [his] lap," in the way the abstractions of Auschwitz and selections suddenly beset Sophie. His hope of remaining aloof, protected by the "armor" he has "wrapped around" himself, is dashed.

Prized from his self-imposed incarceration in art, Stingo becomes involved with Sophie and Nathan. But he retains a degree of detachment, and it is this, the narrator shows us, that gives him a large responsibility for the final tragedy. Nathan, during his telephone tirade before Stingo and Sophie flee south, accuses Stingo of "betraying" him by sleeping with Sophie. His accusation is mistaken at the time, but he is right in believing that he cannot depend on Stingo. Larry had asked Stingo specifically to "keep an eye on Nathan," since he was probably his "best friend." Had Stingo stayed, says the narrator, he might have prevented Nathan's "last slide to ruin." But both then, when he instead went to visit Jack Brown, hoping for sexual fulfillment with Mary Alice, and at the end, when he heads south alone before returning to Brooklyn, he shirks the obligations he has been trusted with.

Sophie's unwillingness to help her "dearest friend," Wanda, with the resistance outside or inside the camp is reprised—at a lower level of risk—by Stingo's unreadiness to help Nathan at a crucial moment. Stingo's instinct is the same as the one Sophie displayed in Cracow and at Auschwitz. The narrator makes that easy to see. When Larry says to Stingo, "I wouldn't ask you to be a spy if Nathan weren't in such a perilous condition," it is necessary only to replace the word *Nathan* with *Poland* or *we* to obtain a remark that Wanda could have made to Sophie. Nathan's unpredictable nature tests Stingo's fiber to the limit and proves it wanting, so the narrator's story is partly a confession of complicity in the tragedy. Just as Sophie was not merely a victim but also an accomplice in events in Poland, so Stingo is both the distraught survivor and a complicit party to the tragedy in Brooklyn.

The discourse toward harmony is still apparent in the main characters of *Sophie's Choice*—in Sophie's and Nathan's failed struggle toward wholeness and in Stingo's attempt "to collect and put back together the shards" of their friendship—but it has been dislodged from its central position as the shaper of the narrative. In prominence now is the price all three pay for harmony through evasion, force, and repression. Sophie's experiences and Nathan's knowledge force Stingo to confront issues he would rather avoid. The urge to harmonize is still alive at the end and is implicit in the narrator, but the narrator also retains his distance from Stingo and ends the novel with more questions asked than answered, and with the accent not on closure but on the future.

Throughout the novel, attempts at harmony are shown to be either largely unworkable or highly ambivalent. Sophie and Stingo both find not only that they cannot avoid the "raw dirty world" but that in trying to avoid it they may contribute to its dirt. Stingo, in his effort to shape events into a coherent picture, shows tendencies as violent as Nathan's. When Sophie's behavior becomes "unruly and difficult" on the final journey south, he finds consolation in saying to himself, "Wait till we're married," as earlier he wanted "to beat the living shit out of " Leslie for not conforming to his plans. Moments like these remind us that to strive to shape the world toward harmony may be a basic human and artistic urge but one that can also lead to violent suppression or to evasion—Lukács' "withdrawal before the contradictory problems thrown up by life"—and so to complicity. It is an urge that, in a sense, the Nazis took to an extreme.

But in *Sophie's Choice*, as in Styron's other novels, despair and affirmation sit together. There is an element of hope even in the deaths of Sophie and Nathan. Given the odds ranged against them, they die to some degree on their own terms. Their bodies are found to the boisterous sound of "Purcell's *Trumpet Voluntary* . . . filled with a resignation almost like joy." Sophie's smile, as seen by Morris only moments before the suicide, suggests a "curious fleeting glimpse of mild amusement," almost a "gentle laugh"—harking back to her "soft peals of laughter as she sank earthward with Nathan" at the fairground in happier days. There is an air of existential defiance. Since, as Nathan says, "Death is a necessity," they go "downward to darkness on extended wings." Consequently, Stingo witnesses not so much their disintegration from health as their courageous rebirth and swan song, as each gives the other a short but memorable stay before the inevitable.

Or is this impression of defiance just a result of the narrator's—and Styron's—need to end on a positive note? The phrasing he ascribes to Morris—the "glimpse of mild amusement"—is really his own, for Morris' eloquence never exceeds his pithy summary of Sophie and Nathan's life together: all they do is "hump and fight." The remark attributed to Morris betrays the narrator's need to discern the possibility of meaning where none may exist. That too, is undercut, however: Sophie and Nathan die in each other's arms in the costumes they wore to celebrate "being human," but Larry warns Stingo not to look at their faces. Yet the mystery of death at least allows the narrator some purchase for avoiding total negation.

Despair is also contained insofar as Stingo ends the novel grief-stricken but in a position to begin anew. If "Sophie's attempts to gain a hold on the confusion of her past" were doomed and Nathan "never got his mind in order," a "fragile yet perdurable hope" of regeneration remains. There are times when nothing but silence is appropriate. After Sophie's revelations, Stingo—fortunately—can "say nothing," and then he resorts to discussing peanuts, in a southern version of Kurt Vonnegut's "*poo-tee-weet?*" in *Slaughterhouse-Five*. He awakens the morning after the funerals from dreams of "speechlessness." But what wakes him are the boisterous shouts of children. Their mimicry of their elders—"Fuuu-ck you!" shouts one, but they have also buried Stingo in the sand protectively—attests the generative cycle that, for Styron, makes tragedy "so provisional." Stingo's eventual arrival among the older generation is promised by his now "frail and rickety" legs. His small recognitions are grounds for optimism that he is on the way to a maturer understanding of his relationship to society and history.

The cleavage between Stingo and the narrator, however, persists to the end. Stingo's archly poetic discourse is set off from the main narrative by italics, punctuating how the clash of voices remains:

It was then that in my mind I inscribed the words: *'Neath cold sand I dreamed of death / but awoke at dawn to see / in glory, the bright, the morning star.*

This was not Judgment Day—only morning. Morning: excellent and fair.

Stingo's focus, as so often, is on himself: it is he who dreams of death, and he who awakens. He is concerned, too, with meter and rhythm—with the artistic form over the subject: hence *'Neath*, and *the bright, the morning*. In contrast, the narrator stresses not the personal but the more generally significant. Open-endedness is what is on the mind of someone who reminds us that Judgment Day is not here. The repetition of *morning*, unlike Stingo's repetition of *the*, has nothing to do with meter and everything to do with renewal and affirmation. The narrator ends not with his own words but with Emily Dickinson's phrase *excellent and fair*. While Stingo struggles for independence from the discourse of other writers, the narrator is content with a turn away from himself and toward another. He is aware that the dialogue must remain open, not merely over Auschwitz but over his, and our, connection with events such as it. For our understanding of the sum and potential of human behavior, it is still only morning.

The allusion to future generations allows the novel to end at least at the junction between hope and despair, between the promise of life and the inevitability of death, the best and worst of human nature and experience. Styron's melding of Stingo's story with Sophie's permits this, but also embeds the horror of Auschwitz in an American context. It lays bare the relevance of that atrocity to the lives of people like Stingo. It also underlines that "absolute evil" is "never extinguished from the world," because its seeds exist not in "monsters" but in the unwitting attitudes of normal people like Stingo, like the victim and accessory Sophie, and like the bureaucrats Dürrfeld and Höss. Stingo, with his self-centered determination, incarnates much of the schizophrenic potential of humanity. When he asks Sophie to "love me . . . love *Life!*" he exhibits the two sides of that potential at once, since he is both selfishly homing in on Sophie for himself and illustrating the necessary optimism of youth.

A sense of rebirth might seem facile on the part of an author who has experienced nothing approaching Auschwitz. But the accounts of survivors demonstrate that even at Auschwitz there were two sides to existence. In *If This Is a Man*, Levi wrote that "sooner or later in life everyone discovers that perfect happiness is unrealizable, but there are few who pause to consider the antithesis: that perfect unhappiness is equally unobtainable." Many survivors of Auschwitz retained their hope in life. If taken literally, Adorno's comment that there is "no poetry after Auschwitz" would be a denial of the human spirit. In any case, it is countered by the facts: Levi begins his account of Auschwitz with a poem, and a spool of writing has been produced by survivors—very often, it appears, as a way of sustaining life. In the camps themselves, inmates gained comfort from storytelling and singing. That is the historical basis for the novel's hopeful, regenerative ending: the idea is that art sustains life, as music does for Sophie—and as it does for Juliek in Wiesel's *Night*, who after the march from Buna to Gleiwitz played his violin for others on the night of his death. That such hope is fragile, however, and that art has its limits are made equally clear.

When the narrator seeks, if not harmony, at least understandable connections between himself and the "suffering Stingo whom I once inhabited, or who once inhabited me," his concerns are far wider than the largely personal preoccupations of Sophie, Nathan, and Stingo. Stingo—prior to his glimmers of understanding—is only fleetingly concerned with the historical context of Sophie's trauma. His desire for her overrides a concern for her feelings. He laps up the "desperately needed" and "vivid encouragement" that Nathan proffers but has little insight into Nathan's madness even after Larry's revelations. The narrator's broader focus takes in the connection between Auschwitz and everyday experience and behavior. At times in the narrative, he—or Styron, as we can call him at such times—dispenses with the characters and amplifies the dialogue.

"For those of us who were not there," the narrator writes, the "nexus" between the differing orders of time that Steiner talks of is "someone who *was* there." Whatever the problems of subjectivity, language, and textual layering, experience is finally nothing if not personal. However impossible it is for us, as James E. Young puts it, "to know these events outside the way they are passed down to us," real people suffered real experiences in millions of personal ways. To mediate some idea of that sort of experience is one of the ends of the novel. But elsewhere Styron—who there becomes one with the narrator—pushes out into wider sociohistorical regions. Sophie's and Stingo's stories recede from the narrative, giving way to a different dialogue conducted in essay form. When Styron brings in books such as Rubenstein's *The Cunning of History* and Steiner's *Language and Silence*, there is a wider purview than the characters', with Auschwitz seen as a historical event recreated through its survivors and commentators.

The short but wide-ranging *Cunning of History* is a disturbing examination of the Holocaust not as an aberration nor as something of preeminently Semitic concern but "as the expression of some of the most profound tendencies of Western civilization in the twentieth century." Writing shortly

after the fall of the Nixon administration, Rubenstein argues that the Holocaust is directly linked both to Western religious traditions and to the
increasing rationalization, secularization, and bureaucracy of Western
society. For Rubenstein, it was an event that, far from being the "work of a
small group of irresponsible criminals," not only directly involved ordinary
businessmen and bureaucrats, who for the most part returned to executive
jobs after the war, but also "required the cooperation of every sector of
German society."

Rubenstein suggests that the mentality behind Auschwitz is still
evident in Western society. He writes that "the American system can be seen
as a link in the process of the progressive rationalization of a system of total
domination that reached its full development in the Nazi camps," since any
system based on "rational efficiency and calculated results" and intent on
"minimum costs and maximum profits" will be subject to pressures to evolve
in this way. In working slaves to death at minimum cost and maximum
productivity, the executives of I. G. Farben "merely carried the logic of
corporate rationality to its ultimate conclusion."

Sophie's two meetings with Walter Dürrfeld, the second of which the
narrator calls a "fragment, among the most odd and unsettling," of her story,
plainly flow from Rubenstein's book. The historical Dürrfeld was a director
of I. G. Farben who survived the war and an eight-year prison term to
become an industrial executive in postwar Germany. The two encounters of
Sophie and Dürrfeld relate to the bureaucratic apparatus of Auschwitz that
managed the production of synthetic rubber. The details that Styron
develops, including the affinities between German and American industry,
are largely from Rubenstein, and constitute still another link between apparently disparate worlds.

It was at the second meeting, at Auschwitz, that Sophie heard Dürrfeld
speak of the "schizophrenia" caused him by trying to reconcile the "Special
Action" of genocide with the "need for labor." But the schizophrenia that
Styron probes is not this, which lends itself to the kind of self-pity about
which Arendt writes, but that arising from the divergence between Dürrfeld's
prewar concerns and his concerns at Auschwitz. Sophie remembered that
when they first met, the attractive Dürrfeld not only did "not in the least
resemble the paradigmatic Nazi" but also "uttered not a word about Jews."
At Auschwitz, in contrast, where he did not recognize Sophie, "almost all
that she heard from his lips concerned Jews and their consignment to
oblivion." Everything Dürrfeld said was couched in terms of bureaucratic
efficiency, to the point that he referred to human beings as "thermal units of
energy." He told Höss, "I am answerable to a corporate authority which is
now simply insisting on one thing, that I be supplied with more Jews in order

to maintain a predetermined rate of production." Styron dramatizes Rubenstein's argument that a few years before the war "I. G. Farben was not an anti-Semitic corporation" and that the Nazis harnessed the outlook and efficiency of ordinary bureaucrats to murderous ends. Both books thus articulate the conviction that what appears disjunctive is really, ominously, in Rubenstein's words, "part of the same world."

Styron is convinced that to see Auschwitz as an aberration—as Bruno Bettelheim does, for example, in *The Informed Heart*—is far more dangerous than to examine the continuities between it and the rest of Western life.

Sophie's actions in the war, and Stingo's friendship with her and Nathan, not least his failure to comply with Larry's request, also illustrate Rubenstein's argument. Complicity through indifference riddles the consciences of both Sophie and the confessing narrator. For both Styron and Rubenstein, the complicity of the victim can be through ignorance. Rubenstein argues that "even the most innocent victim is part of the process of his own undoing by virtue of the fact that he did not or could not take protective measures. The very helplessness or ignorance of the victim is an indispensable part of what takes place." Styron exhibits not only how "absolute evil" is "at the core" of us all but also how our destinies can depend on whether we choose, like the "political neuter" Stingo or the "naïf in politics" Sophie, to empower evil through evasion and apathy or, like Wanda, to fight it. It is also true that the consequences of action and inaction have no guaranteed outcome—there is uncertainty as much in speaking as in keeping silent, as Sophie finds to great cost with von Niemand—but silence, by a social rather than individual measure, must be the more dangerous, since it does nothing to dispel "helplessness or ignorance." There can be no more compelling answer than this to Steiner's musing that the best response to an atrocity like the Holocaust may be silence. The idea that "nothing speaks louder than the unwritten poem" is palpably untrue; unwritten poems do not speak at all.

The Cunning of History also has ties with the novel's dialogizing of the discourse toward harmony and its assessment of the ambivalent worth of ordering activities in the face of historical and political realities. Rubenstein argues, partly by invoking Max Weber, that a movement toward order is in alliance with the logic and progress of capitalism. He endorses Weber's view in "Bureaucracy" that bureaucracy's "*specific nature which is welcomed by capitalism develops the more perfectly the more bureaucracy is 'dehumanized.'*" In *Sophie's Choice*, Höss, with his arms around Sophie, is like a "mechanical fly." When she senses a breakthrough it is like an "aperture clinking open." Höss is part of a system that tries to impose order on Europe: the "first technocratic state, with its *Regulierungen und Gesetzverordnungen*, its electrified filing-card systems and classification procedures, its faceless chains of command and mechanical methods of data processing."

In the novel's musical trope, Nazi order is compared to musical discord—Auschwitz has "symphonic death sounds: of metal clangor, of the boxcars' remote colliding booms and the faint keening of a locomotive whistle"—whereas music itself is Sophie's "life blood." It sustains her from the start against the "discordant strains of her father's obsession." She sees her father as "everything that music cannot be." Contrasting with the sharp dissonance of Nazi technocracy is her memory of "Beethoven's violin concerto played one night at the stadium Yehudi Menuhin with such wild, voracious passion and tenderness that as she sat there alone high on the rim of the amphitheatre, shivering a little beneath the blazing stars, she felt a serenity, a sense of inner solace that amazed her, along with the awareness that there were things to live for, and that she might actually be able to reclaim the scattered pieces of her life and compose of them a new self, given half a chance." This is the urge toward harmony at perhaps its best: the impulse not to impose order on others but only to compose a "new self" better equipped to deal with a world always under threat from drives toward totalitarian order.

The use Styron makes of *The Cunning of History* confirms that the future is a central concern of this historical novel in the same way that, according to Carlos Fuentes, it is a central concern of *The Confessions*. Styron calls Rubenstein's book an "urgent consideration of our own uncertain tomorrows." The object in seeking connections between Auschwitz and Brooklyn must be to reduce the potential of such an atrocity's recurring. As Steiner writes, quoting Kierkegaard, "it is not worthwhile remembering that past which cannot become a present." Styron, like Rubenstein, shows how the individual is at the mercy of events seemingly beyond immediate concern. The implicit conclusion is that we cannot afford to be the political naïfs and neuters that Sophie and Stingo start out as, and that art cannot afford to languish in the deluded vision of an apolitical purity. In 1974, a year before Rubenstein's book appeared, Styron wrote that he could not "accept anti-Semitism as the sole touchstone" by which to examine Auschwitz. In Rubenstein's book, Styron could find spelled out some of the universal implications of the conditions that conduced to the Holocaust.

That Steiner's polemical *Language and Silence* ironically engages in and fans the discussion it purports to reject is recognized by Styron when he says that there is a "touch of piety" in Steiner's call for silence since Steiner himself "has not remained silent." Styron's novel seems to enter into dialogue with three major components of Steiner's argument: his comments on the study of literature, his assertion that much of modern art is a "retreat from the word," and his call for silence.

Steiner asks if, given that a man like Höss can read Goethe and Rilke and then "go to his day's work at Auschwitz," the conception of art as a liberalizer and enlightener is tenable. He goes on to inquire whether a "wide gap" exists "between the tenor of moral intelligence developed in the study of literature and that required in social and political choice:" "There is some evidence that a trained, persistent commitment to the life of the printed word, a capacity to identify deeply and critically with imaginary personages or sentiments, diminishes the immediacy, the hard edge of actual circumstance. We come to respond more acutely to the literary sorrow than to the misery next door." To the first point, it is possible to respond that atrocities by some who read literature do not prove that no one is affected positively by reading it. Meaning exists between the work and the reader; literature is a tool we find uses for. By Steiner's logic, the possibility of killing with knives should call such instruments' social utility into question. But knives can also be used for surgery, and you can strangle someone with a bandage. The second question, however—about whether a commitment to literature diminishes a person's response to the misery next door—requires more than a perfunctory answer.

The second question also has greater pertinence to *Sophie's Choice*, since Stingo's early attitudes seem to substantiate Steiner's suggestion. Stingo certainly begins as one who cares more about literature than people. He deals mercilessly with the hopeful authors who bring their manuscripts to McGraw-Hill, and when he meets Sophie and Nathan, he wants to "nudge them" out of his life because he has other, literary, "fish to fry." But *Sophie's Choice* also affords a partial answer to Steiner. For Stingo begins to learn that art, and the artist, rather than superseding or transcending life, are integral to it. Steiner's argument rests on a monolithic idea of literary study, whereas Styron's novel makes a distinction: Stingo learns the limitations not of the study or practice of literature but of his attitude toward it.

Steiner likens the "retreat from the word" that he sees in literature to developments in postimpressionist and abstract painting and what he sees as the loss of "organization" in modern music. He detects a "retreat from the authority and range of verbal language" in contemporary writing. "The writer today," he says, "tends to use far fewer and simpler words, both because mass culture has watered down the concept of literacy and because the sum of realities of which words can give a necessary and sufficient account has sharply diminished." Only a few writers, suggests Steiner, including Faulkner, Joyce, and Stevens—all influences on Styron—have mounted "brilliant rearguard actions" against the "pressures on language of totalitarian lies and cultural decay."

Language is at the fore in *The Confessions*, and in *Sophie's Choice* there are indications that Styron has in his use of language reacted to Steiner's lament. Not only has Styron mounted a rearguard action of his own but he has done that through a clash of languages, thereby enhancing the textual schizophrenia. Styron's style has often commanded mention by his admirers, critics, and rivals alike. Dorothy Parker, early in his career, said that he "writes like a God," and Norman Mailer remarked that he wrote like "an angel about landscape, and an adolescent about people." More recently, Ruderman has complained that his novels have an "overabundance of words, words, words." Anthony Burgess has a concern about *Sophie's Choice* similar to the one Ruderman has expressed, but he acknowledges that there could be the same concern about "James, Dickens and Melville." In his view, *Sophie's Choice* "is powerfully moving, despite the Southern tendency to grandiloquence, the decking of [Styron's] prose with magnolia blossoms where starkness was more in order." The gravamen of the charge against Styron is usually that, if his eloquent prose is admirable in itself, it either seems to camouflage a lack of substance or is inappropriate to the subject.

There may be truth in the imputation of excess. Unlike much current American writing, Styron's prose has a voluptuous fluidity deriving partly from the grandiloquent southerners Wolfe and Faulkner. But just as there is a subtle use of language in *The Confessions*, there is far less extraneous or inappropriate language in *Sophie's Choice* than many imagine. It is easy to see what Burgess means by magnolian language, both in the narrator's discourse—*thaumaturges, prosthodontia, unguentary*—and rather differently, in the gross hyperbole of Stingo's desperate episodes with Leslie. But it also needs repeating that a novel can have many styles in contest with one another. In *Sophie's Choice*, a variety of styles are enlisted in furtherance of the theme of apparently disparate worlds. What Burgess epitomizes as magnolian phrasing is really a dynamic of differing styles for differing outlooks. In this, Styron highlights the ambivalences but also celebrates the powers of language.

Acquaintance with the novel banishes the idea that the style is uniformly grand—and inappropriate. The long passages of Sophie's narration do not overflow with stylish prose. Consider: "These long years, in 1945, when the war was over and I was in this center for displaced persons in Sweden, I would think back to that time when my father and Kazik were murdered and think of the tears I cried, and wonder why after all that had happened to me I couldn't cry no longer." Nor does the direct discourse on Auschwitz come across as florid, except in irony, as in Höss's description of his house at Auschwitz as making the place seem like an "enchanted bower." The novel is a heteroglossia of competing styles, ranging from Stingo's, in speaking of the need "to stifle [his] monumental anticipation" and "slow [his] galloping pulse," to the reportage of camp conditions: "The stripping and searching of prisoners that invariably took place as soon as they arrived at Auschwitz seldom allowed inmates to retain any of their former possessions. Due to the chaotic and often slipshod nature of the process, there were occasions when a newcomer was lucky enough to hold on to some small personal treasure or article of clothing." Lapses occur in this narrative technique. But given the novel's length and complexity, and the slipperiness of language, it would be remarkable if this did not happen. What is important is that Styron is not subordinating the heteroglossia to one overriding language—as Faulkner perhaps tried to do—but is juxtaposing discourses and levels of experience to bring out connections between them.

Burgess is right to say that in writing about the Holocaust, starkness is in order, but the subject of *Sophie's Choice* is not directly the Holocaust but Stingo's marginal connection with that atrocity. Styron's careful use of language to portray the clash of world views can be seen as an attempt to reaffirm the power of language that Steiner believes attenuated, as well as to incorporate its ambiguities.

Steiner asks whether "our civilization, by virtue of the inhumanity it has carried out and condoned," has "forfeited its claims to that indispensable luxury which we call literature." He argues that silence "*is* an alternative." He suggests that "the best *now*, after so much has been set forth, is, perhaps, to be silent; not to add the trivia of literary, sociological debate, to the unspeakable. So argues Elie Wiesel." Wiesel does indeed argue this. He proclaims, "I write to denounce writing." But the paradox of that proclamation and the oxymoron of Steiner's phrase *indispensable luxury* illustrate that their positions are more nearly gestures of despair than viable proposals.

Steiner, for all his polemics, is not silent, nor is it an advocacy of silence for him to admit that, if nothing else, the "compelling reason" for reading more about the Holocaust is "to make oneself concretely aware that the 'solution' was not 'final.'" Where Styron and Steiner seem to agree is not just in recognizing the personal and national complicity that leads to atrocities but in believing that art is important because it is regenerative. A person can engage in the arts and then "go to his day's work at Auschwitz," but art still has *some* power. As Steiner says, "Men who burn books know what they are doing. The artist is the uncontrollable force." Literature's reputation as a "humanizing force" may be damaged, but great writing springs from the "harsh contrivance of spirit against death."

If Stingo's self-understanding is embryonic at the end of the novel, Styron's focus has been on the transformation Stingo begins to, and must, undergo as man and novelist. The story of Stingo and Sophie means to illuminate what Steiner describes as "the artist's primary material—the sum and potential of human behaviour"—in light of the Holocaust. The focus on the self is not "egotism," as Heath calls it and as Leslie Fiedler implies, but it shows something about egotism, just as the novel is not by but about Stingo.

Sophie's Choice is a journey of recognition—or to the beginnings of recognition—a Bildungsroman perhaps but, really, as David D. Galloway, Rhoda Sirlin, and others say, a *Künstlerroman*. It condenses the path of Styron's career that this study has traced: the movement of his novels away from the stable world of Stingo's father and from Stingo's faith in pure art toward complexity and linguistic ambiguity that continually frustrate any attempt to find a solid base. Above all it charts the distance between Styron's early view "of literature as just pure literature" and his eventual engagement with political and historical topics such as the subject matter of the novel itself. Only by coming to terms with the individual's responsibility through complicity, ignorance, or unrealized potential can we hope to avoid a recurrence of an atrocity on the scale of the Holocaust. The effort, however inadequate, to see the individual in integration with society is necessary and appeals, as Malraux says, to "that element in man which today is fumbling for an identity, and is certainly not the individual." People need to see themselves as part of a wider historical context, and humanity as part of a world structure. Stingo needs to gain an awareness far beyond the "lilac *fin de siècle* hours" with which he begins his career.

If, after all, there seem to be, as Langer suggests, two worlds, or as Steiner says, two levels of existence, all the more reason to try to connect them, however jarringly, into one conceptual frame. The aim must be to locate the points of contact between the best and the worst, between normality and events like the Holocaust that seem to stick "like some fatal embolism in the bloodstream of mankind."

The novel looks not merely to Stingo's future but to "our own uncertain tomorrows," which are ever more insecure—and for reasons now beyond what man can do to man, in view of what humanity is doing to the planet. We cannot say we are not responsible, that we can do nothing, that we have no choice. For one choice we do not have is whether to be involved. If, like Sophie and Stingo, we deny our involvement, the choices that we do have may themselves dissolve.

Rubenstein points out that *Sophie's Choice* "is less a novel about the Holocaust than a novel about how the Holocaust" affects a young writer. Given Styron's southern Wasp background, his response, says Rubenstein, is bound to be different from that of Jewish writers, but "this does not mean that Styron's story is necessarily more or less significant." For Rubenstein, "every honest interpretation represents the weaving of the interpreter's own history and experience with what he or she knows of the event." That, we have seen, is what takes place between the book's two levels—the competing voices of the narrator, Stingo, Sophie, and others on one level, and those of commentators on another. If we can approach any kind of understanding of the Holocaust, it must come from such a textually layered multiplicity of view-points, of which *Sophie's Choice* is now one small cluster among others.

The novel therefore must end with Stingo, and with the morning star—a tired symbol, repeated from *The Confessions*, that perhaps betrays the exhausting effort needed to retain such hope. History, Stingo at last realizes, is not, as Stephen Dedalus would have it, the "nightmare" from which he should try "to awake," nor language something merely to be played with, to immerse himself in like some pleasure-oozing postmodernist bubble bath. History is instead the nightmare that he must awaken *to*, and language—inadequate, flawed, misleading but also powerful—a writer's only means for doing that.

CAROLYN A. DURHAM

William Styron's Sophie's Choice: *The Structure of Oppression*

In the face of repeated objections to the assertion in *What Is Literature* (1948) that a "good" anti-Semitic or racist novel would be a contradiction in terms, Jean-Paul Sartre maintained that whatever the theoretical value of his analysis, no one had yet taken up the practical challenge: "show me a single good novel whose deliberate intention was to serve oppression, a single one written against Jews, Blacks, workers, colonialized peoples." If we judge by his most recent novel, William Styron seems to believe that his own work may represent for some readers an attempt to satisfy Sartre. *Sophie's Choice* incorporates frequent and barely disguised references to the negative critical reception of Styron's earlier novels, which frequently included charges of racism. Such reminders have served as strong evidence for the many reviewers of *Sophie's Choice* who are insistent on identifying its fictional narrator Stingo with William Styron himself.

Thus Nathan Landau notes signs of "ingrained" and "unregenerate" racism in Stingo's first novel, highly reminiscent of Styron's own *Lie Down in Darkness*; and the mature Stingo comments on similar reactions to what is clearly a version of *The Confessions of Nat Turner:* "as accusations from black people became more cranky and insistent that as a writer—a lying writer at that—I had turned to my own profit and advantage the miseries of slavery, I succumbed to a kind of masochistic resignation. . . ." Moreover, Stingo's and

From *Twentieth Century Literature* 30, no. 4. © 1985 by Hofstra University Press.

Styron's current *Sophie's Choice*, for Stingo is writing the novel we are reading, has aroused general critical acknowledgment that its treatment of Jewish experience invites charges of anti-Semitism, even if none has materialized to date.

The textual connections Styron chooses to establish in *Sophie's Choice* among his various fictions do have both aesthetic and ideological significance, not unrelated to Sartre's identification of bad literature with a politics of prejudice. The emphasis this structure places on Styron's literary output as oeuvre, as a body of work dealing with the concept and nature of oppression through the successive examination of particular oppressive systems, can point us toward a richer reading of Styron in general and, in the case at hand, of *Sophie's Choice*. For Styron's work serves of course as an illustration not of Sartre's ironic challenge to skeptics but rather of his original thesis. Styron's novels—and the distinction is important—are not oppressive but about oppression, not racist but about racism, not anti-Semitic but about anti-Semitism, and, I shall argue, not sexist although, in the instance of *Sophie's Choice* especially, are persistently about sexism.

Readers primarily interested in ideology have tended to dismiss formalism as an invalid critical method, choosing to value or to criticize commitment to a cause without concern for the literary means used to convey it. They thus ignore Sartre's fundamental hypothesis that an essential relationship exists between world view and form: "a novelistic technique always reflects the metaphysics of the novelist." Ironically, in this case, early critics of *Sophie's Choice* may be paying both too much and not enough attention to form or, at least, to the nature of its connection to content in Styron's novel. For all of their insistence on equating Stingo and Styron, few reviewers appreciate the structural consequences they subsequently attribute to this intermingling of fiction and autobiography. *Sophie's Choice* has been criticized particularly severely for its organizational weakness: the supposedly chaotic combination of Stingo's sex life with Sophie and Nathan's destructive love; the unjustified comparison of anti-Semitic Poland to a racist American South; the confused linking of Stingo's experience as writer to Nathan's drug-induced madness; and, most importantly, the juxtaposition of all of the above themes to the horrors of the Nazi concentration camps. Those reviewers most sensitive to Styron's novel do glimpse in the multiple riches of *Sophie's Choice* a common pattern, but these critics tend also to see the subject of the novel as too general—Evil—or too specific—the evils of Nazi Germany. That *Sophie's Choice* should be criticized for a lack of structural coherence or for an excess of structural exuberance seems highly ironic; for it is in fact a novel whose very meaning lies embedded in its structure and, even more specifically, in the very concept of structure itself.

Styron attempts to alert us immediately to this important theme by opening the novel with the single chapter he himself has characterized in interviews as autobiographical, and which we may therefore expect to find potentially irrelevant or at least less relevant than others to the story of Sophie Zawistowska. But, in fact, the analysis of the McGraw-Hill publishing house where Stingo begins both his writing career and his narrative provides in its apparent thematic gratuity a paradigm of structure itself and therefore the very foundation of theme in Styron's *Sophie's Choice*. McGraw-Hill represents what Styron understands as *system:* the organized oppression of a given group of people in the name of their deviation from an established norm. Because this original form of systematic or organized evil remains free of any specific ideological content, it sets up a structural pattern that prepares us to comprehend the other systems which form the complex fabric of Styron's novel. Although no doubt pro-Wasp, pro-male, and certainly pro-conservative, McGraw-Hill is neither specifically racist, anti-Semitic, nor sexist; it is merely fundamentally pro-uniformity. Moreover, its function—the publication of good literature—and its fact—the publication of bad—serve from the very beginning of the novel to link Styron's concept of system to his conception of fiction.

Styron subsequently constructs *Sophie's Choice* upon a carefully woven network of parallels and repetitions in which all of the novel's characters gradually prove to share a single common characteristic: the same paradoxical form of prejudice. Only a few years after Auschwitz, the Jewish Morris Fink declares his hate for "boogies." Stingo's father describes his friend Frank Hobbs as a "good solid man," although Hobbs is both an anti-Semite and a racist. Only Stingo's obsession with Nat Turner and with the institution of slavery rivals his interest in the situation of Jews in prewar Poland and in Nazi Germany; yet even Stingo proves capable of brief lapses into both racism and anti-Semitism, and his experience with the Lapidus family amply illustrates the extent to which he harbors remarkably naive and stereotypical notions of Jewish domestic and religious life. Nathan deplores the historic suffering of his fellow Jews, but he does not hesitate to label all Southerners racist. Stingo's father proudly calls himself a liberal Democrat but considers Northerners an ignorant and vulgar caste. German hatred for Jews barely overshadows their horror of "Polacks," and Poles share the barracks of Nazi concentration camps with the Jews they despise. Wanda may best understand the endlessly replicable structure of prejudice and the need therefore to attack the form itself beyond any of its particular contents; she explains to the Jewish Feldshon: "once they finish you off they're going to come and get me."

Although Wanda speaks for herself and her "pretty blonde friend" Sophie only as unlikely victims, it is not insignificant that they are women. In much of his previous work, notably in *Set This House on Fire*, Styron has used the condition of women as a central metaphor for the general degradation of the self and others. In *Sophie's Choice*, sexism serves as a pervasive model of oppression, functioning as do the novel's formal analogies to invite us to see the structural equivalence of all systems of organized evil. Thus sexism proves common not only to the apparently neutral structural shell of McGraw-Hill in which women serve as "mainly secretaries" but to racism and anti-Semitism as well. Stingo's carefully developed comparison between Poland and the American South includes the traditionally double-edged exploitation of females: "domination over women (along with a sulky-sly lechery)." In fact, virtually every chapter of *Sophie's Choice* contains the same consistent structural elements: a system of organized oppression, a particular example of sexism, and a commentary on language or literature, thus creating a structural paradigm in which *sexism* illuminates both the *systems* that oppress society and the *literature* that can lead toward an understanding of how they function.

Two episodes in particular of *Sophie's Choice* can quickly and effectively illustrate the structural and thematic importance that Styron attaches to sexism. Stingo's discomfort at inheriting money from his grandfather's sale of the slave Artiste and his horror at the lynching of Bobby Weed are directly related to racism and, because of the parallels Nathan establishes, indirectly related to anti-Semitism. But more importantly, the two events also reveal a hostility to women which constitutes both their common element and an attitude shared by Stingo and Nathan. Artiste (by his very name an ally of Stingo) must be sold, because "in the first lusty flush of adolescence" (a situation painfully familiar to Stingo), he has made an "improper advance" toward a young white woman who turns out after the sale to be "an hysteric" prone to such false accusations. By the time Bobby Weed is castrated, branded, and lynched years later for the identical and equally nebulous offense, it has become a commonplace: "His reputed crime, very much resembling that of Artiste, had been so classic as to take on the outlines of a grotesque cliché: he had ogled, or molested, or otherwise interfered with (actual offense never made clear, though falling short of rape) the simpleton daughter . . . of a crossroads shopkeeper. . . ."

Such stories impose an absolute double bind—one must necessarily choose to be either racist or sexist: either to condemn blacks for an attitude defined as normal in all other men or to condone the treatment of women as sexual objects. Moreover, whether the women in question tell the truth or lie, whether they are believed or not, they are directly responsible as females for both violence against men and for divisiveness among men. Stingo's attitude clearly implies that women are liars, hysterical, simpleminded, and either obsessed with sex and their own desirability or man-haters afraid of "normal" sexual advances. It is scarcely surprising that in Stingo's later resentment at his own metaphorical castration he should invent for Leslie a comparable racist rape fantasy: "I finished my account with one or two Freudian furbelows, chief among them being one in which Leslie told me that she had been able to reach a climax only with large, muscular, coal-black Negroes with colossal penises."

Among critical objections to the structure of *Sophie's Choice*, or to its absence, distress at the inclusion of Stingo's sexual obsessions, fantasies, and adventures ranks particularly high. Robert Alter's comments reflect a typical discomfort with episodes perceived as tasteless and trivial when combined with the horrors of Nazi concentration camps: "it is hard to see how such concentration on a writhing priapic Stingo helps us to grasp the novel's subject of absolute evil." Ironically, one consequence of a growing awareness of feminist concerns may be to provoke an almost instinctive reaction of hostility to every situation that even hints at the sexual exploitation of women. Yet, as is the case here, specific examples of prejudice, however offensive in themselves, may well function in a larger context to expose and consequently to undermine oppression. To focus our attention on the contextual importance of Stingo's sexual experiences, an issue first raised by his encounter with Leslie Lapidus, Styron has Stingo himself worry about the structural coherence of his novel:

> In itself this saga, or episode, or fantasia has little direct bearing on Sophie and Nathan, and so I have hesitated to set it down, thinking it perhaps extraneous stuff best suited to another tale and time. But it is so bound up into the fabric and mood of that summer that to deprive this story of its reality would be like divesting a body of some member—not an essential member, but as important, say, as one of one's more consequential fingers. Besides, even as I set these reservations down, I sense an urgency, an elusive meaning in this experience and its desperate eroticism by which at least there may be significant things to be said about that sexually bedeviled era.

In defining himself as one of the sexual "survivors" of the fifties, Stingo by his vocabulary establishes a clear parallel between himself and Sophie. Although such a comparison may seem to undermine the importance of Sophie's fight for her sanity and for life itself, it in fact serves to emphasize the centrality of sexual experience in both of their lives, for Nazi Germany and prewar Poland prove no less sexually troubled than postwar America. Stingo's sexual fantasies thus relate directly to Styron's attack on the evil of sexism; those critics who denounce the former as gratuitous or trivial may well regard the latter in the same light.

For Stingo, "Little Miss Cock Tease" epitomizes the era of the fifties and, in general, he adheres to the standard male dualistic view of women. Yet, Stingo's division of the female sex into "cock teasers" or "cock suckers" differs sufficiently from the classic angel/whore dichotomy to reveal usefully the true hostility the latter conceals. The apparent idealization of women as pure and virginal reflects in fact a belief that such women are teases, frigid and inhuman. Thus Stingo's system corresponds to an absolute degradation of women; indeed, as he informs us, he has "not idealized 'femininity' in the silly fashion of the time."

Stingo illustrates this view of women through the repetition of a paradigmatic pattern into which his experience with Sophie eventually fits. The original model provided by Mavis Hunnicutt in the structurally rich opening chapter of *Sophie's Choice* makes it clear that nonsexual relationships with women are inconceivable for Stingo. The "loneliness" on which he insists throughout this period translates unambiguously as sexual frustration: "she could not know what she did to the loneliest junior editor in New York. My lust was incredible. . . ." Through Mavis and her subsequent incarnations in Leslie and Mary Alice, Stingo fantasizes the women as cock sucker and cock teaser in turn, unfortunately in that inverted order. Stingo idealizes the female as sexual initiator or, in any case, as always responsive to male advances; thus, women are allowed volition to want what men do. Invariably, however, women who appear appropriately welcoming ultimately reject Stingo with increasingly dire consequences for him. Merely chagrined at Mavis' imaginary dismissal of him, Stingo falls ill after his failure with Leslie; and Mary Alice—"worse than a Cock Tease, a Whack-off artist"—drives him from his "lifelong efforts at good, wholesome, heterosexual screwing" toward homosexual relations.

Stingo claims a distinction between the women he desires and the women he loves for which, in fact, the novel provides no evidence. Stingo's expression of chaste adoration for Maria Hunt produces a "ferociously erotic" dream in which Maria behaves, to Stingo's delight, with "the abandon of a strumpet." Similarly, although Stingo professes a "poetic and idealistic" passion for Sophie, she too supports the fixed model of sexual identity already established. Stingo's initial encounter with Sophie occurs as Nathan defines her as "cunt" and "whore"; Stingo's attention focuses immediately on her body and her sexuality; his desire "to win the affection" of Sophie marks at best a necessary step toward his real goal: "to share the bed" abandoned by Nathan. Moreover, so that any lingering idealization of the female may be rigorously exorcised, Stingo finds Sophie most arousing when she is least erotic; her most tender, affectionate, and vulnerable moments become an invitation to seduction. When Sophie collapses, shattered by the loss of Nathan and her revelation just moments before of the existence of her son Jan, only Stingo's own fatigue persuades him to forgo a sexual pass: "Lying there, she seemed terribly vulnerable, but my outburst had tired me, leaving me somehow shaken and empty of desire." During the desperate and exhausting flight South to escape Nathan, the sight of Sophie asleep produces in Stingo a similar "seizure of pure lust." Thus, Stingo's synthetic dream in which he makes love to Leslie, transformed in quick succession into Maria and Sophie, has particular significance; it both confirms that love is insepa-rable from lust for Stingo and draws the inevitable conclusion: all women are equivalent and therefore interchangeable.

Yet Sophie does stand apart from other women as an ideal; she is the perfect woman as defined and perceived in a male world. Originally a cock teaser—"a young woman brought up with puritanical repressions and sexual taboos as adamantine as those of any Alabama Baptist maiden"— Sophie has been transformed literally into a cock sucker, "the world's most elegant" according to Nathan, thereby proving the male maxim that women, however much they may initially resist, really welcome sexual advances. Moreover, Sophie's behavior perpetuates the particularly vicious myth that women respond to physical and mental violence as pleasurable. In the midst of an orgy of abuse, Sophie blissfully sucks Nathan's cock; and after hours of torture involving physical beating, verbal abuse, and psycho-logical assault, she welcomes immediately and without hesitation Nathan's invitation "to fuck."

Nathan misdirects his jealousy of Sophie, since its justification lies not in her attraction to other men but in their obsessive interest in her; for every man she encounters, however briefly or infrequently, Sophie becomes an object of desire, a seducible prize. But in the sexist world that Styron portrays, once Sophie has allowed herself to be seduced, she must be degraded as the whore she has become. Her very submission to Nathan confirms the justice and accuracy of his accusations, and marriage logically becomes the prize that Nathan proffers or withdraws on the basis of his current beliefs about Sophie's sexual fidelity. Stingo, tormented for months by his desire for Sophie, nonetheless characterizes her seduction of him on the beach as "forthrightly lewd," and the episode illustrates with particular clarity the incredible double standard to which women are subjected, the inescapable vicious circle in which they are trapped. When Sophie initiates lovemaking, immediately after her latest revelations about her past, Stingo implicitly condemns her for frivolity, capriciousness, an inability to feel deeply: "The shift in mood—the grisly chronicle of Warsaw, followed in a flash by this wanton playfulness. What in hell did it mean?" But when Sophie returns to her story after Stingo's premature ejaculation, his renewed horror is heightened. Sophie's failure to be appropriately affected by their recent intimacy, to live this sexual adventure as "cataclysmic" and "soul-stirring," offers evidence of an insensitivity far greater than any Stingo had yet imagined and leads him to one of the novel's relatively rare generalizations about "women": "Could women, then, so instantaneously turn off their lust like a light switch?"

Styron's careful construction of a globally sexist world provides a context in which the events of Sophie's arrival at Auschwitz cannot possibly be dismissed as an aberration. However great our shock and our horror, the "choice" that the Doctor Jemand von Niemand imposes on Sophie marks the logical extension of all male behavior toward women recorded in *Sophie's Choice* up to that point. Despite Stingo's elaborate attempts to "understand" the Doctor's action, to offer an explanation that inevitably becomes a defense, Jemand von Niemand fits into a clearly established pattern. He makes Sophie the same proposition that virtually every other man in the novel, implicitly or explicitly, has made her—"I'd like to get you into bed with me"—and when she fails to respond, he destroys her. For with tragic irony the perfectly pliant Sophie, who has always understood the necessity of female submission in a male world, fails to react quickly enough at the single moment when the metaphorical survival of the female becomes literal. Yet, the greatest horror recounted in *Sophie's Choice* may be less the cruelty of the Nazi doctor than its perpetuation in Stingo. For Stingo's reaction to the story of Eva's death is virtually indistinguishable from Jemand von Niemand's behavior during the actual event: Stingo too wants to go to bed with Sophie. The fact that she clearly initiates their night of inexhaustible sex changes nothing in a world in which women are required to be both prey and predator, except perhaps to confirm once and for all how well Sophie learned her lesson at Auschwitz.

The role of sexual oppressor that links all men and the use of sexism as paradigm to connect Nazi Germany to postwar America extend to the reader as well. One of the most remarkable successes of Styron's attack on sexism comes from his ability to implicate the reader himself in the system that victimizes Sophie; the male pronoun is for once authentically generic since all readers, male or female, will be forced to view Sophie from a masculine perspective. Our limited, popular, and generally sensationalist knowledge of history prepares us to suspect Sophie's involvement in sexual crimes or experiments at Auschwitz, and the mysterious secret announced in the novel's title encourages us to believe she participated more as collaborator than as victim. Moreover, Nathan serves as our representative in the text. He gradually plants the idea that Sophie's survival at Auschwitz is linked to her sexual behavior; this insidious process, reinforced by Sophie's evident obsession with her own guilt, culminates in his identification of Sophie with Irma Griese: "hey Irma how many SS pricks did you suck to get out of there, how much master race come swallowed for *Freiheit*?" Styron's technique effectively exposes the reader as participant in the same system of sexism the novel as a whole reflects; for at the moment we learn the true nature of Sophie's "choice" or "crime," we are forced to confront the discrepancy between the truth and our assumptions.

Women can ultimately be reduced to interchangeable sex objects, because sexist society denies them a personal identity, a sense of self. Styron's novel, consistent with much feminist theory, locates the origin and the model of female oppression in the father dominance of the traditional family. In general, Sophie's father reduces her to "virtually menial submission," but his most significant assault is aimed at Sophie's love of music, the representation throughout the novel of her identity, her individuality. As a significant prelude to her account of her arrival at Auschwitz, Sophie relates a dream in which she explicitly identifies her father's will to deny her access to music with the death of the self:

> "So in the dream that has returned to me over and over I see Princess Czartoryska in her handsome gown go to the phonograph and she turns and always says, as if she were talking to me, 'Would you like to hear the Brahms *Lieder?*' And I always try to say yes. But just before I can say anything my father interrupts. He is standing next to the Princess and he is looking directly at me, and he says, 'Please don't play that music for the child. She is much too stupid to understand.' And then I woke up with this pain. . . . Only this time it was even worse, Stingo. Because in the dream I had just now he seemed to be talking to the Princess not about the music but about . . ." Sophie hesitated, then murmured, "About my death. He wanted me to die, I think."

On at least three occasions in the novel, Sophie repeats the most fundamental of her lies and the one most puzzling to Stingo: she makes of her father a decent, brave, and loving man. Because Sophie has no sense of self—because her identity is entirely relational, alienated in that of the men who control and protect her—her only opportunity to experience self-esteem, however vicarious and reflected, is to belong to men of whom she and others can think well. Logically, when her hated father and the husband who is his mirror image are murdered, Sophie grieves not for their death but for her own: "Her entire sense of self—of her identity—was unfastened." Nathan offers Sophie an exact replica of her relationship with her father: she receives protection and identity at the price of "childlike dependence," a total self-alienation that Nathan correctly identifies: "My darling, I think you have absolutely no ego at all." In this context, the story of Blackstock and his wife Sylvia, structurally gratuitous if the unity of Styron's novel is situated elsewhere than in the institution of sexism, serves a central metaphorical function. Blackstock's adoration for Sylvia turns her into a pet, a doll, a pampered child whose total irresponsibility is not merely tolerated but encouraged; and Sylvia destroys herself in an automobile accident, the head she has never had occasion to use severed from her body and lost.

Styron continually places Sophie in impossible situations which have particular metaphoric significance for women: if they prove appropriately selfless, they participate in their own alienation and destruction, but any claim they make for the right to self instantly backfires by proclaiming them to be selfish. Not only does Stingo openly condemn Sophie; she traps herself in her own narrative. For example, Sophie justifies her attempt to seduce Höss as the disinterested and courageous effort of a mother to save her son, but until all hope is clearly lost, we hear Sophie ask Höss only for her *own* freedom; we are in fact still unaware that she has a child. Sophie demands what she desperately needs and deserves—the right to exist—but she does so in a morally ambivalent context in which we are led to condemn her for her egotism, for failing to live up to the ideal of female selflessness: motherhood. But Sophie cannot win, for when she acts as the good mother, she is also condemned for the same female sin of selfishness. Both Sophie's refusal to help the Home Army in Warsaw, out of fear for her children's safety, and her inability to steal Emmi's radio, lest she lose her last chance to save Jan, demonstrate the selfless other-orientation traditionally required of women. But through our identification with Wanda and the Resistance movement, we come to regard Sophie as not only morally weak and irresponsible but indeed as selfish for her inability to put the plight of the Jewish people before her own, suspecting as well that she uses her children as an excuse to hide her own cowardice. Condemned for her maternal role, whether she fulfills it adequately or not, Sophie ultimately must act as the quintessentially bad mother: she becomes a Medea, morally guilty of infanticide. Not only has she implicitly preferred one child to another in a society in which maternal love is by definition unconditional and all-encompassing, but she whose value as woman is based upon her ability to give life has sent one of her children to death.

Although Styron uses the concept of a slave world, common to the Nazi concentration camps and to the history of the American South, to examine the condition of women as well, slavery serves him as contrast as much as comparison. For Styron understands the limits of the analogy even if in his existential world it may in some terrible sense be preferable to remain an absolute slave. The ultimate horror of the situation of women rests precisely on the two factors that distinguish them from the Negro slaves and from the Jewish inmates of Auschwitz: *choice*, however limited, and *collaboration*, however enforced. Sophie may have been prepared to act in a particular way at Auschwitz because of her gender identity: "she had been a victim, yes, but both victim and accomplice, accessory." Certainly Sophie's understanding of her "complicity," not only in her own oppression but in a world in which systematic oppression is possible, long predates the war. The typing and distribution of her father's murderous tract force her to acknowledge her tragic responsibility: a volition too strong to allow her the comforting status of victim but too weak to permit her to revolt:

> "And this terrible emptiness came over me when I realized just
> then there was nothing I could do about it, no way of saying no,
> no way possible to say, 'Papa, I'm not going to help you spread
> this thing.' . . . And I was a grown woman and I wanted to play
> Bach, and at that moment I just thought I must die—I mean, to
> die not so much for what he was making me do but because I had
> no way of saying no."

Certainly Sophie's enforced choice between her children represents the ultimate tragic dilemma, for she is made to choose in a situation in which no meaningful choice is possible: any decision will produce morally and emotionally identical results. And yet Dr. Jemand von Niemand is not totally wrong to call Sophie's right to choose "a privilege"; for as Sophie herself understands, without choice as possibility or concept, women would remain helpless victims, unable to institute change. Ultimately, Sophie can choose for herself only on choosing suicide, but the importance of that decision should not be underestimated. Not only, as Phyllis Chesler has pointed out, does physical action—including suicide—remain extraordinarily difficult for women, but Sophie selects death over a new loss of identity in the marriage and motherhood that Stingo offers.

Throughout *Sophie's Choice*, all questions of sex and sexism are linked to language and literature: to Stingo's vocation as writer, to the construction of the novel we are reading, to the creation of the story of Sophie. For Stingo, writing and sex are inseparable, indeed indistinguishable. In the key first chapter of *Sophie's Choice*, Stingo professes "an affinity for the written word—almost any written word—that was so excitable that it verged on the erotic." The urge to masturbate invariably accompanies Stingo's one creative task of the moment, the composition of jacket blurbs; and the fantasy garden parties he imagines from his window are not only dominated by his lust for Mavis but peopled with famous authors: "In these demented fantasies I was prevented from immediate copulation on the Abercrombie & Fitch hammock only by the sudden arrival in the garden of Thornton Wilder. Or e. e. cummings. Or Katherine Anne Porter. Or John Hersey. Or Malcolm Cowley. Or John P. Marquand." To Stingo as hero, the equivalence of language and sex becomes a source of almost unbearable frustration. He consistently finds himself a sexual eavesdropper, a sort of oral voyeur, for whom knowledge of the act of love is limited to the words other people pronounce during sex. With comic irony, the woman Stingo selects as his sexual initiator has a totally lingual sex life: Leslie only kisses and talks about sex, and the single concrete result Stingo gleans from the adventure is an inflamed tongue.

But to Stingo as writer, sex is language in the most positive of senses: both the source and the subject of art. Susan Gubar and Sandra Gilbert in *The Madwoman in the Attic* postulate that the pen acts as "a metaphorical penis"; and Stingo illustrates particularly well their thesis that male sexuality is the essence of literary power. The opening chapter of *Sophie's Choice* sets up a paradigmatic model of male bonding through art: an older male, denied a writing career, devotes himself instead to the support and encouragement of a younger and more gifted "son" or "brother." Farrell's intention to write is transformed into the nurturing of his talented son, subsequently replaced by Stingo: "Son, *write your guts out*." Nathan, a gifted mime and storyteller, has also wanted to write and becomes instead a "supportive brother-figure" for Stingo and the only reader and critic of his novel. Even the narrative technique of *Sophie's Choice* contributes. The dialogue between the old and the young Stingo provides an affectionate father/son tone which guarantees a constant framework of male bonding in the joint pursuit of the ultimate male task of artistic creation:

> "How I now cherish the image of myself in this earlier time . . . supremely content in the knowledge that the fruit of this happy labor, whatever its deficiencies, would be the most awesome and important of man's imaginative endeavors—the Novel. The blessed Novel. The sacred Novel. The Almighty Novel."

On the other hand, the relationship of women to language in *Sophie's Choice* reflects their negative status with equal accuracy. Women are not only degraded by the sexist language men use to reduce them to their sexual anatomy—for example, "a piece of ass"—but women are obliged to degrade themselves through their own use of language. Leslie's uninhibited sexual language is her greatest "turn-on," since "this concubine's speech" serves to assure Stingo that the Jewish princess is in reality only a whore. The degradation of Sophie, whose linguistic ability far surpasses that of any male in the novel, illustrates particularly well the obstinate determination of sexist society to deny women any authentic use of language. Fluent in German, Polish, French, and Russian, Sophie finds herself in a situation where she must speak English, the single language in which Stingo and Nathan retain total superiority. Indeed, at our first encounter with Sophie, Nathan is berating her for the parallel female sins of sexual and linguistic infidelity: "I *can't* be a cunt, you dumb fucking Polack. When are you going to learn to *speak* the *language*?" Stingo periodically quotes Sophie's speech verbatim so that we may observe for ourselves that it is indeed "fetchingly erratic," that is, riddled with lexical and syntactical errors. Moreover, Sophie essentially parrots Nathan: "All at once I became aware of the way in which Sophie echoed so much of Nathan's diction." The one linguistic skill for which we hear Sophie consistently praised is her perfect command of German, an ambivalent accomplishment at best given the historical setting of the novel; the writer Stingo, on the other hand, commands the "gorgeous" English tongue.

If Nathan in his roles as knowledgeable reader, critic, and literary historian predicts the coming of Jewish Writing to replace Southern Writing, certainly neither he nor Stingo ever foresees a tradition of Women's Writing. By the time Sophie expresses the astonishing desire to write a novel about her own experiences, her linguistic incompetence has been sufficiently proven to make her project seem not only improbable but almost comic; should any doubt remain, we are treated immediately to the single sample of her writing included in the novel: "it was testimony indeed to the imperfect command of written English of which Sophie had so recently lamented to me. . . ." Since Sophie nonetheless retains a terrible obsession with her personal history, she must delegate her story to a man.

Although Stingo apparently accepts the passive role of listener, comparable both to the religious confessor and to the analyst, for Sophie there is ultimately neither redemption nor cure. The story she believes she is assigning to Stingo's pen is in the process stolen from her. As Gilbert and Gubar point out, not only does a writer "father" his text in Western literary tradition but "the chief creature man has generated is woman." Stingo, who places himself in the category of writers who exploit the tragedies of "others," that is, of women, continually generates the same female story of self-destruction: in every important sense, Maria Hunt is already Sophie Zawistowska. Moreover, the female story ultimately turns out to be in the service of and subservient to that of the male. Stingo sees in Sophie the experience of love and death he must have to mature into a writer as he reads *Sophie's Choice* as his own picaresque novel.

The peculiar interplay of the narrative voices in *Sophie's Choice* illustrates particularly well the respective roles of men and women in a sexist literature and society. Not only is Sophie's narrative punctuated with reminders of Stingo's presence, but in most cases Stingo and not Sophie actually recounts her past. As "herstory" becomes "History," a clear narrative pattern emerges to distinguish the female from the male narrator. Sophie tells her own story only when she is lying or confessing previous lies. Thus, Sophie's major interventions involve her creation of a false childhood in Cracow, a misleading portrait of Nathan as a supportive and loving "Prince Charming," her malignant misrepresentation of Wanda, and so on. Not only is unreliability thus attributed to the female, but the male voice becomes in contrast the voice of Truth. Indeed, the male narrator is consistently obliged to identify the female as liar: "But now it again becomes necessary to mention that Sophie was not quite straightforward in her recital of past events. . . ."

At other times, Stingo uses the opposite but functionally identical technique of the insistent assurance that Sophie tells the truth, or rather—and the distinction is important—that Stingo believes her. Not only are Stingo's reassurances suspiciously overdone, not only do they imply that Stingo did not believe her at other times and thus remind us that Sophie lies, but they make it clear that truth is male-defined and that to merit belief, Sophie's story must receive male validation.

Moreover, Sophie's lack of credibility is directly and significantly linked to her alleged lack of fidelity: women are whores and liars. We should carefully note the context in which the issue of Sophie's credibility is first raised:

> Blackstock was a truly happy man. He adored Sylvia more than life itself. Only the fact that he was childless, he once told Sophie, kept him from being *absolutely* the happiest man on earth. . . .
>   As will be seen in due course (and the fact is important to this narrative), Sophie told me a number of lies that summer.

By juxtaposing the first mention of Sophie's lying to the protestations of Blackstock that he is a truly happy man who adores his wife, Stingo at least suggests by association that Sophie's "lies" may include her denial of sexual involvement with Blackstock. In any case, Sophie's initial lie to Stingo falsely represents her sexual fidelity: "I note that Sophie told me a lie within moments after we first set eyes on each other. This was when, after the ghastly fight with Nathan, she leveled upon me her look of desperation and declared that Nathan was 'the only man I have ever made love to beside my husband.'" The possibility that Sophie may be lying about her fidelity is further reinforced by Nathan's accusations, and this extraordinary promotion of Nathan to a figure of authority permits Styron to expose the irrational bias of systematic sexism. For insane or not, pathological liar or not, Nathan is established as credible, given the insistence elsewhere on his prescience, his insight, his power to predict correctly, and by his general association with the representation of the male as the possessor of knowledge.

While Sophie remains obsessed with her personal life and story, Stingo seeks to place the former in its historical and theoretical context. The female lies; the male provides statistics, information, facts. Styron portrays the male in general as the learned, objective, neutral scholar; for the liar Nathan, who inexhaustibly researches Nazi anti-Semitism and the Civil War, fulfills this vision as much as Stingo. Ironically, of course, Sophie's lies essentially concern men. She accepts her female role as their promoter and protector, perpetuating to the best of her ability one of the central myths of a world in which men dominate, namely, that men are *good:* Sophie's father risked his life to save Jews; Casimir was a generous, loving, intelligent husband; Nathan is a gentle and tender savior, Stingo a devoted friend. And yet, or so a system founded on sexism would have it, Sophie is a liar, and Stingo and Nathan, who perpetuate harmful and degrading misrepresentations of women, are not only imaginative and creative but factual and reliable.

Although Styron has been repeatedly accused of exploiting the experience of others for his own personal and literary benefit, no one seems yet to have questioned his right as male to usurp a female life. Stingo himself expresses some concern that he may have "intruded" on Sophie's privacy, but his scruples involve Sophie not as woman but as the survivor of a concentration camp. In fact, Styron demonstrates that the experience of women can be a particularly effective means of understanding an experience of oppression otherwise foreign. In part, Sophie's life attracts Stingo as the possibility for a story because of certain similarities between the two of them: both are non-Jews isolated in a Jewish community; the war leaves both to suffer from some degree of survival guilt; both feel shame for the racial or religious prejudice of their compatriots; and so on. Such parallels serve not to trivialize Sophie's experience, as many critics have suggested, but to insist on the important generic sense Styron means ultimately to attach to her life. Mary Daly has no doubt correctly identified the technique of "universalization" as one means used to deny the reality of the specific oppression of women. Styron uses the opposite method of particularization: the situation of women becomes the basic model through which a general concept of systematic oppression can be illustrated. In seeking a confrontation with the reality of twentieth-century dehumanization, Styron has understood the usefulness of women whose intermediate position between victim and collaborator permits him to illustrate the necessity of choice and responsibility for the liberation of the self. Thus does Stingo appropriately feel rage and sorrow at the end of *Sophie's Choice* not just for Sophie but for all "the beaten and butchered and betrayed and martyred children of the earth" who have peopled his fictional world.

WILLIAM HEATH

I, Stingo: The Problem of Egotism in Sophie's Choice

A case can be made for the idea that William Styron is the foremost novelist of his generation. His first novel, *Lie Down in Darkness* (1951), was widely acclaimed as a masterpiece, a structural and stylistic tour de force whose tragic power belied the author's twenty-six years. In a bravura challenge to his literary predecessors, Styron took on Faulkner, Fitzgerald, Warren, Wolfe, Lowry, and Joyce, absorbing their influences while asserting his own voice and vision. In *Set This House on Fire* (1960), he demonstrated a determination to move beyond his southern heritage, choosing an Italian setting and an existential situation. Inverting Henry James's International Theme, Styron's Americans proved to be not so innocent, committing murder and rape for reasons reminiscent of Dostoyevsky and philosophizing on The Meaning of It All straight out of Sartre. Turning next to the tragic core of American history, he wrote *The Confessions of Nat Turner* (1967), in which he dared to enter the consciousness of his black hero, showing that Nat's motivations, as well as the evils of slavery, were a tangle of private frustrations and public injustices, of love, hate, guilt, and misunderstanding. Despite a heated controversy over Styron's portrayal of Nat, the book was both a popular and critical success and was awarded the Pulitzer Prize. Twelve years later Styron published his most ambitious work yet, *Sophie's Choice* (1979), which amplified the meditation on slavery in his previous

From *Southern Review* 20, no. 3. © 1984 by Louisiana State University.

novel into a confrontation with the most appalling crime of our century—the
new world of total domination that was Auschwitz. By telling the story of one
scarred survivor, an elusive and captivating woman named Sophie, he was
able to approach the Nazi atrocity obliquely, and thus to personalize and
dramatize a horror so monstrous that the human component is usually lost.
All four of these novels have been praised for their stylistic mastery, their
structural virtuosity, their creation of multifaceted characters, and their
courageous depiction of private griefs as well as public dilemmas. At a time
when most American novelists have engaged in needlework, nit-picking, and
navel-gazing, Styron has affirmed his belief in real people, actual places, and
the most harrowing facts of modern history. Surely, one can argue, his is an
achievement that must be called major.

On closer examination, however, the question of Styron's merit and
reputation proves to be problematical. After an initial whirlwind of puffery
and praise, each of his books has received more reserved critical estimates.
On rereading it is clear that *Lie Down in Darkness*, for all its impressive
evoking of place and creation of character, dissipates the brilliant promise of
its exceptional opening chapters, failing in the end to achieve the tragic effect
Styron was aiming for. Once the stage is set and the principals introduced,
he seems at a loss how to dramatize their predicament. Instead the characters stand around feeling sorry for themselves and blaming each other for
their failures. The drunken father haunted by the cynical quips of *his*
drunken father, the neurasthenic mother substituting piety for a dry heart,
the idiot child inadequately loved, the hypersensitive daughter cursed to
commit suicide to expiate familial doom, the funeral procession, the God-
fearing blacks as choral witnesses to white decline and fall—what is this but
a retelling of tales Faulkner has definitively told? The same problem of
imitation is evident in the country club scenes—where Styron sometimes
does Fitzgerald better than Fitzgerald—and in Peyton's long deathward
dramatic monologue, which sounds like Quentin Compson ad-libbing Molly
Bloom. In sum, Styron is all too enmired in his sources, which frequently
swamp his own considerable talents.

Set This House on Fire and *The Confessions of Nat Turner* are even more
obviously flawed. The first slips into melodrama, relies upon stereotypes,
strains too hard to be topical and profound at the same time, fails to see the
essence of its main characters, and imposes an unconvincing up-beat
ending which exposes the glib uses Styron was making of his borrowed
existentialism—"As for being and nothingness. . . ." In spite of some vivid
and dramatic scenes, the book seems finally an unnatural mating of *Tender
Is the Night* and *The Marble Faun* with *Being and Nothingness* and *Crime and
Punishment*. The central problem with *The Confessions of Nat Turner* is the

unfortunate choice Styron made to tell Nat's horrendous story in stilted pseudo-Victorian rhetoric which smothers the slave's life in a prodigal and prolix language that is foreign to his mind and actions. Furthermore, Styron's sense of Nat's personality and motivations, which are questionable at best, suggests that in truth we are reading the confessions of William Styron. Critical reappraisal, in short, indicates that Styron's career has not been the triumphal procession his admirers have insisted on; rather, there is substantial evidence of floundering, of failing to fit technique to theme and find an eloquence appropriate for his important subjects. In truth Styron's fictions serve to illustrate Randall Jarrell's witty definition of a novel as a long piece of prose that has something wrong with it.

This brings us to the difficult critical conundrum presented by *Sophie's Choice*. Most reviewers praised the novel as a superior achievement, even a masterwork of American fiction, citing Styron's valiant grappling with the evils of Auschwitz, his moving recounting of Sophie's sufferings, and his intricate blending of her story with Stingo's loss of innocence and Nathan's descent into madness. But others had grave reservations. John Gardner questioned whether Styron's transferring the techniques of Southern Gothic to a topic as unique as the Holocaust didn't "seriously alter the thing seen," while John Aldridge asserted that the "soaring grandiloquence of Styron's prose," which portends "some large and apocalyptic meaning," was completely out of key with the "sad comedy" of his story. Jack Beatty attacked the book as "a palimpsest of self-canceling intentions," finding Sophie "insufferably coy," Nathan "fudged," Stingo "masturbatory," the style "sluggish and self-indulgent," the structure "rambling," and Styron's moral sense "purblind" and "promiscuous." Almost as harsh was Robert Towers, who thought that Sophie remained "a parcel of fragments," that Nathan was merely "a confection from the gaslight era," that significant themes were "insufficiently dramatized," and that the style at its worst was "elephantine." Although Towers admitted that the Auschwitz sections were "memorable," he also felt that the book was so flawed it could not even be considered "a noble failure."

Is it possible, amid all these conflicting claims, to elaborate a more convincing interpretation? It seems to me that the key to a satisfactory evaluation of *Sophie's Choice* is the problem of Styron's characterization of Stingo, a central figure in the novel, its narrator, and the author's alter ego, his "brother-self." Stingo plays a double role in the novel; as a twenty-two-year-old budding novelist and reluctant virgin he learns the ways of the world largely through his encounter with Sophie and Nathan, and as a narrator in his fifties he recalls his youthful experiences and adds his own commentary on everything from the contents of medicine cabinets to the meaning of Auschwitz. Both the younger and the elder Stingo are obviously based upon

Styron himself, who has chosen to imbed fragments of his own autobiography in the larger edifice of the novel. Apparently, the purpose of this method is to establish an authenticity based on Styron's life in 1947 from which he can lure the reader into accepting the grand fable he is creating about Sophie and her ordeal at Auschwitz. Unfortunately Styron is not always clear about what his stance toward his persona should be; ironic detachment yields to nostalgic identification, satiric comedy is superseded by apologetics, and the entire relationship between Styron and Stingo becomes hopelessly confused.

Styron himself has described *Sophie's Choice* as "a funny, split book" which merges Stingo's "raw curiosity about the world, his naivete, his groping, and his yearning" with the demonic story of Sophie's life, which is "past any American concept of what horror is." Stingo is "a kid coming up against this inferno, of which he's only had the vaguest hint. And this girl being the filter through which it is rendered." In other interviews Styron has insisted that Stingo is, for the most part, a stand-in for himself: "The novel is plainly autobiographical," he told James Atlas, "but it shouldn't be taken as God's truth about my life." And to Valerie Arms he said, "I wouldn't feel happy unless they immediately identified Stingo as a man who is masquerading as Bill Styron. That is central to the whole strategy of the book."

The problem is not with the use of an autobiographical persona as such, but with the fact that Stingo as presented seems too vain, callow, and self-deceived to be Styron himself; yet the author makes only fitful attempts to differentiate himself from his character. The reviewer Edith Milton was convinced that Stingo is not at all autobiographical, regardless of the fact that his history is "identical" with Styron's, claiming that what we are witnessing is a "breathtaking" balance between fiction and fact with Styron moving "from confession to invention, from deeply felt compassion to glibness, from wisdom to asininity, in the most brilliant display of pyrotechnics in the uses of the narrator since Byron's *Don Juan*." I find this reading too clever by half—Styron, after all, is not Borges. It is tempting to separate Styron from Stingo completely, but the text simply does not support that kind of interpretation. Robert Towers has stated the problem best:

> Is it possible that Styron is playing a complex literary game of some sort, endowing Stingo with the externals of his own career, using him for purposes of self-parody, establishing him at an ironic distance from himself? Or is the whole thing an exercise in self-castigation? Alas, there is no telling, for Stingo's voice is the only voice we hear.

Let us listen, then, to Stingo's voice to see what we *do* hear.

When we first meet Stingo he is an ambitious young novelist of twenty-two who is experiencing his first case of writer's block—"I had the syrup," he says, "but it wouldn't pour." His dreams are of destined fame, but his lowly job involves reading unsolicited manuscripts for McGraw-Hill. With the spite that seems to make the literary world go around, Stingo rejects every single submission, "all of them so freighted with hope and club-footed syntax," taking a sadistic delight in his work: "I honestly enjoyed the bitchery and vengeance I was able to wreak upon these manuscripts. . . . Oh, clever, supercilious young man! How I gloated and chuckled as I eviscerated these helpless, underprivileged, subliterary lambkins." In his smug zeal he even casts off *Kon Tiki*. Were this novel about anything but the Holocaust, the "supercilious" ironies of this episode would be plain enough, but when we juxtapose Stingo's attitudes toward *this* selection process with the choices of life and death involved in the Final Solution, suddenly all the language becomes acidic—"clubfooted," "helpless," "eviscerated." Whether Styron is aware of these added ironies, and the commentary they make on his narrator, is not clear. What is clear is that when Styron is talking about his persona, Stingo, he tends to forget that the central story of the novel is Sophie's tragedy, not Stingo's "voyage of discovery." Instead of using Stingo's sexual yearnings and novelistic ambitions as an understated ironic counterpoint to Sophie's more significant fate, Styron makes the two tales compete with each other. Although the novel's title is *Sophie's Choice*, Styron gets so caught up in his fable of how his narrator writes his novel, wins his manhood, and conquers grief that the novel might just as well be called *Stingo's Progress*.

Obviously there is a strong element of nostalgia in Styron's portrayal of Stingo; like Whitman singing a song about himself, it is only natural that Styron/Stingo celebrates himself as well:

> How I now cherish the image of myself in this earlier time. . . .
> Oh, Stingo, how I envy you in those faraway afternoons of First
> Novelhood (so long before middle age and the drowsy slack tides
> of inanition, gloomy boredom with fiction, and the pooping-out
> of ego and ambition) when immortal longings impelled your
> every hyphen and semicolon and you had the faith of a child in
> the beauty you felt you were destined to bring forth.

If I am right in my contention that Styron's career has been floundering almost from its inception, then there is an added poignancy in this attempt to reinvigorate his mid-life stagnation by reincarnating his younger, more confident, self—a young man who can boast, "Move over, Warren, this is

Stingo arriving," and who takes enormous pride in "the sheer *quality* of what I had put into the book."

The book in question, apparently, is *Lie Down in Darkness*, and Styron's compulsion to tell how that book got written is the key to why Stingo's story tends to subvert Sophie's. Stingo is aware that he is "unacquainted with love and all but a stranger to death," and that until he has understood these things he cannot hope to be more than "a skinny, six-foot-tall, one-hundred-and-fifty-pound exposed nerve with nothing very much to say." At this point three important things happen which foster Stingo's ambitions: his father sends him the necessary money (improbably derived from the sale in the past of a slave named, ironically enough, "Artiste"), Stingo learns of the death of a childhood crush named Maria Hunt ("she was beautiful enough to wreck the heart"), and he meets Sophie and Nathan. With the money he can quit his job and devote full time to writing, using the death of Maria as his tragic subject and finding in his turbulent new friends the companionship and experience he has been longing for. At first Stingo resists their overtures for fear of "getting sucked toward the epicenter of such a volatile, destructive relationship," declaring that "I, Stingo, had other fish to fry," determined as he is to "write my guts out," and not get trapped into playing "the hapless supernumerary in some tortured melodrama."

As it turns out, the tragedy is theirs and the melodrama is his, but Stingo never seems to realize that, always upstaging the more significant action. His obsession is with "poor dead Maria, doomed and a victim from the outset through all the tangled misunderstandings, petty hatreds and vindictive hurts that are capable of making bourgeois family life the closest thing to hell on earth"—a statement that Auschwitz renders absurd. Stingo's eye, however, is not on the sufferings of others, but his own. He tells us, after his failure with Leslie, that "I was a writer, an artist," who would not allow "some misplaced notion of the primacy of the groin to subvert grander aims of beauty and truth. *So onward*, Stingo, I said to myself, rallying my flayed spirits, onward with your work." "Flayed" as he may be, Stingo still has the certitude that "the wrenching anguish endured in the crucible of art would find its recompense in everlasting fame, and glory, and the love of beautiful women." Admittedly, there is a degree of irony here, but none when Stingo speaks of "spilling quarts of my heart's blood" after a morning of "especially fruitful work." Similarly, when Nathan claims priority over Sophie, Stingo dismisses his love for her as "futile woolgathering" and returns to his novel, "intensely aware that I had my own tragic chronicle to tell." Even at the end, when he has triumphed over his rival and has Sophie in his arms, Stingo's mind is on his all-important career: "I hugged Sophie softly and thought of my book."

From Stingo's point of view, then, Sophie and Nathan are merely crewmen on his own voyage of discovery. They teach him about the complexity of human nature, the evils of Auschwitz, the splendors of love, and the horrors of madness. They become, in a sense, a surrogate family for Stingo, nurturing his talent as they initiate him into the Freudian depths of life. The elder Stingo, in describing his preparations to tell Sophie's story, displays the same egocentric pattern as his younger self. He stresses how he had to "torture" himself "by absorbing as much as I could find of the literature of *l'univers concentrationnaire*," and he pinpoints his own "time relation" to the Holocaust—"as Sophie first set foot on the railroad platform in Auschwitz, it was a lovely spring morning in Raleigh, North Carolina, where I was gorging myself on bananas." Once again Stingo's ego gets in the way, comparing the sufferings of the Jews with his own torturous reading of George Steiner.

Nathan's role in "Stingo's Progress" is equally ironic. Styron goes to great lengths to convince us that Nathan is a polymath and a prophet. Mad though he may be, his breakdown is also a breakthrough; he sees, Stingo alleges, things the rest of us miss. Nathan's prophecies range from the trivial—the advent of unbreakable records—to the profound—the coming years of "madness, illusion, error, dream and strife." But as far as Stingo is concerned, all the indicators of Nathan's sagacity are only preparations for his augury of Stingo's future artistic preeminence. "That's the most exciting hundred pages by an unknown writer anyone's ever read," Nathan proclaims, and Stingo becomes an instant believer: "How could I have failed to have the most helpless crush on such a generous, mind-and-life-enlarging mentor, pal, savior, sorcerer? Nathan was utterly, fatally glamorous." Thus while Nathan the Mad goads Stingo with the aspersions of his harshest critics, that he has "a pretty snappy talent in the traditional Southern mode" with "all the old clichés," Nathan the Wise is there to reassure him that he had created a "fresh vision of the South" which transcends the admitted influence of Faulkner and is "uniquely" and "electrifyingly" his own.

However self-serving Styron's characterization of Stingo's artistic ambitions may be (he even suggests that his book on Nat Turner disproved the demise of the novel), I can appreciate some of the author's indulgence—after all, writing a novel is an enormous challenge and the first hundred pages of *Lie Down in Darkness* are astonishingly good. But Stingo's presentation of himself as an "aspiring swordsman" is a complete miscalculation. In an effort to aggrandize Stingo's lust Styron unlooses the floodgates of his rhetoric, pompously celebrating Stingo's vain efforts to get laid as a quest of epic proportions. In consequence, what should be light comedy and ironic contrast competes with and undercuts Sophie's unfolding tragedy.

One clue to Styron's lack of stylistic control may be found in the affinities he perceives between sex and language. Written words, Stingo tells us,
fill him with erotic feelings, so that even reading a telephone directory can
cause him a "noticeable tumescence." Likewise, when Stingo is at a loss for
words he feels "foreshortened, shriveled" on one occasion and "feeble, impotent" on another. He thinks of his novel as "a cathartic instrument through
which I was able to discharge on paper many of my more vexing tensions,"
and when he is contemplating writing about the evils of Auschwitz, he
declares that the topic is "impenetrable only so long as we shrink from trying
to penetrate it." Not surprisingly, then, Stingo feels grateful to Nathan for
purging his prose of "onanistic dalliance." Indeed, masturbation plays a large
role in Stingo's life. He sees himself as "sacrificed on the altar of Onan" and
"reduced to performing furtive pocket jobs"; he even prides himself on a
"surprisingly witty" essay on the best manual lubricants which he has
confided to his journal. Sartre has argued in *What Is Literature?* that "to speak
is to fire"; it would seem that the corollary for Stingo is that to write is to
"shoot off."

In writing about Stingo's lust, Styron is misled by the classic American
assumption that bigger is better. A giganticism dominates his prose which
combines the worst mannerisms of Thomas Wolfe and Edgar Allan Poe.
Stingo tells us that his lust was "incredible—something prehensile, a groping
snout of desire, slithering down the begrimed walls of the wretched old
building, uncoiling itself across a fence, moving with haste serpentine and
indecent," and he pictures himself as "a godforsaken organism in absolute
thrall to the genital urge, capable of defiling a five-year-old of either sex." He
is "a recumbent six-foot-long erogenous zone," in a nearly constant "stal-
lionoid condition," whose gargantuan sexual need is "immeasurably huge."

While Stingo swoons over the "various undulant roundnesses" of the
women of his dreams, nothing is more blatant, and vulgarly inappropriate,
than his "dorsal fixation." Leslie is praised for her "darling behind" and Mary
Alice for having "the most gorgeous sweetheart of an ass"; but the trophy, of
course, goes to Sophie's "achingly desirable, harmoniously proportioned
Elberta peach of a derriere," which is as "sumptuous . . . as some fantastic
prize-winning pear" and is "the paragon of world behinds." Readers may
take their pick from the fruit metaphors and speculate about how the world's
best behind is chosen, but when Stingo finally enjoys Sophie's body, and finds
himself "thrusting into the cleft between those smooth white globes," he, for
one, is convinced that it is now necessary to redefine the meaning of "God."

The spirit of Poe haunts Stingo's imagination. In anticipation of his
visit to "the dark gods" with Leslie he zooms in to admire "the orthodonti-
cally fashioned perfection of her sparkling incisors" in language that recalls

how Ligeia's mad husband extols the width of her nostrils and the height of her forehead. Stingo kissing Leslie is described as though it were a shoving match between creatures of the deep: her tongue "plunged like some writhing sea-shape into my gaping maw . . . it wriggled, it pulsated, and made contortive sweeps of my mouth's vault." Given this grotesque Poe-like magnification, it is apt that Leslie's tongue should taste like "Amontillado." Even more disturbing is Stingo's fascination with necrophilia. He delights in imagining bouts of "stormy lovemaking" with Leslie, Maria Hunt, and Sophie all at once. What makes these dreams particularly enticing for him is the thought that they are all dead—"not truly dead . . . but in effect extinguished, defunct, kaput, so far as each of them concerned my life." Certainly part of Stingo's attraction to Sophie is the fact that she is damaged goods; Alvin Rosenfeld has even suggested that Stingo's lust for Sophie perpetrates an "Erotics of Auschwitz," with Sophie's "abused and broken body" dramatizing the appeal of "the Mutilated Woman." Overstated as that may be, clearly Stingo's sexual yearnings, as presented by Styron, are impossibly heavy-handed and offensive, if not downright perverse.

Nevertheless it is precisely Stingo's greedy libido that Styron presents as his chief claim on our sympathies. Stingo, we are repeatedly told, suffers; his balls ache like no others; for him purity is "an inwardly abiding Golgotha." Even if *Sophie's Choice* were not a novel about the Holocaust, Styron should have had enough sense of proportion to stay away from such inept comparisons, but instead he glories in them. Stingo describes hearing Sophie and Nathan making love in the room above him as "another nail" to "amplify my crucifixion," and his fumbling sessions with Leslie as "a Passion Week" which concluded with "my time on the Cross in the small hours of Friday morning." He bemoans "the torture she inflicted on me," and cries out, "Oh Lord, how my balls hurt," and asks himself, "Could John the Baptist have suffered such deprivation?" But how can he explain such torments to a silly girl? "It's tough on a guy," he whines to Leslie. "It's terrible. You can't imagine." Yet Stingo forgives Leslie, since she knows not what she does, and predicts that she found "her full meed of happiness" in a "multiorgasmic" life.

Later in the novel Stingo endures the same mock-ordeal with Mary Alice. Once again he "writhes inwardly" and complains that his "poor John Thomas" was "as moribund as a flayed worm." Enraged by her "prissy chagrin" he shouts, "You cock teasers have turned millions of brave young men, many of whom died for your precious asses on the battlefields of the world, into a generation of sexual basket cases!" Then he goes back to his room to have his first homosexual dream. Obviously, all of this should be played as low comedy, but Stingo insists that his sufferings must be taken as seriously as Sophie's. When he mourns with her after his failure with Leslie, he feels that "her grief met mine in some huge gushing confluence"; and after he has been "flayed" by Mary Alice, he is convinced that he has now experienced "the horror of existence," and he prays that Sophie will come to help "relieve my angst." When she does arrive, he insists that they were both "bleeding to death with . . . gaping wounds," and shortly thereafter Stingo and Sophie flee together—as though Stingo through his sexual suffering had earned the right to share his fate with hers.

What does Styron hope to accomplish by such a bombastic treatment of Stingo's sexuality? Are Stingo's pseudo-agonies inflated to the size of Sophie's genuine ones so that he can win her love and have the last word? Styron's explanation for including Stingo's erotic escapades seems an exercise in apologetics. He claims that to cut out this part of the novel would be like "divesting a body of some member" and that he senses "an urgency, an elusive meaning in this experience and its desperate eroticism" which says something significant about the "sexually bedeviled" 1940s:

> A lot in the way of bilious reminiscence has been written about sex by survivors of the *fifties*, much of it a legitimate lament. But the forties were really far worse, a particularly ghastly period for Eros. . . . For the first time within reckoning society permitted, indeed encouraged, unhindered propinquity of the flesh but still forbade the flesh's fulfillment. For the first time automobiles had large, upholstered back seats. This created a tension and a frustration without precedent in the relationship between the sexes.

As social history this is hardly convincing, yet Styron appears to take it seriously, depicting mid-century America as "a nightmarish Sargasso Sea of guilts and apprehensions" which "the ensuing decades, with their extraordinary scientific progress in terms of the care and maintenance of the libido" have wonderfully transcended. As proof of his thesis he cites the fact that now for five dollars he can "freely and without anxiety . . . view sex like the conquistadores beheld the New World: . . . jumbo-sized dreamy-faced wet-lipped young Pocahontases" and so forth—as if pornography were the cure for all the terrible tensions caused by those big back seats! Stingo contends that the story of how he lugged his "engorged penis across the frozen sexual moonscape of the 1940's" provides a "nice counterpoint to the larger narrative," but a close reading of the text does not support his argument. Rather his tale seems to be an ill-considered indulgence and a narcissistic attempt to sabotage Sophie's much more significant chronicle.

Further evidence of Styron's confusion of purpose is found in the use he makes of Stingo's journal. Once again we are given self-deceiving excuses:

> Although I promised myself not to inflict upon the reader too many of the voluminous jottings I made that summer (it is a tiresome and interruptive device, symptomatic of a flagging imagination), I have made an exception in this particular instance, setting my little memorandum down just as I wrote it as unimpeachable testimony to the way some people talked in 1947.

As the novel progresses, Stingo makes several more "exceptions," and so we get to sample quite a few of his jottings. After presenting his first selection—"I have turned on her the pure flame of my intellect,"—Stingo confesses that he is "a little mortified" to see that his younger self wrote without "the faintest trace of irony," but when he comes to quote his notations again two chapters later, his evaluation is much higher. Now these writings are compared to Gide's *Journals:* it is plain to see, Stingo announces, that their style "continues to possess an unruffled, wryly sardonic, self-anatomizing quality which Gide might have admired." A few phrases, however, refute Stingo's appraisal:

> I am so beside myself with plain old hog lust. . . . Never before have I known that kissing can be so *major,* so expansive. . . . In the soft light of the foyer my membrum, betrousered, is truly rampant. Also a spot of "dogwater" there, pre-coital seepage, as if a puppy had peed in my lap.

Gide, of course, would never have admired such trite musings—I imagine his saying something like "*Qui est ce fou là?*"—but Stingo maintains that his journal is filled with "vivid and valuable passages" which have a "legitimate place" in the narrative.

Stingo's relationship with Sophie—how through loving her and learning the story of her life he comes to understand that "absolute evil is never extinguished from the world"—is at the core of the novel. In order to analyze some of the difficulties Styron has with his hero/narrator in these central sequences, I want first to note some of the salient traits of Stingo's personality. As I have already shown, Stingo is a very ambitious young man with an overheated and misdirected sex drive. Certainly he is not averse to praising his own merits, admitting to "a spacious and sympathetic intelligence," *et cetera*, but he is also aware of at least some of his crucial short-comings. As an only child he was "classically though not immoderately spoiled," and the easy success of his life enables him to say "I was fortune's darling if there ever was one." He is aware that his privileged position is a mirror of America's auspicious status in an iniquitous world—"Our glut of good fortune was enough to make us choke." He also knows that despite his "staggeringly puerile inexperience" he has a tendency to turn pontifical and didactic. In sum, Stingo is not lacking in self-criticism, yet I think he is largely insensible to his most detrimental traits: his condescension to "inferiors," his latent potential for violence, and, most importantly, his tendency to retreat from difficult situations into a self-satisfied complacency.

I have already shown Stingo's contempt for unfit manuscripts and the nasty connotations such an attitude implies; frequently he betrays the same disdain for people—from the "series of reptilian desk clerks" in the first chapter to the "clots of thuggish policemen" in the last. Stingo has inherited his condescension from his father—a man he praises for his "abiding belief in good manners and public decency," but also a man who scorns New York as a hellhole and who is baffled by the "feisty Hibernian umbrage" of a taxi driver he has tipped a nickel. Given such "umbrage" on the part of the lower orders, Stingo himself is often tempted to "acts of near-violence." He thinks that his situation in Brooklyn is "closely analogous" to Raskolnikov's in St. Petersburg and speculates on the consequences to himself were he to kill his landlady. Women who frustrate him, those "loathsome little vampires," also trigger off murderous urges. When Leslie fails to fulfill her sexual promises to Stingo, he wants to "belt the living shit out of her" and to ram a "priceless Degas down around her neck." With Mary Alice, whose caresses lack affection, he has an "overpowering longing to perpetrate a rape." Even the ineffectual minister at Sophie's funeral brings out his "homicidal potential." Stingo demonstrates, in short, the pattern of dehumanizing people through contempt and then wishing to destroy them with the impunity that has been the fatal curse of modern history.

Not surprisingly, therefore, Stingo lavishes an indiscriminate "understanding" on Rudolf Höss and Dr. Jemand von Niemand, inserting explanations for the feelings and motivations of these two important Nazis which are remarkably at odds with his narrative dramatization of them. Stingo tells us, for example, that Höss is a man who is profoundly "tormented" by his job: "A convulsive despondency, megrims, anxiety, freezing doubt, inward shudders, *Weltschmerz* that passes understanding—all overwhelm Höss as the process of murder achieves its runaway momentum. He is plunged into realms that transcend reason, belief, sanity, Satan." Yet the Höss we meet in the novel, and as far as I can tell, the Höss of history, is very much the ambi-

tious petty bureaucrat of banal evil that Hannah Arendt has so aptly
described. A selection from Höss's journal shows how much he is merely a
man of smug mediocrity:

> I was no longer happy in Auschwitz once the mass extermina-
> tions had begun. . . . When I saw my children happily playing or
> observed my wife's delight over our youngest, the thought would
> often come to me: How long will our happiness last? My wife
> could never understand these gloomy moods of mine and
> ascribed them to some annoyance connected with my work.

The soulless obliviousness of this passage is beyond commentary. And as for
the Weltschmerz of Höss's megrims, what the narrative demonstrates is that
his headaches are the product of logistics, not ethics; he complains to Sophie
that "They seem to have no knowledge of the incredible numbers involved
in these Special Actions."

The portrait of the doctor who forces Sophie to make her most
terrible choice is equally skewed. The scene of the choice itself is taut and
laceratingly effective, but Styron immediately follows it with a cockeyed
homily on the doctor's motivations. It seems he was looking for "some
tender and perishable Christian" upon whom he wanted to inflict "an
unpardonable sin":

> Was it not supremely simple, then, to restore his belief in God,
> and at the same time to affirm his human capacity for evil, by
> committing the most intolerable sin that he was able to conceive?
> Goodness could come later. But first a great sin. One whose
> glory lay in its subtle magnanimity—a choice.

This interpolation is a serious artistic blunder; Styron deflates the power of
the decisive scene his novel has been building toward for nearly five hundred
pages by foisting on us the so-called "religious strivings" of a bored mass
murderer who misses God. It is as if Shakespeare were to interrupt the
climax of *King Lear* for a disquisition on how and why a slave came to be
Cordelia's hangman.

The contradictions in Stingo's character, as well as the split between
how skillfully he tells his story and how poorly he interprets it, are best illustrated by his infatuation with Sophie, which combines vanity and empathy,
attraction and repulsion. Stingo is truly moved by Sophie's distress, yet he
also wants to use her for his sexual relief; he is more than willing to play her
father confessor, and to help alleviate her survivor's guilt if he can; but he also

wants to turn her tragedy to his own artistic advantage, and he reserves the right to suppress her disclosures if they become too threatening. Indeed, nothing is more striking in Stingo's personality than his tendency to elude difficulties, to retreat, to escape.

Stingo states that as a writer he is drawn to "morbid themes;" yet when he is actually confronted with Nathan's madness, for example, he finds himself suddenly transformed into "a triumphant paradigm of chickenshit," and all he really wants to do is "curl up and take a nap." In other scenes we find him abdicating responsibilities, not listening to the problems of others, and deliberately forgetting disquieting events. The archetype of all these evasions is found, I believe, in the revealing anecdote Stingo tells about how he once neglected to care for his dying mother. Instructed to stay at home and keep a fire burning for her, Stingo goes joy-riding instead; when he returns one look tells him that she has almost frozen to death in his absence:

> Those hazel bespectacled eyes and the way that her ravaged, still terrified gaze caught my own, then darted swiftly away. It was the *swiftness* of that turning away which would thereafter define my guilt; it was as swift as a machete dismembering a hand. And I realized with horror how much I resented her burdensome affliction.

As punishment Stingo's father makes him spend two hours in a freezing shed, an ordeal Stingo welcomes because he believes he can expiate his crime by suffering in exactly the same way his mother has. A few weeks later his mother dies "a disgusting death, in a transport of pain," and he is left to wonder whether his actions hastened her death and if his mother ever forgave him. He describes his resultant guilt feelings as hateful, corrosive, and toxic, and he seeks a convenient excuse to be rid of them and to "think of sex" instead.

Several clues to Stingo's motivations are suggested in this episode. Most striking is the idea of *equivalence*—that if he reenacts and imitates what his mother endured he will be able to purge himself of guilt. At the same time we see that he resented his mother's sickness, hated his pangs of guilt, and would rather contemplate erotic pleasures. Later in his life Stingo is compelled to encounter tragedy, to witness the appalling truths of life, and then to lay claim to and impersonate equivalent disasters, in order to be free of the dire situations he himself has sought out. We have already seen how Stingo tries to pit his sexual frustrations against the far more profound agonies of Sophie, thus pretending that he has earned the right to share her sufferings and her love. In general, Stingo's pattern is to transform tragic empathy—with its burden of guilt, fear, pity, and pain—into what he takes to be a comparable self-dramatization, which serves to neutralize the bane and permits him to slip back to his customary complacency. The result is a thwarting of authentic tragic catharsis by self-serving mimicry and evasion.

Stingo's entire relationship with Sophie is restricted by the egocentric limits of his response. When he learns that Sophie needs a father confessor, he is sure that "I, Stingo, handily filled the bill," but he also admits that he is acting on "a strictly self-serving scheme" to steal her away from Nathan. Yet when Sophie tells him how terribly Nathan has been treating her, Stingo's basic response is personal—"'. . . what about me? Me? *Me?*' I began to smite my chest to emphasize my own involvement in the tragedy. 'What about the way he treated *me*, this guy?'" A similar prideful insistence is seen when Stingo, talking to himself in the shower, rehearses his proposal—"So now love me, Sophie. Love me. Love *me!* Love life!" Nonetheless when Stingo the life-force first has a chance to love Sophie, he glumly confesses that "kissing was *all* I could manage," and he is devastated when she describes his penis as "sweet" rather than "gigantic." He also resents that, minutes after masturbating him, Sophie's thoughts wander back to a dead lover from her past. "Could women, then, so instantaneously turn off their lust like a light switch?" Stingo asks, offended that he is not the alpha and omega of her world. Shortly afterwards Sophie tells him that "some day you will know what it is to be in love," a statement Stingo rejects as "infinitely boring," and one which he thinks reveals a "profound failure of sensibility." But Sophie, of course, knows what she is talking about; Stingo's selfish lust is a far cry from love, and the failure of sensibility is his.

Even after Stingo has supposedly fallen in love with Sophie and learned some of the most dreadful truths about the Holocaust, he facilely decides "to hear no more about Auschwitz," not to let Sophie obsess him as "a love object," and to "put her story out of my mind." Informed by Larry that Nathan is clinically insane, and asked to keep a close eye on him, Stingo goes running after Mary Alice instead, abandoning Nathan and Sophie to their fate. Predictably, Nathan has one of his sinister rages, prophetically accusing Stingo of the seduction he has not yet accomplished, and, in effect, forcing Sophie into his arms, as they both flee from Nathan's mad wrath.

Thus Stingo is given his great opportunity, but he proves inadequate to the situation. Nowhere is his basic complacency of mind more apparent than in this crucial sequence. Rather than rising to the occasion he subsides into "a remarkable tranquility" and "equanimity," thinking more about his career than Sophie's anguish. He basks in the prospect of his future fame, priding himself on the hard work and the "occasional freshets of grief" that have combined to enrich his novel. When he has a moment of gloom, it concerns not Sophie but the question of whether he will be able to summon the necessary passion and insight to write his climactic scene—the suicide of Maria Hunt. Clearly, in the story of "Stingo's Progress" it is Sophie's job to provide those essential "freshets of grief" and her suicide inspires him to complete his masterpiece. All of this is wonderfully presaged in an anecdote Stingo tells Sophie about how as a boy he once won a pile of nickels and, in his passion to horde them, managed to lose them all. "It is a cautionary tale," he acknowledges, "about the destructive nature of greed."

As if to shock Stingo out of his narcissistic complacency, Sophie finally tells him the story of the horrid choice she was forced to make at Auschwitz. But, as we have already seen, Stingo seems to be more interested in the motives of the doctor than the death of Sophie's child. Rather than take the tragedy to heart, he seeks "the blessed release of witless diversion," prattling away to her "with brainless unrestraint" about how happy they will be on Stingo's farm in Virginia. He tells us, with astonishing self-delusion, that they then "drank, ate crab cakes and managed to forget Auschwitz"—as if Sophie could ever forget. That night she initiates Stingo into the "varieties of sexual experience," putting him through his paces with a passion he finds as "boundless" as his own. With typical hyperbole, Stingo presents their lovemaking as an Olympian event which for Sophie was an "orgiastic attempt to beat back death, but for him was a chance to win the laurel of Sophie's praise—"Your [sic] a great lover Stingo."

Sophie rejects Stingo's questionable life-force, choosing in the end Nathan's malign death wish, and Stingo is left to recover from and make sense of their tragedy. Characteristically, Stingo's part in this fatal sequence begins with an evasion—he heads South instead of immediately going to Brooklyn to try to save Sophie. He is perplexed by his action—it is almost as if he *wants* to share the guilt for her death: "To the guilt which was murdering her just as surely as her children were murdered must there now be added my own guilt for committing the sin of blind omission that might help seal her doom as certainly as Nathan's own hands?" By claiming complicity in Sophie's death, Stingo is able to expand his role in the final scene so that it is his soliloquy which has stage center at the end. "I was determined," Stingo tells us, "that before our last leave-taking Sophie and Nathan would hear my voice."

Stingo calls his last words on the tragedy "A Study in The Conquest of Grief," but how much grief is actually felt and how well it is conquered are questionable. That Stingo wants the spotlight all to himself is made obvious by his "homicidal" resentment of the Reverend DeWitt, whom Stingo tries to upstage by swearing and talking out loud during the funeral service. Next he drinks beer all the way to the cemetery, feeling a "euphoric, inebriate

glee" and a "hilarity . . . mixed with grief," in a pathetic effort to call attention to himself and compete with the funeral of his best friends. His eulogy
to them, with the exception of the enigmatic poem by Emily Dickinson, is
platitudinous and insufficient. Stingo quotes three passages from his journal,
each of which discloses how little he has learned.

"*Someday I will understand Auschwitz*," the younger Stingo asserts,
which his elder self revises to "*Someday I will write about Sophie's life and death,
and thereby help demonstrate how absolute evil is never extinguished from the
world.*" This modification is more within an author's scope; but it tends to
reduce the complex fabric of the novel to a pat moral, and it evokes the
Gothic notion of "absolute evil." The next words of wisdom which "the
suffering Stingo" has for us are "*Let your love flow out on all living things*," a
precept which Stingo, as we have seen, rarely practices. Nevertheless, Styron
presents it to us without irony as "the only remaining—perhaps the only
bearable—truth," and he claims that in uttering such deep thoughts Stingo
is in the company of "Lao-tzu, Jesus, Gautama Buddha and thousands upon
thousands of lesser prophets." However prophetic universal love may be,
clearly for Stingo it is a cliché which has no bearing on his conduct; and the
debate which ensues about whether or not Auschwitz has blocked the flow of
"titanic love," and whether we can still love a "rabies virus" is sheer sophistry.

For his final phrase Stingo chooses a line of poetry, his own, "'*Neath
cold sand I dreamed of death / but woke at dawn to see / in glory, the bright, the
morning star*," a verse which seems to mourn the dead but whose real purpose
is to call attention to the fact that Stingo is *still* alive. What the novel ends
with, then, is not Stingo's conquest of grief, but his mock death and pseudo
resurrection; thus the focus is switched from Sophie's tragedy to Stingo's
woe, as we see him weeping for "the beaten and butchered and betrayed and
martyred children of the earth." And so it is as a man of constant sorrows that
we are meant to see Stingo as he lowers himself "to the sand on legs that
suddenly seemed strangely frail and rickety for a man of twenty-two," where
he lies all night "as safe as a mummy" until he rises like a man reborn,
blessing his "resurrection" and stating that "this was not judgment day—only
morning. Morning: excellent and fair." These words, of course, echo Emily
Dickinson's apt poem, but for Stingo they serve to imply a conquest of grief
which the woman who wrote "I like a look of agony / Because I know it's
true" would have found, I suspect, fraudulent.

What, then, are we to make of Stingo the character and Stingo the
narrator, and what do they tell us about Styron the author? I think it is clear
that both Stingos are narcissistic, with traits which enable them to exploit
others, avoid unpleasant truths, and celebrate the imperial self. As a result,
Sophie's Choice, which at its best is a tragedy of great power, is sabotaged and

replaced by "Stingo's Progress," which draws upon Sophie's sufferings and Nathan's prophecies in order to proclaim Stingo a Great Lover and a Great Writer. To what degree Styron is aware how "funny" and "split" a book he has written is difficult to tell. Certainly there are places where his ironic distance is perfect, as when he terms Stingo's encounter with Leslie "a scratching match between two virgins" and when Sophie condemns the "unearned unhappiness" of Nathan's Jewish friends. Furthermore, my exclusive focus on the liabilities of both Stingos should not blind us to the superb sequences in the novel which deserve extensive praise. But still the evidence does suggest that at many points in *Sophie's Choice* there is a problem not only of an unreliable narrator, but also a problem of an unreliable author as well, and that Styron in certain critical scenes blends with his hero/narrator and fails to heed the fundamental Socratic dictum to "Know Thyself."

ELISABETH HERION-SARAFIDIS

Sophie's Choice: *In the Realm of the Unspeakable*

> But in order to make you understand,
> to give you my life, I must tell you a
> story.
> —Virginia Woolf, *The Waves*

> For me, if literature cannot change the
> world in a radical way, it can, all the
> same, penetrate deeply into human
> consciousness.
> —William Styron, Braudeau interview

Replay
The Autobiographical Impulse

The extent to which William Styron can be considered, in the words of psychoanalyst Clarence Crafoord, to have "made himself his project"—to have involved himself in a project of self-exploration in his writing—is suggested by the increasing frequency with which he draws on personal experience, engaging aspects of himself and incidents from a personal past in

From *A Mode of Melancholy: A Study of William Styron's Novels.* © 1995 Elisabeth Herion-Sarafidis.

his art. Also, in interviews he has consistently drawn attention to this auto-biographical strategy. An example of this is his telling Valarie Meliotes Arms that his fourth novel, *Sophie's Choice*, started out in a purely autobio-graphical mode. About one quarter of the way into the narrative, the fictionalizing process, the invention of episodes, commenced; all the same, he would not feel "happy unless [readers] immediately identified Stingo [the narrator of *Sophie's Choice*] as a man who is masquerading as Bill Styron. That is central to the whole strategy of the book." It is a strategy, I believe, at work in all of the novels: most of his characters, Styron observed in an early interview, "come closer to being entirely imaginary than the other way round. Maybe that's because they all seem to end up, finally, closer to being like myself than like people I've actually observed. I sometimes feel that the characters I've created are not much more than sort of projected facets of myself. . . ." What Carolyn Durham calls Sophie Zawistowska's "terrible obsession with her personal history" would seem to have a parallel in William Styron's desire to reactivate aspects of his own past in his works of fiction. One way of approaching these narratives, then, is to read them as a writer's attempt at discovering the "truth" about himself in the voicing of that truth—an endeavor which invites comparison with the psychoanalytic project.

In *Sophie's Choice*, the writer appears not only as a persona in his own text, as an earlier rendition of himself, a protagonist whose journey to emotional maturity is one of the thematic pursuits, but also as the filtering and welding consciousness of the narrator: the writer here quite explicitly makes himself his topic. Ostensibly, the reason for the incorporation of the adventures of young Stingo hinges on the narrator's need to distance himself from the part of his story which directly involves the atrocities of the Nazi death camps, whose evil he has set out to comprehend. "*Sophie's Choice* is Stingo's tale," Styron told an interviewer. "This is why Stingo is so utterly essential to the whole story. . . . [The story] had to be told through the eyes of this young man. . . . Perhaps it's a story not so much of Auschwitz but of discovering evil. It's a time-honored technique to have the young man revealed through a reminiscence by the older man of his youthful experi-ence." In one respect a portrait of the artist as a young man, then, the text of *Sophie's Choice* is loaded with the narrator's references to and comments on his younger self—the insecure, ignorant and vulnerable young man—as well as the social/sexual mores of the United States in the early postwar years. The book also contains several entries from journals, purportedly kept by young Stingo, entries, writes the narrator, which he has kept and incorpo-rated into *Sophie's Choice* "less for any intrinsic worth than for what they added to the historical record—the record, that is, of myself."

The sheer number of autobiographical references—the different kinds of "texts" that Styron can be seen to have constructed—indicates the complex relation between this writer and his work and suggests emotional release as one of the functions of his narratives. In *Sophie's Choice,* for example, as the narrator muses on the role of writing in his life, he focuses particularly on its centrality for his twenty-two-year-old alter ego. Realizing not only how "intensely discontented, rebellious and troubled [he had been] at that age," he emphasizes the extent to which "writing had kept serious emotional distress safely at bay, in the sense that the novel I was working on served as a cathartic instrument through which I was able to discharge on paper many of my more vexing tensions and miseries." Thinking back on his work in progress, the older man remembers having at one time "felt so serenely secure in the integrity of this novel that [he] had already fashioned for it an appropriately melancholy title: *Inheritance of Night,*" which, it will be remembered, was the working title for what became *Lie Down in Darkness.* This fits well with Styron's observation in a 1979 interview with Michiko Kakutani, where he sees his fictional characters, the fact that "so many . . . are neurotic, unable to cope, frustrated and obsessed," in the light of an "attempt to get rid of my own frustrations and obsessions." While the narrator of *Sophie's Choice* reveals that the focal character of his first book was modeled on Maria Hunt, a childhood acquaintance of his, a young woman whose suicide he learned of that summer in New York, in the Kakutani interview, William Styron volunteers additional sources of an even more private nature for his first novel: at liberty to speak about these matters since the death of both his stepmother and his father, he points out that to a large degree "[Peyton's] plight was based . . . on his own adolescent gropings and struggles with a stepmother who was as close to the wicked stepmother image as one can possibly imagine."

In addition to this conscious strategy to incorporate autobiographical material the narratives also reveal, I would argue, the presence of an unconscious element. Re-encountering, as it were, his own texts many years after their creation, having recently emerged out of a severe depression, Styron confesses, as will be remembered from the discussion of *Darkness Visible,* to profound astonishment at how his younger self could have written with such insight about a state of melancholia with which he was supposedly unacquainted at that time: "In re-reading . . . sequences from my novels . . . I was stunned to perceive how accurately I had created the landscape of depression in the minds of these young women, describing with what could only be instinct, out of a subconscious already roiled by disturbances of mood, the psychic imbalance that led them to destruction." In an interview given shortly after his breakdown, Styron addresses the searing sense of guilt that is such an irresistible force in all of his narratives. Acknowledging—in words that seem to emanate from one of Cass Kinsolving's monologues—his personal experience of this mood, he explains how, in the acute state of depression, the stricken person is assaulted by feelings of devastating and utter worthlessness, convinced that "'[e]verything I have ever done is a bloated monstrosity of my ego, and I have committed atrocities against my fellow man that are unpardonable. . . . Little insults you've committed become crimes, and all your achievements, in your own mind, are reduced to a mound of ash.'" Not only could these words have been spoken by Cass in *Set This House on Fire:* very similar ones are voiced by Stingo in *Sophie's Choice* in relation to the mother who died of cancer when he was thirteen—as did the mother of the narrator of "A Tidewater Morning" as well as the mother of William Styron.

When exploring, to borrow Eudora Welty's phrase, "the solitary core" of William Styron's vision, a reader becomes increasingly attuned to the dichotomy located there: while the surface texts of the narratives appearing after *Lie Down in Darkness* can be read as a consistently affirmative gesture shaped by the quest for recollective insight, the attempts to tear away the "mask and the symbol" are, ultimately, resisted and undermined by dark swirls of melancholy, by a corrosive conviction of the essential condition of human existence as one of solitary confinement. As Styron's texts consistently court the release of guilt through narration, storytelling as an act of exploration is freighted with great significance, and language is endowed with therapeutic powers in the attempt to rescue meaning. Such a strategy would seem to be grounded in a conviction that, as Arnold Weinstein puts it in *Nobody's Home*, "all storytelling is inherently generative. . . . Narration is akin to Genesis; it is a rejection of closure, a denial of death, an engendering of presence, a preferring and a conferring of life." But as we can see, ultimately, there is no hopefulness in Styron's texts: rather, in the manner of an incantation, they encircle and yet evade the darkly alluring pull of death, the narrator in each case composing, to speak with Paul Whitehurst, "such other words as would distract me from the moment's anguish." The story "A Tidewater Morning" can be seen to provide a key to Styron's fictional *oeuvre*, as the writer, devising a means of escaping from the intolerable in the manner attempted by Paul Whitehurst (one of the names of Styron's paternal grandfather), enlists the power and magic of words in his quest for retrieval and reconstruction—as if in the clear light of retrospection, by some act of linguistic alchemy, reality could be transformed through and in the act of writing. Although Styron's texts are generally preoccupied with and played out in a realm which borders on the unspeakable, perhaps this is especially true of *Sophie's Choice*.

In the final analysis, however, argues Michael Kreyling in "Speakable and Unspeakable in Styron's *Sophie's Choice*," Styron can be seen "relentlessly maintaining the speakable nature of the universe" by creating a narrator who "would rather have language, even with its myriad thorns of irony and double meaning, tone and connotation, suggestion and play, than the ominous silence in which and because of which Auschwitz robs man of humanity in robbing him of his speech." It is true that Styron will not accept that some subjects—such as the absolute evil visible in Auschwitz—are considered too sacred or too torturous to be treated fictionally: "I cannot accept [George] Steiner's suggestion that silence is the answer, that it is best 'not to add the trivia of literary, sociological debate to the unspeakable.'" But a discussion of *Sophie's Choice* must not, I believe, take into account only the storyline that charts Stingo's way to maturity and reflects the organizing, speculating and connection-making endeavor of the narrator, the middle-aged writer. In the other storyline, Sophie can be seen to achieve a liberation of sorts through recollection and voicing, facing the truth exposed by the reassembled fragments of her life. Yet the ultimate vision inherent in this storyline is, surely, one of the utmost bleakness and hopelessness: the sole way out for Sophie is shown to lie in a termination of life. Thus the life-affirming nature of the project of recollection, to reach a kind of acceptance by mastering one's past, is turned into its dark negation—Sophie's tormented untangling of psychological constraints amounts to a preparation for death rather than life.

A Landscape Revisited

The architecture of *Sophie's Choice* is one the seasoned reader has learned to recognize in William Styron's books, one in which the interplay between repression and revelation makes up the structural matrix. When Richard Law observed that part of the argument of *Sophie's Choice* is that the "direct and unmediated encounter with the heart of darkness is not only dangerous, but may, by its very nature, prevent comprehension," he might, in fact, have been speaking about either *Set This House on Fire* or *The Confessions of Nat Turner.* It is indeed part of Styron's narrative strategy to shun the head-on confrontation; he prefers a degree of deviousness. The psychological landscape of *Sophie's Choice* is also a familiar one; this is another text seared with emotions of wretchedness and states of depression—where two of the three main characters are severely emotionally disturbed—a text about (self-)destruction, human betrayal, guilt, and actions of such inhumanity that they amount to manifestations of absolute evil.

As many critics have noted, Styron's texts play out variations of the complexities of human interrelations, of the ways in which human beings use each other. The focus is often on victimization; in the words of Styron himself: "I'm always concerned with themes that have to do with human domination. Slavery in its active form is probably the most powerful example of that." In this context, he once remarked to other interviewers that *Sophie's Choice*, "in a curious way is an extension of *Nat Turner.*" The *leitmotif* of slavery, the treatment of the margins of human existence, this time with the focus on genocide and the Nazi death camps, is one of the obvious thematic ways in which Styron's fourth novel can be considered a continuation of the previous book. But *Sophie's Choice* is also, again, a narrative deeply engaged in exploring consciousness, in speaking the unspeakable—in the charting of a quest for self-knowledge: the Sophie of the title is yet another fragmented self, one more protagonist tortuously enmeshed in feelings of guilt, like Nat Turner "pursued by an obscure, unshakable grief . . . shiver[ing] in the knowledge of the futility of all ambition." What he sought to recreate, Styron explained in an interview, was the "agony" of the life of the woman who was the inspiration for Sophie. The extent to which his Sophie is an emotional cripple, someone whose identity has been irrevocably shattered, is a matter which is disclosed only gradually to the young Stingo whom she befriends one summer in New York and whom she entrusts with her story— and, for a moment in time, also with her life. In a courageous yet doomed effort at reconstructing her life, Sophie narrates episodes from her past, confessions that reveal memories and insights which she has blocked, relegated to obscure regions of her consciousness. This recollection of her past—"an aria of unending bereavement"—is offered in a series of confessional installments, as Sophie evasively, even mendaciously at times, voices shreds of her life-story to Stingo. In a comment relating to the circuitously revelatory narrative technique of his text, Styron suggests that

> [f]irst through her lies, then through her confession, one discovers several states in her evolution, in her tragedy, several levels of horror, with a choice at each level. To be for or against the Nazis, for or against the anti-semites. To be a member of the Resistance or not. Finally to choose to live or to die. Not forgetting the choice she must make to save only one of her two children.

Sophie's confessions are like boxes within boxes—secrets within secrets that are presented to Stingo one after the other as Sophie herself is able to untie them. The circumstance that in the United States she has, as Samuel Coale writes, "reconstructed a past that parallels the same sexual and suicidal patterns of her present, one feeding the other so completely that there can be no way out in life," is a truth that will be gradually exposed in her mnemonic pursuits—unfolded, sieved through the consciousness of the middle-aged narrator whose younger self some thirty years earlier served as her confessor. In these recollections she bores down through intricately layered memories, each of which is centered around a choice, as Styron explained. As the older Stingo speculates on Sophie's reasons for telling her story in the way she did, he focuses on the sense of shame and guilt he, at the time of narration, understands to have been at the heart of her darkness.

> Sophie was not quite straightforward in her recital of past events. . . . I would learn this later, when she confessed to me that she left out many crucial facts in the story she told Nathan. She did not actually lie. . . . Nor did she fabricate something or distort anything important. . . . Why, then, did she *leave out* certain elements and details that anyone might reasonably have expected her to include? . . . the word "guilt," I discovered that summer, was often dominant in her vocabulary, and it is now clear to me that a hideous sense of guilt always chiefly governed the reassessments she was forced to make of her past.

These paralyzing feelings of guilt, interlaced with her self-hatred, that prey on her have their roots, Stingo learns, not merely in a survivor's guilt, but also in an awareness of her own complicity: her sins, as John Lang has observed, were "sins of both omission and commission." Penetrating one emotional barrier after another, she thus forces access to the innermost, secret recesses of her psyche, and arrives finally at the heart of the matter, at what she has been unable not only to voice, but, until then, it is suggested, even to confront in the privacy of her thoughts—the choice whose burden she is unable to bear, whose voicing irresistibly propels her towards death. Her *ultimate* choice is thus a suicide pact with her lover Nathan, the crazed, demon-ridden American whom she regards as both savior and destroyer.

Having stared down the Medusa, and in one sense, spoken herself whole, having painfully and painstakingly reassembled the free-orbiting fragments of her self, Sophie, then, instead of being freed into life, seeks out oblivion. Rather than coming as a surprise to the reader, however, this final choice emerges as the inevitable destination towards which she has been journeying, unconsciously, ever since her experiences at Auschwitz, and perhaps even earlier. A vital aspect of the text is the way in which the narrator invariably associates her appearance with references to doom and destruction. Thus when the twenty-two-year-old Stingo first sets eyes on the lovely woman who is Sophie, although her beauty renders him almost speechless, he associates her with tragedy and despair, with a young woman of his acquaintance, a recent suicide: "what is still ineffaceable about my first glimpse of [Sophie]," writes his older alter ego, "is not simply the lovely simulacrum she seemed to me of the dead girl but the despair on her face worn as Maria surely must have worn it, along with the premonitory, grieving shadows of someone hurtling headlong toward death." Significantly, too, Sophie is not alone when Stingo first encounters her: she is involved in a fierce quarrel with Nathan in the hallway of the boardinghouse in Brooklyn where they all live. A witness to her attempts at stopping Nathan from walking out, Stingo overhears her cry of despair, "We need each other," and he also hears the retort, which sounds like a malediction, but will prove to be a prediction: "I need you like *death*. . . . *Death*!" Later that first night, as Stingo lies in bed in his room he hears Sophie seek solace in what he will learn is her chief source of comfort, classical music, then weep despairingly after Nathan has stormed out of the house. Stingo finally drifts off to sleep, but wakes suddenly "just before dawn, in the dead silence of that hour, with pounding heart and an icy chill staring straight up at my ceiling above which Sophie slept, understanding with a dreamer's fierce clarity that she was doomed." Spinning a fine, yet irresistible weave of premonition out of the tenacious threads of melancholy that envelop Sophie, the narrator links her to death three times before she has even properly assumed her role in the story. And yet another such hint follows immediately as, on Nathan's subsequent return to the boardinghouse and Sophie, Stingo hears his voice through the ceiling, "booming, with the ponderous, measured cadence of booted footfalls, and [crying] out in a tone that might have been deemed a parody of existential anguish had it not possessed the resonances of complete, unfeigned terror: 'Don't . . . you . . . see . . . Sophie . . . we . . . are . . . dying! *Dying*!'" In this manner, the text foregrounds the way in which shadows of death and self-destruction stalk not merely Sophie but also Nathan: the way in which these two gravitate not only towards each other, but towards the specter of self-destruction as well, is one of the central concerns of this narrative.

In a similar fashion, the sinister qualities pertaining to Nathan are emphasized from the beginning. His special kind of madness, the split self—that he is a diagnosed schizophrenic will become clear only much later—is suggested shortly after the scene in the hallway as one of the other boarders likens him to a *golem*, a Jewish monster which, although it looks human, is made of clay: "'you can't control him. I mean, sometimes he acts normal, just like a normal human. But deep down he's a runaway fuckin' *monster*. That's a golem.'" Although Stingo becomes instantly and incurably infatuated not merely with Sophie but also with Nathan (who assumes the role of a wise, experienced, and wonderfully charming older brother) and becomes the third party in their intense relationship, he is made vaguely uneasy even during their first time together, as "[b]eneath all the jollity, the tenderness, the solicitude, I sensed a disturbing tension in the room," a tension which seems to emanate mainly from Nathan. This unspecified sense of premonition and doom, one that never really leaves young Stingo, but one he generally elects to disregard, will not merely remain a presence in their relationship, but a subtext of increasing palpability in the narrative.

Developing Storylines

The confession has an equally important function in *Sophie's Choice* as in *The Confessions of Nat Turner* and *Set This House on Fire*. For *Sophie's Choice* too, is a text structured as a series of confessions: this time there are three layers of narration, the nethermost one consisting of Sophie's revelations, which are then filtered not once but twice through Stingo's consciousness. Since the narrator's meditations concern not only Sophie's story but also the younger version of himself, the aspiring writer questing for theme as well as voice, the structure also involves two intersecting storylines. Although it is clearly Sophie's revelations that provide the narrative propulsion, structurally, the book is an intricate mesh of, on the one hand, her recollections and, on the other, depictions of young Stingo's thwarted attempts at losing his virginity—all of which is, then, re-visioned by the middle-aged narrator. As both storylines consist of sense-making projects, the arbitrary nature of knowledge and interpretation emerges as a central concern: the task of the narrator, it would appear, is to comprehend both the nature of the evil to which Sophie had been exposed—in the form of the death camp—and to determine what the confrontation, through her, with that evil meant to his younger self.

The task Sophie appears to have assigned herself during that long-gone Brooklyn summer is equally highly charged. The process of coming to terms with her life requires a carefully orchestrated homing in on unbearable truths, the most harrowing of which is the choice referred to in the title of the book. This is why the model of narrative organization in *Sophie's Choice*, what Samuel Coale refers to as the "web of complicity and self-deception," is an intricate movement between revelation and concealment. The narrating Stingo seeks to explain the psychological necessity behind her lies, evasions, and silences, the circumstance that she simply does not dare disturb the memories that lie nested within her—in Horneyan terms, she opts for a strategy of solution rather than resolution. Contemplating her inability to confront certain areas of her life, Sophie once wishes that she "could unlock the past even a little. . . . But the past or guilt, or something, stops up my mouth in silence." Since each of Sophie's revelations not only introduces new information, actually offering amended versions of her previous recollections—as she admits to evasions or outright lies concerning certain painful aspects or incidents of her past life, and about her relationship with Nathan—Stingo is forced into constant revisions and readjustments of his view of her. Again and again, the deceptive nature of appearances is brought home to him: what he conceived to be the truth proves to be boggy ground, indeed. As Sophie's story exposes to him, the naif, the horrors and evil of which mankind is capable, she assumes another dimension in his eyes. Thus the circumnavigatory fashion in which *Sophie's Choice* is narrated reenacts not only Sophie's own gradual acceptance of certain insights but also Stingo's equally gradual realization of the immense tragedy of her life—or so the narrator would have it. There are, however, numerous instances which appear to belie such a reading, instances which instead suggest either that Stingo—a child of what is referred to as a "sexually bedeviled era"—is simply too immature and self-preoccupied to be able either to comprehend or to feel in his heart the "unspeakable nature" of what is bared to him, or that he actively blocks a full comprehension. As a confessor, judging by his reactions to the recollections to which he is privy, reactions which the narrator dwells on in fond indulgence, he would seem to leave a great deal to be desired. Concerning his role in Sophie's life that summer, the mature Stingo ventures the speculation that "quite unbeknownst to herself she was questing for someone to serve in place of those religious confessors she had coldly renounced. . . . Then when she was the most vulnerable, her need to give voice to her agony and guilt was so urgent as to be like the beginning of a scream. . . ." This clearly suggests the unimportance of the identity of her listener, her confessor: letting herself voice the past, she speaks to herself out of an inner compulsion in what is, in fact, a preparation for death, and she talks to Stingo simply, because, as he says, "I was always ready and waiting to listen with my canine idolatry and inexhaustible ear." The fact that during the main portion of Sophie's mnemonic confrontations, Stingo is lost in erotic fantasies, or dreaming about coming chivalrously to her rescue, is, perhaps, not a truly serious offense. A matter of considerable gravity, however, is his very real failure to comprehend the depth of her despair. "Naturally," the narrator explains, "it was impossible not to remain haunted and, to some extent, intermittently depressed over what Sophie had told me about her past. But generally speaking, I was able to put her story out of my mind. Life does indeed go on. Also, I was caught up in an exhilaratingly creative floodtide and was intensely aware that I had my own tragic chronicle to tell and to occupy my working hours."

The most blatant example of Stingo's empathetic ineptitude occurs when Sophie's anguished inner journey has almost reached its completion. On a stop-over during their panicked, headlong flight from the ragingly murderous Nathan, Sophie and Stingo spend the night cooped up in a small hotel room in Washington, D. C. . A measure of the confusion and anguish in which she lives at this point is the fact that among the random assortment of clothes she hastily threw into her suitcase as she and Stingo ran away is the wedding dress Nathan had just bought her. Drinking steadily, in need of some kind of prop as her recollective endeavor plunges her ever deeper into emotionally mined territory, Sophie now makes herself voice what she has never touched on before, not to anyone. She must, she claims, finally, tell someone, because even though she has bared so much of her shame and guilt to Stingo, he will still not be able to understand her if he does not also know that when she was sent to Auschwitz she had been accompanied not merely by her son but also by her youngest child, her daughter. On their arrival at the camp Sophie had been told that she could only "keep one of [her] children. . . . The other one [would] have to go." Forced to make a choice, she was thus compelled to assign one of them to death, and she had only a minute in which to make this decision: if she faltered, she was told, both of her children would be sent to the gas chambers. The instant Sophie cried out, "Take the baby! . . . Take my little girl!," Eva was led "away into the waiting legion of the damned," holding on to her flute and her teddy bear. Because of her loss of Nathan, the one human being, however flawed, whom she depended upon, the compulsive need to come to peace with herself that has been at work all through her relationship with Stingo becomes more insistent, and by this mutedly anguished last confession, Sophie has finally opened up the "realm of the unspeakable." Still, it is possible to see a subtext to what she has just voiced, concerning the nature of her choice, something she refrains from taking up. What does Sophie's choice reveal about her? Was the little girl less loved because she was a girl? Are there reverberations in Sophie's choice of her own lack of self-esteem; was it an inevitable reflection of the treatment she herself had received as a child, an acting out of the relationship between herself and her father? Is this the ultimate root of her feelings of guilt?

On the train journey to Washington, Stingo busies himself not merely with entertaining daydreams about marrying Sophie and moving to his inherited peanut farm in the South and having children, but actually also with trying to sell her this dazzling prospect—to a woman who is now drinking steadily, crying and unmistakably about to come apart. Later, when she has talked herself into a state of exhaustion and numbness in their hotel room, Stingo seeks to "distract" her with stories about the South and the Virginia countryside where they are heading, and to take her out to dinner. Judging by the narrator's astounding choice of words—"Through various conversational stratagems, including more agricultural wisdom leavened by all the good Southern jokes I could extract from memory, I was able to infuse Sophie with enough cheer to make it through the rest of the dinner. We drank, ate crab cakes and managed to forget Auschwitz"—he appears to believe himself successful. A statement like that, however, unavoidably invites the question about what it is that young Stingo actually learns through his exposure to the immeasurable evil and pain of the world. Do his actions and responses bear out the narrator's claims of his having become initiated into the "realm of the unspeakeable"? The textual evidence appears, in fact, to contradict such claims. *Sophie's Choice*, then, would be better read as a book about how the mature narrator learns by telling the parallel stories of his youthful self and of Sophie.

Actually, the role of the narrator of *Sophie's Choice* is a bone of critical contention. A substantial part of the adverse criticism in Robert Towers' review in *The New York Review of Books*, his considering the book a "highly self-conscious performance, full of autobiographical references . . . narrated by a man called Stingo whose career parallels Styron's in many particulars," thus hinges on his view of the role of the narrator. "The weakest element in the novel," in Towers' view, is the "voice and personality assigned to the narrator." Generally, the critical discussion of *Sophie's Choice* has centered on two areas, one thematically and one structurally related. Some members of the Jewish community, like Elie Wiesel and Cynthia Ozick, feel strongly that Styron violates "sacred ground" by writing about the Nazi death camps, that—as a Christian and non-survivor—he does not have the "moral right" to speak about matters of "absolute evil." The bulk of the critical essays and reviews, however, concerns matters related to Towers' criticism—whether the story can be said to "belong" to Sophie or to Stingo, and, in this connection, what would be the function of the narrator, the older Stingo. William Heath, for instance, who is severely disturbed by the many autobiographical elements of the text, voices his displeasure in "I, Stingo: The Problem of Egotism in *Sophie's Choice*": "Unfortunately Styron is not always clear about what his stance toward his persona should be; ironic detachment yields to nostalgic identification, satiric comedy is superseded by apologetics, and the entire relationship between Styron and Stingo becomes hopelessly confused." Heath obviously misses the point here—the relationship is confused, and intentionally so.

The storyline that charts Stingo's journey towards a questionable maturity, his encounter with the dark forces of human existence, and the inclusion of what has been referred to as superfluous material, have spawned substantial discussion, the argument being that the seriousness of the subject matter of genocide is "trivialized" by the extent to which the story is concerned with young Stingo's obsessively self-centered quest for sexual experience, what Heath calls Styron's "bombastic treatment of Stingo's sexuality . . . [his] pseudo-agonies." Ralph Tutt finds that "[o]n the autobiographical level, *Sophie's Choice* can't decide whether it wants to be picaresque sex comedy or a serious *Künstlerroman* relating Stingo's sexual blockage to his writer's block." Tutt believes himself finally to have identified an authorial mood of self-defense rather than self-parody, and he offers the suggestion that Styron has "armor[ed] himself with personality as a guard against critical disparagement for having written another old-fashioned novel in an era of accelerating experimentation with language, form, and the idea of history."

Other critics take a different position and assign, with Samuel Coale, primary importance to "Stingo's tale of self-discovery." Arguing that the depiction of Stingo's development constitutes the heart of *Sophie's Choice*, Coale asks: why does the narrator make the structure

> directly imitate Sophie's repressive way of revealing her secrets? He knows the facts before he writes, of course. The truth must lie with his ultimate point of view, that of focusing on the younger Stingo's discovery of Sophie's fate and consequently his loss of innocence. It also lies with the narrator's focusing on reproducing Stingo's discovery of a tragic person and theme to write about, with revealing why Stingo became the writer he did and what needed to happen to him in order to become that writer. The narrator's true story, then, is Stingo's tale of self-discovery, of his shock of recognition concerning absolute evil, the crush of history, and the horrifying realities at the heart of the middle of the twentieth century. That recognition for the narrator is obviously more important than the fact of Sophie's death—could really have done anything to save her?—and explanations of how to live in a post-Holocaust world.

To critics like Coale and others, more than simply a picaresque, *Sophie's Choice* is the story of Stingo's development, a story of initiation: on this level it is explicitly concerned with the search for an artistic voice, with charting the emergence of a writer. Thus, reading Styron's book as "a *Bildungsroman* in which the organizing axis of narrative is Stingo's quest for knowledge," Richard Law, who finds that "[a]ll of the elaborate excursions and digressions contribute to that developing line," would surely concur with Carolyn Durham's observation that as *Sophie's Choice* is a "novel whose very meaning lies embedded in its structure and, even more specifically, in the very concept of structure itself", it is indeed ironic that it has been criticized for a lack of structural coherence or for an excess of structural exuberance.

Occupying a middle ground, rather than privileging one storyline over the other, a number of readers find, with Daniel Ross, that the "two plots of *Sophie's Choice* are not 'separate and unequal' but unified and interrelated; indeed, the novel is itself a narrative born from the seemingly incompatible coupling of Sophie's and Stingo's life-histories." For varying reasons still other critics foreground Sophie's story, and read the text from this perspective. William Heath, in fact, chastises Styron, the author, for failing to understand that, ultimately, the story is Sophie's: "What is clear is that when Styron is talking about his persona, Stingo, he tends to forget that the central story of the novel is Sophie's tragedy, not Stingo's 'voyage of discovery'." Although my own reading of *Sophie's Choice* also focuses on Sophie's agonized recollective endeavor, it seems to me that there are, after all, satisfactory explanations for the strong presence of young Stingo in this text.

Guilt-Ridden Journey

In Sophie Zawistowska, Styron has, for the first time, created a protagonist who travels to the end of the road to self-discovery, who probes the depths of her own guilt and despair and finally keeps her eyes unflinchingly on what is brought to light. Although both Cass Kinsolving and Nat Turner are involved in similar recollective mind-journeys, seeking, in a sense, to speak themselves free, ultimately, I have argued, they falter as, unable to bear the guilt and anguish that their venture unearths, the nature of human life as solitary incarceration, they "fantasize it out of existence." Sophie, however, is a different kind of protagonist; when her past threatens to engulf her, and her memories force a confrontation with the origin of her own guilt, she pursues to the very end the road of the search for self, opening herself to the grim core of anguish lodged inside. In the re-activation of her desperately courageous attempts at beating "back death," the story of her psychic inventory is a depiction of an inevitable progression towards (self-)destruction. When the unspeakable, finally, has been spoken, her pain and guilt unearthed, her cowardice and complicity in the horrors of her life confronted, Sophie is "free" to make her ultimate choice: her suicide is thus not an act of confused despair, but one of premeditation—something the narrator, in truth, goes to some length to demonstrate. Although her end puts the reader in mind of the

death of the haunted and confused Peyton Loftis, there is a significant difference between the final fate of Peyton—an anguished and lost daughter of
parents who have abandoned her—and that of Sophie, a woman who acts on
the realization that for her there is, ultimately, no salvation: that she can
neither be saved nor save herself.

The portrayal of Sophie shows her lovely exterior to be a mask
stretched tautly around an inner core of despair, or rather, a self fragmented
to the point where it has been rendered practically devoid of a core. After
years of malnutrition, Sophie's body is still in a precarious state of repair
although Nathan has provided her with a "superb new set of dentures," and,
having diagnosed her severe anemia, is feeding her the vitamins and massive
doses of iron that cause her skin to glow and her hair to shine. The text
provides a most graphic illustration of this lack of correspondence between
the radiant façade and the hollowness that is her inner being in a scene to
which Stingo becomes the inadvertent witness. Stealing into Sophie's room
unannounced one time, he finds her in preparation for the outing they have
agreed on, combing her hair in front of the mirror. As she becomes aware of
his presence, she "turned from the mirror with a startled gasp and in so doing
revealed a face I shall never in my life forget. Dumbfounded, I beheld—for
a mercifully fleeting instant—an old hag whose entire lower face had crum-
pled in upon itself, leaving a mouth like a wrinkled gash and an expression of
doddering senescence. It was a mask, withered and pitiable." This brief
drama serves not merely as a foregrounding of the theme of dissolution, but
also as a link to a related theme of significance for the portrayal of Stingo.
The deceptive nature of appearances is one of the many facts of life that the
inexperienced and innocent Stingo has to confront: here it is exemplified by
the circumstance that the "old hag" to whom he is suddenly exposed is also
the sensuously beautiful woman whose face and body send him into raptures.
This passage also provides a significant clue to Stingo's relation to reality:
protecting himself from the darker sides of existence—as witnessed by his
obliviousness of the suffering that must have lain behind the loss of teeth in
this young woman—he here refers to Sophie's real face as "a mask."

The theme inherent in this scene—the disparity between appearance
and reality, the inclusion of mirroring effects and the double, the *Doppel-
gänger* motif—is one of the constants in Styron's narratives generally: it is
also, as Gwen Nagel has noted, a thematic aspect of considerable significance
in *Sophie's Choice*. It is from this perspective that the beautifully tailored
period costumes which it is one of the joys of Sophie and Nathan to don
should be viewed: they are a manifestation of their fragmented selves. Originally, Nathan tells Stingo, it was Sophie's idea that they have matching
costumes, made from different epochs, but he himself took readily to her

game and showed himself equally delighted by dressing up on weekends and going about town peacock-fashion. It is, of course, not unnatural that a long-time deprivation of such things in a sensuous woman could bring about the childlike pleasure Sophie takes in finery, and in the lovely textures and colors of the tailor-made costumes. Nagel, however, points to the significant aspect of the "mask" in this connection: the circumstance that the costumes have a more important function for Sophie and Nathan than simply to dazzle and delight. They both suffer from severe psychological disturbances, albeit in different ways—"she is devoid of a sense of herself, he has many identities"—and the clothing, argues Nagel, is a means of creating "new fantasy selves." That their fascination with dressing up could be read as a desire to escape the reality that is theirs seems to be corroborated by the fact that their preparations for death include dressing up in one set of these fancy suits; thus "gaily costumed" they invoke in death a sense of wholeness and carefreeness they did not possess in life.

When this theme is pursued in relation to Sophie, it becomes clear that one of the significant components of the complex origin of her self-loathing is connected to her early relationship with her father. In her talks to Stingo, Sophie often reminisces about her years of growing up in peaceful, pre-war Cracow, describing in a quietly glowing way the passionately humanistic man that was her father, the happy family she and her parents made. Recollecting how he saved "Jews from a Russian pogrom at peril to his life," she creates, in Stingo's words a "perfect little cameo of paternal rectitude and decency: the fine socialist paterfamilias fretting over the coming terror, a man haloed with goodness." But as she narrows in on Auschwitz in her attempts at mastering her past, Sophie has to admit to having lied about her father, to having provided her audience, Stingo, with

> a fabrication, a wretched lie, another fantasy served up to provide
> a frail barrier, a hopeless and crumbly line of defense between
> those she cared for, like myself, and her smothering guilt. Would
> I not forgive her, she said, now that I saw both the truth and her
> necessity for telling the lie?

The truth of the matter is that her father, a puny, authoritarian, and severely limited man wholly lacking in imagination and insensitive to the point of cruelty, was not merely an oppressor of Sophie and her mother, but also most violently anti-Semitic, the author of rabid pamphlets advocating the extinction of Jews even before the Nazis appeared on the Polish scene. In every respect, then, the real man and the emotional world of her childhood can be seen to differ from the ideal image conjured up by Sophie. The ensuing voicing of the "discovery" of her hatred for her father is a significant rung on the ladder leading up to her real self. She tells Stingo how once, when she acted as her father's secretary, the realization that she actually hated him had come upon her so forcefully that it was like an assault. The incident which triggered her reaction seems hardly grave, more like a crystallization of every petty insult of which he was guilty, but it suddenly made her see with unmistakable clarity that she, his daughter, was of absolutely no importance to him. In the words of the narrating Stingo:

> There are rare moments in life when the intensity of a buried emotion one has felt toward another person—a repressed animus or a wild love—comes heaving to the surface of consciousness with immediate clarity; sometimes it is like a bodily cataclysm, ever unforgettable. Sophie said she would never forget the exact moment when the revelation of the hatred she felt for her father enveloped her in a horrible hot radiance, and she could find no voice, and thought she might faint dead away . . .

That the grief and guilt that accompany the realization of the actual nature of their relationship, a "knowledge" thus far blocked by Sophie, are internalized can be seen, for instance, by her creation of an idol, a kind and loving father and husband, in lieu of the actual man. Indelibly imprinting itself on her psyche, the contempt she breathed from her early years thus becomes the seed of her self-loathing, and, consequently, of the process of disintegration which, ultimately, comes to an end in a Brooklyn boardinghouse.

Another part of her devastating guilt originates in a sense of cowardice, of culpability and complicity in the terrible events that took place in Poland when she was a young woman. She exposes her feeling of shame that, during the time she lived in Warsaw, after the arrest of her father and husband, she had been grateful that the Germans were persecuting the Jews with such terrible vigilance—because that meant, she had been convinced, temporary safety for herself and her children. Even worse than the awareness of her cowardice, writes the older Stingo, was the fact that "she could not wriggle out from beneath the suffocating knowledge that there had been this time in her life when she had played out the role, to its limit, of a fellow conspirator in crime. And this was the role of an obsessed and poisonous anti-Semite. . . ."

Sophie's guilt, shame, and sense of worthlessness result in a neurotic submissiveness, an aspect which has received insightful treatment by Carolyn Durham in a discussion of the oppressive nature of the patriarchal, sexist societies of pre-war Poland and post-war America. The sole way for Sophie to feel self-esteem, Durham suggests, is to completely nullify herself, to seek to "belong to men of whom she and others can think well." It is undoubtedly true that Sophie's strategy for survival in Poland as well as in the United States tends towards the self-effacive. Giving a psychological explanation for the complex origin of such a strategy, Karen Horney writes that

> [t]here is scarcely any neurosis in which the tendency to get rid of the self does not appear in a direct form. . . . Whether the neurotic subjects himself to a person or to fate, and whatever the kind of suffering which he allows to overpower him, the satisfaction he seeks seems to be the weakening or extinction of his individual self. He ceases then to be the active carrier of actions and becomes an object, without a will of his own.

This last phrase, "without a will of [her] own," provides an apt description of Sophie's relation with Nathan. From the moment she met Nathan, she tells Stingo, she put her fate, unhesitatingly, in his hands, letting him do with her whatever he pleased, giving herself up completely. And as he showers her with clothes and gifts, teaches her the delights of splendid wines, and any manner of extravaganza, she succumbs to his will and powerful gift for life (when sane), becoming a wonderfully receptive and obedient pupil, even to the point of adopting his idiosyncrasies of speech. This quality of submissiveness—of self-annihilation, in fact—is a feature also of their love-making; in Stingo's words, the sexual satisfaction Sophie experiences is clearly tinged with a desire for oblivion: "an almost sinister final losingness of herself has been achieved, a sucking death like descent into caverns during which she cannot tell whether she is lost in herself or in him, a sense of black whirling downward into an inseparability of flesh." It appears Sophie herself is aware of this dark desire as she tells Stingo that the Polish words she whispered— "mysteriously, spontaneously"—while making love meant "Take me, take me," and not "*fuck me*" as she had told Nathan. It is as if, when he diagnosed her illness and coaxed her back to physical health, she granted him the right to her life. When madness overtakes him, as on the trip to Connecticut, "an unending delirium" of pain and violence, in which fearful demons stalk them both, she stays close like his shadow, masochistically ready to let him "piss on me, rape me, stab me, beat me, blind me, do anything with me that he desired." Insanely raving—"We must die!" and "Death is a necessity"—on a manic pill-induced high from which he crashes, he comes within a fraction of having them both swallow the cyanide capsules he carries with him. If Nathan's abuse of Sophie, as Richard Law has suggested, be seen as an extension of Auschwitz, the revelation of his madness is crucial: The "discovery of the cause of Nathan's behavior—or rather, this definition of it—forces us to revise our understanding of the relationship between Sophie and Nathan and its role in Sophie's impending doom." Perhaps, for Sophie, his attraction is composed equally of an omnific zest for life and the, at times, almost irresistible pull of death.

Sophie's recollective endeavor, the circling in on different aspects of her heft of loss and guilt, comes to a head in the scruffy, "darkening shoebox" of a hotel room in Washington; not only does Sophie here reveal the existence and death of her daughter Eva, but she also tells Stingo about her "*recurring* dreams" about her father, which, she explains, have returned to her "over and over" since childhood, even there, in Washington. Her father has remained a "presence" in her life. And this time, the terrible truth lurking in this dream is bared to her, allowing her access, in Alice Miller's words, to her own truth, the truth about the childhood that was hers. Reactivating a blissful incident from her girlhood, the dreamscape is initially suffused by a mood of exaltation and joy related to what in life has always provided Sophie with her greatest happiness—music. As she listens to a record of some breathtaking Brahms *Lieder* she has never heard before, she is filled with an aching desire to hear them again, a wish that would seem to be granted as the acquaintance of her father's who owns the records promises to play the lovely music again. But then Sophie's mood of pleasure and expectation is abruptly shattered by her father's intervention: it is useless, he says, to play such music to her since she is much too stupid to understand it. Although this dream has been a frequent visitor throughout the years, in Washington it takes on the grisly hue of a true nightmare since she realizes that her father is talking about something other than music—about her death: "He wanted me to die, I think," she tells Stingo. Music to Sophie was (and is) like her own heartbeat, and to want to deny her access to music is tantamount to wanting her death. Her recreation of this dream scene—less for the benefit of Stingo than for herself—exposes the truth about her relation to her father in all its ugliness, a truth she has not only denied, but actually rewritten. Although blocked from her conscious mind, the knowledge that Sophie voices here has been lodged deep inside her ever since childhood: the internalization not only of her father's contempt, but of the fact that her own father had actually desired her death, laid the foundations for her self-loathing, one aspect of which is her longing for extinction, for death.

The innermost center of Sophie's despair and guilt, however, which Stingo has to know, or, she tells him, "you wouldn't understood anything about me at all," revolves around the choice she was forced to make involving her daughter Eva. The verbal reenactment of this unspeakable core of Sophie's existence amounts, I believe, to a final "settling of affairs," a rite of preparation for death. Samuel Coale contends that "[o]nce she reveals her secret, her most horrible choice, she in effect signs her death warrant. She has lived to tell her tale, and the very telling of it ensures her demise." Coale's reading reflects his view that Sophie's story carries less significance than Stingo's development: her function here is to provide Stingo with the kind of "raw material" he needs to become an artist. But Sophie's final choice is less the result of her having "revealed" her tragedy—that because of circumstances wholly beyond her control she was forced to send her girl-child to the gas chambers—than, I believe, of her having voiced her innermost guilt, thereby allowing herself full access to what has been done to her, the agony of her existence. It is obvious to the reader, as indeed also to the narrator, though not, it seems, to young Stingo, that she has actually been courting oblivion for a long time: she remembers how, once in Auschwitz, she lost touch with herself to the extent that she was unable to remember her own name—"'Oh, God, *help me!*' she called aloud. '*I don't know what I am!*'" One facet of the death wish she has been struggling with for a long time is suggested by some words she repeats to Stingo in Washington, words her friend Wanda uttered many years earlier in Warsaw. Talking about Conrad's *Lord Jim*, Wanda had said: "I think you've forgotten how in the end the hero redeems himself for his betrayal, redeems himself through his own death. His own suffering and death."

Intersecting By-Line

In what must be read as a humorous intertextual gesture, the narrator invokes one of the mightiest metaphysical quests in American fiction, Moby-Dick, early on in the first chapter of *Sophie's Choice*. Having introduced himself, Ishmael-fashion, with the phrase "Call me Stingo," he proceeds to provide the origin of this nickname, the far from complimentary "Stinky," after which he devotes the entire chapter to a depiction, as it were, of the lay of the land—a description of young Stingo's character, his social and financial situation, and his burning desire to become a writer, as well as other burning desires connected with the mores of the post-war years. About *Moby-Dick*, Styron said to Rhoda Sirlin that the entire "'first chapter has nothing to do with the issue at hand. It's just there.'" Perhaps in what he felt to be an emulation, his own lengthy, circumstantial first chapter of *Sophie's Choice* is designed "'to let the reader know that he's in the hands of someone who has had this kind of experience, a disaffected young man with a certain mindset, who is rebellious to a certain degree. Without all that, you wouldn't understand what's going to happen when he meets Sophie and Nathan in

Brooklyn.'" The point of the chapter, then, is to make the autobiographical connection, creating the persona, a lonely young man "assaulted by Kierkegaardian dread."

While Sophie dwells mainly in the past—and even when she does not, her course of action in the present is determined by the past—young Stingo has his mind set on the future. He hungers for different kinds of experience: for sexual experience, since his life thus far has been almost wholly devoid of such pleasures, and for experiences pertaining to the complex and shadowy recesses of human existence. Although he had "traveled great distances for one so young," explains the narrator, his "spirit had remained landlocked, unacquainted with love and all but a stranger to death," the knowledge of and exposure to which are necessary for a presumptive recorder of human life. At the time of his encounter with Sophie and Nathan, he had absented himself from both human passion and human flesh in his "smug and airless self-deprivation." In the narrator's tone of humorous indulgence when describing his younger self, young Stingo emerges as something of a voyeur, someone who learns about life second-hand through the experience of others—in matters of sex as well as of psychic obsessions and torment. His first "encounter" with Sophie and Nathan comes, consequently, through exposure to their lovemaking, which is of such a riotously joyous nature that it threatens to send their bed crashing through the floor—his ceiling—into his room. The more immediate or light-hearted side of young Stingo's quest as it is presented by his narrating older self, comes, however, to a blissfully satisfactory end, as Sophie, on that memorable night in Washington, finally delivers him from the painful limbo of carnal deprivation.

But although even knowledge of the evil of the world comes to him secondhand, specifically through the mediation of Sophie, young Stingo is no stranger to guilt. The origin of his psychic pain, his sense of "ineradicable loss," is connected to the death of his mother when he was a boy, and to the unforgivable crime of omission he committed when, as she lay painfully dying of cancer in the coldness of an unheated house one winter afternoon, he selfishly forgot the task assigned him of fueling the fireplace. He abandoned her. The mature Stingo recollects, how, upon the return of his youthful self to the house,

> one impression captured my soul so completely as to seem to
> envelop the room: her eyes. Those hazel bespectacled eyes and
> the way that her ravaged, still terrified gaze caught my own, then
> darted swiftly away. It was the *swiftness* of that turning away
> which would thereafter define my guilt; it was as swift as a

> machete dismembering a hand. And I realized with horror how much I resented her burdensome affliction. She wept then, I wept, but separately, and we listened to each other's weeping as if across a wide and desolate lake.

The narrator suggests that this incident—young Stingo's sense that his "crime was ultimately beyond expiation, for in my mind it would inescapably and always be entangled in the sordid animal fact of my mother's death"—has colored his entire outlook, not only his view of himself but also of human existence; there is a strong sense of "the solitude of the self" alive in that last sentence. His guilt comes to the surface of his consciousness in his dreams, most of which seem to have in common that they are connected to his mother's death, that still unhealed wound, the childhood trauma. Still haunted by this memory—"grief drove like a spear of ice through my chest when I recaptured the fright in my mother's eyes, wondered once again if that ordeal had not somehow hastened her dying, wondered if she ever forgave me"—Stingo measures every pain he experiences by what he felt when his mother died. When Nathan and Sophie, after a terrible quarrel, seem to have disappeared from his life never to return, Stingo says that "the melancholy which had taken hold of me when I left [the boardinghouse] and journeyed by subway to stay with my father in Manhattan had been as close to creating an excruciating physical malaise as any I had ever known—most surely since my mother's death." There is a quality strongly reminiscent of Cass Kinsolving's inner torment in young Stingo's bouts of "Kierkegaardian dread," his devastatingly omnific sense of guilt, and the haunting nightmares.

Sophie's Choice, like Styron's earlier narratives, also privileges dreams as carriers of insights blocked: "in dreams," writes Karen Horney, "we are closer to the reality of ourselves; . . . they represent attempts to solve our conflicts, either in a neurotic or a healthy way; . . . in them constructive forces can be at work, even at a time when they are hardly visible otherwise." Looking for connections between Sophie and Stingo, Samuel Coale, taking his cue from Daniel Ross, locates these links primarily in their nightmares: "[i]n that border realm, that subconscious crossroads, they both dream of death, sex, and guilt in often ghastly incarnations." In Horney's terms, this would mean that there are strong connections also between their psychological realities. On the subject of dreams, Stingo himself writes that "[b]y their very nature dreams are, of course, difficult to access through memory, but a few are forever imprinted on the brain. With me the most memorable of dreams, the ones that have achieved that haunting reality so intense as to be seemingly bound up in the metaphysical, have dealt with either sex or death." Generally, these two areas are actually connected, as in his dream about Maria Hunt—the young model for the protagonist of his novel, and the person he was reminded of when he first saw Sophie—when he has learned about her suicide. This "erotic hallucination" affected him more strongly, he says, than any dream since the haunting nightmare

> soon after my mother's burial, when, struggling up from the seaweed-depths of a nightmare, I dreamed I peered out the window of the room at home in which I was still sleeping and caught sight of the open coffin down in the windswept, drenched garden, then saw my mother's shrunken, cancer-ravaged face twist toward me in the satin vault and gaze at me beseechingly through eyes filmed over with indescribable torture.

As Sophie's dreams can be seen frequently to have turned on guilt-ridden or painful memories of her father, so Stingo's dreams almost always have to do with his own private image of the intolerable—the illness and death of his mother, and his guilt-infested part in these.

The ultimate connection between Sophie and Stingo is found, of course, in the text of *Sophie's Choice.* In a bequeathal of sorts, Sophie tells him in Washington that her desire to learn not only to speak but to write English properly is motivated by her need to write about her experiences at Auschwitz:

> maybe I could write it as a novel, you see, if I learned to write English good, and then I could make people understood how the Nazis made you do things you never believed you could. . . . They made me afraid of everything! Why don't I tell the truth about myself? Why don't I write it down in a book that I was a terrible coward, that I was a filthy *collaboratrice,* that I done everything that was bad just to save myself?

Sophie herself would never write her life, but since she had spoken it that task could fall on Stingo. In the final pages of *Sophie's Choice* the narrator retrieves this thread, suggesting that the book about Sophie's life and death that he is about to finish has not, as he had naively written in his diary on the night of Sophie's and Nathan's burial, helped him understand Auschwitz—the metaphor for absolute evil—but that it will rather "*help demonstrate how absolute evil is never extinguished from the world.*" Of the entries young Stingo made in his journal on the night of the burial, there are only a few lines that the mature man wants to preserve: "*Someday I will understand Auschwitz,*" and "*Let your love flow out on all living things.*"

End of the Line

William Styron, Rhoda Sirlin argues, "challenge[s] the moral and intellectual complacency of his readers with fiction that demonstrates that there is no rational order in existence, that human beings are at risk of extinction, and that rebellion, therefore, in a post-Holocaust world is critical to our survival as a species." It will be remembered that a number of critics read Styron's work through a prism which gives off redemptive and life-affirming fractions, mistaking, I believe, the "willed" quality of stoicism or optimism of the endings for the moral vision of the work. Thus engaged, Sirlin compares *Sophie's Choice* and *Moby-Dick*, discussing these books in terms of "tragedies of madness and acts of metaphysical rebellion," and "acts of resistance against our evil potential." Melville and Styron both, Sirlin argues, provide a "vision of brotherhood as our only salvation, a vision which shapes the artistic endings of *Moby-Dick* and *Sophie's Choice*." Invoking another literary parallel, she argues that "for Styron and Camus, to be fully human is to doubt. One either chooses the creative present, this world, or one chooses death. Finding spiritual sustenance in our modern wasteland is the job of the living. Resisting nihilism, therefore, is one of Styron's most urgent themes." In a similar vein, Valarie Meliotes Arms, while spicing her interpretation with the irresistible Southern connection, contends that *Sophie's Choice* is an "attempt to affirm life with a moral point of view. . . . Using an international subject matter, Styron has found a new prism that allows him to extend the Southern view of man. . . . Styron's particular presentation is the unique outgrowth of a Southerner who could not escape his roots, but could and did extend himself in a viable way."

My own reading of this narrative does not bear out any of the above claims: I find instead that Styron, a writer who consistently rejects overt multiplicity and anxiously forces closure on his texts, does so also in *Sophie's Choice*. And as in the previous novels, the ending of *Sophie's Choice* also presents a problem, since, again, the final pages read as a kind of postscript blocking or denying the "sense of life or the outlook that reveals itself in the structure of the text taken as a whole," to recall the words of Martha Nussbaum prefaced to the present project. How should the almost euphoric overtones of the "final entries," what the narrator calls "A Study in the Conquest of Grief" of *Sophie's Choice* be understood? What should the reader make of the exuberant joy at being alive manifested by Stingo on the day of Sophie's and Nathan's burial, and what of the very last sentence—"This was not judgment day—only morning. Morning: excellent and fair"—a disturbing echo of the phrase which intimated the way in which Nat Turner averted *his* gaze from the intolerable?

The narrator describes how young Stingo wanders off on his own after the funeral services, a grief-stricken "being whose very survival was in question for a time," cries "warm rivulets" of tears not only for Sophie and Nathan but mourning all those "who during these last months had battered at my mind," and falls into a drunken sleep on a Coney Island beach, dreaming about

> being split in twain by monstrous mechanisms, drowned in a whirling vortex of mud, being immured in stone and, most fearsomely, buried alive. All night long I had the sensation of helplessness, speechlessness, an inability to move or cry out against the inexorable weight of earth as it was flung in *thud-thud-thud*ing rhythm against my rigidly paralyzed, supine body, a living cadaver being prepared for burial in the sands of Egypt. The desert was bitterly cold.

Waking the following morning, "safe as a mummy" beneath the coat of sand with which he has been covered by some unidentified children, Stingo has been miraculously relieved of his despondency of the night before, and "[b]lessing [his] resurrection," in his mind he inscribes the words: "'*Neath cold sand I dreamed of death / but woke at dawn to see / in glory, the bright, the morning star*.'"

It is the contention of Rhoda Sirlin, and others, that "Stingo's inner journey does lead somewhere—to a fuller understanding of history as refracted through Sophie and to a fuller understanding of the self, the all-too-innocent American self." Certainly, Sirlin's contention that Stingo "is the lone survivor learning how to conquer grief and despair so that he can go on living, the only character not destroyed by his suffering," sounds like a paraphrase of what the narrator implies when he writes about his younger self that it was "as if the suffering Stingo whom I once inhabited, or who once inhabited me, learning at firsthand and for the first time in his grown-up life about death, and pain, and loss, and the appalling enigma of human existence, was trying physically to excavate from that paper the only remaining— perhaps the only bearable—truth. *Let your love flow out on all living things*."

But is such a reading really borne out by the text? Having "preserved those words as a reminder of some fragile yet perdurable hope," the narrator obviously suggests that, from the perspective of young Stingo, the encounter with Sophie and Nathan has amounted to a rite of initiation: the aspiring writer whose "spirit had remained landlocked, unacquainted with love and all but a stranger to death" has been released into artistic expression through the confrontation with evil, pain, and madness. But the story about Sophie's slow and tortured confrontation with her own guilt and anguish and Nathan's sadly twisted and violent existence, their only release to be had in death, would appear to be wholly alien to vapid sentiments like "*Let your love flow out on all living things.*" The actual psychological terrain of this text is, again, one of a crippling sense of guilt, of emotional failure, of struggles "with the demon of [one's] own schizoid conscience," and while the pursuit of the text has been to free that consciousness, the final outcome is still self-destruction. The key phrase, therefore, of the quotation is "to excavate . . . perhaps the only bearable truth," a sentence which calls to mind the one from "A Tidewater Morning"—"We each devise our means of escape from the intolerable." Incantation remains the sole, and ineffectual means to cope with the unspeakable, for Stingo no less than Nat Turner, Cass Kinsolving, or Paul Whitehurst. Significantly, in the words Stingo chants to ward off an onslaught of the cruelty, pain, and evil of the world, words that he had "memorized as a boy: *And God shall wipe away all tears from their eyes. And there shall be no more death, neither sorrow nor crying, neither shall there be any more pain . . .*," the reader recognizes the epigraph (from Revelation) to *The Confessions of Nat Turner*. Like his fictional predecessors, William Styron's persona Stingo can here be seen to be willing away the paralyzing realization of the tenuousness of existence.

MICHAEL KREYLING

Speakable and Unspeakable in Styron's Sophie's Choice

One of the first acts of David after he was anointed king of Israel was to retrieve the Ark of the Covenant and return it to the Citadel in Jerusalem. David did not need a media adviser to know that the ark was the religious and civil center of the nation over which he hoped to rule; possession of the ark was possession of the incorporating power of the nation.

The author of 2 Samuel reminds his readers of the actuality of that power vested in a central sign, if they had forgotten during the preceding turmoil. The ark, he writes, "bears the name of Yahweh Sabaoth," which is to say the ark *is* Yahweh Sabaoth. Then he follows with a brief narrative exemplum to illustrate the crucial distinction between *is* and *stands for*.

Two sons of Aminadab have been deputed to accompany the ark on its ride back to Jerusalem. Uzzah, one of the sons, walks alongside while a great celebration, consisting of harps, lyres, tamborines, and David himself cavorting before the ark, entertains the crowd. As the oxen pulling the ark labor over the entrance to Nacon's threshing house, the cart tilts and seems about to dump the ark onto the floor. Uzzah stretches out his hand to steady the ark—a simple reflex action. "Then the anger of Yahweh blazed out against Uzzah, and for his crime God struck him down on the spot, and he died there beside the ark of God" (*The Jerusalem Bible*). David, the author records, was "displeased"; the sudden death of Uzzah must have thrown a pall over the new king's first

From *Southern Review* 20, no. 3. © 1984 Louisiana State University.

public demonstration. But there was nothing anyone could do. Uzzah was dead, one of the more intriguing casualties of Yahweh's quick wrath, and all concerned went on chastened and, supposedly, refreshed by the lesson of the identity of God and Word.

The unfortunate Uzzah forfeited his life for neglecting, in an instant of ordinary consciousness, the extraordinary nature of the thing which seemed about to crash to the floor of Nacon's threshing house. The ark not only bore the name of Yahweh, but in fact was the thing it named, God: his potency, person, and presence among his people. The ark is more than symbol to the chosen people, and yet it is not an idol—not like the Dagon of the Philistines, that cannot remain upright in the presence of the ark. The ark of Israel is both object and logos, word and actual presence, signifier and signified. Touching it outside of ritual sanction, Uzzah broke its mystery by treating it as any other cargo that might have shifted in transit. He violated community, too, for he stepped beyond the boundaries set by Yahweh for the definition of his people even though, perhaps especially because, no conscious choice was involved. The community exists independent of the individual act of thinking of it.

Uzzah also tampered with the writing of God—the ark contained the tablets on which the law was inscribed. For the people of Israel, identity and distinctiveness in history, against the threats of a host of immediate foes and the ultimate fate of eternal oblivion, was a matter of written contract: God's promise to them housed in language. The central signifier was kept away from the profane touch of the everyday so that the omnipotence and truth of God would survive as the one and only language in which mankind's history would be written. Uzzah was a writer who, stretching out that fatal hand as if to revise the sacred and unspeakable with the mundane and momentary, unwittingly played the part of the usurper of the Word.

William Styron brings Uzzah back in the character of Stingo, hero-narrator of *Sophie's Choice*, but the world sanctioned by the certainty of the central word of Yahweh is so corrupted that Stingo's Uzzah's touch to *Auschwitz* aims to resuscitate the human community, the body of mankind. Stingo's call to this prophetic office is no less dramatic than that of Samuel himself. Farrell, the failed priest, tells Stingo "'Son, write your guts out'" and from that moment the young writer's mission is clear: he must abolish *l'univers concentrationnaire* by reconnecting the character of the word to the human community. Auschwitz, which Styron often considers as a human condition beyond its limits in actual time—the logos or continuing character of a lifeless void—is the great unspeakable that fattens on man's silence. This Uzzah's touch will bring life.

Language, then, is the medium and subject of *Sophie's Choice*. The danger, as Stingo sees it, lies in the very silence that critics such as George

Steiner suggest as the fitting response to the enormity of the evil of Auschwitz. Stingo would rather have language, even with its myriad thorns of irony and double meaning, tone and connotation, suggestion and play, than the ominous silence in which and because of which Auschwitz robs man of humanity in robbing him of his speech. As writer, more pertinently as southerner and writer, Stingo is convinced that telling his story of becoming a writer is also telling the story of how the Holocaust came about. Denying the unspeakable any ground, Styron aims to drag Auschwitz back into the public forum of the speakable. To accord it the sanctuary of the unspeakable is, in Styron's verbal universe, to surrender to it the power to haunt, to kill, to blight the human community that survives by speaking.

Steiner's admonition, taken up by Styron near the midpoint of *Sophie's Choice*, operates by implication from the beginning of the novel. Robert Towers, reviewing the novel in the *New York Review of Books*, thought enough of the aside on Steiner to place it at the crux of his review. Here is Styron's passage:

> Yet I cannot accept Steiner's suggestion that *silence* is the answer, that it is best "not to add the trivia of literary, sociological debate to the unspeakable." Nor do I agree with the idea that "in the presence of certain realities art is trivial or impertinent." I find a touch of piety in this, especially inasmuch as Steiner has not remained silent. And surely, almost cosmic in its incomprehensibility as it may appear, the embodiment of evil which Auschwitz has become remains impenetrable only so long as we shrink from trying to penetrate it, however inadequately; and Steiner himself adds immediately that the *next* best is "to try and understand." I have thought that it might be possible to make a stab at understanding Auschwitz by trying to understand Sophie, who to say the least was a cluster of contradictions.

Styron's usage of Steiner's language eventually gives way to his own usage, a sort of serious play, alternately clownish and pregnant, admitting the radicals, associations, and double meanings of the very weapon he brandishes in the face of the incomprehensible.

Styron seems unconcerned that the handle is very slippery. According to Kevin Sack, Styron once commented:

> "I've always thought that English was a wonderfully rich and descriptive language. . . . It's wrong not to exploit it to the hilt, even if it courts criticism of overwriting—which I have been accused of. I find the use of extraordinary words valuable. It

keeps the mind going. You have to use discrimination. But I
would rather err in the usage of more ornate language than with
language which has no vitality and color."

Words are close to being living things, with color, movement, and vitality.
They are warm, they make noise—Stingo mumbles them to get the prose
rhythms right. Using words makes us part of the body of man; allowing
words to go unspoken leads that body to atrophy, to Auschwitz.

Styron, in rebutting Steiner, twice uses the word *penetrate* and once
stab to sexually characterize the act of writing by which he hopes to fathom
Sophie and Auschwitz in the same act. To *shrink* from the challenge is
unmanly, he implies. From the early pages of the novel describing Stingo's
arid life at McGraw-Hill and his frustrated celibacy at the University Resi-
dence Club, we are carried along on the double currents of sex as language
and language as sex, not immediately certain that the destination is
Auschwitz.

Outside Stingo's window is a "ravishing garden"—nicely ambiguous
phrase—into which, like a horny Giovanni Guasconti, Stingo gazes with
starved libido and the concomitant creative viscosity of molasses in January.
Recalling Gertrude Stein on the latter point, Stingo says of himself that he
had the syrup but it wouldn't pour. Given the spurts, gushes, and deluges of
his later orgasmic achievements, we are alerted to Stingo's idée fixe: luxuriant
seminal liquidity means verbal fluency. Stingo's occluded currents of sex and
literary creativity are undammed in his verbal conquest of the maid in the
ravishing garden. Spying the shapely woman of the house across the way,
Stingo transforms his lust into a figure of language, which then aptly slithers
into the garden where Stingo, safe in his hermit's cell, "fucked her to a frazzle
with stiff, soundless, slow, precise shafts of desire." Or of language, being
honed to penetrate and stab no less precisely and slowly (*Sophie's Choice*
unwinds to 515 pages) the unspeakable enigma of Auschwitz.

Stingo confesses that his obsession with words is almost "erotic," and
Styron's affection for this type of play runs to raunchy uproar rather than to
chaste awe at the ravishing phrase. But the faith in language is of no less
crucial importance to *Sophie's Choice*. Readers may differ on the degree of
Styron's "discrimination" in approaching such a subject as Auschwitz armed
solely with the English language, with help from phrases from a few others.
But that is what he does.

In his youthful hormonal and literary maelstrom Stingo must choose
between moving Venus pencils (Tannhauser of the yellow legal pad) across a
blank sheet of paper, or masturbating. Masturbation, in fact, is one of the
prime distractions from the writing Stingo desperately wishes to complete.

Writing his "snotty" manuscript evaluations for McGraw-Hill, he has to fight off the temptation to masturbate; every second he abandons pen for penis is one more second he is delayed from reaching the company of Melville, Dostoyevsky, Faulkner, Warren, or any of the dozen or so literary idols he wants to knock off.

Stingo, for his sins of self-abuse, becomes something of an authority on lingual and manual venery—not that a connoisseur's knowledge brings him a scrap of joy. With Leslie Lapidus and Mary Alice Grumball he learns that sex and speech are contiguous parts of the whole human organism.

Leslie enters Stingo's life first; her sex-talk literally inflames Stingo. But her "totally lingual" sexual performance smothers the flames. "Her [Leslie's] sex life is wholly centered in her tongue. It is not fortuitous therefore that the inflammatory promise she has been able to extend me through that hyperactive organ of hers finds correlation in the equally inflammatory but utterly spurious words she loves to speak." Stingo found no fulfillment with Leslie, but blessed her future. Mary Alice Grumball, whose maddeningly workmanlike services as a "whack-off artist" Stingo endures for a term of three nights, fares less well. Her hand is a clammy and unnatural substitute for the proper organ of copulation; in that, she is not much more foolish than Leslie. Mary Alice's language, however, condemns her more sternly than Leslie's. Only a few years after millions of victims had been incinerated in Nazi furnaces, Mary Alice Grumball, American, complains to Stingo that the reason she will not go all the way is that she "got burnt so badly" when her fiancé left her at the altar. Just this trick of vocabulary Styron faces head on by relentlessly maintaining the speakable nature of the universe. The risk is huge, for the medium of his narrative—words—has the power, by an unpredictable double meaning or errant association, to overturn itself. There is something mysterious yet fecund in language that makes the female, Sophie, the end of Stingo's sexual and linguistic yearnings.

With Sophie sex and language are always a different matter, and often the same matter. From the outset Stingo's obsession with Sophie is fraught with muted resonance as he tries to interpret her with an energy second, it seems, only to that he pours into the story of the doomed Maria Hunt. Sophie is her speech, her self-recreation in a new tongue. Characteristically, the first shouting match between Nathan and Sophie dwells upon the appropriate usage of a word, *cunt*. Nathan belabors Sophie with her erroneous usage of the female epithet for him. More telling, however, is Stingo's reaction to Sophie's language. He too corrects her in the American idiom, all the while maintaining that Sophie's speech carries an elusive essence: "Without overdoing it, I will from time to time have to try to duplicate the delicious inaccuracies of Sophie's English. Her command was certainly more than adequate and—for me, anyway—actually enhanced by her small stumbles in the thickets of syntax. . . ." Sophie's body registers the same "delicious" charm as her speech:

> As she went slowly up the stairs I took a good look at her body in
> its clinging silk summer dress. While it was a beautiful body, with
> all the right prominences, curves, continuities and symmetries,
> there was something a little strange about it—nothing visibly
> missing and not so much deficient as reassembled. . . . Despite
> past famine, her behind was as perfectly formed as some fantastic
> prize-winning pear; it vibrated with magical eloquence. . . .

Sophie's voluptuous, fleshly "eloquence" merges with her "delicious" speech, so that talking or standing still she is an object to be savored on the tongue. Her self-proclamations in skewed syntax, X-rated malapropisms (e.g. complimenting Stingo on his handsome appearance in a "cocksucker" suit), or the tortured confessions of her choices in Auschwitz literally embody her, for her flesh is her story, the text in which her sins are recorded. The book of her life shows the heavy patronage of men, too; each use is rudely stamped.

It is essential to see Sophie as created by and netted in language. A series of men appropriate her through the imposition of a superior language. Her father, the minor league fascist Professor Bieganski, imprisons Sophie within the language of his anti-Semitic pamphlet. The word *Vernichtung*, which he surreptitiously slips into the manuscript that Sophie types, penetrates her mind and memory with more destructive force than the phantom finger that rapes her in the New York subway. This word becomes the vacant center into which her life vanishes.

Her first meeting with Nathan is also commemorated by the special mediation of language. The Brooklyn College librarian literally slams Sophie to her knees with his harsh words for her misapprehension of the name "Emily Dickinson." Nathan soothes Sophie with his own voice, later puts names on all of her maladies and deficiencies, and eventually brings on a semblance of health. When Nathan is not cooing to Sophie, though, he is scourging her with words. His verbal abuse is no less aching than the blows and kicks he lands, for the bruises to the body will heal.

As tortured and melodramatic as the pact between Nathan and Sophie is, Sophie's encounter with Höss is more laden with meaning for the quest of the novel and Stingo. In Styron's protracted dramatization of the scenes between Sophie and the commandant of Auschwitz, the relevance of language to the unspeakable evil, indications of the origin of a curse beyond the immediate horrors of the camp, and the possible efficacy of silence in the healing of the body of mankind are central to the theme. Sophie is, first of all, Höss's amanuensis, as she was her father's, his hands in the drafting of letters and his liaison with the world. Sophie translates the world of local priests and camp suppliers for Höss, and revises his own verbal presentations to his superiors in Berlin.

Sophie, for example, handles the correspondence when Höss begs Berlin to relax the pace of mass death in his crematoria. The ovens, Höss fears, will not hold up under the steadily increasing stream of human victims shipped in for extermination. Sophie types his unoriginal and awkward prose: "The mechanism for Special Action at Birkenau having become severely taxed beyond all expectation, it is respectfully suggested that, in the specific matter of the Greek Jews, alternative destinations in the occupied territories of the East . . . be considered." Aware of "the reality behind these euphemisms," Sophie automatically strips the official, passive prose of its betrayal: "'The Greek Jews being such a pathetic lot and ready to die anyway, we hope it is all right that they have been assigned to the death commando unit at the crematoriums, where they will handle the corpses and extract the gold from the teeth and feed bodies to the furnaces till they too, exhausted beyond recall, are ready for the gas.'" Sophie "finished [Höss's] letter without a mistake," typing the official text while the true one spoke in her mind. Language undermined her moral ground, tainted her with complicity, doomed her to a life without hope even in survival. She participated in the act of betrayal by which a word is uttered but its natural bond of meaning in the world is ignored. This is a blasphemy against language, for it negates the human connection of language and relegates it to the sphere of knobs, switches, and keys—the manufactured world that has usurped the human. And it also constitutes a misuse of the tongue—the organ of speech. The sexual handicaps of Mary Alice, Leslie, and others find their more serious cognates here.

Sophie is corrupted by language misused; the agent of her personal *Vernichtung* is, appropriately, the tongue. Rape by the oafish Wilhelmine is more than graphic: "the brutish muzzle and the bullethead of a tongue probed into what, with some dull distant satisfaction, she realized was her obdurate dryness, as parched and without juice as desert sand." Stingo makes this point with a succession of modifiers, each one reinforcing the same impression: passion and life are wet; death-in-life is parched, arid, dry. Wilhelmine's tongue, brutish as it is, must probe deep into Sophie's psyche as well as her body. As the words *Vernichtung, Special Action, Final Solution,* even the word Holocaust itself, penetrate or stab at the vast void of Auschwitz, they belittle it with verbal utterance, ignoring the awe-full assumption that an evil so absolute might not be compassable in a human word. We all are doomed to the usage of language, however; even in our attempts to name the absolute we displace it into the human sphere of language and thereby falsify. To avoid this necessary falsification Steiner counsels silence. *Auschwitz* is the word that negates the Word, the darkness that finally extinguishes the Light of the World. We can, therefore, understand Sophie's hatred for religion, her truly desperate cry: "'I hate religion. It is for, you know, *des analphabètes*, imbecile peoples.'" Language is always revealing; Sophie associates religion with those people who have no language. Once we have language, we have Auschwitz.

In this shadowed world, dimmed by the clouds that float out from Birkenau—an atmosphere of despair that Styron had used similarly in *Lie Down in Darkness*—the wise suspect doom comes with the act of speech. To be a hero, to counter Höss and his numerous clones in the SS, one must, Styron pleads implicitly, inject meaning back into the womb of silence. Figuratively, then, the male writer's priapic urges and verbal libido are phases or aspects of his foreordained calling to sow the world with meaning.

Perhaps the southern writer is best positioned to see this facet of the world of words and relations in language. Stingo certainly fields and dodges most of the assumptions about southern life and writing which have been the pride and bane of generations of southern writers. But the immersion in the word for the southern hero-writer is more complex than the mere record of a literary situation in any given time and place, and Styron sees through to its important function in his quest for the return of the speakable world in the aftermath of Auschwitz.

Stingo is the southern man of letters in a radical sense: he is a man whose very character is composed of words. His father, significantly, appears in the novel first in the language of his epistles to his exile son. The first letter to Stingo introduces themes of sex, slavery, and money that reverberate throughout the novel. The father's letters are the distant preparation for the assault on *Auschwitz*.

The ultimate cause for Stingo's hope in the efficacy of language is the "Southern Lord Chesterfield," his father, whose symmetrical prose is part and parcel of a universe in which all can be named and ordered in a moral as well as a linguistic grammar. What cannot be thought is never said, and therefore does not exist. Stingo's experiences in the world beyond this linguistic and moral arcadia teach him that too much has been repressed or simply excised from the verbal record to support the perfect world of the father. The lynching of Bobby Weed, with which Nathan taxes Stingo, is a gruesomely apt event: "While he was still alive Bobby Weed's cock and balls had been hacked off and thrust into his mouth, . . . and when near death, though reportedly aware of all, had by a flaming blowtorch received the brand on his chest of a serpentine 'L'—representing what? 'Lynch?' 'Lula?' 'Law and Order?' 'Love?'" The white mob conveniently fits into the linguistic-sexual motif of the novel, for their torture of Bobby Weed renders him sexually null and unable to speak with the same act of barbarity.

Preceding and accounting for Stingo, in the person of his father, is a universe of the known, utterable world. The father's world, however, is not portable, does not travel across time and space. His visit to Stingo in New York confirms the limited boundaries of this once and former universe.

The father, from deep in his past, had nursed "an undying hatred for the vicious monopoly capitalism that tramples the little man." He carried his antipathy to the modern city made by that capitalism, New York, and into a cab driven by one Thomas McGuire. McGuire, with the sullen linguistic aggressiveness we all recognize, rejected the father's five-cent tip and called him a "fucking asshole." The father is at first taken aback, then quite carefully requests that McGuire repeat himself, his words. The father then blasts McGuire with words he probably had never heard: "detestable scum," "sewer rat," one who "disgorg[es] . . . disgusting filth" and "spew[s] . . . putrid language upon fellow citizens." At this McGuire abandons his tenuous footing in the world of verbal discourse and slugs the father.

Stingo takes the episode with a mixture of dazed concern and tired resignation. He is a few sheets to the wind already, deeply depressed over Nathan and Sophie, and unsurprised that his father had virtually sought out the lowest of the lower orders in the Northern Babel. The episode is also Boschian in its richness and fertility for the novel. The father, hating the modern order from the distance of a past and agrarian enclave (although he does work in a shipyard, his antiquarian pursuits and dreams of the Southampton peanut farm are stressed in Stingo's narrative), hurls himself directly at the corruption of the tongue in Babel. McGuire has uttered words that, save by a tortured process of sociolinguistic explication, cannot be said to carry any meaning. They not only carry the force of a sexual insult; by their obscene coupling of antitheses, they negate the erotic act of language itself. The father flies into his tirade, heaping scorn on the unnatural oral and linguistic perversity of McGuire's offense, for he sees that the offense inheres not in the speaking of "dirty words," but in the blasphemy against the human act of speech and the betrayal of the community naturally and lovingly to be engendered by its right use. McGuire is the vulgar apparition of Höss.

About one hundred pages earlier, Stingo had limped to the defense of Theodore Bilbo, race-baiting Mississippi demagogue, whose mouth cancer seemed, both to Nathan and to Stingo, strikingly apt punishment for a lifetime of name-calling. Stingo's refusal to equate Bilbo and Hitler, however, is weakened by his earlier lukewarm farewell to Bilbo: "Glad to see you go, you evil-spirited old sinner." The father takes a harder line when he recognizes the signs of human corruption in the corruption of the word.

Styron's fixation with language, the physiology of its formation by the mouth and tongue, and the symbolic and actual links between language and its instruments and sex and the same instruments, fills *Sophie's Choice* with ornate and vital—if minimally discriminated—associations and images. The echoes and double entendres are never totally escapable; somehow, through a raunchy wisecrack or a solemn pronouncement, language always turns up as the sacramental act in question. If, as Auschwitz seems to prove, the mystery and sacred potency has been filched from man's tongue, then we are indeed in a universal death camp, a totally new form of human society.

The supercharged use of language is nowhere more intensely pressed for meaning than in Styron's ultimate assault on the central signifier of death-in-life: *Auschwitz*. Auschwitz, in *Sophie's Choice*, and in the modern Judeo-Christian world that has survived the butchery, is more than a mere word. It is the articulation we use to signify an otherwise inexpressible trip into nullity. The killing, Styron ventures, was a peculiar result of a modern cancer—boring, unimaginative yet efficient, and utterly without symbolic import. The executioners of Bobby Weed had more claim to meaning something. Auschwitz stands at the beginning of a wholly new scripture; when Morris Fink asks Stingo "'What's Owswitch?'" the author of *Sophie's Choice* makes his central point: American Jews and Gentiles alike operate in a naive dispensation, are in a sense *des analphabètes*, illiterate in the new covenant of absolute nothing. The new Uzzah enters to topple the evil covenant of silence.

For Americans, Stingo asserts, the names of all concentration camps are "stupid catchwords," the usage of which signifies a shallow, puerile sense of history and morality. The elderly cricket's voice of H. V. Kaltenborn, from whom Sophie and Nathan listen to the news from Nuremburg, seems an appropriately thin voice, with a whiff of Disney, for the degree of reality Americans are capable of mustering to the Nazi horrors. With Auschwitz a new language looms in the world of man—a language now spewed forth, as the novel periodically claims, by a carcinoma on the soul of the technologically efficient society that has replaced the human community. Stingo's father, and Sophie's uncle in the ill-fated Polish cavalry, recognize the contagion, but neither is any match for the onslaught.

Styron thrusts at the tremendous evil of Auschwitz in a variety of movements, each one having to do with a crucial lapse, corruption, or betrayal of language. One revolves around the attempt by Sophie to seduce Höss, after her own ill-defined reasons, away from the stark realm of his sclerotic language and into a living realm where the link between word and thing, speaker and lover, has not been erased. She wants to put them both back into a condition where lips, hands, tongues—and the words they make—are used for eros, not death. Crucially, the utterance that might have drawn Höss away from the mechanistics of his obsession with death is never given voice. Sophie confesses to Stingo that, after a pause in her stenographic work for Höss, she tried to compose herself, to make herself look "'as if I wanted to fuck. Looking as if I wanted to be asked to fuck.'" Höss never says the word; he remains in the cell of disembodied language.

The absolute poverty of Höss's moral and verbal world is revealed in his reaction to Sophie's request that she be permitted to see her son Jan. Höss's words cap a tortured chapter (chapter 10) in which Sophie tells Stingo of her attempts to seduce Höss, the failure, and her pleading for her son. Höss responds with his own disgust for most sex, and to Sophie's plea turns what he no doubt believes to be a benign and assenting face. Stingo gives Höss's words in both German and English: "'Glaubst du, dass ich ein Ungeheuer bin? Do you think I am some kind of monster?'"

Höss is a monster; that he does not suspect this testifies to the thorough inversion of language that enabled Auschwitz. For Styron to put on Höss's lips the single word, *monster*, most frequently used to name the Nazi horrors, is a touch of verbal irony. At the base of the problem facing the redeeming writer-hero is the failure of language to hold the natural human community together in a world of reality. Once the Adamic check upon word and thing is lost, the route to the death camps is open. No one in *Sophie's Choice*, with the possible exception of Stingo, knows a way back.

Nathan is peculiarly doomed, for he is as riddled with the monstrous Nazi contagion as any SS functionary. His excessive worship and fascination for science, and particularly for the pharmaceutical miracles of the Pfizer company, pushes him perilously close to the bloodless horrors he loathes. Stingo gathers from Nathan's boasting that he and his research team are creating life in a test tube, a somewhat boozy conclusion but nevertheless uncomfortably close to the monstrous. Nathan's infatuation with cyanide, the capsule of which bears the conspicuous logo of the Pfizer company, apes Herman Göring's suicide and is the probable source of Nathan's choice for his self-destruction. Nathan is destroyed by his obsession with the Nazi technology; at one of Morty Haber's parties he listens as if transfixed to the news of fresh discoveries of "the Nazi handiwork." God's "Hände Werk," so joyously celebrated in the music that Nathan and Sophie play, has been demolished.

Perhaps more tragically than Sophie, then, Nathan is a victim of Auschwitz. As deranged, imaginary scientist, he manifests the sinister curse of scientific progress that Styron locates in the Nazi enterprise. In *One-Dimensional Man: Studies in the Ideology of Advanced Industrial Society*,

Herbert Marcuse has identified its residue for the world after Auschwitz:

> Auschwitz continues to haunt, not the memory but the accomplishments of man—the space flights; the rockets and missiles . . . the pretty electronic plants, clean, hygienic and with flower beds; the poison gas which is not really harmful to people; the secrecy in which we all participate. This is the setting in which the great human achievements of science, medicine, technology take place; the efforts to save and ameliorate life are the sole promise in the disaster.

For Marcuse, Auschwitz is the central fact in the post-Holocaust world Western man has made for himself. Not even the atomic bomb supercedes it. Inseparable from the consciousness of his accomplishments is the horror at the ease with which we can and will use our marvels for more heartless killing. And we twist the language to shield us from our handiwork. If Nathan is a paranoid schizophrenic, it is not because of chemical imbalances in the hippocampus of his brain. He carries the post-Holocaust disease: identification with the victim, envy of the evil manipulator.

The world that Styron proposes in order to render Auschwitz speakable and readable in *Sophie's Choice* is a version of the modern world Marcuse calls "Advanced Industrial Society." Putting severe burdens on his narrative logic, Styron tries to establish this world by first introducing Stingo's father as a capitalist hater and then much later bringing on the character of Walter Dürrfeld, boss of IG Farben. Styron nearly trivializes the novel by suggesting that the root of the evil is in the organization man.

In "Hell Reconsidered," a 1978 essay collected in *This Quiet Dust*, Styron broaches the argument that light could be shed on the hellish darkness of Auschwitz through attention to the advanced industrial ends to which it and other camps were set up. In the essay Styron tries out many of the theories later advanced by Stingo in the novel. The form of slavery practiced by the Nazis in the camps, for instance, is understandable as existing on a "continuum of slavery which has been engrafted for centuries onto the very body of Western civilization." A southerner, especially one with the convenient memory of the slave Artiste, is thus ideally situated to decode the ominous monolith of Auschwitz.

The type of slavery the Nazis made, Styron continues in his essay, having been accelerated in degree of harshness, suddenly became different in kind:

> Slaving at the nearby factory of I. G. Farben or at the Farben coal mines (or at whatever camp maintenance work the SS were able

to contrive), the thousands of inmates initially spared the gas chambers were doomed to a sick and starving death-in-life perhaps more terrible than quick extinction, and luck was more often than not the chief factor involved in their survival.

That the Nazis, whom Styron glibly describes as "among this century's leading efficiency experts," are squeezed into the position so often reserved for Yankee mill owners in unreconstructed defenses of slave society (in fact, to the detriment of the novel, Stingo gratuitously likens New Jersey factories to the crematoria at Birkenau), places Styron and the novel in jeopardy. By first advancing toward the assertion that the Nazi death camps were a uniquely different *kind* of slavery, and then resorting to shopworn comparisons between "efficiency experts" and SS officers, Styron undermines his achievement by grasping at the easy answer. Stingo had tried the same disappearing act when he refused to toast Bilbo's death with Nathan. Southerners owned slaves, and lynched some of them: so far the parallel with Hitler that Nathan pushes. But, Stingo insists, the numbers were fewer, and Bilbo pushed some good social legislation. Nathan will not allow him the unearned piety of absolution through the higher average of good. Nathan's madness is not without its flashes of insight, and the numbers trap is one of them.

Another example of this facile maneuver appeared on the editorial page of the *New York Times* for October 16, 1946—about eight months before time present of *Sophie's Choice*. In a series of brief editorial commentaries linked by the motif of batting averages, the editorialist moves from baseball to the American record on the Negro to the Nazi horrors. Even though a few American blacks have been lynched, the editorialist admits, the numbers are negligible compared to the millions murdered by the Nazis. Our national moral purity remains, in the terms of the image, unsullied:

> It is a distorted arithmetical sense, a completely atrophied sense
> of proportion, which insists that because of the mote in our own
> eye we are estopped from taking note of the monstrous beam in
> a stranger's eye.

Happily, we as a nation retain our moral right to judge others, especially those "strangers" on trial in Nuremburg, because we have the higher batting average. The word *estopped*, letting in the slightly musty odor of antique diction reminiscent of Stingo's father, hints back to the father's moral universe: simple, honorable, real, symmetrical.

Basing morality on average numbers of good or bad actions, though, seems to be a damning signal. Nathan, crazy bellwether that he is, sees it.

Numbers serve as the basis for the Farben enterprise administered by Dürrfeld through Höss, the gloss that Stingo hopes will explain Auschwitz.

Dürrfeld is introduced very late in the narrative, chapter 13. Sophie's father sycophantically shows him around the industrial and cultural sites of Cracow even as the Farben boss and family man makes veiled glances at the young and pretty Sophie. The next time Sophie and Dürrfeld meet she is an inmate of Auschwitz, so wasted that he does not recognize her. But she knows him by his voice. The scene has the thin feel of "Great Coincidences in History," but Styron's quest for the unlocking insight into Auschwitz carries him over the thin narrative ice before it breaks.

Sophie overhears some rather trumped up conversation in which both Höss and Dürrfeld discount "that mind doctor in Vienna" but go on to repress their direct complicity in mass murder: "'But when it comes to failure of production, do you think I can plead sickness—I mean schizophrenia—to my board of directors? Really!'" Dürrfeld is already deeply schizophrenic; his usage of *production* for the actually correct *destruction* (for the inmates are systematically destroyed) is conclusive proof of the division of language and mind.

Later in the novel, in the climactic episode of Sophie's encounter with the SS doctor who forces her to choose between Jan and Eva, Stingo brings up IG Farben once again. In trying to assess the personality of this anyone-no one doctor, Stingo attributes an unspecified segment of his motivation to the military-industrial complex: "Besides, he was at bottom a vassal of IG Farben."

How much evil can be explained by this route of reasoning? Is the military-industrial complex, or something like it, truly at the bottom? Dürrfeld and the Farben connection do not carry enough weight to answer these questions. Within the pattern of language usage and corruption, the Farben excursus *seems* to work. Industrial man has been forced to adopt a new grammar. The privilege of the word in naming the world has been revoked. Hence Höss himself gropes for "circumlocutions" to deflect the actuality of murder and to give a false resonance to his claim to be a person, not a monster. Dürrfeld calls the extermination of human beings by the name "production" and justifies slave labor by a half-jocular allusion to his board of directors. "It would be pleasant," says the character of a Polish resistance fighter Styron uses late in the novel, "to speak a language other than that of an oppressor." That grace is not vouchsafed our new community, for Auschwitz signifies the accomplishment of a technologically efficient industrial order that has abolished the human world. The central sign is the separation of speech from the body. Stingo tries manfully to reinstate the erotic joy of speaking and hearing, but his success is incomplete.

Still, we must acknowledge Styron's huge gamble in flinging himself at the monolithic and inscrutable sign of the time, Auschwitz, with good faith, sincere emotion, and the English language. We must also acknowledge his considerable subtlety in diagnosing the malady in our tongue. He imagines a redemption for Höss. Staring at Harlekin, the Polish Arabian that gambols in a corral at Auschwitz as the soot of thousands of human beings settles softly to the earth, Höss nearly completes a passage that leaves Sophie speechless as she tells it and Stingo as he listens. Sophie cannot say what Höss might have meant, but she can repeat his exact words: "'To escape the body of man yet still dwell in Nature. To *be* that horse, to live within that beast. That would be freedom.'" "What?" Stingo implores when Sophie cannot say what these words mean. Is this a way out, or the route into the death camps? Is it a wish for release into the transcendent realm beloved of Western mystics from Augustine on? Or is it a self-contradicting and ulti-mately perverting dream of pseudo-life without the flesh—a dream falsely accorded the status of the real and then used in the "monstrous," unspeakable foundation of the crematoria of Birkenau? Here is yet another of Sophie's choices.

RICHARD G. LAW

The Reach of Fiction: Narrative Technique in Styron's Sophie's Choice

In *Sophie's Choice*, the telling of the tale is contrived to display the capacity of fiction to illuminate a subject that baffles ordinary inquiry and to test the claims of art against perhaps the extreme form of knowledge: the meaning of Auschwitz. The novel also makes imperious demands on the reader, who is lured into constructing a text of the Holocaust—a process which, while productive of insights that are perhaps available in no other way, comes at the cost of a painful imaginative involvement. An essential part of the "argument" of *Sophie's Choice*—and of the implied claims for fiction which are embodied in it—is that the direct and unmediated encounter with the heart of darkness is not only dangerous, but may, by its very nature, prevent comprehension. Given a subject which cannot be confronted without danger of engulfing the viewer, the controlled distancing of art may be a necessary component of understanding.

Accordingly, the novel alternates between intense glimpses of its subject and moments of great psychological distance and abstraction, drawing the reader into a rhythm of confrontation and evasion. One of the primary means by which the reader's encounter with Auschwitz is controlled and manipulated is through the alternation complementary but quite different narrative perspectives. Stingo's point of view provides a direct though naive experience, approaching Auschwitz more or less accidentally and unwillingly. Through

From *Southern Literary Journal* 23, no. 1. © 1990 by the Department of English of the University of North Carolina at Chapel Hill.

Stingo, the reader has a direct glimpse not of Auschwitz, but of the delayed *effects* of Auschwitz on another. Stingo's experience is supplemented by the point of view of the mature authorial voice of the narrator, who offers a retrospective, frequently satirical reconstruction of his younger self's encounter with Sophie and her past. This retrospective view is informed by a broad scholarly rumination on the records of and commentary about the Holocaust, including extensive quotations from both victims and Nazi officials. In this way the book gives expression to many voices (no one of which can presume to capture "Auschwitz") even as it assimilates them to its own ends.

I

The subject of the Holocaust represents a test case for exploring the limits of what we conventionally call knowledge. It is hard to "know" Auschwitz. The experience of the camps exists so far outside normal human frames of references that the very facts of the case are, in a sense, unimaginable. As Styron himself has asserted, "Auschwitz can be compared to nothing"; "Auschwitz must remain the one place on earth most unyielding to meaning or definition." Moreover, the mind has defenses against such horror which are not easily overcome. It is no small task, then, to attempt to link the incommensurate with the familiar, to bring what lies at such an extremity within range of our ordinary powers of vision. What can be known of the phenomenon of industrialized mass murder is also complicated by the different senses by which we understand the word "knowledge." One kind of knowledge is the historian's, which is abstract and retrospective—its value deriving in part from its very distance from the events themselves and from the extent to which the events can be processed (interpreted) for general use. Quite another kind of knowledge is, of course, to have been there: "Only survivors of Auschwitz know what it meant to be in Auschwitz." Such knowledge is untranslatable and incommunicable; it not only transcends interpretation but defies attempts to make sense of it.

Between the former kind of knowledge and the latter, of course, lies an enormous distance which the novel invites us to contemplate. As Styron was aware, formidable commentators like Elie Wiesel have advised that fiction writers not even try to deal with the subject—that to make it a subject of fiction is somehow a desecration of the memory of the victims. Similarly, George Steiner has asserted that the only proper response is silence. Styron's novel, however, is directed squarely at the Steiner-Wiesel position that art can only trivialize an experience like the Holocaust. The "ultimately transcendental and important thing about art," Styron has claimed, "is its ability to do anything—that's the definition of art. It can deal with any experience—past, present, or future. . . ." In dramatizing the position that silence will not do as an answer to the camps, the novel has as much to say about the nature and capabilities of art as about Auschwitz. It is as if the novel accepts its subject as a challenge: if *Sophie's Choice* can provide a medium in which Auschwitz can, in some meaningful sense, become known, then literature can treat anything; no subjects are off-limits; no veils may be drawn across any area of human experience.

Styron's act of writing the novel, then, involves a monumental presumption and irreverence. He refuses to concede any privileged area to "insiders" or to bow to any form of proprietorship—a stance which had embroiled him earlier with some members of the black intelligentsia over *The Confessions of Nat Turner*, just as it has antagonized some Jewish readers of *Sophie's Choice*. But the novel embodies a kind of reverence as well, in that Styron's position, regardless of the components of personal arrogance or humility in it, implies that the imagination can function in a saving way at the very margins of human experience.

II

If *Sophie's Choice* is as preoccupied with the problem of knowledge as is *All the King's Men* or *As I Lay Dying*, it also attempts to overcome the obstacles to knowledge with techniques familiar from those precedents: it explores minutely a particular instance (Sophie's season in Hell) as a synecdoche of the Holocaust. The text draws a familiar distinction between abstract and concrete knowledge, the historian's knowledge vs. the victim's, and it relies heavily on the power of imagery to combine both, to fuse concepts and emotions, the general and the particular, in complex, highly charged dramatic actions. Like Faulkner's *The Sound and the Fury*, Styron's novel is constructed around a powerful germinal scene which the rest of the work may be said to gloss. Styron has referred to the genesis of the novel as a waking dream which imposed itself on him and became the controlling metaphor for the whole work. The image which troubled Styron involved a young woman on the platform at Auschwitz being forced to choose between her children. That image focused and contained several decades of his pondering on the meaning of the death camps: "I suddenly realized that this had to be the metaphor for the most horrible, tyrannical despotism in history, that this was a new form of evil. . . ." This single scene defines the world the Nazis made; it explains the secret wellspring of Sophie's mystifying behavior and the source of the irrational guilt which destroys her. It also dramatizes—by a process this essay will explore—as much of the heart of the darkness as is possible to dramatize.

It is critical to note that the reader encounters the core scene of Sophie with her children on the platform at Auschwitz only on page 484 of a 515-page text, by which point the narrative, through the powerful spectacle of her suffering, has converted the reader's initial gossipy interest in Sophie into a profound sense of empathy. Knowledge of her "choice" is withheld until the reader is prepared for it, subtly, by sensing in her attempts to start a new life in New York the consequences of some unknown event—the shadow of some unspeakable experience in her past—which has left Sophie obscurely crippled. In the meantime, by becoming gradually acquainted with Sophie and her story, the reader has descended, step by step, through layer after layer of her psychic pain, each layer worse than the last—and each, in a sense, unimaginable, unevocable, except by the process and in the context of the tale in which we have become immersed.

Because of its literally almost unspeakable subject, the manner of the unfolding of the tale is an exercise in overcoming, or putting to sleep, reader resistance. To keep the reader's imagination from evading the nature of Sophie's experience, Styron employs a variety of stratagems, some simple and others Byzantine in their elaborateness. The unfolding of the narrative, then, is a kind of trick which simultaneously carries us toward and hides its destination. The whole narrative is skillfully crafted to get us in a frame of mind where we cannot evade, or fail to imagine, the experience of genocide from the point of view of one of its victims.

Given the gruesome opportunities of the subject matter, there are very few actual scenes of Auschwitz, and few of them are particularly sensationalized or physically brutal. Although his portrayal of the camp is carefully based on surviving documents, Styron resists, for the most part, direct representation of its most sensational features. A careful reader of Emily Dickinson, Styron evidently holds with her that, because of its power to blind, "the Truth must dazzle gradually." Accordingly, most of the brutal realities of the camps are realized by suggestion, by brief direct glimpses, and by analogy. We acquire a sense of the degree to which Sophie has been brutalized in the camp from the way her father, an ardent fascist, treats her before the war and from the way her lover, Nathan Landau, treats her afterwards; we sense something of the camp's limitless oppression and dehumanizing impersonality from the anonymous digital rape of Sophie in the subway in New York. Similarly, from Stingo's haunted conscience about failing his cancer-stricken mother, we acquire the barest inklings of Sophie's sense of guilt—just the faintest sense of that open oven door of memory she encounters when she thinks of her children.

Such reserve and indirection are characteristic of the narrative strategems generally in *Sophie's Choice*. The experience of direct, scalding pain is, of course, not the object of the narrative, but rather a sympathetic intuition of the dimensions of Sophie's agony. Styron uses very shrewdly his art form's ability to move toward insight by the "stairway of surprise." By careful preparation and frequent deception, the narrative takes us up to one threshold of revelation after another and then stops, the narrator seeming always just about to show us things or tell us things. By such means it manages to take us places we would refuse to go if we sensed the destination. The components of the victim's experience of Auschwitz are vividly suggested in the narrative, but the task of assembling and understanding them belongs to the reader.

Sophie's Choice is presented in the form of a *Bildungsroman* in which the organizing axis of the narrative is Stingo's quest for knowledge. All of the elaborate excursions and digressions contribute to that developing line. Stingo is presented as a characterization of Styron himself at 22: a lonely ex-Marine with both literary and amorous ambitions seeking his fortune in the city. Stingo's is a familiar tale of initiation in which a callow, superficial sense of self and world is demolished by his "education." Stingo's attainment of a more mature and adequate perspective is not dramatized, although his having arrived at it is implied in the presence of the mature authorial voice, who has somehow survived and come to terms with the knowledge that Sophie represents. In reminiscing about the summer of 1947, the mature narrator speaks to us out of a successful career as a writer—a success which has, by some means difficult to fathom, been engendered by the experience that overwhelms his younger self. In mediating between the reader and the traumatic experience which constitutes Stingo's education, the mature narrator plays an unobtrusive but significant role in assembling the tale and controlling reader responses. Using the guise of confessional autobiography, the mature narrator dramatizes his younger self's failure to comprehend and assimilate his education while simultaneously taking the reader on a tortuous journey almost to the center of that experience.

The narrative he constructs of his early shortcomings is self-consciously intertextual; it casts Stingo as a twentieth-century version of Melville's Ishmael, setting out in Brooklyn on a "voyage of discovery": "my spirit had remained landlocked, unacquainted with love and all but a stranger to death." In a technique also reminiscent of *Moby-Dick*, the narrative has a double story line with dual protagonists and dual centers of interest, so that Stingo's own story emerges out of his telling us the story of the second figure, Sophie, whose name means "wisdom." The narrative is structured so that for Stingo to discover the answers to the riddle of Sophie, to know Sophie, as it were, would amount to a resolution of his quest. What Stingo acquires by way of an education is an experience of "evil," which is also the subject of the mature narrator's brooding enquiry.

Styron gives Stingo's initiation story important twists: his education involves gaining a perspective adequate for his ambition to become a writer. The narrative therefore recounts Stingo's discovery of both a subject and the resources within himself to treat it—the *knowledge*, presumably, to interpret it. Organized in this way, the fictive world which emerges in the narrative has a bearing on and provides a partial definition of the writer's craft and calling. However, Stingo's education consists largely of discoveries—in scenes such as the revelation of Nathan's madness—of the invalidity or unrealiability of his knowledge.

Learning of Sophie's past and observing her eventual death constitute the chief means through which Stingo acquires an experience of evil. The two mysteries, Sophie and Auschwitz, are telescoped together, with Sophie serving as the focal point through which the mystery of Auschwitz can be glimpsed: "I have thought that it might be possible to make a stab at understanding Auschwitz by trying to understand Sophie. . . ." However, the youthful Stingo is too stunned to assimilate, even vicariously, Sophie's experience of evil. A product of a safe, white, middle class, Protestant Tidewater Virginia upbringing, Stingo appears an unlikely candidate for either mature understanding or Parnassus. He suffers from a peculiarly American innocence, epitomized by his "virginity," which not even a hitch in the Marine Corps in World War II could alter. Naive, frequently obtuse, and sexually obsessed, he is, for much of the narrative, essentially a comic figure, providing a kind of bizarre (but often welcome) relief from the unfolding horrors of Sophie's past.

But it is important to note that the mature narrator, even in his retrospective account, is not readily able to follow the track of Sophie's experience to her nightmare encounter on the platform either. One index to the difficulty the narrator has in assimilating the knowledge that Sophie represents is the manner of the telling of Sophie's tale, which is as circuitous in its own way as the telling of *Absalom, Absalom!* To an extent, the narrative technique dramatizes not just Stingo's repeated failures to comprehend, but the older narrator's cautious approach toward the death camps. Aspects of her past, or aspects of what is known of Auschwitz, are worried at length, as if no context could be large enough to encompass and no background sufficient to explain the impending revelation. Typically, key information is offered up piecemeal, in fragments which have to be assembled by the reader, or as generalization separate from context or details. Events and information come jumbled together in baffling counterpoint, sometimes juxtaposed as if to comment on one another, and at other times seemingly to retard the action, as if to post-pone the platform encounter.

The gradual unfolding of Sophie's past is structured around a number of moments of revelation which require revisions of Stingo's previous esti-mates of her. These moments function as mileposts in the narrative's approach toward the secret of her life. The need for continual revision is partly a result of Sophie's reticence about things and partly of her active duplicity. She lies about her unhappy marriage and her relationship with her father, fabricating a parent who is a kindly paragon of virtue and learning, rather than a fanatical anti-Semite who had imagined and passionately advo-cated for others the kind of fate which overwhelms his daughter and grand-children. She suppresses her wartime experiences in Warsaw and the fact that she had a son at Auschwitz and a daughter also. Last of all, the revelation that she was forced to choose between them comes only slowly, after many evasions, so that each revelation forces Stingo to construct a new interpreta-tion of her past and therefore of her "present" character and situation. Also absent from early accounts of her past is the "fact" that, in the moral quag-mire that was Auschwitz, Sophie was not simply a victim of the Nazis, but, in a complex and extremely tenuous way, an accomplice.

But the need for revision is also partly a result of the strangeness and enormity of what is to be understood. Preoccupied by his own sexual enter-prises and blinded by his infatuation with her, Stingo is obviously not very astute in his reading of Sophie. He is taken in by her evasions and fails to comprehend her real needs for assistance. For example, after his comically disastrous attempts with Leslie and Alice, Stingo has his longed-for sexual encounter with Sophie, but the act is a grim parody of intimacy, and it fails to effect the magical changes in himself that he had hoped for. In fact, the loss of his "virginity" is largely ancillary to his education, and it certainly does nothing for his powers of observation. Stingo fails to realize that, for Sophie, the experience is merely a brief anodyne for her pain, which is intense enough to make death desirable. Stingo, the aspiring novelist, is not astute enough to recognize how little his offer of a Southern pastoral retreat, complete with matrimony and an on-looking Protestant community, could appeal to Sophie in these circumstances. He also fails utterly to grasp the dual roles Nathan has played in her life as healing savior and the pursuing demon of her conscience. By presenting himself in the role of yet another male savior, Stingo shows himself insensitive to the elements of her life of struggle for independence of male domination. Finally, he is oblivious to her dread of having more children. His catalog of missed signals is great enough to suggest that another, less tragic outcome might have been possible, had he truly *known* Sophie.

Stingo misunderstands Nathan as thoroughly as he does Sophie, oscillating until nearly the end between admiration and loathing of this older, mysterious figure. In one typical revelation, Sophie confides to Stingo that Nathan was addicted to drugs. "How blind I had been!" Stingo exclaims, in the throes of a complete reinterpretation of Nathan's past behavior. For a time, Nathan's demon acquires a specific shape and rationale in Stingo's mind, only to be expunged as an explanation by Larry Landau's further revelation of Nathan's madness a hundred pages later. But these failures of Stingo to comprehend critical issues throughout the narrative are not merely illustrative of his flaws of character. They dramatize the elusiveness of the understanding he seeks. And because the mature narrator does not share with the reader the benefits of his own hindsight, but withholds information and silently encourages false or incomplete appraisals, the reader is left equally at sea—therefore sharing with Stingo multiple experiences of disquieting misapprehension, revision, and reinterpretation. This technique involves the reader intimately in Stingo's experience, in Stingo's "voyage of discovery." By such means, as we shall see, the narrative encourages in the reader a sense of involved discovery which is closely akin emotionally to actual experience. Drawing the reader into constructing the text also has the function of bringing into consciousness the provisional nature of the kind of knowledge at issue here: the "truth" is invariably grimmer and more complex than the reader's first estimates of it. At the same time, the center of attention in the novel is subtly shifted from the events themselves to the process of interpreting experience *as* text and to the writer's act of reconstituting experience *in* the text. Thus, the technique also illustrates the arbitrary nature of the discourse in which knowledge is ordinarily framed.

III

Larry Landau's disclosure, "the truth is that my brother's quite mad," is one of the most significant expectation-shattering revelations in the novel. Like the revelation of Darl's insanity in *As I Lay Dying*, it has the effect of dramatically overturning the reader's previous estimates and forcing a fundamentally different reconstruction of the narrative. The revelation about Nathan's clinical history of insanity demolishes the most fundamental interpretative paradigm of the narrative as the reader had been led to conceive it—the novel as essay on the nature of evil. Nathan's violent abuse of Sophie had had the function throughout most of the narrative of embodying the principle of evil that has deformed Sophie's life and prospects. As Sophie's torturer in the New World, Nathan is presented, seemingly, as a "mirror" or extension of

Auschwitz. By bringing atrocity on a mass industrial basis down to a recognizable human scale, Nathan had also served as one of the means by which the reader is empowered to imagine the larger "absolute evil" of the camps. Consequently, Dr. Landau's description of his brother Nathan's diagnosis— "Paranoid schizophrenic, or so the diagnosis goes, although I'm not at all sure if those brain specialists really know what they're up to"—is a transforming event which wrenches the frame of reference onto an entirely different plane. The terms of explanation shift: "insanity" is suddenly substituted for "evil"; the language of morality is replaced by a discourse which is secular and scientific.

This discovery of the cause of Nathan's behavior—or rather, this definition of it—forces us to revise our understanding of the relationship between Sophie and Nathan and its role in Sophie's impending doom. Having been invited by the narrative to construct an indictment of Nathan as brute and torturer, the reader finds this indictment suddenly quashed. It is no longer clear, given this revelation, whether Nathan functions as a moral extension of the camps—or whether the camps, too, represent a manifestation of collective madness (an idea which is hinted at once, in a thought attributed to Nathan). The "fact" of Nathan's madness therefore leaves the reader unhooked from any certain set of terms or interpretive frame and unsure of how to judge what has happened. Schizophrenia, that mysterious and tragic ailment, is an acid capable of dissolving even complex moral judgments—thus denying us the moral judgment of Nathan which we had been permitted to make and robbing us of the precious sense of comprehension that condemnation of Nathan had provided.

The operative definition of evil—the version of it which presents itself as an issue in the text—is domination: evil consists of exalting either self or some abstract value into the supreme or sole value and reducing all else, including others, to instruments. In the autobiographical testament of Commandant Höss, for example, "real evil" appears as a kind of twisted piety, joined with an egotism which directs all natural pity away from one's victims and toward one's self. Simone Weil and Hannah Arendt are quoted on the "true nature of evil," which is allegedly "gloomy, monotonous, and boring." Whether boring or flamboyant, evil appears to consist of one human being's ruthless use of another, with the Nazi concentration camps, with their total and utterly uninhibited domination of human beings, illustrating evil in its ultimate or "absolute" form. This definition allows the narrator to place American slavery, Professor Biegański's treatment of Sophie, and Nathan's behavior as her lover in a moral continuum.

The paradigm of evil demands, as terms of discourse, some axiomatic concept of value (e.g. human life), a perversion of privation of that value, along with the concept of choice. The paradigm of mental illness, on the other hand, implies a determinative chain of causes and effects operating uniformly in a physiological system. In the latter kind of discourse, value and choice can scarcely enter into the operations of "indifferent nature"; thus, any supposed agency responsible for "evil" recedes into the recesses and obscure chemical transactions of Nathan's brain.

By a kind of Faulknerian irony, almost immediately after the revelation of Nathan's insanity, Nathan finally succeeds in seducing Sophie into suicide. Or at least they both die. Like Cash Bundren witnessing his brother Darl trussed up and carted off the Jackson, the reader is forced to confront the tenuousness of the connections between our language and the world which it organizes for us—particularly the arbitrariness of our collective definitions of "sane" and "insane," and of the terms of discourse which they evoke. Denied the explanation of evil, the reader must grope for some alternative interpretive map, for a language past the "sanity and insanity" of human doings but adequate to our "horror and astonishment" at both. Thus, this "epiphany" does not so much enlighten us as bring us up short against the limitations of our perceptual templates and the poverty of our explanations. This encounter with a paradigm-shattering event is especially significant in a narrative which identifies Auschwitz as a kind of ultimate object of knowledge, because it appears to problematize the narrator's meditations on the nature of the "evil" which Auschwitz represents in so ghastly a form.

IV

By these means, the question, what can be known of Auschwitz? is transformed by the novel into a kind of meta-question: what is the *form* of such knowledge? What can be said about Auschwitz as an object of knowledge which is uniquely the province of fiction? And what does conventional discourse about evil tell us about how we make sense and meaning out of experience? These highly abstract issues are set loose by the narrative precisely at the point that the reader is most baffled about the immediate, tangible, and quite unabstract issue of Nathan's role in Sophie's fate.

As we have seen, one part of Styron's strategy of conveying the incredibly ugly reality of Auschwitz as it "really" was is to set before us the excruciating experience of a survivor, realized dramatically through her memories and through the effects of that experience on her subsequent life. Another strategy involves a thorough appropriation of the abstract, scholarly overviews of what happened, to show what Auschwitz means by exploring the sense others have made of it. In the service of that aim, the narrator summons up an impressive array of the scholarship, commentary, and eye-witness accounts of the Holocaust, including Bruno Bettelheim, Elie Wiesel, and George Steiner. The works of Simone Weil and Hannah Arendt are consulted on the nature of totalitarian societies, the banality of evil, and the psychology of mass murderers. The autobiographical statements of Auschwitz Commandant Höss are even quoted at length. The most curious and unexpected source of ideas in the book is probably Wilhelm Reich, whose theories about the relation between sexual and political repression pervade the narrative and provide an intellectual framework linking Sophie's childhood under the sway of her tyrannical Polish Catholic father, her experience at Auschwitz, and her suffering under the domination of her periodically insane lover.

This material is employed in tension-breaking digressions and speculative meditations by the mature narrator as he closes in, slowly and reluctantly, on the sources of Sophie's pain. At one level, this assembled erudition is highly satisfying; it speaks to what we usually mean by understanding. As Philip W. Leon has pointed out, Styron's narratives convey ideas. And it is obvious that the narrative of *Sophie's Choice* presents, in its smallest as well as largest details, a carefully worked out and complex view of the nature and meaning of Auschwitz. *Sophie's Choice* dramatizes not just the historically established verities about Auschwitz, but the threat it poses for the future by incorporating the conclusions of one of the most searching of recent scholarly meditations on the meaning of the Holocaust—Richard Rubenstein's *The Cunning of History: The Holocaust and the American Future*. Both Styron and Rubenstein reject an eschatological reading of the camps and place them in an essentially secular context, as an example of *genocide* rather than as a *holocaust* (in the primary meaning of the word, a burnt offering, and hence, by extension, a pagan sacrifice and therefore an event in an on-going sacred history). To view the camps in terms of human rather than Divine history means that the horrifying events enacted in them touch upon the mystery of human nature rather than upon the mystery of God's will. One of the paradoxes of a theocentric view of the camps is that the calculated destruction of the Jews is, in a sense, a ratification of the Jews' special status as the Chosen People, just as it ratifies the status of the Gentiles as people appropriately left outside the covenant. It is that sense of moral vindication through persecution which presumably renders such a heritage of suffering "precious" (a view explicitly rejected in the novel). Even while acknowledging that the Jews were the chief targets of this instance of "genocidal fury," Styron and Rubenstein see the Holocaust as a general conflagration, the flames of which continue to threaten humankind in general. "Anti-Semitism," Styron has asserted, "is not the sole touchstone" by which to examine the phenomenon of the death camps; rather, in their ultimate depravity, they were "anti-human. Anti-life."

Furthermore, according to Rubenstein, the death camps were neither a unique event—a claim implicit in some theocentric views—nor were they contrary to or a denial of the essential features of the Judeo-Christian tradition. These horrors were, rather, a full flowering and expression of central tendencies in that tradition and civilization: "*we are more likely to understand the Holocaust if we regard it as the expression of some of the most profound tendencies in Western civilization in the twentieth century.*" Auschwitz, in this view, represented not just a place of execution but a "new form of human society," a "society of total domination," and an ultimate form of slavery uninhibited by taboos about the value of human life. Rubenstein extends the observations of Max Weber earlier in the century concerning the tendency of modern Western culture to "rationalize" more and more of its experience, to remove more and more areas of activity from the inhibitions of custom, taboo or religious scruple, while at the same time developing both the techniques and an impersonal, rational, and amoral ethos of bureaucracy. By the Second World War, this "all-conquering rationality" had acquired an enormous momentum in precisely the most "civilized" of the Western nations. If this development has made possible a "society of total domination," Rubenstein argues (again drawing on Weber's insights), this outcome is itself the legacy of Judeo-Christian civilization. The Nazi's program of industrialized slaughter, he concludes, is therefore an extreme, but probably repeatable, expression of that cultural legacy. The camps were thus far more of a "permanent threat to the human future than they would have been had they functioned solely as an exercise in mass killing."

These views find expressions in the narrative of *Sophie's Choice* in ways too obvious to require much illustration: in the choice of Sophie as protagonist, in the narrator's comparisons of the camps with American slavery and with sexism, and through such minor characters as Sophie's friend Wanda and the I. G. Farben executive, Walter Dürrfeld. Through these means, Sophie's experience at Auschwitz dramatizes a generalized threat of dehumanization and destruction which is aimed, potentially at least, at the reader. But this reading of the past also involves the reader as potential perpetrator as well as victim. Such an indictment is implicit in Rubenstein's disturbing assertion that the camps were manifestations of the basic religious traditions of the West, not departures from them. The Nazi ideology of a master race, he suggests, is a caricature of the Biblical concept of the Chosen People and also represents a recurring tendency in Western culture—what he calls that "night side" of the Judeo-Christian religious heritage. "What makes the problem so serious is that there is no escape from [this] . . . ethos of exclusivism and intolerance . . . as long as our fundamental culture is derived from a religious tradition that insists upon the dichotomous division of mankind into the elect and the reprobate." To divide humankind with its infinite shades of gray into sharp categories of black and white is, to Rubenstein, a basic feature of "the illness we call Judeo-Christian civilization." It follows, then, that the forms of perception common in our culture—particularly our assumptions about the nature of good and evil—are critical to understanding the historical and moral significance of genocide and the lethal potential in Western culture to repeat it.

Rubenstein's book, then, profoundly affects the manner of the telling of *Sophie's Choice* as well as its content. While Styron has been attacked in some quarters for emphasizing the humanity of the mass killers, it is, following this de-mythologized and non-demonized view of the Holocaust, precisely in the human qualities of the organizers of genocide that the mystery of Auschwitz lies. Moreover, rather than presenting the "absolute evil" of Auschwitz in rigidly dichotomous terms, the narrative continually presses (to borrow the language of one of the novel's epigraphs, from Malraux) toward "that essential region of the soul where absolute evil confronts brotherhood." It is a feature of the narrative to suggest, paradoxically, by means of the language in which it is constituted, the original, undifferentiated, seamless flow of experience *prior to conceptualization in language*. Similarly, the narrative approaches the subject of Auschwitz through a consideration of the nature of evil, but at the same time subjects that very consideration to an acid bath of irony. One of the points Rubenstein makes about apparent extremes actually residing within and coexisting within a complex whole may offer a clue to Styron's narrative technique: "It is an error to imagine that civilization and savage cruelty are antithesis. On the contrary, in every organic process, the antitheses always reflect a unified totality, and civilization is an organic process." To dramatize the whole, to express the unified totality of any complex situation or concept, the writer must present the extremes, the antitheses—"*Die Schizophrenie*," if you will— which are in fact encompassed within it. Antitheses, apparent incompatibles, are, in a sense, a projection of the observer; they emerge almost as by-products of meaning-endowing acts of interpretation.

It follows, then, that "schizophrenia" is not merely the unsettling diagnosis of Nathan Landau, but a motif implanted in the narrative, like a jarring fragment of discord in a musical composition or a recurring pattern of shadow in a painting. Stingo puzzles over the "centuries-long, all-encompassing nightmare spells of schizophrenia" in the histories of both Poland and the South, where the "abiding presence of race has created at the same instant cruelty and compassion, bigotry and understanding, enmity and fellowship, exploitation and sacrifice, searing hatred and hopeless love." We observe Sophie struggling with a "schizoid conscience" a page later; we learn that Hans Frank, governor-general of occupied Poland and a key figure in the destruction of Poland's Jews, was himself a Jew; we overhear Commandant Höss and Walter Dürrfeld, the I.G. Farben executive in charge of slave labor, discussing the inconsistencies in Nazi policy concerning the use or disposal of undesirables. One ministry desires them for slave labor; another snatches them away for "special action":

> "The result is a split—completely down the middle. A split—
> You know . . . what is the word that I mean? That strange word,
> that psychological expression meaning—"
> "Die Schizophrenie."
> "Yes, that's the word," Höss replied. "That mind doctor in
> Vienna, his name escapes."

Throughout the book, we see a pattern of schizophrenic doubleness and contradiction: Nathan's worst psychotic depressions flow out of exuberant "highs"; his insane accusations of Sophie proceed out of quite sane questions; Sophie's vitality is nearly always juxtaposed against premonitions of her death. Extremes meet, perversely, everywhere in the narrative. In fact, the whole of Nathan and Sophie's relationship exemplifies this kind of split or doubleness, in its simultaneous fusion of devotion and cruelty, healing and rending, *eros* and *thanatos*. Nearly everything in the narrative presents itself in terms of a contradictory or paradoxical doubleness: Sophie, we recall, is both victim and accomplice, Nathan both savior and *golem*; Höss, who as commandant at Auschwitz, retains, even there, some absurd fragments of bureaucratic scruple: "Do you think," he asks Sophie, apparently without irony, "[that] I am some kind of monster?" The blasphemy contained in Sophie's suicide note is a revelation not just of the vehemence with which she has rejected her childhood faith, but evidence of how much of it she has retained.

Even Stingo's vocation as a writer is subjected to this corrosive irony: the disparity between Stingo's ideal of authorship as a high calling and his "ghoulish opportunism" is apparent from the beginning. His early acquaintance with Sophie coincides with his discovery of the subject of his youthful novel, the suicide of Maria Hunt. His developing friendship with Sophie and Nathan stimulates him to pursue a subject that involves a number of parallels with Sophie's situation, including a tangle of "unresolved guilt and hatred" and the tragic death of a beautiful young woman. Sophie, who possesses a "distant but real resemblance to Maria Hunt," provides not only a "lovely simulacrum of the dead girl" but an image of the "despair . . . worn as Maria surely must have worn it, along with the premonitory, grieving shadows of someone hurtling headlong toward death." To Stingo, Maria's death seems "perfectly marvelous, a gift from the sky," while Sophie's pain provides a convenient gloss on Maria's: "*scratch scratch* went the virginal Venus Velvet."

"Consider, Sophie love," Nathan says at another point,

> consider how intimately life and death are intertwined in Nature, which contains everywhere the seeds of our beatitude and our dissolution. This, for instance, HCN, is spread throughout Mother Nature in smothering abundance in the form of glyco-sides, which is to say, combined with sugars. Sweet, sweet sugar. In bitter almonds, in certain species of these autumn leaves, in the common pear, the arbutus. Imagine, then, when those perfect white porcelain teeth of yours bite down upon the delectable macaroon the taste you experience is only a molecule's organic distance removed from that of this [cyanide capsule]. . . .

In this world spun cunningly out of the novelist's language, opposites inter-mingle, surprise lurks in the nature of things, death in the midst of life, like the "choking core of a sweet apple."

One such moment of extreme paradox occurs in the scene of Sophie's choice on the platform at Auschwitz. The scene as presented is a fiction within a fiction, the narrator's extension of what his younger self had heard and been unable to comprehend. Upon Sophie's account, upon the "facts" of the case, the narrator has constructed a wholly conjectural account of the motives and state of mind of the Nazi doctor. The narrator gives the man a name—Dr. Fritz Jemand von Niemand—and endows him with a past and aspirations for the ministry which were frustrated by a domineering father. Serving the Nazis, he "had to replace God with a sense of the omnipo-tence" of the business and the state for which he worked. But the caprice (or schizophrenia) of Nazi policy, which periodically forced him out on the platform to make "selections," or alternately spared him this "duty," had begun to destroy him:

> The renewed horror scraped like steel files at the doctor's soul, threatened to shred his reason. He began to drink, to acquire sloppy eating habits, and to miss God. *Wo, wo ist der lebende Gott?* Where is the God of my fathers?

At some point, the hypothetical Dr. Jemand von Niemand realizes that the absence of a sense of sin about what he is doing is connected with his sense of the absence of God in his life:

No sin! He had suffered boredom and anxiety, and even revulsion, but no sense of sin from the bestial crimes he had been party to, nor had he felt that in sending thousands of the wretched innocent to oblivion he had transgressed against divine law. All had been unutterable monotony. All of his depravity had been enacted in a vacuum of sinless and businesslike godlessness, while his soul thirsted for beatitude.

Was it not supremely simple, then, to restore his belief in God, and at the same time to affirm his human capacity for evil, by committing the most intolerable sin that he was able to conceive? Goodness could come later. But first a great sin.

This *fictional* extension of Sophie's account of what happened to her not only gives the epitome of "absolute evil" a human face, but joins the motif of "*die Schizophrenie*" to the novel's consideration of evil. "I have always assumed," the narrator tells us, "that when he encountered Sophie, Dr. Jemand von Niemand was undergoing the crisis of his life: cracking apart like bamboo, *disintegrating at the very moment that he was reaching out for spiritual salvation*" (emphasis mine). The doctor's atrocity, then, is inextricably bound up with his conception of good, and his act of ultimate evil is presented as born of an impulse toward the good. In its very doubleness, this definition of the encounter on the platform connects "ultimate evil" with the other, smaller acts of evil in the book; it joins it to the familiar without making it less mysterious—or less repugnant. Moreover, it displaces the mystery of evil from Auschwitz to the reader, who could be "anyone from anywhere."

The motif of schizophrenia, then, is a way of dramatizing tendencies in the way we perceive the nature of things. We organize our experience, the novel suggests, in "dichotomous divisions"; we convert the spectrum of actual experience into extremes of black and white; we write our personal histories and we dress our historical experience in the clumsy, ill-fitting garments of morality plays. We slaughter each other in the name of our highest values. In a sense, the values create the slaughter, but without ceasing to be values.

Consequently, the novel's definition of evil, like the young Dr. Jemand von Niemand, disintegrates precisely at the moment it finds absolute expression. Evil appears most elusive, most baffling in nature, in the very language which sets it before us in its most palpable form. Furthermore, the mystery of evil is inextricably linked in the narrative with the even murkier issue of guilt. The novel dramatizes, most notably in Sophie, the pitiless tenacity with which individuals *hold themselves* accountable—even knowing, as Sophie does, that her guilt is a consequence of how she was treated at Auschwitz, not of what she has done: "This guilt is something I cannot get rid of. . . . And because I never get rid of it, maybe that's the worst thing the Germans left me with." Styron quotes Simone Weil's astute observation about the effects of great suffering: "Affliction stamps the soul to its very depth with the scorn, the disgust and even the self-hatred and sense of guilt that crime logically should produce but actually does not."

To the mystery of iniquity and the phenomenon of guilt, often irrationally founded, Styron adds the concept of "collective guilt." Together the three issues—evil, guilt, collective guilt—form links in an endless circular argument that mocks the usual sense we make of things. The concept of collective guilt is succinctly expressed in George Steiner's assertion: "Treblinka *is* both because some men have built it and almost all other men let it be." By this familiar formulation, "almost all the men" share responsibility for the genocidal acts of the Nazis. Sophie overhears a friend of Nathan's express a logical extension of the concept: "It is the German people who should be themselves executed—they who allowed these men to rule them and kill Jews." The Poles, in his view, are hardly less guilty—a charge that the daughter of Professor Bieganski feels incapable of refuting. Nathan shares the extreme view of collective guilt and, in moments of paranoia, holds Sophie responsible for the crimes of the Holocaust. Unfortunately for Sophie, Nathan's raging accusations objectify her own unrelenting inner voice, which torments her beyond the capacities of her most sadistic oppressors—thus making her again, though in a sense that defies analysis, an "accomplice" of the Nazis. However, perhaps to prevent us from absolving her completely from guilt, we learn in the account of Sophie's past not only of the anti-Semitic cultural environment in which she was raised but of her own insensitivity to Jews and to the climate of growing hostility toward them: "They simply did not concern her." While she does not share her father's extreme views, her indifference *could* be construed, following Steiner's formulation, as consent. The problem with such an argument is that it engages in a crude group stereotyping which is little different from the anti-Semitism of the Nazis.

Nathan also periodically charges Stingo, as a white Southerner, with complicity in the racial oppression in the South, holding him responsible for the grotesque death of Bobby Weed and the political career of Mississippi's Governor Bilbo. In spite of the ludicrousness of the specific charges, the comparisons drawn between the two environments of racial hostility, Poland and America, are uncomfortably apt. If we are to believe Stingo (who is being supported in Brooklyn on the proceeds of the sale of a family slave named Artiste), history—or mere distance in time—effectively absolves one of complicity in evil. If we are to believe Sophie, however, one is absolved by nothing.

What saving knowledge, then, can be wrested from experience in such a world? The Stingo who emerges from his grave of sand on the beach that morning after the funeral of Nathan and Sophie is chastened and subdued at the same time he is cleansed and exalted. By some strange compensatory economy in the nature of things, his loss is a gain, somehow energizing his career as a writer. If the deaths of Sophie and Nathan and his own symbolic death constitute Stingo's rite of passage, the cost would seem incommensurate with any imaginable gain. But by a logic now familiar in the novel, the triumph of life would necessarily be intimately conjoined to death, as joy is to pain. Such success is doubly ironic in that one of the chief pieces of knowledge that Stingo has acquired is an awareness of evil in himself—including his monumental self-centeredness and his capacity to use others as instruments. Ultimately, then, rather than providing a definition of the most spectacular historical manifestation of evil, the narrative demonstrates what Styron has called the "ecumenical nature" of evil and its omnipresence in human experience. In effect, rather than resolving the mystery of the evil which Auschwitz represents, the narrative displaces the mystery from its form as monstrous other to the familiar and near, and from external world to self.

In spite of the book's implicit claims advanced early in the narrative, *Sophie's Choice* has not, by the ending, truly "dealt" with Auschwitz. On the other hand, by not dealing with it (in the sense of resolving or putting to rest the issues it presents), the narrative has forced the reader to encounter Auschwitz imaginatively on many levels—even to consider in a self-reflective way the manner by which we conceptualize Auschwitz. Stingo's encounter— and the mature narrator's re-encounter—with the seamlessness of experience, with the nature of things beyond our language for it, paradoxically affirms the need for speech, for coherence and meaning, and therefore for art, at the same time that it demarks their limitations and acknowledges their frailty. The subtle changes dramatized in the mature narrator represent a recognition of those limits. Early in the book, the authorial voice had ventured to assert: "I have thought that it might be possible to make a stab at understanding Auschwitz by trying to understand Sophie." The humbler speaker at the end of the book has abandoned such ambitions: "*Someday I will understand Auschwitz.* That was a brave statement but innocently absurd. No one will ever understand Auschwitz. What I might have said with more accuracy would have been: *Someday I will write about Sophie's life and death, and thereby demonstrate how absolute evil is never extinguished from the world.* Auschwitz itself remains inexplicable."

LARS OLE SAUERBERG

Fact-Flirting Fiction: Historiographical Potential or Involuntary Parody?

In his biography of Charles Dickens from 1990, Peter Ackroyd startles the reader by confronting him with a number of interludes in which he introduces an element of fantasy not expected in what is on the whole signalled as another hefty volume of carefully documented and objectively delivered discourse on the life and circumstances of the Victorian novelist and literary entrepreneur. Categorically, the five interludes belong to fiction, both regarding conventional markers—dialogue, etc.—and their obvious incongruity with documentable authenticity, such as the meeting between Little Dorrit and Dickens (between chapters four and five) or the conversation between Chatterton, Wilde, Eliot (T.S.), and Dickens (between chapters fourteen and fifteen). That Ackroyd trespasses upon the ground of the fictional in his otherwise non-fictional life of Dickens is somewhat cautiously and indeterminately presented as a positive trait in the flap-cum-hype text on what to expect from the content:

> Peter Ackroyd is a celebrated novelist and biographer who brings to Dickens his proficiency in both disciplines. Based upon an extensive examination of original sources, and animated throughout by the historical imagination he displayed in *Hawksmoor* and *Chatterton*, Ackroyd's latest work is one in which

From *European Journal of English Studies* 3 no. 2. © 1999 by Swets & Zeitlinger.

the true figure of Charles Dickens and the moving spirit of his
age are for the first time faithfully combined.

One notes the eagerness to assure the reader that this 'celebrated novelist
and biographer' actually based his work on original-source research, only
then to go on to praise the catalytic function of the 'historical imagination';
all in aid of the faithful combination of the 'true figure of Charles Dickens'
and the 'moving spirit of his age'. How exactly such notions as 'true figure'
and 'moving spirit' correlate with the empirical data available to the biographer is left out of account. However, one senses the urge to catch 'everything
that got away, that fled with the last deathbed exhalation of the biographee'.

   Peter Ackroyd's life of Dickens life is exceptional in its integration of
the fictional into the non-fictional. But the exceptional is in the technique
rather than in the aim. The gap between the available empirical data and the
actual presence of a person is unbridgeable, since texts and other kinds of
documentation will never let us have the impression of the whole of that
person. It is nonetheless the ambition of all biographers to re-create as much
of the whole person as possible, and in that perspective the fictional short-
circuiting attempted by Ackroyd is understandable and, under the circumstances, quite legitimate.

   If Ackroyd makes intermittent use of the fictional in an attempt to get
closer to what it was really like in a narrative context otherwise respecting the
conventions of the history, the attempt to make history come alive is the
motive force behind the efforts of most historical novelists. In contrast to
biographers, to whom historical truth is synonymous with historical facts,
historical novelists subject historical facts to the generation of the kind of
truth which novelists aspire to and which is perhaps best, if somewhat curso-
rily, described as that which is recognizable as the generally human. The
further biographers stray from the specific circumstances of their subject—
in Aristotle's words, the possible—to make the specific cohere with what we
as readers would like to have been the case—the probable—the more they
enter the domain of the fictional, and we as readers judge the narratives
accordingly: not in relation to factual truth, but according to the truth of
likelihood. The reconstructions of the past offered by a Sir Walter Scott, a
Robert Graves, or an Allan Massie are generally true to historical detail as
they are to major historical events, but between these two margins of the
historically given, they exercise their inventive freedom and create characters
and occurrences following the dynamic of the invented narrative rather than
the dynamic of the narrative given by history.

   It might be said that history as a text enjoying special status in relation
to the reality of which it is assumed to be the verbal reflection is the last

bastion of a battle already lost. It is well known to literary historians and critics that the novel in its stages of formation and consolidation was invariably constructed so as to dupe its readers into believing that it offered history rather than story. Only in recent times has this convention been given up in favour of another which suggests precisely the opposite: that the novel is indeed an imagined narrative, a construction of texts forming and re-forming in carnivalesque fashion from a never exhaustible stock of available narratives. Peter Ackroyd's treatment of Dickens could be seen as a—strikingly unconventional—concession to this principle, from the quarter of the non-fictional. However, the principle has been much more contagious among novelists than among historians. The reason is not hard to find. Whereas the historian traditionally considers himself a scholar working within a well-defined area and on the rock bottom of empirical data, combining them in systematic ways that will sustain colleagues' re-examination, the novelist is the scavenger always on the lookout for bits and pieces which he can accommodate according to his 'inner' needs in the imagined universe under construction. The more the historian attempts to argue in favour of an idea, the more he will resemble the novelist, for whom the idea is indeed that which regulates his universe and which in consequence functions as the sorting mechanism for his materials. The meeting ground of the historian and the—realistic—novelist is the small and the large of the world of fact. But for the historian there is no opportunity for free play in a space between them, because the factualities of the small and the large will meet in the middle. The novelist, including the historical novelist, will insist on his right to make use of, perhaps even widen out, this free-play space between the factualities of kitchen utensils and kings. Entering into this free-play space means abandoning the domain of the factual as the point of resort and instead handing over to the inner necessity of the fictional universe. Once this domain is entered, any kind of reference to facts or even passages of historical texts lose their claim to the world 'outside' the text, because they are now part of a new textual whole, which has its own phenomenological kind of relationship with factual reality.

Of course, reference to facts in the space of free play only in principle loses its claim to referential meaning. It retains some of it, because the reader will be aware of the double nature of such references as simultaneously relating to the imaginative construct of the fictional work and to the factuality beyond it. In most cases the references to facts in a space of free play appear as being in accord with the factual world, or at least not in any gross opposition to it. Many such references will be unmarked, in the linguistic sense of the word. But there are cases in the fictional universe of the free-play space in novels where such references are deliberately marked so as to stand out conspicuously, challenging the reader's urge to accept them as part of the imaginative construct. Sometimes this challenge results in a degree of parody never intended by the novelist. In the following I shall consider some concrete examples for the purpose of discussing the reference to facts in a free-play space as something that may involuntarily result in parody. A comparative analysis of three novels—Thomas Keneally's *Schindler's Ark*, William Styron's *Sophie's Choice* and D. M. Thomas's *The White Hotel*, which all feature the atrocious events of the Holocaust—will serve to demonstrate the delicate balance between the novelist's attempt at establishing a sense of existential urgency and the inherent risk of undermining it in a reader-phenomenological perspective.

In the first chapter of his *Slaughterhouse-Five*, Kurt Vonnegut insists on the impossibility of writing a regular novel about an outrage like the saturation bombing of Dresden, which he experienced as a prisoner of war. The bombing and the subsequent cleaning up he tried to form into a novel, but found himself stopped by the paradoxical tendency of novels to celebrate what they try to deplore. The only way to respond to a unique event like that is to write a unique novel, an anti-novel: 'It is so short and jumbled and jangled . . . because there is nothing intelligent to say about a massacre.' Thomas Keneally's solution, in a similar situation, was to choose the comparatively neat narrative format of the traditional, realistic novel. Now there is, of course, a difference in the focus of Vonnegut and Keneally insofar as *Slaughterhouse-Five* attempts to present the madness of war in general by drawing metaphorically on the collective death of 130,000 people in a German city towards the end of World War Two, whereas *Schindler's Ark* is about an individual caught up in the inferno of the Nazi slave-labour system. But the two writers share the need to make the insanity of the situation immediately felt by the reader. Vonnegut's 'irrational' narrative is meant to discourage any easy familiarization with irrational events. Keneally's approach, the combination of documentary and novel, allows him to integrate references to fact, since this is in the traditional nature of the novel, but at the risk of upgrading the entertainment function by his chosen format. By adopting the novelistic format he hopes, however, to be better able to draw a correct picture of the historical person Herr Schindler, since 'the novel's techniques seem suited for a character of such ambiguity and magnitude as Oskar'. Keneally does not specify what he means by 'the novel's techniques', but his ambition is quite clearly to be able to re-create the person of Herr Schindler as the rounded and often contradictory kind of character we know from realistic fiction. The ambiguity of his 'hero' would probably be the most characteristic feature in a wholly documentary mosaic of Herr Schindler based on extant written and photographic material. The novelist has the liberty, which the historian has not (but nonetheless often resorts to), of connecting the elements which make for this ambiguity when he subordinates possibility to plausibility.

Keneally sets out to tell a 'true story' in the shape of a novel devoid of all fiction, 'since fiction would debase the record', and he declares his intention to 'distinguish between reality and the myths which are likely to attach themselves to a man of Oskar's stature'. The novelist allows himself to 'make reasonable constructs of conversations of which Oskar and others have left only the briefest record'. But, he claims, 'most exchanges and conversations, and all events, are based on the detailed recollections of the *Schindlerjuden* (Schindler's Jews), of Schindler himself, and of other witnesses to Oskar's acts of outrageous rescue'. These remarks obviously aim to reassure the reader of the historical authenticity of the narrative, which, in traditional generic terms, may be said to straddle the historical novel and the social novel.

The reader will readily appreciate the 'novel's techniques' in *Schindler's Ark*. The *in medias res* opening of the prologue ensures that the reader is hooked at once in the way familiar from countless other novels, not least from highly dramatic ones like thrillers. We accompany Herr Schindler on his way to a dinner party in the forced-labour camp at Plaszow outside the Polish city of Cracow, at the invitation of SS *Hauptsturmführer* Amon Goeth some time in the autumn of 1943. Here we witness the contrast between the life led by the members of the *Herrenvolk* and the wretched plight of the prisoners working for the commandant. But we also immediately get a glimpse of Herr Schindler in his role as saviour, as he clandestinely promises to transfer a girl and her younger sister to his factory, at which he uses camp-labour, but at which there is safety in comparison with the camp proper. The authorial voice, which is throughout of the intrusive kind, justifies his choice of this particular opening by suggesting that an immediate offering of an example of Herr Schindler's 'strange virtue' may be the best approach to a tale about goodness, a notoriously difficult theme to handle in stories. This device of the *in medias res* opening will likewise be well known to readers of fiction.

After this prologue, we are taken back in time to learn about Herr Schindler from his birth in 1908 onwards. The chronology of the protagonist's life becomes the story as well as the plot in Forster's sense of the terms. The suspense effect relies on the reader's curiosity to know the *how* rather than the *what*, as of course there can be no surprise hidden in the outcome, a circumstance which the author acknowledges both by his explicitness in the prologue and his frequent anticipations of future action during the narration. The suspense effect is heightened, as, in the latter half of the narrative (from p. 269 which mentions April 28, 1944), the author becomes increasingly lavish with date references: obviously the race against the inevitability of historical facts spurs the writer's and hence the reader's absorption.

The epilogue has a double function as narrative device. Structurally, together with the prologue it suggests some kind of framework creating an aesthetic distance, and in terms of plot it tells the story, as in the familiar Victorian-novel closure, of what happened to the main characters after the primary action; a conventional means of ensuring the plausibility of the fiction.

Perhaps it is the point of view where the narrative is most typically felt to be the traditional realistic narrative which it was Keneally's intention to write—or, rather, the combination of authorial omniscience with plot progress, because the two are aspects of each other. One explanation of Keneally's frequent anticipations of future action and events, and surely the explanation most in accordance with the intentions expressed in the prologue, is the factual nature of the material: as this is history, the outcome is already known (example: 'Later in the year they would send poor Szepessi to Auschwitz for being so persuadable'); as a recurrent stylistic element the modal expression 'it would' implies the inevitable). But at the same time this device is one of the traditional signals of realistic novels. Rather than seeing history unfolding, the reader may feel that, as when reading a novel by Thomas Hardy or George Eliot, he is witnessing the master narrator presenting and *controlling* his tale.

Although Keneally set out to write a novel, not a history, and so felt justified in leaving out any references to documentation beyond his 'word of honour' in his *Author's Note* that the factual foundation is sound enough, there are traces throughout of an obligation to remind the reader of the factual basis of his tale. Attention has already been drawn to the foreshadowing technique in the plot, which, however, is of an ambiguous nature, since in combination with the authorial omniscience it is easily 'mistaken' for a signal of fiction. But there are other, and much more obvious, instances of the will to document—or to point to the lack of sources to document what is told in—this 'fictionless' novel. The closest the novelist comes to regular source-citation is in the references to a letter from the central SS administration in Berlin to commandants of the concentration camps, a short-hand transcript of Schindler's speech to his workers at the liberation, the transcripts of Schindler's testimonies before the German Federal Justice Department, a German TV documentary about Schindler from 1973, and a copy of Schindler's list. These are all instances of verifiable information, with the implication that if the reader has the curiosity and energy, he can go and look for himself, just as he may visit Schindler's widow in Argentina. But there are many more instances of untraceable references, such as: 'Those who knew

Oskar in those years speak of . . .', 'From the little that Oskar would say of
his childhood, there was no darkness there', 'Whatever his motives for
running with Henlein, it seems that as the divisions entered Moravia . . .'.
Sometimes the novelist/historian weighs different kinds of evidence against
each other, as in this passage: 'His leaking of the news to Stern, far more than
the unconfirmed Nussbaum story, goes some way toward proving his case.'
But it is not only in such more or less circumscribed references to verifiable
history that we see the quasi-historian at work. Sometimes the style chosen
reveals the professional historian's distance growing out of his duty to
present facts only, as in the paragraph closing chapter twenty-one:

> More than 4,000 people were discovered overnight and executed
> in the streets. In the next two days their bodies were taken to
> Plaszow on open-platform trucks and buried in two mass graves
> in the woods beyond the new camp.

Stylistically, this is the opposite of the loaded expressions mentioned above.

Among the documentary material consulted by Keneally are
photographs. Some of them show Schindler with German officers, but
there is also a collection in itself of remarkable interest, since they were
taken surreptitiously by an Austrian official supervising a factory in
Plaszow. The history of these photographs is told at some length in a story
within the story. The reader guesses from the acknowledgements page that
they may be found either at Yad Vashem or are in the possession of a Mr.
Leopold Page. It must be these pictures that the lay-out people at Penguin
Books, USA, used in the American edition as the background against which
several chapter numbers appear. They are reproduced in such a way,
however, that they present dimmed images, from which the reader can only
perceive an outline. If the photos had been reproduced and inserted in the
usual way, either here and there in the text, or gathered together somewhere in the book, the pull towards the historical text would perhaps have
been too strong. As they are placed now, they have a force, however, which
is ornamental rather than documentary.

On the whole, the frequent—undocumented—reminders of the
reality behind the narrative ought not to impair the status of *Schindler's Ark*
as a novel. After all, such assurances are part and parcel of traditional
realism, with the aim of furthering plausibility. The reader is not meant to
stop and check, but to endorse in principle the insistence on the possibility
of links with verifiable facts. The problem with a narrative like Keneally's,
however, is its contradictory nature: insisting explicitly (*Author's Note*) and
implicitly (in its novelistic characteristics, including the assumption of a

factual foundation) on an ontological status usually associated with fictional kinds of narrative, it will create a certain distance from its subject-matter by its self-contained universe, in which internal consistency conventionally has priority over external relations. The author betrays an intermittent aware-ness of this problem, not, as observed above, in his insistence on faithfulness in representation, but in his meta-commentary. (Meta-commentary should not be mistaken for the omniscient and intrusive author persona's interfer-ence with the story. This is an integral part of the narrative itself. Meta-commentary is the *author's* display of opinions of and attitudes to the text as a whole, including the author persona.) An instance of this type of comment occurs at an early point in the narrative, where an attempt is made to describe Schindler's youth. There would have been a certain fictional consistency if the German industrialist's rescue work during the late phase of the war could be traced back to a traumatic experience at an early time in his life:

> Oskar's later history seems to call out for some set piece in his childhood. The young Oskar should defend some bullied Jewish boy on the way home from school. It is a safe bet it didn't happen, and we are happier not knowing, since the event would seem too pat.

The repeated and declared efforts to distinguish between reality and myth/story/legend have a similar effect, and another instance is the cross-novel reference to William Styron's *Sophie's Choice* in order to expose quite briefly the difference between the Auschwitz commandant Rudolf Höss as experienced on the one hand by the Schindler women arriving at the extermination camp ('reality') and, on the other, as portrayed in Styron's novel ('fiction'). The meta-commentary pulls in a direction different from both unintended fiction and intended documentary, in that it draws atten-tion to considerations about conventional plot lines, to deliberations about narrative concepts and terminology, and to an awareness of 'competition' in the world of fiction.

As in Thomas's *The White Hotel*, it is the inadequacy and irrelevance of fiction in the face of the 'fictitious presentation' of the Nazi genocide and their invention of the experience of *l'univers concentrationnaire* that prompts the use of documentary material. The Sophie plot of *Sophie's Choice* would have been the proper stuff of melodrama if not acted out in the context of the perverse logic of Nazi ideology and camp ethos. In a universe devoid of traditional ethical distinctions the choice with which Sophie is presented by the drunken—and symbolically named—Dr. Fritz Jemand von Niemand on the ramp is, in the narrator's interpretation, a desperate act of a man daring

God to show himself by pushing to still further extremes an already all too extreme situation. This interpretation is emblematic of the difficulties faced by those who, for the umpteenth time, try to describe the realities of the Nazi regime without falling into the trap of merely rehashing the already familiar: '. . . the jaded reader surfeited with our century's perdurable feast of atrocities will be spared here a detailed chronicle . . .'. Referring to the detailed testimony offered by a range of Holocaust survivors, the narrator announces his choice of the particularized, without, however, making it clear that the particularization is not only a new attempt at defamiliarization but also, of course, an inevitable function of the fictional. Like all realistic fiction, Styron's novel consolidates its own fictionality through insistence on its factuality, but as the device of documentary realism is to carry to extremes such insistence, it is a question of very delicate balance whether the reader will feel that the particularization of individual experience against an emphatically verifiable background enhances the totalization which is the primary claim of fiction, or whether the foregrounded factuality of the Holocaust horror forbids a fictional treatment. The narrator is aware that there is a problem of 'writerly ethics' involved, but does not distinguish between its two aspects: on the one hand there is the problem about the 'right' of outsiders to write about the Holocaust, and on the other the admissibility of introducing fictional elements into the world of historical fact. There would have been less of a problem if the subject-matter had been something other than the Holocaust and related phenomena. In realistic novels set in an everyday context, the fictional elements are inconspicuously placed alongside factual elements. But in the case of unique events, there is often a transformation in the status of the fictional from the merely fictitious into the frivolous. In other words, the problem of mimesis ceases to be an aesthetic one, becoming instead a complex aesthetic-and-ethical one. The narrator invites the solution of the second problem by the conventional measure of postulating the 'fact' of Sophie's existence—technically by not drawing any attention to her fictitious existence—and thus merges fact and fiction on traditionally fictional premises. The mechanism of the merging appears clearly from one of the concluding passages, in which the senior narrator is reviewing his diary notes from the time when he was with Sophie and Nathan:

> *Someday I will understand Auschwitz.* This was a brave statement but innocently absurd. No one will ever understand Auschwitz. What I might have set down with more accuracy would have been: *Someday I will write about Sophie's life and death, and thereby help demonstrate how absolute evil is never extinguished from the*

> *world*. Auschwitz itself remains inexplicable. . . . I did not weep
> for the six million Jews or the two million Poles or the one
> million Serbs or the five million Russians—I was unprepared to
> weep for all humanity—but I did weep for these others who in
> one way or another had become dear to me.

The first problem concerning the 'right' to write as an outsider about the
subject-matter in hand branches out into two. The one is the general
problem of imaginative scope. Certainly this is a kind of problem which can
only be dealt with pragmatically by pointing to the circumstance that some
authors have stuck consistently to autobiographical sources, while others
invent their narratives quite freely. The other is the specific problem of using
Holocaust material at a second remove. It is interesting to note that,
although he discusses the opposition to the 'novelization' of the Holocaust
voiced by Elie Wiesel and George Steiner, and although he confesses to
having been haunted by an 'element of presumption in the sense of being an
intruder upon the terrain of an experience so bestial', the narrator never
proposes a firm distinction between fictitious Sophie and factual Holocaust.
In principle we have to do with an approach parallel to the one adopted by
Keneally in *Schindler's Ark*. Keneally chose to present his factual figure as a
fictional character, because that would give him a larger scope to underscore
the man as a composite being. Sophie contributes exactly the same quality to
Styron's narrative, because, as 'a cluster of contradictions', she epitomizes the
evil of a place and a regimen like Auschwitz. Partly sufferer, partly (involuntary) collaborator, she contributes to our acceptance of evil's first premise:
that, despite our preference for seeing it as something absolute, it is a highly
complex phenomenon. The use of Sophie's self-contradictory character as
simultaneously a key to and a symbol of the nature of evil is to suggest an
avenue towards understanding.

   The senior narrator intrudes into the narrative to justify the recourse to
quotation from and paraphrase of his main source, the memoirs of Rudolf
Höss, the commandant of Auschwitz 1940–43, as well as texts by Simone
Weil, George Steiner, and Richard L. Rubenstein. The need for the documentary is explained in detail at the point where the Höss–Sophie plot starts,
when Sophie sees a picture in the American magazine *Look* of Höss just about
to be executed. The narrator—logically the senior one, since Höss's memoirs
referred to were not available in English until 1959—insists on the importance
of Höss's writings as offering the truest possible insight into the nature of evil:

> Certainly it should be read throughout the world by . . . anyone
> concerned remotely with affecting the consciousness of his

fellowman—and this would include our own beloved children, those incipient American leaders at the eighth-grade level, who should be required to study it along with *The Catcher in the Rye*, *The Hobbit* and the Constitution. For within these confessions it will be discovered that we really have no acquaintance with true evil; the evil portrayed in most novels and plays and movies is mediocre if not spurious, a shoddy concoction generally made up of violence, fantasy, neurotic terror and melodrama.

Before venturing into a brief account of Höss's life, the narrator quotes Simone Weil on the difference between the common but wrong conception of evil and the real kind represented par excellence by the Nazi world-view and behaviour: 'This "imaginary evil . . . is romantic and varied, while real evil is gloomy, monotonous, barren, boring."' Styron's use of documentary material, primarily from Höss's biography, bears out Weil's assertion. There is a stark contrast between Sophie's suffering, gradually unveiled until the culmination which gives the book its title, and the domestic idyll of the camp commandant's household in the midst of Auschwitz. The idyll would have been unbelievable if presented as a product of the imagination. The insistence on the documentary source to form the basis on which the novelist may construct his fiction of Sophie forces the reader to accept the reality of the contradiction-filled life in the concentration camp, at the same time as the novelist signals his creative impotence; a technique which in itself foregrounds the enormity of the situation.

The three intertwined plots of *Sophie's Choice*—the events leading up to Sophie's choice, the Sophie-Nathan relationship, and the narrator's own sexual comedy—are all hinged on the historical fact of Nazi infliction of mass suffering, and together they form the dramatic enactment of the perhaps most important single thematic issue in the novel: the contrast between American innocence (symbolized by Nathan and the narrator Stingo) and European experience (symbolized by Sophie and Höss). The word 'guilt' appears time and time again in the narrator's preoccupation with the contrast between the events in Europe and his own relatively comfortable life in a United States hardly affected by the war. It is possible to read the twists and turns in Stingo's unfulfilled erotic career as a symbolic underscoring of not only the individual but also the national immaturity which meets the experience of those directly involved in the war, for whom the concept of evil as something absolute is meaningless. Höss's incapacity as a bureaucrat to make ethical distinctions, as he himself sees it, and Sophie's singleminded urge to survive in a man-made hell and to constantly repress her painful memories are pragmatic lessons in the dynamics of evil. Stingo's—and the reader's—

lack of comprehension can be traced back to the frustrated expectations of conventional evil and the lack of heroic action to curb it. Those, like Sophie, who have experience of evil, can, according to Styron, testify to the gloominess, monotony, barrenness, and boredom of which it is constituted.

There were several reasons why D. M. Thomas's novel *The White Hotel* created a stir on its publication in 1981. Some readers were disgusted by what they saw as deliberate pornographic speculation, others were puzzled by the exacting multi-tiered structure of the narrative. But the academic discussion centered first and foremost on the use that Thomas had made of Sigmund Freud and of an eye-witness report of the German massacre of Russian Jews at Babi Yar.

All the passages attributed to Freud and his correspondents were made up by Thomas in a style identical with source documents, whereas the eye-witness report was changed only very little to fit into the narrative rhythm of the context. Thomas's critics could tolerate his handling of Freud, putting it down as pastiche, which is a conventional and therefore acceptable literary device. With the Babi Yar account, however, it was different. Although Thomas had duly acknowledged his loan on the copyright page, he found himself accused of plagiarism. Putting aside legal considerations, we have a narrative signalling itself and being signalled by its publisher as a work of fiction, a novel. In his free-play space Thomas made use of extensive reference to facts: in the case of Freud, fake references; in the case of the eye-witness report, a reference for which there exists a source document, the account of Dina Pronicheva as related to a gatherer and publisher of such accounts. To the reader not able immediately to spot the fake nature of the Freud passages, they will have exactly the same impact and function as the eye-witness report. Both elements will be absorbed, with readerly awareness split between an appreciation of them for their function in the totality of Thomas's fictional work and as elements inviting attention to their own contextual factuality.

As in the case of the well-known narrative technique of embedding a fictional narrative in some kind of frame, intended to enhance the authenticity of the embedded 'document', the inclusion of fact-reference elements in a clearly signalled fictional narrative gives the illusion of upgrading the general verisimilitude of the fictional. Given the implicit Platonic premise that the value of a text depends on its degree of authenticity, a fictional text supposedly stands to gain with every inch it can approximate to 'reality'. In the case of Thomas's narrative with regard to its inclusion—almost verbatim—of the eye-witness report, there is indeed a difference if the reader approaches the text with an awareness of the documentary nature of the report: that is, bearing in mind the information given on the acknowledgements page, or if he simply plunges into the text with expectations of just another novel with a lot of fictional content in the free-play space. Thomas could have chosen to foreground the authentic quality of the report by applying some kind of transitional device foregrounding the shift in validity. It was his decision to provide instead a seamless transition that provoked a reaction on the part of some critics, to the effect that Thomas had tried to get away with plagiarism, all the more disgusting considering the kind of experience. Thomas could get away with his Freud pastiche, since the general erotic import of his narrative is fully commensurable with the psychoanalyst's teachings. However, to lodge the enormity of the Babi Yar massacre in this erotic dynamic was felt to be just short of sacrilege.

We have Thomas's own assurance that he felt a need to refrain from imaginative flights in the face of events more gruesome than the imagination could possibly devise. So the only way out was to incorporate 'reality itself' in the form of the eye-witness report, duly acknowledged on the credits page, but disguised in the text with no markers to signal where fiction ceases and fact takes over. Considering Thomas to be in good faith about the reason for his extended quotation, his was indeed an honourable act: to stand back modestly and let history speak. Thomas's solution would have been applauded by Plato, and is probably also applauded by the intended model reader attentive to all the information offered in the book, including the small print on the prenarrative copyright page. But to many readers, and some articulate critics, the alleged incommensurability between the narrative's erotic drive and the subjection of the events and characters in the novel to a libido principle overruling all Thanatos urges, opens up space for a reading which places the authorial voice at odds with the author's in a position whence its effect is not in the service of enhanced verisimilitude, but of—unintended—parody.

There is no doubt that novelists who choose to upgrade the reality content of the traditionally quite fictitious free-play space of their narratives walk a tightrope. Their balance is kept if their embedded historical texts or references to real events sustain the import of the narrative universe. But the balance is lost when the reader begins to entertain a feeling that there is a discrepancy between what the novelist has set out to do and the nature of his chosen factual references. When the novelist fails to maintain his balance, the result is often an unintended self-parodic effect. Despite Styron's penchant for the sentimental, his *Sophie's Choice* seems on the whole to manage the tightrope walk. The universe in that novel has a nightmarish atmosphere in the gradual revelation of the unspeakable events of the Holocaust to the innocent narrator. To have revealed Hell as a matter of trivia and arbitrariness is underlined by the incorporation of factual references to that effect. In comparison with Styron, both Keneally and Thomas run the risk of having their narratives received as unintended parodies. Keneally does not employ historical texts in his Schindler narrative but adopts the novelist's stance, while assuring the reader that his story was thoroughly researched. There is in the traditional, realistic novel a tendency, which is a function of the limited cast required to carry through a minimum action of conflict, to elevate the protagonist, and, in consequence, to make him or her into an interesting figure. Even in the case of a decidedly anti-heroic figure, the reader is lured into a relationship by which he engages in a 'contract' with the protagonist and which may range from repulsion via suspicious attraction to undivided sympathy. But it is beyond debate that the protagonist is always the star; sympathetic or repulsive, the protagonist always commands our attention, in a system of degrees of fascination. It is precisely this stardom, inherent in the protagonist's role, that in the case of *Schindler's Ark* threatens to make Herr Schindler into a hero figure, in the light of which the text may easily be experienced as a romance kind of narrative with melodramatic overtones. I do not wish to suggest that Keneally deliberately betrays his material, nor that he is insincere in stating his intentions in the preface, but merely that this potential exists by virtue of the very selection of the novel format. Romance with melodramatic overtones can be a highly effective mixture, as the canon of adventure stories and thrillers testifies, but *Schindler's Ark* invites the question whether the author's intention of presenting the 'pragmatic triumph of good over evil' in the ethical anarchy of the Holocaust is indeed best served by his particular brand of documentary realism.

In the case of *The White Hotel*, readers can hardly be blamed for responding negatively to Thomas's subordination of Dina Pronicheva's eye-witness testimony to his celebration of the libido. Although this, as we have seen, was not at all Thomas's intention, the text does not allow for a reading which sees a mocking of enormous suffering for the somewhat unfocused purpose of celebrating the life urge in terms which many readers would judge as improper under the circumstances. In consequence, Thomas's use of his historical passage invites a change of status into involuntary and rather macabre and tasteless parody.

When novelists choose to incorporate bits and pieces from reality into the space which traditionally allows for the free play of the imagination, they run the risk of no longer being in full control of their material. It may be that what they have imported with a view to strengthening their imaginative efforts turns against them in mocking parody, of which they themselves are the very targets. To determine whether this is so in the individual case is a matter of holding up the text to the mirror of its own fictional universe and the cultural background of its readers, to find out if there is a satisfactory degree of commensurability among all the elements in the narrative. In this perspective, the intentions of the well-meaning novelist seem singularly irrelevant.

RHODA SIRLIN

Sophie's Choice: *An American Voyage into the Mystery of Iniquity*

Styron, a Southerner by birth, was naturally influenced by the Southern literary tradition, particularly by the novels of Faulkner, Robert Penn Warren, and Thomas Wolfe; indeed, his first novel, *Lie Down in Darkness*, published in 1951, is heavily indebted to the themes and styles of Faulkner and Warren. Some critics hailed Styron in the early 1950s as the heir apparent to Faulkner's throne. These same critics, however, were disappointed by Styron's subsequent fiction because it was not "Southern enough," arguing that Styron had abandoned his true calling, his Southern roots. When asked if he considers himself part of a tradition of Southern writing, Styron responds that he does not feel committed to the Southern tradition largely because the South has changed. Styron has been living in the North for over three decades, and while he acknowledges an attachment to and knowledge of the South, his non-Southern literary influences are formidable, including, among others, Shakespeare, Marlowe, Flaubert, Conrad, Joyce, Dostoevsky, Tolstoy, Melville, Fitzgerald, Camus, Malraux, Gide, Bellow, and Roth.

Despite this, some critics persist in pigeonholing Styron, particularly irksome because he is one of our least parochial novelists. Samuel Coale, author of several articles on Styron, calls *Sophie's Choice* a piece of "Southern Gothic fiction," in which the guilt is so overwhelming that attempts to transform it appear ludicrous and evasive. Coale concludes that feeling guilt is all

From *William Styron's* Sophie's Choice: *Crime and Self-Punishment.* © 1990 by Rhoda Sirlin.

there is in Styron's novel. To make matters worse, Coale insinuates that Styron is cowardly because his protagonists (here he is thinking of Nat Turner and Stingo) escape this nightmare vision all too easily, escape unscathed because the Gothic romance tradition does not embrace absolute evil, demanding the waking from the nightmare, a return to normality; Coale, therefore, sees Stingo's resurrection at the end of the novel as forced, a cowardly evasion. Styron, he told this writer, "avoids the contraries"; he insists that Styron is a "provisional rebel in Christian masquerade." Pauline Kael, the film critic for *The New Yorker*, calls *Sophie's Choice* Styron's "Holocaust Gothic." She further asserts that the novel is all come-on, a striptease, sweetened along the way with "Gothic goodies like the Pink Palace." The novel, for her, is garish and titillating, playing the readers for suckers.

What is important about these two assessments is not only that they are inaccurate, but that they obscure the meaning and importance of the novel, first by placing it in the wrong genre—Southern Gothic—and second by condemning the limitations of that genre. Styron's Pink Palace is light-years away from Faulkner's decaying mansions, from Gothic romance. To understand the symbolic structure and meaning of the novel we would be better served if we turned our attention away from the Southern literary tradition, as Styron urges us to do, to more solid and fertile ground, specifically to two great symbolists: the nineteenth-century American novelist and poet Herman Melville and the twentieth-century French novelist and essayist Albert Camus; *Sophie's Choice* owes more to Melville and Camus than it does to the great "Dixie Special"—Faulkner. If we do not assess these influences, we cannot possibly appreciate the novel's architecture or understand the profound implications the novel has for contemporary readers. Let us begin with an exploration of the Melvillean overtones in *Sophie's Choice* and how these contribute to the novel's characters, action, and ideas, demonstrating that far from "avoiding the contraries," *Sophie's Choice* reveals the urgency and necessity of ramming right into them.

When asked in 1977, while writing *Sophie's Choice*, which novelists continue to mean the most to him, the first writer Styron mentioned was Melville. Already in the second paragraph of *Sophie's Choice* the reader is forced to make a connection with Melville since the paragraph begins with "Call me Stingo," echoing the famous beginning of *Moby-Dick*, "Call me Ishmael." Is this merely a rhetorical device? In a 1980 interview when asked why he chose to make the book partly autobiographical, Styron responded:

> I realized that this was very important in order to make this story
> as seductive as I could make it, as dramatically compelling. I had
> to back off and give the reader—from the very first page—a sense

of who was talking, which is a very good dramatic device and an old-fashioned one, but one that if done properly almost never fails. It's at the heart of storytelling and is the art of the novel— to establish oneself with a great authority as the narrator who's going to tell you a very interesting story, but who has not gotten around to telling you the story yet. A good example of this device is *Moby-Dick* where Ishmael goes through a long, wonderfully comic episode in New Bedford right before he gets you on the ship. He establishes the right to dominate your attention. I didn't do this with anything so obvious as *Moby-Dick* for a model, but just used a device that has been used many, many times.

Clearly, Stingo and Ishmael are youthful stand-ins for their creators. Both Melville and Styron strive for authority in their narrators; the fact that both narratives are told in the first person lends an intimacy and directness, and the fact that both narratives are told as reminiscences gives them greater richness. Beginning the novel with "Call me Stingo," therefore, is more than a safe rhetorical device. First, it tells us something about the character of the young, twenty-two-year-old narrator: that he is imaginative, literate, and a bit cocky. The tone is meant to be a bit mocking, comic. The name Stingo, after all, was derived from the nickname Stinky, referring to the narrator's hygiene. The beginning of the novel, then, is self-mocking, the older, more accomplished writer looking back at his younger, naive self. As such, *Sophie's Choice* is a *Künstlerroman*, a novel chronicling a writer's artistic development.

The implications of this link to Melville go much deeper than rhetorical strategies. It will be shown that *Moby-Dick* and *Sophie's Choice* share much in common in terms of their characters, ideas, themes, action, and overall architecture, that both novels are actually tragedies of madness and acts of metaphysical rebellion. Both Melville and Styron share Ishmael's view of mankind: "Heaven have mercy on us all—Presbyterians and Pagans alike—for we are all somehow dreadfully cracked about the head, and sadly need mending."

The first chapter of *Sophie's Choice* is reminiscent in many ways of the first chapter of *Moby-Dick*, entitled "Loomings." Both Stingo and Ishmael are young narrators with little or no money in their purses, without much stake in society, hostile to social institutions. They are both feeling a November in their souls. Stingo tells us that his youth at twenty-two "was at its lowest ebb." He could not produce a novel, he was out of work, had no money, and was a Southerner self-exiled in New York. It was, in short, a "morbid and solitary period." To keep the wolf from the door, Stingo becomes a reader for McGraw-Hill but feels a spiritual ache while working for this "soulless empire." Stingo is a lonely outcast, a "Southerner wandering

amid the Kingdom of the Jews," suffering the "pain of unwanted solitude."
Curiously, Stingo tells us he would like to be a writer someday with the soaring
wings of a "Melville, Flaubert, or Tolstoy." To ease his solitude when not at
work, Stingo tells us he is reading "The Bear," *Notes from the Underground*, and
Billy Budd; that is, when he is not gazing out of his window consumed by sexual
fantasies. Stingo is indeed "still very much feeling his oats." He knows enough
at twenty-two, however, to know that he dislikes any "tidy, colorless and arch-
conservative mold," and chafes at unthinking, mechanical, conforming men.
Stingo refuses to wear a hat when ordered to and will not read the acceptable
New York newspapers to conform to his boss's demands. Stingo is, then, an
idealistic, ambitious youth on a spiritual quest, a rebellious voyager in search
of the knowledge of good and evil, of knowledge of the self.

Stingo's view from the twentieth floor of his midtown office building
gives him "spasms of exhilaration and sweet promise that have traditionally
overcome provincial American youths." It is the Hudson he sees, and water
imagery is important in this first chapter. We must remember that Stingo
has just returned from the sea, having been a U.S. Marine in World War II,
stationed in the South Pacific. Stingo sees a misty and obscure future when
staring at the Hudson; his coworker Farrell stares often at the Hudson, his
water gazing emblematic of terrible spiritual longing, having recently lost
his son Eddie in Okinawa. When Stingo tells Farrell that he has been fired,
Farrell responds, "People have been known to drown in this place." Stingo,
normally a landsman, will be confronted by the destructive power of water
but will also seek the purifying comfort of Coney Island after the deaths of
his two closest friends.

We learn that Farrell sees Stingo as the promising writer his son can no
longer be, whereas Stingo feels he has been deprived of something terrible
and magnificent, having arrived in Okinawa after the shooting had ceased.
Stingo muses on the incomprehensibility, the absurdity of time, of fate,
which allowed Eddie to die in Okinawa while he, Stingo, was somehow
spared what could have been that same fate. This realization causes him to
conclude that all ambition is sad, that he carries a "large hollowness" within
him, having been, until twenty-two at least, Fortune's darling. Stingo's self-
assessment at the beginning of his voyage is this: "It was true that I had traveled great distances for one so young, but my spirit had remained landlocked,
unacquainted with love and all but a stranger to death." Stingo knows he
needs a "voyage of discovery," but little did he suspect at twenty-two that he
would so quickly become acquainted with love and death in so strange a place
to him as Brooklyn in 1947.

Ishmael, the isolato, experiences deep spiritual despair at the beginning
of *Moby-Dick* and knows that he, too, must no longer remain landlocked. He

takes to the sea to keep his madness under control, to "drive off the spleen and regulate the circulation," having been "involuntarily pausing before coffin warehouses and bringing up the rear of every funeral [he meets]." Ishmael in the insular city of the Manhattoes knows that the streets take you waterward, that thousands of men are "fixed in ocean reveries." "Meditation and water are wedded for ever." What unites men, Ishmael muses, is their need to get as close to the water as they can without falling in. We see ourselves in all rivers and oceans. "It is the image of the ungraspable phantom of life; and this is the key to it all." Ishmael, also normally a landsman, is a meditative, restless voyager needing to unlock his landlocked spirits. We could say, then, that *Sophie's Choice* and *Moby-Dick* are spiritual autobiographies, with Stingo and Ishmael the heroes who observe and participate during their voyages.

We also learn that Ishmael is like his creator in that they both were country schoolmasters, hailing from old established families and therefore unused to taking orders, yet he feels compelled to go on a whaling voyage, being ruled by "the invisible police officer of the Fates." Like Stingo, he is aware of the role of Fate in our destiny, aware that we are not entirely in control. While he does not understand fully at the beginning why the Fates have ordered him to go on this whaler, he knows it is somehow necessary to his development. Ishmael tells us that he is tormented with an everlasting itch for things remote. He "loves to sail forbidden seas and land on barbarous coasts." Both Stingo and Ishmael, then, establish themselves as lonely, sensitive, adventurous romantic questers in search of "things remote," knowing that they somehow must confront a "portentous and mysterious monster," not content with safe routines. Both leave their jobs to explore their souls. The opening chapters of both *Sophie's Choice* and *Moby-Dick*, therefore, are full of portentous loomings for the strange journeys that are to follow, metaphysical voyages into the mysteries of evil, madness, love, and death. Neither Stingo nor Ishmael ignores what is good, but Ishmael knows and Stingo will come to know how important it is "to perceive a horror" and "be social with it . . . since it is but well to be on friendly terms with all the inmates of the place one lodges in." Both Ishmael and Stingo discover that "unless you own the whale, you are but a provincial and sentimentalist in truth." Both will for a time be mesmerized by fatally glamorous heroes, Ahab and Nathan, will indeed identify with them.

It is not surprising, then, that Stingo is reading *Billy Budd* at the beginning of his journey or that he compares himself to Ishmael even mockingly or that one of Styron's and Stingo's favorite novelists is Melville. There are profound intellectual, emotional, and philosophical connections between Styron and Melville and, therefore, between Stingo and Ishmael, their

youthful alter egos. The most profound similarity is their interest in metaphysical questions, their pondering the nature of being. Unsurprisingly,
then, the problem of evil haunts both writers and spawns a moral quest, a
search for values amid the stark realities of pain and suffering. Both writers
stalk the riddles of personality and the riddles of existence, dramatizing
human tensions without necessarily resolving them neatly. It is much easier
for a twentieth-century novelist to do this than it was for Melville, who met
a hostile response with the publication of *Moby-Dick*.

Why did he meet with such hostility during his lifetime? The overwhelming answer is that Melville was out of step with the prevailing mood
of mid-nineteenth-century America, which was optimistic, expansionistic,
and still terribly naive, an America that had won the War of 1812 and had
more recently won the Mexican War, an overconfident, young America. It
was an America that believed itself the chosen land, destined for some
future unrelated to the vast flux of history, the city on the hill, a beacon of
hope, an alternative to European Machiavellianism. The prevailing philosophy to match those soaring spirits was Transcendentalism, a belief in the
goodness of the universe and God, a belief in the emblematic nature of the
universe in which nature and spirit are one. Transcendentalism searched
for reality through spiritual intuition. In short, it was a visionary, idealistic
philosophy which held that human beings are related to all nature; they are
not aliens. Its leading proponents were, of course, Emerson, Thoreau, and
Whitman—three rugged individualists who believed wholeheartedly in this
new democratic experiment, who believed that evil was merely the privation of good, that people were at peace with their environment since matter
and spirit were one, that divinity lay in all living things, a primitive
Pantheism; thus, Emerson could write the following in his journal during
the middle of the Civil War, November 1863:

> We, in the midst of a great Revolution, still enacting the sentiment
> of the Puritans, and the dreams of young people thirty years ago;
> we, passing out of the old remainders of barbarism into pure
> Christianity and humanity, into freedom of thought, of religion, of
> speech, of the press, and of trade, and of suffrage, or political right;
> and working through this tremendous ordeal, which elsewhere
> went by beheadings, and massacre, and reigns of terror,—passing
> through all this and through states and territories, like a sleep, and
> drinking our tea the while. 'Tis like a brick house moved from its
> old foundations and place, and passing through our streets, whilst
> all the family are pursuing their domestic work inside.

Melville, however, could not subscribe to this view, nor could his friend and neighbor Hawthorne. The two writers launched an all-out attack on such dangerous naivete, their writing revealing their passionate conviction about the omnipresent existence of evil in human beings and nature, and their deep belief that such innocence was not only naive but potentially dangerous. Melville saw good and evil as independent forces at war for control, closer to Zoroastrianism or Manicheism, courageously rebuking the prevailing empty optimism in American thought, viewing man as a stranger, an orphan, exiled and abandoned in dangerous waters.

Such an insistence on man's darker side had its consequences and still does today. Styron, too, insists that we look at our darker selves, our potential for evil and destruction; if we neglect to do so, we are doomed. In twentieth-century America, however, pessimism is an easy commodity, this century having been particularly barbaric. While Americans can argue that Auschwitz was a European phenomenon, Styron knows that Americans cannot claim innocence; in 1979, when *Sophie's Choice* was published, America had just withdrawn its forces from the undeclared, bloody, protracted war in Vietnam. The older Stingo knows this when telling his story of Nazi horrors, horrors which did not end with the fall of the Third Reich. The younger narrator knows nothing about the concentration camps at the beginning of his journey, but by the end he can no longer claim ignorance as an excuse. Morris Fink's 1947 question, "What's Oswitch?" would no longer be acceptable since such ignorance is fatal. Styron, too, pays for his beliefs; he is appreciated much more in Europe than in this country precisely because he is candid in his criticism of American innocence and naivete and insistent about our necessity to experience evil within us, a potentially liberating experience. He demonstrates that Americans are not chosen people, just painfully ignorant of history and, therefore, overly optimistic. Some critics called Styron's second novel, *Set This House on Fire*, more French than American, and Styron himself calls France his spiritual home. Essentially, Styron's vision is more European, more Manichean, more aware of our duality. *Sophie's Choice* reflects this European outlook. In 1984, Styron was awarded the medal of the Commander of the Legion of Honor for his work, the highest honor the French government bestows; in France *Sophie's Choice* is considered one of the most significant novels to have emerged since World War II.

Melville had to obscure his real meanings in *Moby-Dick* and his subsequent fiction to make it more palatable for his readers. Styron does not use disguises, and has been heavily criticized during the last twenty years for his unflinching portrait of slavery in America in *The Confessions of Nat Turner* and his portrait of anti-Semitism, sexism, and racism in *Sophie's Choice*. The mystery of iniquity does indeed haunt Melville and Styron, permeating their fiction and their tragic view of human existence. Styron explained why Americans balk at this viewpoint in a 1962 interview in France for *L'Express*, right after *Set This House on Fire* was published to great acclaim in France but met with a lukewarm response in America:

> American society is an overly optimistic society. Except for the Civil War, it has never known tragedy and horror on its own soil. . . . It is more difficult for America than for Europe to conceive of tragedy. Americans do not like being told that people can be unbalanced, desperate, sometimes corrupt, that life can be horrible. . . . And they reject any tragic representation of life, not realizing that this representation can be a catharsis, that to accept a tragic picture of life on the artistic level can indeed free one from the horror so that one may enjoy life more.

Obviously, then, Melville and Styron share an important philosophical way of perceiving the world and human nature, a view acutely aware of human history and our potential, a view which is difficult and at times dispiriting but also potentially freeing. Both Melville and Styron, at least the Melville of *Moby-Dick*, provide a way out of future barbarisms, a way towards the regeneration of our souls. It is a humanistic, not a religious resurrection, however, a vision of brotherhood as our only salvation, a vision which shapes the artistic endings of *Moby-Dick* and *Sophie's Choice*.

Melville and Styron also share a curious personal history regarding slavery, which prompts them to address questions of racial divisiveness in their fictions. We must not forget that *Moby-Dick*, published in 1851, was written in a time of great national crisis over the slave question. Slavery was the dominant issue being debated in 1850, and Melville and others feared the slavery issue would tear the Union apart—which, of course, it did just a short decade after *Moby-Dick* was published.

Melville was not just abstractly aware of the slavery crisis; his own father-in-law, Judge Lemuel Shaw, was the first Northern judge to enforce a rigorous 1850 fugitive slave law providing for interstate extradition for escaped slaves and heavily penalizing anyone aiding fugitive slaves. He ordered the return of runaway slave Thomas Sims to his master. Judge Shaw also upheld the Boston Primary School Committee's right to enforce segregated schooling, which was to establish a basis for the separate but equal doctrine. We could speculate that Melville harbored tremendous guilt about his family's close connection to promoting slavery, especially since Lemuel

Shaw often supported Melville financially. It is not surprising, then, that race figures prominently in Melville's fiction. Melville understood that slavery deforms its victims and victimizers, generating an endless cycle of vengeance, a theme explored fully in his 1856 novella, *Benito Cereno*. The Civil War, as Melville predicted in *Moby-Dick*, would engulf all Americans, guilty and innocent, white and black, Northern and Southern.

Like Melville, Styron has a close personal link with slavery. Recently, Styron wrote a tribute to his late friend, writer James Baldwin, acknowledging that Baldwin's "soul's savage distress" helped shape and define his own work and its moral contours. Styron muses, "this would be the most appropriate gift imaginable to the grandson of a slave owner from a slave's grandson" ("Jimmy in the House"). Styron's paternal grandmother, Marianna Clark, born in 1848, owned two small black handmaidens throughout the Civil War. This tainted inheritance shows up fictionally in the guise of Artiste, a slave child the sale of whom provides Stingo with a small income which enables him to continue writing. Although Stingo is desperate for money at twenty-two while trying to write his first novel, he is nevertheless secretly happy when his apartment is burglarized and Artiste's money is stolen.

Also linking Styron with slavery is the place he grew up: Southampton County, Virginia, the same county in which Nat Turner led his slave revolt. Styron knew when quite young that he would one day write about this remarkable man. In 1967, he published *The Confessions of Nat Turner*, engendering a Pulitzer Prize and a good deal of hostility from black readers and from critics who accused him of being a racist. Styron's ambivalence towards the South appears in some of his fiction, as in Stingo's occasional yearning for the old bucolic South in contrast with the reality of the new, industrially blighted South. Styron feels compelled to tackle the stain of slavery in his fiction and nonfiction. Curiously, Melville and Styron are white writers who have written fictions about slave rebellions from the slave's point of view, trying to understand the victims and the victimizers of this tragedy, perhaps exorcising some of their own sense of shame. Styron is aware that his *Confessions of Nat Turner* is part of a tradition in American literature based on an awareness of racial division. He expanded on this in a 1968 interview shortly after his novel was published:

> I think the *Confessions* is just a continuation of a tradition which we're going to find more and more of. An important strand of American literature is based on a consciousness of this division in our culture, this racial division. Melville had it; Mark Twain had it; Faulkner certainly had it; Sherwood Anderson had it; and Richard Wright had it. To some extent, it's been a large, impor-

tant stream in the Mississippi River of our literature. I think that
my book will have its place as part of this consciousness that we
all share, black and white. Ralph Ellison's next novel, which has
been a long time in preparation, shows a daring boldness on his
part to penetrate into the white consciousness. Without such
efforts, I visualize an America where we will not be able to exist
unless we exist together. I fully believe this; I don't believe we can
exist apart. The awareness of this, I think, will only come
through literature which allows both black and white to courageously venture into each other's consciousness. I think it's a
denial of humanity, of our mutual humanity, to assume that it is
pretentious and arrogant and wrong for a white man to attempt
to get into a black man's skin.

What is important about this biographical information is that *Moby-Dick* and *Sophie's Choice* are not obviously about slavery, but if we investigate more closely, slavery—that is, the propensity for human beings to dominate others—is a crucial theme in both novels. Both novels are cautionary tales about this evil propensity and how a society may not allow this domination without being at risk of moral and physical collapse. Symbolically, the destruction of the *Pequod* suggests the destruction of the Union. Ahab ulti-mately rejects Pip; Stubb demeans Fleece and abandons Pip to the pitiless ocean. The harmony that does remain is Queequeg's friendship with Ishmael, suggesting that interracial harmony is not just an admirable, abstract ideal but a necessity for human survival. Similarly, in *Sophie's Choice*, Stingo understands that he must not profit from the sale of the slave Artiste. More importantly, Stingo learns that hatred of a race or ethnic group leads to Auschwitz. The older Stingo explains that Auschwitz was a system based on the view that life is totally expendable.

Sophie's Choice links, then, the two horrors of modern times—slavery and genocide in the American South, and slavery and genocide in Nazi Eastern Europe, demonstrating that Auschwitz was a part of a long history of global slavery, unique, though, because of the added concept of the absolute superfluity of human life which authorized mass extermination; Styron, therefore, draws a daring parallel between the Old South and Nazism. In this sense, *Sophie's Choice* can be read as a continuation of *The Confessions of Nat Turner*.

Essentially, Melville and Styron both subscribe to Melville's dictum: "To write a mighty book you need a mighty theme." Both writers are aware of the sinister forces in history and modern life which threaten all of humanity, thus giving their fictions larger tragic dimensions. Melville and

Styron share an existential vision, urging that we must search for faith and certitude, for values, in a pandemonious world symbolized by bondage and oppression, a world hostile or at best indifferent to our needs. We must, then, always be in spiritual revolt against the evil and chaos in the universe.

This brings us to Ahab and his connection to *Sophie's Choice*. There were mythic fictional heroes in revolt before Ahab. We think automatically of Prometheus, who challenged Zeus's authority, the Satanic Hero, cast out of heaven by Michael, and the romantic Byronic hero. Certainly, Melville had these heroes in mind as well as the biblical wicked King Ahab, slave-master and worshiper of false idols, when he created Ahab. While Ahab is an admirable character in many ways, rebuking life for its incompleteness because of death and its wastefulness because of evil, he is also terribly dangerous to himself and others. Melville points out the limits of the Byronic and Satanic heroes, heroes whose strong will to power can lead to narcissism and despotism. His portrait of Ahab also rebukes his contemporaries, Emerson and Carlyle, by dramatizing the dangers of blind hero worship and total self-reliance. In 1837 Emerson read Carlyle's review of the *Mémoires* of the French Revolution's statesman Mirabeau and noted in his journal:

> Then he is a worshipper of strength, heedless much whether its present phase be divine or diabolic. Burns, George Fox, Luther, and those unclean beasts Diderot, Danton, Mirabeau, whose sinews are their own and who trample on the tutoring and conventions of society, he loves. For he believes that every noble nature was made by God, and contains, if savage passions, also fit checks and grand impulses within it, hath its own resources, and however erring, will return from far.

Shortly thereafter, Emerson wrote his famous essay "Self-Reliance," a manifesto urging us to believe in the dignity and sanctity of the self, in individualism above all else. Transcendentalism encouraged what we now call charisma. A few quotations from his essay give the flavor of his manifesto:

> To believe your own thoughts, to believe that what is true for you in your private heart is true for all men—that is genius. Speak your latent conviction, and it shall be the universal sense. (Whicher 147)

> Whoso would be a man, must be a nonconformist. He who would gather immortal palms must not be hindered by the name

of goodness, but must explore if it be goodness. Nothing is at least sacred but the integrity of your own mind. Absolve you to yourself, and you shall have the suffrage of the world. (Whicher 149)

No law can be sacred to me but that of my nature. Good and bad are but names very readily transferable to that or this; the only right is what is after my constitution; the only wrong what is against it. A man is to carry himself in the presence of all opposition as if every thing were titular and ephemeral but he. (Whicher 150)

What I must do is all that concerns me, not what the people think. This rule, equally arduous in actual and in intellectual life, may serve for the whole distinction between greatness and meanness. It is the harder because you will always find those who think they know what is your duty better than you know it. It is easy in the world to live after the world's opinion; it is easy in solitude to live after our own; but the great man is he who in the midst of the crowd keeps with perfect sweetness the independence of solitude. (Whicher 151)

And truly it demands something godlike in him who has cast off the common motives of humanity and has ventured to trust himself for a taskmaster. High be his heart, faithful his will, clear his sight, that he may in good earnest be doctrine, society, law, to himself, that a simple purpose may be to him as iron necessity is to others! (Whicher 161)

Does this not sound like Ahab—"And it truly demands something godlike in him who has cast off the common motives of humanity and has ventured to trust himself for a taskmaster"? We can view the portrait of Ahab as Melville's answer to Emerson and Carlyle. As such, *Moby-Dick* is a Transcendental parody. Ahab is the incarnation of the self-reliance doctrine gone mad. What Melville wants us to see is that strong leaders, strong individuals, do not have to be great ones; they can be selfish and destructive by casting off the common motives of humanity, such as survival and brotherhood. Ahab demands to be recognized as a distinct personality in the midst of the personified impersonal, and we admire his ability to assert his individualism; however, Ahab is essentially tyrannical and manipulative, with a will to power that will cause the destruction of the *Pequod* and its thirty isolatoes, exclusive of Ishmael. Ahab is grand but also fatally glamorous. While we admire his rebelliousness, his ability to feel profound outrage at life's injustices, we must also be frightened and outraged by his shameful recklessness, his disregard for human life, his evil. In short, Ahab is the era's "most fully developed oxymoronic character, attaining a kind of universality from the magnitude of the contrary impulses he embodies."

It is not surprising that *Moby-Dick* has greater appeal for twentieth-century readers than for nineteenth-century readers. In 1887, only 4,000 copies of *Moby-Dick* were printed and sold. There were heavy sales, however, from 1921 to 1947. Our century responds to Melville's restless, puzzled, questioning spirit, to his intuitive understanding of the power of the unconscious, of the primitive within us. Melville understood there was no resolving the tensions between Transcendentalism and Empiricism, between religion and science, faith and skepticism; his spirit is essentially modern: alienated, divided, skeptical.

Melville scholars are reinterpreting Melville in light of feminism, Freud, the proletariat, Eros, and Nazi Germany. There has even been an argument advanced that *Moby-Dick* is a novel of political prophecy; that is, Melville's portrait of the charismatic yet tyrannical Ahab prefigures twentieth-century fascism. It is in this regard that *Moby-Dick* has eerie parallels in *Sophie's Choice*. Christopher S. Durer has written a provocative piece originally presented before the Melville Society in the summer of 1986 entitled "*Moby-Dick* and Nazi Germany." Durer begins his essay by acknowledging the recent interest in the political world of Melville's writings, making us more aware of Melville's stature as a liberal thinker and of the political and economic tensions which shaped his writing. This new political criticism, which began in the 1960s and has grown stronger in the 1980s, sees *Moby-Dick* as

> growing out of the aftermath of the Mexican War, with its rabid political and economic expansionism, the burning issue of the treatment of the Indians, and the apparently insoluable problem of slavery. The interregional and interracial society on board the *Pequod*, the structure of power which she exhibits, and numerous political allusions establish her as the ship of state in mid-nineteenth-century America.

Durer takes this political criticism one step further by arguing that *Moby-Dick* is a book of political prophecy, "this time pointing to the inhumanities of twentieth-century totalitarianism, especially the National Socialist regime in Germany between 1933 and 1945." He develops this analogy in two ways: first, by describing Ahab's propagandistic techniques, similar to those used in Nazi Germany, and second, by exploring Melville's understanding of the "very psychology and psychosis of power in a totalitarian state, such as Nazi Germany." For Durer, then, *Moby-Dick* anticipates, psychologically and politically, the tragedies of our century. It "projects a macabre vision of twentieth-century fascism and offers a schema and typology of this fascism—its precarious beginnings, its growth and zenith, its death rattle, and its demise." Durer shows how demagogues begin with limited powers and then obtain greater dominion by fomenting fear and hatred. Like Hitler, Ahab reaches for the "folk-soul" of the crew and manipulates their minds with sinister skill. A charismatic leader can tap and redirect primitive hatreds and racial animosities. Here is Melville's description of the *Pequod* crew under Ahab's rule: "Like machines, they dumbly moved about the deck, ever conscious that the old man's despot eye was on them." "They were one man, not thirty . . . and were all directed to that fatal goal which Ahab their one Lord and keel did point to."

Again, paralleling the transformation of the German nation under the Nazis, the crew of the *Pequod* becomes "a folk organism and not an economic organization," since Ahab rejects the commercial benefits of whaling for a collective psychological fulfillment, resulting from the revengeful pursuit of one whale, seen as the enemy of the state. The mystique Ahab creates for himself is similar to Hitler's psychological enslavement of the German nation and his notion of himself as the leader; consequently, rather than being a type of pre-twentieth-century absolute ruler, Ahab is in reality a prototype of a twentieth-century fascist dictator, someone like Adolf Hitler. *Moby-Dick*, according to Durer, is both a cry of anguish and a dark historical prophecy.

Essentially, Durer demonstrates that ideology deadens and depersonalizes; human beings become robots, resulting from a particular political ethos. The crew functions like a machine, with lifeless obedience amounting to political automatism. Captain Ahab identifies the white whale as the enemy of the state, a threat to the collective will; Moby Dick, however, is merely an archetypal victim on whose hump Ahab piles "the sum of all the general rage and hate felt by his whole race from Adam down." To preserve its monolithic character, a group needs an enemy that gives it security and cohesion. Melville presents to us those who would be susceptible to excessive authority—mongrel renegades, castaways, and cannibals—the dispossessed and the violence-oriented; therefore, *Moby-Dick* depicts the soil in which fascism can flourish. There can be no redemption or self-fulfillment in obedience; the crew must share some of the guilt for the destruction of the *Pequod*, for their own destruction. This kind of evil defies rational solutions. Interestingly, Ahab and Hitler end up as suicides when their empires collapse. Mythic heroes are usually rehabilitated or redeemed, but there can be no redemption for Ahab. We need Ishmael's recounting of this tragic story so that we might be redeemed. Durer sums up the importance of *Moby-Dick* as follows:

> *Moby-Dick* portrays deep subterranean social forces—the different dynamics of society, the psychologies of the crowd, ruthless pursuits of power, the frailties of social organisms under pressure—all of which pose monumental problems and ultimately defy solutions, pointing at the same time to the catastrophies and cataclysms of the twentieth century.

We must remember that every ship was, in those days, a tyranny; nevertheless, Ahab's story has profound social and political implications, not only for America in 1850 but also for twentieth-century readers. The connection to *Sophie's Choice* is both obvious and subtle; Ahab is a prototype for twentieth-century dictators, for the Third Reich we confront in *Sophie's Choice*, but he also resembles one of the three main characters in the novel—Nathan. The biblical Ahab was a wicked king, but the biblical Nathan was the prophet who rebuked King David for his murder of Uriah. We are meant, therefore, to conceive of Nathan as a moral exemplar, and, in some ways, Nathan is quite literally a gift to humanity as his name suggests; however, Nathan, like Ahab, like Hitler, is determined to rid the world of what he considers to be evil, to fight evil with evil. Ahab wanted to destroy Moby Dick and thereby cleanse the world of malice. Hitler wanted to rid the world of undesirables—Jews, homosexuals, Slavs, Gypsies, Poles, the handicapped—to create a purified Aryan race. Nathan wants to destroy the evil the Holocaust represents, wants to rid the world of torturers, tyrants, anti-Semites, and collaborators, as his battering of Sophie indicates. The profound connection between Ahab and Nathan is that they both see the overwhelming malice in the universe and feel outraged by its power and capriciousness; they understand that our highest goal is to strike through the mask. They do not, however, stop at feeling outraged by life's injustices and cruelties. Both Nathan and Ahab incorporate the evil into themselves, use the "enemy's" methods; that is, they are dependent somewhat on the evil and their spiritual revolts take on a murderous edge.

Though outraged by life's cruelties represented by the inscrutable and ubiquitous whale, Ahab becomes capricious and cruel himself, forsaking human fellowship for diabolical ends. We might contrast here Ahab's reaction to the loss of his leg with the response of Jack Brown, Stingo's friend, who lost his leg during the Second World War. Jack Brown had a "mad and

sovereign stoicism that prevented him from falling into suicidal despair."
Ironically, the artificial leg which replaces the one torn off Ahab by Moby
Dick is made of whale jawbone, so that Ahab's mobility is literally owed to a
dead whale. Though Starbuck, Pip, and other ships' captains warn him of the
folly and futility of his chase, Ahab will not swerve from his ill-fated course;
he has fallen into the abyss. Still, Melville wants us to feel that Ahab's clever
villainy is preferable to society's established hypocrisy.

Nathan, like his biblical namesake, takes a strong stand against murder
but ultimately becomes evil himself. We must remember, of course, that
Nathan is quite literally mad. Diagnosed as a paranoid schizophrenic, he has
been in and out of mental institutions for much of his life; his is not a rational
mind, whereas the appalling nature of Ahab's and Hitler's crimes was indeed
their incredible rationality, their deliberateness, their efficiency. Nathan's
crimes are irrational, his attacks on Sophie often induced by drugs or
madness, his fits of jealousy and violence sudden, unplanned, impulsive. We
must remember that Nathan fears genocide in this country, becoming
increasingly enraged when he hears about the camps, the Nuremburg trials,
and Göring's suicide. The awful, bitter irony, however, is that Nathan, who
rages against the Nazis' use of cyanide gas to destroy millions of Jews, swallows a cyanide tablet to kill himself, uses, in effect, the Nazis' methods, their
technology of death; Nazi evil, therefore, becomes his evil. Psychologically,
some have described this phenomenon as a victim's identification with his
victimizer, which creates a horrible chain of compulsive behavior affecting
generations. Both Ahab and Nathan would have done well to read Augustine's *Confessions:* "I sought whence is evil; and sought it in an evil way; and
saw not the evil in my very search."

Part of the power of *Sophie's Choice*, then, lies in its dramatization of
what the Holocaust has done to a generation of people, Americans and Europeans, and how it continues to cause anguish, pain, unforgettable evil, and
torment. We see what the Holocaust has literally done to Sophie and what it
imaginatively has done to Nathan, whose schizophrenia represents the
world's wounds, and we see how the innocent Stingo learns about the
unspeakable horror through his love for Sophie and friendship with Nathan.
All this adds up to a rich texture of horror, and as readers we respond to the
novel as we would a Greek tragedy, with awe, pity, and fear.

Both *Moby-Dick* and *Sophie's Choice* dramatize how all of us are
enveloped in whale-lines, how we all walk into the jaws of the whale; it is the
human condition. There is no comfortable wisdom, and this truth makes us
sorrowful. Melville tells us that the truest of all men was Solomon, the Man
of Sorrows, who despaired of solving the mystery of the universe; Stingo
prefers to read Ecclesiastes and Isaiah, not the Sermon on the Mount,

because Hebrew woe seemed more cathartic. Styron, like Melville, sees the value in suffering, indeed sees suffering as a moral quality that can drive human beings to self-understanding and give them the chance of purification and transformation, leading them to freedom and human dignity, symbolized by Melville's Catskill eagle in "The Try-Works" chapter.

Too much sorrow, however, is destructive. Ahab has "his humanities" but will ultimately abandon his kindred spirit, Pip. Nathan is most attracted to Flaubert's *Madame Bovary* because of Emma's suicidal resolution and sees suicide as the legitimate option of any sane human being after the Third Reich. Stingo and Ishmael, however, after coming as close to the water's edge of despair as is humanly possible, learn how to conquer their grief. This is not to say that the two narrators are no longer sorrowful men, for they are, but they have earned their unhappiness and gain dignity and strength from their short stay in the abyss. The Greeks understood that there is no wisdom without suffering. Both Ishmael and Stingo, and Melville and Styron by extension, urge us towards this hard-earned wisdom, towards the wisdom that is woe, an uncharacteristically American view.

What happens, however, when that woeful wisdom becomes intolerable? Ahab's murderous monomania and Nathan's suicidal schizophrenia are obvious results. But there are two characters less obviously devastated by wisdom, one minor, one major: Pip in *Moby-Dick* and Sophie. Both Pip and Sophie are dealt blows which they are incapable of surviving: theirs is the woe that is madness, both victims of life's wantonness. Pip is the black cabin boy whose tambourine music uplifts the *Pequod*'s crew. Superficially, Pip appears to be the stereotypically happy, music-loving slave. Actually, Pip is closer to Lear's wise fool, warning against folly. Pip is stung by life's injustices, but his passive response is in direct contrast with Ahab's vengeful protests. Pip's madness is acquiescence. Pip has been thrown overboard to the sharks symbolically. Hours later, by chance, not design, Pip is rescued by the *Pequod*, but by this time he has, it seems, lost his mind. This crucial chapter in *Moby-Dick*, called "The Castaway," dramatizes most graphically the narrator's feelings that the universe is a "heartless immensity." Ishmael hints that Pip's madness is caused by the fact that the sea carried him

> down alive to wondrous depths, where strange shapes of the
> unwarped primal world glided to and fro before his passive eyes;
> and the miser-merman, Wisdom, revealed his hoarded heaps;
> and among the joyous, heartless, ever-juvenile eternities, Pip saw
> the multitudinous, God-omnipresent, coral insects, that out of
> the firmament of waters heaved the colossal orbs. He saw God's
> foot upon the treadle of the loom, and spoke it; and therefore, his

shipmates called him mad. So man's insanity is heaven's sense; and wandering from all mortal reason, man comes at last to that celestial thought, which, to reason, is absurd and frantic; and weal or woe, feels then uncompromised, indifferent as his God.

The universe, Ishmael suggests, is absurd, frantic, indifferent, a realization too overwhelming for some. True wisdom—that is, an accurate perception of God's malice—is maddening. Ahab's response is to strike through the pasteboard mask of appearances. But how many would want to strike through the mask if on the other side were nothing? Pip's madness is terror, and is less noble than defiance, but is still superior to "right reason." If the universe is indifferent, it is wise to celebrate the value of human friendship, of love. At weak moments, Ahab almost abandons his maniacal course when he allows himself to identify with Pip's suffering, to empathize with other human beings. Pip shows us the importance of human solidarity in a universe in which human beings are strangers, aliens, the pitiful waste of Ahab's antisocial, antilife behavior. An essential question *Moby-Dick* poses, then, is how can the innocent, symbolized here by Pip, protect themselves from the sharks without adopting evil methods themselves. The answer suggested is by going mad and not by doing evil. This question has profound importance for the twentieth century and brings us to Sophie Zawistowska.

Sophie, as her name suggests, is wise; she has fully experienced life's sharkishness. Sophie, more than most, has been forced to stare into the face of evil and not only come up cold against the inferno but live in it, forced to make infernal choices. How is one to survive such "wisdom"? What *Sophie's Choice* dramatizes is that no one can stare into the face of evil that long and survive. Sophie physically survives her twenty months in Auschwitz, but it is clear from the beginning of the novel that part of Sophie is already dead, and the remaining part longs for total annihilation. One of the most profound implications of *Sophie's Choice* is that survivors of the Holocaust can never totally recover, can possibly survive physically but not emotionally or spiritually. While psychologists give this condition a name—post-traumatic shock syndrome—the truth is that Sophie's "illness" is more than a syndrome, more than shock waves following the experience of war. Both *Moby-Dick* and *Sophie's Choice* urge us to acknowledge cosmic evil and the shark within, to be curious about and familiar with it. Dwelling on the horrors of existence, however, will produce madness, which can take a passive form, as in the cases of Pip and Sophie, or a very active form, as in the cases of Ahab and Nathan.

Sophie begs Nathan to abandon his mad quest, which is seemingly a quest to destroy Sophie but is actually a quest to destroy evil. Sophie, to

Nathan, is a living reminder of all those who died in the concentration camps, his pain exacerbated by the fact that she is a Gentile survivor. In striking Sophie, Nathan is attempting to harpoon his own Moby Dick, the incarnation of the world's evil. Sophie, he feels, is a Nazi collaborator and is, therefore, a Nazi herself. At first, Nathan views Sophie as the unfortunate victim of a horrific era and nurtures her lovingly back to health. Anytime Nathan reads or hears about the camps or the SS, however, he takes out his rage against Sophie, who metaphorically has stolen a piece of Nathan: she lives while Nathan's "Jewish brothers" have perished. We must remember, of course, that Nathan is a schizophrenic and drug addict and represents the world's wounds. There is no way, then, for Sophie to deter Nathan, a fact which ultimately leads to her own destruction as well. Pip, too, is destroyed because he cannot deter Ahab from his course. The difference is that Pip is killed along with the other crew members when Moby Dick proves mightier than Ahab, but Sophie chooses to die. She can neither live with nor live without Nathan; he is merely her final torturer. Like Pip, Sophie can never really recover from life's blows anyhow, from the accuracy of her perception of the world's malice. Stingo is right when he says that Sophie would be able to endure any hell in the afterlife.

Sophie had attempted suicide right after the liberation of Auschwitz and flirted with it during a weekend in Connecticut with Nathan where he dangled a cyanide capsule in front of her mouth; she also tried to drown herself at Coney Island and was rescued by the innocent Stingo, determined to save her at any cost. Sophie, however, had seen the heartless immensity of the universe; the infinite of her soul had been drowned long before the actual suicide. Sophie saw the indifference of nature, of God, and knew that God was dead; either he abandoned her or she abandoned him. She did not have the ability to revolt against the chaos and evil in the universe; having been too maimed by the inferno, she was no longer able to believe in a future. Through Sophie, Stingo experiences the inferno firsthand and begins to recognize the appalling enigma of human existence. Like all of us, Stingo is forced to consider whether Auschwitz was "a fatal embolism in the bloodstream of mankind." Is loving an absurdity after Auschwitz? Interestingly, *Moby-Dick* asks a similar question a century before the Holocaust: Are friendship and love possible in a sharkish world? The answer is a fragile yet real half-blind yes.

The other curious similarity between Pip and Sophie is the fact that they are slaves of sorts, Pip because of his color in mid-nineteenth-century America, and Sophie because she is Polish in Europe in the 1940s. Both love music and are capable of feeling and expressing ecstasy, yet Pip and Sophie are both considered commodities, both incarnations of the two horrors of modern times—slavery and genocide in America, and slavery and genocide in Nazi Eastern Europe, two victims of racial madness, of bigotry, of systems that dare to think of themselves as "brotherly," as paternal. Stubb orders Fleece to serve him and abandons Pip to the vast ocean. Dürrfeld, the German industrialist, says to Höss: "I am answerable to a corporate authority which is now simply insisting on one thing: that I be supplied with more Jews in order to maintain a predetermined rate of production. . . . We must have the coal. . . . I must have more Jews." Both Melville and Styron provide alternatives to authoritarian "brotherhood," to systems which degrade and demean the dignity of human life, to systems which "commodify" human beings.

The links between Ishmael and Stingo, Ahab and Nathan, and Pip and Sophie have been demonstrated. The obvious character excluded is the whale itself—Ahab's powerful antagonist—with its parallel in *Sophie's Choice*—the Holocaust. A little more than a quarter of the way into the novel, Melville devotes two entire chapters to Moby Dick—an attempt to grapple with the reality and meaning of this whale—"Moby Dick" and "The Whiteness of the Whale." Ishmael as narrator has been interested in exploring what Moby Dick means in retrospect, *Moby-Dick* being told as a reminiscence. All the material presented about whales and whaling, then, is an attempt to discover the meaning of Ahab's quest and Ishmael's own experience as a crew member of the *Pequod*. Ishmael sees naught in that whale but the deadliest ill. Unlike Ahab, Ishmael does not consider Moby Dick his enemy. Ahab, however, believes that the world is controlled either by a vicious God who operates through visible objects represented by Moby Dick, or is controlled possibly by nothing—that there is nothing behind the mask. We must remember how blasphemous these two beliefs were in Melville's pious century, which explains why Melville depended on irony and evasiveness so much. Actually, much of what is thought about Moby Dick is based on hearsay, rumor, fears, and superstititions; legend has it that Moby Dick is ubiquitous and immortal. What is true for certain is that Moby Dick is powerful, larger than most sperm whales, with a snow-white forehead, a high white hump on his back, and a deformed, scythe-like lower jaw.

In the famous "Whiteness of the Whale" chapter, Ishmael tells us that for him, Moby Dick's whiteness was the most appalling characteristic and suggests that the whiteness provokes terror in humans because it cannot be explained or grasped. Whiteness is awful because "by its indefiniteness it shadows forth the heartless voids and immensities of the universe." Whiteness, therefore, suggests annihilation, meaninglessness, universal indifference. The fear whiteness provokes, then, is primal, beyond rationality. Ishmael warns us not to be too curious about this leviathan since it is one creature in the world which must remain unpainted to the last. Moby Dick's voracity is seen as natural; that is, the sea is full of universal cannibalism. Ishmael suggests that we are part of this universal cannibalism; therefore, Ahab wants to destroy a force that has been a natural part of the universe long before human beings existed, when the whale was king of the earth.

Whatever moral or metaphysical significance Moby Dick might have, it is its physicality, its sheer omnipresence, that must be recognized. Ishmael views Moby Dick with a sense of mystery. Here is a phenomenon of existence that defies rational explanation; thus, it is to be regarded with respect, an object of profound curiosity. The whale, in short, is terrifying, powerful, inscrutable.

What Ahab fails to realize is that much of the evil perpetrated is caused by human beings. There are indifferent evils like natural disasters and disease, but Ahab projects evil onto visible objects, thereby abdicating any personal sense of responsibility for evil in the universe. Ironically, it is Fleece, the aged Negro cook, bossed around by the mindless Stubb, who understands the connection between humanity and sharks (he calls the sharks "fellow-critters"). In the "Stubb's Supper" chapter, Fleece preaches to the sharks to govern their sharkishness, for "all angel is not'ing more dan de shark well goberned." "Your woraciousness, fellow-critters, I don't blame ye so much for; dat is natur, and can't be helped; but to gobern dat wicked natur, dat is de pint." The chapter ends with Fleece's sage ejaculation about Stubb: "more of shark dan Massa Shark hisself." The lines between master and slave and predator and prey certainly become blurred. While it is easier to project evil onto others, Melville insists we must recognize the shark within us and try to govern it, not eliminate it, since that is against nature. As Melville said in *Mardi:* "All evils cannot be done away. For evil is the chronic malady of the universe; and checked in one place, breaks forth in another." Here Melville is echoing Hawthorne's view about evil, a decidedly anti-Transcendental one, which is the theme of Hawthorne's famous short story "Young Goodman Brown": "The fiend in his own shape is less hideous than when he rages in the breast of man." Goodman Brown, like Ahab, Pip, Nathan, and Sophie, is destroyed by the knowledge of demonism in the world.

This brings us to the portrayal of evil in *Sophie's Choice*, an evil that remains frustratingly mysterious for all of us—the Holocaust—represented by Sophie's "all but incomprehensible history." Like Moby Dick, the Holocaust is not mere symbol but a terrifying physical reality. The big difference, however, is that Moby Dick is a natural phenomenon, and the crematoria were created by human beings. Both novels ponder the mystery of iniquity, insisting that evil will always remain mysterious. Auschwitz must remain the one place on earth most unyielding to meaning or definition. How the Holocaust occurred is well documented; why it occurred remains a mystery, but that does not mean we must stop trying to come to terms with our evil potential. When the Nazis were not killing people, they were turning them into animals. Perhaps the worst legacy is that those who managed to survive feel guilty for having done so. Sophie's "badness" "pursued her like a demon"; she has a "schizoid conscience." Stingo finally acknowledges at the end of his voyage that Auschwitz will remain inexplicable to him and to all of humanity; absolute evil is never extinguished from the world. Styron said this about evil when asked why he chose Malraux's quotation about absolute evil to serve as one of the novel's epigraphs:

> But what mystifies me, and it's very hard to express, is that we are all of a species, you and I and all of our ancestors, we came from the same womb, the same source and we are in effect brothers. But all the horror and suffering, aside from natural disasters which there is no way to explain, are caused by man, by our own species, acting in evil ways towards himself. It's a very simple, but a very complex equation. Nature is indifferent. You could say much of the evil that we feel is a product of irrational nature, disease, let's say cancer. There's no way of explaining it. It happens, and it's evil. And an earthquake, you could say, is a kind of indifferent evil, or a flood. These things are part of the natural scene, but, basically, the unhappiness and the things we all consider to be evil derive from ourselves.
>
> We who are supposed to be brothers are the authors of the pain and oppression of the world. And it's a mystery, because one would think that, theoretically, a species such as we are with our capacity for love and goodness and friendship, which we all have, most of us, unless we're crazy, so often are mechanized and twisted through society, politics, through a thousand different ways, into causing evil and suffering. It's a mystery but I think that's what a writer has to deal with. And I have.

Melville had to write *Moby-Dick* partially in code since his vision was so blasphemous in 1850 in America. He said he had written a wicked book and felt proud. His reading of Shakespeare, particularly the Shakespeare of *King Lear* and *Hamlet*, confirmed his sense of the dark forces, of selfishness and cruelty, in human beings; he came to acknowledge that there was something arbitrary and irrational in the very structure of things. Melville had the courage to look at life without illusions, to demonstrate the dangers of refusing to question, revealing in the process the nobility of defiance. Too many Americans had opted for an empty innocence, an ignorance of evil, which is actually immaturity or spiritual cowardice; Starbuck's pious view, his "right reason," is revealed as shallow.

Just five years after the publication of *Moby-Dick*, Melville published *Benito Cereno*, an even darker tale about the dangers of ignorance and innocence. Yankee Captain Amasa Delano was another American with a "singularly undistrustful good nature, not liable, except in extraordinary and repeated incentives, and hardly then, to indulge in personal alarms, any way involving the imputation of malign evil in man." Captain Delano thinks Don Benito should be ecstatic because his life has been spared in the course of a slave mutiny on board his ship. Delano says, "You are saved," but Benito replies, "The negro." As long as human beings have memory, they can never be happy or innocent; innocence is cowardice.

This is critical for an understanding of Sophie. Her life has been spared, but she has memories to haunt her eternally despite her attempts to block these memories through alcohol, music, and sex. The young Stingo, with his "delusionary dreams about a Southern love nest" shared with Sophie, is a kind of Captain Delano, a present-oriented American, divorced from history, from maturity. Stingo thinks he can erase her past by sweeping her away to his peanut farm in Virginia, marrying her, and having children with her. The thought of becoming a wife and mother again, however, causes Sophie to feel ill: she has too many horrific memories of losing her children to the crematoria and her husband to a Nazi firing squad. How can a woman like Sophie truly start over?

There are many survivors today who have seemingly started over, but their nightmare world continues to haunt them. Many survivors suffer extreme psychic disorders and, sadly, sometimes pass their pain on to their children. Many children of survivors have trouble reading *Sophie's Choice* objectively, accusing Styron of anti-Semitism and intruding immorally on their territory. Their parents' pain has thoroughly become their pain; they find it obscene to try to understand those who perpetrated this pain. In fact, a meeting of children of survivors in New York City recently condemned Styron for giving a Gentile, Sophie, the "luxury" of a choice. Clearly, the evil that is the Holocaust continues to cause suffering and madness. For many, the Holocaust is the central event of the twentieth century with which we must grapple. Stingo cannot weep for eleven million people, but he can weep for Sophie, Nathan, Jan, Eva, Eddie Farrell, Bobby Weed, Artiste, Maria Hunt, Nat Turner, and Wanda, "just a few of the beaten and butchered and betrayed and martyred children of the earth." Melville and Styron show us that war is indeed humanity's madness, a fall from our inborn creative potential.

Those who dive too deeply, those whose sense of evil is so inflexible and adamant in their refusal to admit any existent good, come perilously close to a love of evil, to a queer pact with the devil. Ahab's last words are: "Oh, lonely death on lonely life! Oh, now I feel my topmost greatness lies in my topmost grief." Ahab and Nathan, Promethean in their defiance, push the quest too far. Both *Moby-Dick* and *Sophie's Choice* demonstrate that our greatness must not lie in our topmost grief. After experiencing the most profound rage, sorrow, and despair, after fully understanding our lonely, abandoned place in the universe, we must still conquer grief and affirm the dignity of life. Both Ishmael and Stingo learn this by the end of their journeys.

Sophie, and many other Holocaust survivors, can never conquer their grief and fully rejoin the living. How can they forgive their tormentors, forgive the murder of millions? It is hard not to recall the recent suicide of Primo Levi, the Italian novelist, chemist, and Holocaust survivor, or the many Vietnam veterans who will never fully rejoin the living. One of the most bitter legacies of the Holocaust is that many survivors feel evil and guilt-ridden themselves. Sophie, therefore, does not have the choice that Ahab has.

A recent book called *Haing Ngor: A Cambodian Odyssey* by Dr. Haing Ngor, the Cambodian physician who won an Academy Award for his performance in the film *The Killing Fields*, grapples with the human capacity for evil. His book explores Cambodia's exercise in auto-genocide. The Khmer Rouge tried to exterminate or at least deliberately work to death a majority of the population systematically, a regime which makes even less sense than the Third Reich. Ngor admits he does not understand the Khmer Rouge, his own people. Confronting the Cambodian capacity for evil, we cannot but wonder about our own. For most of us, "the face of evil will remain as blank as the stare of a patrolling shark."

Another new book, a novel entitled *The Immortal Bartfuss* by Aharon Appelfeld, Israeli novelist and Holocaust survivor, paints a portrait of a man who survived the Holocaust and now resides in Israel. Appelfeld explores a survivor's mysterious and hallucinatory private being, reminiscent of Camus' *The Stranger*, but even more extreme in its vision of alienation. Bartfuss is called immortal because "there are fifty bullets in his body." We are to understand Bartfuss as being not so much alive as merely undead. He feels like a shadow and hates his wife for having given birth to children who force him to become more than a survivor, a stranger. Bartfuss thinks that he could have been happy were it not for his wife and children, if he could live on an island alone. However he discovers a need to love, to give, to reenter the human family through his daughter Bridget. Bartfuss offers to buy his daughter a watch, acknowledging the value of time, the fullness of human existence. He can still act, can still love. Appelfeld shows the need for survivors and, in effect, for all of us, to live as if—as if there is a way out of the nightmare. In an interview with Philip Roth, Appelfeld said his latest novel "offers its survivor [Bartfuss] neither Zionist nor religious consolation." Bartfuss has "no advantage over anyone else, but he still hasn't lost his human face. That isn't a great deal, but it's something."

Melville and Styron offer neither Zionist nor religious consolation in their dark novels. *Moby-Dick* begins Christmas day, but evil remains despite the birth of a savior. Our lives are "encompassed by all the horrors of the half known life." Yet both *Moby-Dick* and *Sophie's Choice* have somewhat optimistic epilogues, both of which have been misinterpreted. Many critics have argued that the only reason Ishmael is rescued at the end is so that there can be a survivor to tell the tale. That misses, however, the important symbolism of the brief epilogue. Ishmael is literally buoyed up by Queequeg's coffin, so that the ship *Rachel*, searching after her missing children, "only found another orphan." Ishmael is still the lonely outcast he was at the beginning of the novel but with one major difference: he has experienced firsthand the meaning of love, death, evil, and madness. He undergoes a conversion to the subversive. Metaphorically, Ishmael is saved because he has fully accepted his humanity, adopting a doctrine of racial and social community as an ideal to set opposite the isolated individual; Ishmael's embrace of a black pagan represents a protest against civilized hypocrisy. Queequeg is loyal to his beliefs and friendships. He has risked his life to save his shipmate Tashtego and, of course, his symbolic loyalty at the end of the novel, his coffin, saves Ishmael's life. Through his friendship with Queequeg, Ishmael feels a melting. "No more my splintered heart and maddened hand were turned against this wolfish world." Ishmael comes to respect the "common continent of men." If we all walk into the jaws of the whale, lucky is any person who has a real friend. We are indeed enveloped in whale-lines, lines which link whalesmen to their prey and can destroy them as it does Ahab, but which also link Ishmael to Queequeg, to communal effort, to loyalty, to love; we have both options.

We must remember that Ishmael is reborn, but he is still an orphan. Ishmael's survival is absurd in a universe ruled by a capricious God or no God at all; alienation remains the central theme. What is important, though, is that Ishmael makes a pro-life choice while conscious of his dissatisfactions, yearnings, and homelessness, conscious that all of us are limited by necessity and chance; he has conquered his suicidal despair. Melville suggests that there is a certain kind of serenity in knowing one's limits and maintaining one's dignity, in accepting one's destiny as an orphan in the universe. Ishmael learns to accept the world without understanding all of it. Melville, then, saves Ishmael from pious Christianity and primitive Pantheism.

Ishmael's acceptance of his vulnerable humanity is reflected in the vision of nature in the epilogue: "The unharming sharks, they glided by as if with padlocks on their mouths; the savage seahawks sailed with sheathed beaks." The symbolic linking of Ishmael and Queequeg projects an ideal of interracial harmony, a power to counterbalance the sharks and seahawks, the way to "gobern" the shark within. It is a power that comes from a defiance of, not submission to, Christian orthodoxy. The resurrection at the end of *Moby-Dick*, then, is humanistic and accidental, not religious; the pulpit does not lead the world. That is the meaning of Ishmael's voyage of discovery. Only a humane, broadly tolerant view and defiance give meaning to a life that seems a meaningless, unfriendly ocean.

Similarly, the longer epilogue in *Sophie's Choice*, which Stingo calls "A Study in the Conquest of Grief," reveals the meaning of Stingo's voyage of discovery. Stingo is sickened by the hypocrisy and witlessness of the Reverend DeWitt, who delivers the eulogy for Sophie and Nathan, both of whom he did not know, pompously declaring Sophie and Nathan "lost children. Victims of an age of rampant materialism. Loss of universal values. Failure of the old-fashioned principles of self-reliance." What a bitter irony to blame their deaths on the failure of self-reliance. Did not Sophie and Nathan suffer because of self-reliance gone mad, individualism turned into totalitarian madness, the blind will to power? Religious consolation is nothing more than hypocrisy, immaturity, and mendacity.

Stingo, therefore, will not let the Reverend have the last word. He reads the poetry of Emily Dickinson, the poet who brought Sophie and Nathan together, appropriate as well because Dickinson's poetry reveals her own profound religious doubts. Stingo knows how much classical music meant to Sophie and Nathan and was, therefore, appalled that "no one had bothered to consult about the music, and this was both an irony and a shame." The grandeur of Brahms was replaced by the peevishness and vulgarity of Gounod's "Ave Maria." Stingo knows that it is art, not religion, that affirms our existence, our dignity.

Stingo tells us that his very survival was in question after the deaths of Sophie and Nathan. It is at this extreme point of suicidal despair that Stingo comes to understand that no one can understand Auschwitz, that absolute evil will never be extinguished. The sharks and seahawks will always be there. If there is any hope, any bearable truth, it is in loving all living things. "Let your love flow out on all living things." Is this possible after Auschwitz? Did not Auschwitz alter the nature of love entirely? Is not love absurd in a world "which permitted the black edifice of Auschwitz to be built"? Stingo admits it is too early to answer that question, but he remembers "some fragile yet perdurable hope."

Stingo wants to lose himself after the funeral and goes back to Coney Island. Wanting to drown, he begins to cry instead. He now has the wisdom that is woe, the painful memories, the rage and sorrow for all the butchered children. Stingo falls into a disturbed sleep and dreams of drowning in a whirling vortex of mud, buried alive, almost drowned in a vortex like Ishmael. When Stingo awakens, however, he discovers he has been covered with sand, not suffocating mud, by children trying to protect him. Stingo has been spared annihilation because of the instinctive compassion of children, who find randomly, like the *Rachel* did, another orphan. Stingo blesses his resurrection, understanding that this was "not judgment day—only morning. Morning: excellent and fair." For a while at least, the sharks have padlocks on their mouths, and the savage seahawks sail with sheathed beaks. Again, the resurrection is not religious but humanistic; *Moby-Dick* and *Sophie's Choice* are essentially anti-Christian novels. If there is to be any resurrection, it will come from an affirmation of human dignity despite an awareness of the wisdom that is woe, a wisdom that Ishmael and Stingo initially try to avoid but later come to embrace.

It is interesting to note here that Stingo is reading *Billy Budd* at the beginning of his journey. It is at the end of his journey that he will be fully able to understand that novella about paternal and fraternal love gone astray, about the dangers of submission and obedience. Billy is falsely accused by fellow shipmate Claggart and condemned to hang by Captain Vere, whose rigid formalism overshadows his paternal feelings for Billy, the foundling. Both Melville and Styron dramatize the horrors of malicious or illegal authority and the subsequent need for and dignity of revolt, be it a revolt against a cruel cosmos as in *Moby-Dick* or human tyranny as in *Billy Budd* and *Sophie's Choice*.

This brings us to Styron's link to Camus, the twentieth-century writer whose work is closely associated with the need to affirm human dignity in the face of a meaningless universe, and Camus' link to Melville. Camus, like Styron, was influenced by Melville's mighty themes; he was more comfortable in his unbelief, however, than Melville. All three novelists can be called obstinate humanists, affirmative and moral in the face of a Machiavellian universe. Camus' favorite American novelist was Melville, and the only twentieth-century American writer he admired was Faulkner. Twentieth-century American literature for him was guilty of crude realism, a *littérature de l'élémentaire*. Camus felt that nineteenth-century grandeur, as exemplified by the works of Melville, was replaced by magazine writing in which the interior life was simply ignored, in which human beings were described but never explained. Twentieth-century American literature was documentation, not art, which he attributed to the commercialization of literature.

Camus was profoundly influenced, however, by *Moby-Dick*, which he called a truly absurd work. He read the novel in 1941 in the Gallimard edition shortly before he wrote his novel *The Plague*. From Melville he learned how symbol could be raised to the universal quality of myth. To dramatize the problem of evil, Camus chose a plague which was, like the whale, a symbol of evil. Camus, too, was intrigued by the character of Ishmael, the lonely, sea-loving wanderer. He wrote essays about Melville, his literary brother in pain, psychologically identifying with him. The interesting historical connection is that *The Plague* was written during the German occupation of France, and *Moby-Dick* was written when the Union was being torn apart by the slavery crisis. It is not surprising that both novelists would emphasize the need for human solidarity in their work. When Camus visited New York, he was most moved by the Bowery and not the skyscrapers. He was disturbed by the American attitude toward the black race, another link to Melville, and saw to it that Richard Wright was translated and published in Paris. Having been born Algerian, Camus was particularly sensitive to illegal and malicious authority, to feeling victimized because of race. And having been a part of the Resistance movement in German-occupied France, Camus was fully acquainted with evil and death, acquainted in a way most Americans are not.

Aware of the horrors of existence, Camus preached revolt, but not Byronic or Marxist revolt: that way lies nihilism and police terror. A person who refuses to lie, for Camus, is a person in revolt. Rebellion, then, implies tension, incompletion, and no absolutes. Most rebels, he claimed, choose the comfort of tyranny or servitude. While intelligence must always be in revolt against a hostile universe, tyranny which authorizes murder is unacceptable, and nihilism, which values nothing and flirts with the apocalypse, leads to suicide. Camus had contempt for the cowardice of submission. The answer to murder and suicide is a rebellion against suffering to promote healing. Human love must be thought an end in itself.

Camus criticized American authors who created characters with no memories and no understanding of the past and future, characters defined only by immediate sensations. Melville and Camus, however, were able to dramatize the tragedy of human existence while also providing limited but honest affirmations. Underneath a Melville or Camus is a rigorous idealism, but one which has been painfully extracted, not the "unearned unhappiness" Sophie bitterly rebukes in the Americans she meets in 1947.

It was unusual for a nineteenth-century American writer, for Melville, to understand that Americans cannot transcend or escape history, to rebuke America for its resistance to the painful process of growing up. Many American writers of the nineteenth century preferred their heroes to be liberated from family and social history, morally prior to the world, American Adams. *Moby-Dick* is actually a total blasting of the vision of innocence of the moral childishness of the hopeful. In Melville's works we see Adam gone mad with disillusion. This is all the more remarkable since the era of the 1840s was a time when hopefulness was all the fashion, like this century's 1940s. Melville deeply felt the agony of living in an America where empty-headed cheerfulness was a religion, and so he leaned on European tradition, on a tragic conception which understood that creativity itself is associated with a monstrous vision of evil, that artists get their strength from an acknowledgment of evil.

Similarly, *Sophie's Choice* is a total blasting of the vision of innocence which demonstrates the impossibility of escaping or transcending history. The novel is set shortly after World War II, a time of great hopefulness and prosperity. Americans were heroes, with America having emerged as the major superpower. At the beginning of the novel, Stingo has just returned from his stint in Okinawa. To many Americans, the Second World War was a war against the Japanese. What Stingo learns in that hopeful era of the 1940s is that while he was gorging on bananas in April of 1943, in an attempt to meet the minimum weight requirement for the U.S. Marines, Sophie and her two children were being carted to Auschwitz. America had been spared occupation, bombing, and invasion, but to be a European was to have experienced all three. Stingo must confront his, and, by extension, America's painful ignorance and childishness.

Stingo learns he is ignorant on many counts. He thought he would never hear another shot fired after World War II. He had never heard of Höss before he met Sophie. He thought Nathan's outbursts were a "shocking failure of character, a lapse of decency, rather than the product of some aberration of mind." Drug addicts were ax murderers to Stingo. He did not know enough to connect Nathan's dilated pupils with drug addiction, and madness to Stingo was "an unspeakable condition possessed by poor devils raving in remote padded cells." His ignorance and innocence was America's in the 1940s: "What Americans had been spared in our era. . . . How scant our count of fathers and sons compared to the terrible martyrdom of those unnumbered Europeans. Our glut of good fortune was enough to make us choke." Recently, the broadcaster Eric Sevareid said that news on television "has become part of the daily entertainment of a rather bored society. . . . If you had another great war or great depression, that would change matters, but that would be too high a price" ("Sevareid Assails TV News").

A tragic awareness must be forced if a civilization is to survive. In this, Styron most closely resembles Camus: both are twentieth-century writers who have accepted both the death of God and the meaninglessness and indifference of the universe while simultaneously affirming the values which the Nazis denied their victims. There may be no salvation, no eternal justice, but revolt can establish justice. While evil is mysterious, we must still resist its pull; the role of the artist is to look into the abyss, forcing a level of consciousness which has the potential for constructive action, not a nihilistic vision which denies action, denies the will. Camus and Styron paradoxically urge rebellion and moderation, eternal struggle, yet limits and incompletion. They are writers closer to the Greeks who knew that human beings are limited, closer to a Promethean vision of mankind's deliverance.

A speech Camus delivered in 1946 to students at Columbia University might very well serve as the philosophy that lies at the heart of *Sophie's Choice*, a viewpoint only a European living in occupied territory during World War II and active in the Resistance movement could have. It is this viewpoint that Stingo comes to share, prompted first by his association with Sophie and Nathan and later by experiencing the 1950s, 1960s, and 1970s—"wretched unending years of madness, illusion, error, dream, and strife." Camus said:

> We were born at the beginning of the First World War. As adolescents we had the crisis of 1929; at twenty, Hitler. Then came the Ethiopian War, the Civil War in Spain, and Munich. These were the foundations of our education. Next came the Second World War, the defeat, and Hitler in our homes and cities. Born and bred in such a world, what did we believe in? Nothing. Nothing except the obstinate negation in which we were forced to close ourselves from the very beginning. The world in which we were called to exist was an absurd world, and there was no other in which we could take refuge. The world of culture was beautiful, but it was not real. And when we found ourselves face to face with Hitler's terror, in what values could we take comfort, what values could we oppose to negation? In none. If the problem had been the bankruptcy of a political ideology, or a system of government, it would have been simple enough. But what had happened came from the very root of man and society. There was no doubt about this, and it was confirmed day after day not so much by the behavior of the criminals but by that of the average man. The facts show that men deserved what was happening to them. Their way of life had so little value; and the violence of the Hitlerian negation was in itself logical. But it was unbearable and we fought it.
>
> Now that Hitler has gone, we know a certain number of things. The first is that the poison which impregnated Hitlerism has not been eliminated; it is present in each of us. Whoever today speaks of human existence in terms of power, efficiency, and "historical tasks" spreads it. He is an actual or potential assassin. For if the problem of man is reduced to any kind of

"historical task," he is nothing but the raw material of history, and one can do anything one pleases with him. Another thing we have learned is that we cannot accept any optimistic conception of existence, any happy ending whatsoever. But if we believe that optimism is silly, we also know that pessimism about the action of man among his fellows is cowardly.

We oppose terror because it forces us to choose between murdering and being murdered; and it makes communication impossible. This is why we reject any ideology that claims control over all of human life.

It is curious that Camus was more admired here than in France for a time, having been criticized, especially by Sartre, for his anticommunist stand. Also, he rebuked France for its imperialism in his native Algeria, warning as early as 1939 what would happen if Algerian suffering continued to be ignored. Styron, who has been critical of the United States, has been criticized in America but has been terribly popular in France. Obviously, writers express thoughts their own readers hide from themselves. This certainly explains the popularity in France of Poe, Melville, and Faulkner as well. The best writers try to give body and voice to the tragic elements that society officially wishes to ignore.

Styron's career, in fact, resembles Camus' more than it does other American novelists. Styron is not only a novelist but a committed essayist, confronting the important political, social, and moral issues of his day. A collection of his moving nonfiction prose entitled *This Quiet Dust* was published in 1982 and closely resembles Camus' *Resistance, Rebellion, and Death*. Revealing Styron's engagement and commitment to public life, *This Quiet Dust* addresses such issues as the death penalty, slavery, pornography, and the Holocaust. His fiction and nonfiction, like that of Camus, demonstrate a sense of moral responsibility, a knowledge of the sinister forces in history and modern life which threaten all of us. Not typically American, Styron does wed politics and literature, public and private concerns. Like Camus' essays, *This Quiet Dust* could serve as an entryway to Styron's fiction. Ironically, however, *This Quiet Dust* was diminished by some critics. One reviewer asserted that Styron's powers are largely rhetorical, that his eloquence and passion do the work of thought. Melvin J. Friedman, contributor of many pieces on Styron and a book-length study of his fiction, however, said this about Styron's fate as an artist:

This least parochial of contemporary American writers appears fated to have each of his books underestimated and misunderstood at home and then warmly accepted abroad, especially in

France. *This Quiet Dust* will surely one day have a place next to Mann's *Essays of Three Decades*, Valéry's *History and Politics*, and Camus's *Resistance, Rebellion, and Death*—where it belongs.

What is important here is that *Sophie's Choice* owes more to European philosophy than to American thinking, a fact which enables Styron to dramatize and criticize the American myth of Adamic innocence. It should be obvious that calling *Sophie's Choice* "Southern Gothic fiction" or "Holocaust Gothic" is painfully off the mark. Styron certainly does not "avoid the contraries" in his fiction. At the heart of the stark visions of Styron and Camus is "an invincible sun," not the Hollywood kind, but the kind that asserts that the universe is full of evil, and whatever good exists, exists in people. Still, life is a trial, and suffering and death are certain. Revolt alone can establish justice: revolt against the servitude of hope.

Here Camus and Styron are most at odds with Emerson, particularly Emerson's concept of compensation. Essentially, Emerson asserted that nobody can harm one but oneself, that nothing can be given or taken without an equivalent. It would be instructive to quote his short poem "Compensation" in its entirety:

> Why should I keep holiday
>   When other men have none?
> Why but because, when these are gay,
>   I sit and mourn alone?
>
> And why, when mirth unseals all tongues,
>   Should mine alone be dumb?
> Ah! late I spoke to silent throngs,
>   And now their hour is come.

Emerson also believed one's fortune, one's fate, to be the fruit of one's character. "The event is the print of your form," he wrote. As such, an individual's fortunes can never be inappropriate, cruel, or undeserved; we are all equally compensated. There is no room, then, for innocent suffering. *Sophie's Choice* stands as a rebuke to such a Transcendental view, revealing the horrific inequities of fate and the overwhelming suffering it causes. Sophie's fate is certainly not just the fruit of her character, nor was the fate of the millions of Jews and non-Jews gassed in the crematoria under Hitler's reign. The speaker in "Compensation" asks why he should be happy if others are not. The response is that when others are happy, he will "sit and mourn alone." Stingo, however, realizes the absurdity and horror of his having gorged on bananas while others were being gassed in Auschwitz; the simultaneity of events staggers his imagination. Should Stingo rest easy because some day he might know some unhappiness to compensate for the millions gassed? There can be no Emersonian compensation. Melville knew that the black race did not deserve its fate in nineteenth-century America, and Styron knows, as does the older Stingo, that millions of innocent people were victimized by totalitarian madness, that the twentieth century has been a particularly barbaric one of overwhelmingly undeserved suffering.

It is not enough just to rebuke Transcendental thought, to abhor the American tendency towards mindless optimism. Styron, like Camus, offers an alternative. In "The Myth of Sisyphus," Camus addresses the most basic question: if life has no meaning, if nature is indifferent and God is dead, why live? Addressing the question of suicide, "The Myth of Sisyphus" ultimately asserts that the only way we can transcend our absurd existence is by protesting against it. Revolt, then, is the key to Camus' thinking, to his notion of happiness, the meaning of life, and artistic creation. Since there is no religious salvation, no afterlife, Camus urges us to love this life, to love struggle, to live a life in which happiness is based on sacrifice and personal responsibility. Stingo tells us he is an agnostic brave enough "to resist calling on any such questionable gaseous vertebrate as the Deity even in times of travail and suffering." We could say that Camus and Styron are pessimists about humanity's destiny but optimists where the individual is concerned.

Camus said that contemporary belief is not based on science as it was in the late nineteenth century, but rather that it denies both science and religion. It is not the skepticism of reason in the presence of a miracle but passionate unbelief. We must, Camus insists, think of Sisyphus as being happy as he struggles once more to push that rock up the hill. The temptation of nihilism will always be present. The attempt to fight nihilism, however, can be seen in all of Styron's fiction, and it reaches a most poignant intensity in *Sophie's Choice*, given the Holocaust as its subject matter. Styron urges us to resist the temptation of absolutes as answers to the pain of existence. The Resistance worker in *Sophie's Choice*, Wanda, says that whether the Resistance saved Jews or not, they tried, and that is satisfaction. Likewise, the defiance behind Ahab's spear-hurling gesture is more significant than the gesture's futility.

Camus was acutely aware of our potential lethal will to power. Melville intuited this danger, and *Sophie's Choice* dramatizes the consequences of those who rationalize or justify absolute power. The new revolt must be a rebellion against the will to power. Evil, for Camus and Styron, stems from diffused guilt and the fatal mistake of the will to power. We must accept our orphaned state with its inevitable suffering and defeat and occasional triumphs. Hiding from this reality will result in either self-destructive or aggressive behavior, a need to dominate others. Melville says in *White-Jacket* that murder and suicide are the last resources of an insulted and unendurable existence. The resistance shown to the works of Melville and Styron in the United States reveals how uncharacteristically American is this view.

Styron has said that all of his fiction concentrates on victims of one sort or another and on the possibility for beauty in this absurd existence. *Sophie's Choice* confronts the victims of the Holocaust and offers the possibility of beauty and love after Auschwitz, a heroic stand. Most despair, including current cynicism, is fed on ugliness and violence. Camus and Styron insist that we must not exile beauty and love. Camus said, "There is beauty and there are the humiliated. Whatever may be the difficulties of the undertaking, I should like never to be unfaithful either to one or to the other." If we compare this to what Styron says about the role of the novel we can see just how closely allied he is with Camus:

> In this fantastic world the claims on our emotions and our intellect are so urgent, so persistent and clamorous, that it is no longer either sufficient or rewarding to curl up with yet another cleverly written, well-crafted novel which describes, say, the beginning and the end of a love affair. During the novel's serene heyday the changes and varieties on this theme—and a score of other themes— might readily engross the reader's attention, but in our day they no longer suffice; we've been there too many times before.
>
> Sartre was wrong. For me, if literature cannot change the world in a radical way, it can, all the same, penetrate deeply into human consciousness. Millions of people can read, and I believe that a book can work on their consciences. As a writer I have no other goal.

Writers must continue their search for significant themes, but characters must not be allowed to succumb to theme. Melville, Camus, and Styron have sometimes allowed characters to succumb to theme, but *Sophie's Choice* is Styron's most satisfying novel in the sense that character, theme, and action are ideally blended to produce a great work of art which readers can regard with awe and have something in their lives that did not exist before. *Sophie's Choice* is that rarest of fictions: a novel which explores our national character that is not journalistic, ideological, or parochial.

Styron and Camus know that a period "which, in a space of fifty years, uproots, enslaves, or kills seventy million human beings should be condemned out of hand"; however, they both argue that this period and its culpability must be understood, that a belief in nothing justifies everything. As Camus says, "we would be free to stoke the crematory fires or to devote ourselves to the care of lepers." Evil and virtue must never be considered mere chance or caprice. *Sophie's Choice* is an act of metaphysical rebellion protesting the human condition "both for its incompleteness, thanks to death, and its wastefulness, thanks to evil." Camus feels the real passion of the twentieth century is servitude, a negation of everything, a rush towards an impossible innocence. In this sense, Camus can condemn Hitler's Germany and Stalin's Soviet Union, any utopian messianism, and, of course, America's own brand of innocence which, rather than seeing history as supreme, ignores its importance altogether. Rebellion is the refusal to be treated like an object, the refusal to be reduced to simple historical terms. When we put limits on history, we are giving birth to values. Camus states that "instead of killing and dying in order to produce the being that we are not, we have to live and let live in order to create what we are." The novel, then, must be the literature of rebellion, not the literature of consent.

We can see the quest for unity, for affirming interior reality, in the novels of Melville, Camus, and Styron. If "art is an impossible demand given expression and form, there is no genius in negation and pure despair." Art teaches us that human beings cannot be explained solely by history, and *Sophie's Choice* is proof that we will never understand Auschwitz just by reading historical accounts of this tragedy, that horror can be apprehended only obliquely, through artistic distance. Artistic rebellion will always exist because falsehood, injustice, and violence will always exist. Stingo is finally able to conclude at the end of his journey that absolute evil is never extinguished from the world. The older Stingo knows that we continue to pay for slavery, for the sale of human beings, that the black edifice of Auschwitz will always haunt mankind. Since there will always be suffering, there will be outrage at that suffering; art and rebellion will die only with the last human being.

Sophie's Choice demonstrates artistically that none of the evils that totalitarianism claims to remedy is worse than totalitarianism itself. Totalitarianism is based on faith in a perfect future (a rush towards innocence) and murder. Melville, Camus, and Styron are artists who have eased the various forms of bondage weighing upon us, overcoming the temptation of hatred. Ishmael and Stingo, maddened by their anti-Christian perceptions, must overcome their potential for suicide. In 1957, Camus said the wager of his generation was to accept everything: "If we are to fail, it is better, in any case, to have stood on the side of those who choose life than on the side of those who are destroying." The loftiest work will always be that which maintains an equilibrium between reality and the artist's rejection of that reality. If, as Camus asserts, an artist's only justification is to speak up for those who cannot do so, Styron is amply justified with his *Sophie's Choice*, a novel which speaks up for "but a few of the beaten and butchered and betrayed and martyred children of the earth." The emancipatory force of art, then, threatens tyrants of the Left and the Right.

Melville, Camus, and Styron have written mighty works because they have been drawn to mighty themes, particularly the themes of absurdity, evil, slavery, revolt, and love. All three have looked into the abyss and forced their narrators to come up cold against the inferno while maintaining an affirmative vision of the "common continent of men." All three novelists assert that although we cannot comprehend the mysteries of existence and iniquity, we can resist iniquity's tug.

It would be instructive here to discuss briefly Conrad's disturbing turn-of-the-century novella, *Heart of Darkness*, which has interesting parallels with *Moby-Dick* and *Sophie's Choice*. Conrad was an early favorite of Styron, who at thirteen wrote an imitation Conrad short story entitled "Typhoon and the Tor Bay," and whose unfinished novel, *The Way of the Warrior*, abandoned when Styron felt compelled to write *Sophie's Choice* instead, has been compared to *Lord Jim*. Conrad, Styron told this writer, has saturated his thought and has been a helpful influence on his work. Whereas *Moby-Dick* is a revolt against a cruel cosmos, *Heart of Darkness* and *Sophie's Choice* are more concerned with the varieties of human evil, acknowledging the "heart of an immense darkness." *Moby-Dick*, *Heart of Darkness*, and *Sophie's Choice* are symbolic journeys into our darker regions, written as reminiscences so the cool light of intelligence can play over them.

Besides similarities in theme and narrative strategies, there are fascinating connections among the characters in these three works. Kurtz, a man relieved of all social and civilized restraints, touches bottom after committing himself to the total pursuit of evil and depravity. He is a Promethean protagonist, grandly demonic, a man whose grandiose, idealistic mission degenerates into barbarism and domination. Ahab and Nathan are also grandly demonic figures whose observations tear them apart. Marlow is in the middle; he is shaken by peering into the abyss but does not go mad like Kurtz. He is also philosophical like Ahab, but he does not let his observations tear him apart, although he comes perilously close to the edge by his own admission, drawing back his foot from the precipice of madness. Marlow's confrontation with an individual's capacity for evil leaves him sober, disturbed, meditative, and obsessed with relating his story. Similarly, Stingo and Ishmael, the lone survivors of their tales, are left shaken after their confrontation with demonism but come to accept our potential for evil and good. Ishmael, Marlow, and Stingo, while irrevocably changed because of their journeys, leaving them little to cheer about, emerge nevertheless affirming human dignity. Though these narrators escape, they learn wisdom at a price—the wisdom that is woe. Their rejection of fantacism, their wisdom, makes these narrators seem pale and anonymous in comparison with the charismatic figures of Ahab, Kurtz, and Nathan. *Moby-Dick*, *Heart of Darkness*, and *Sophie's Choice*, then, explore our capacity for evil as well as our ability to resist it, the necessity for restraint (to "gobern de shark"), and the need to conquer grief.

Despite the tragic nature of our existence, Melville, Camus, and Styron doggedly assert the dignity of humanity against the inexorable flux of history. If life copies art, it is possible these humanistic values will be emulated—the only antidote to the murders and suicides that flood the fictions of these novelists and our daily newspapers. The only way for us to become more human is for artists to create audacious works of fiction which make the human face richer and more admirable, lest we all drown in the vortex of atomic fallout.

We must remember that *Sophie's Choice* was written from 1974 to 1979, a time of moral bankruptcy—the post-Vietnam, post-Watergate era. It is, therefore, a weary voice we hear in the older Stingo who tells a story about the 1940s but reflects the madness of the whole post-Holocaust era as well. If we read Styron's collection of essays, *This Quiet Dust*, we can glimpse Styron's concerns in the 1970s when he was writing *Sophie's Choice*. The Vietnam War's degeneracy was represented, for Styron, by Lieutenant Calley, whom he compares to Eichmann—two banal, witless nobodies claiming to be cogs in great machines. Styron writes that Calley had a choice, especially since other officers refused to follow Captain Ernest Medina's orders to kill everything in My Lai. Calley had no remorse. Evil is shown as a kind of diffused guilt, but even in war there must be codes, especially since for many men war is still the ultimate adventure, a means of escaping an ordinary existence. *Sophie's Choice* dramatizes the poet Marianne Moore's feelings, "There never was a war that wasn't inward." War is the madness in humanity. Styron has dedicated himself to writing about this catastrophic propensity of human beings to dominate and destroy each other, becoming an analyst of evil, claiming that Auschwitz is embedded in our cultural traditions, a sleeping virus which did not end with the destruction of the crematoria in 1945. We can never rest easy because totalitarianism is a constant threat to the human family. To attempt to come to terms with Auschwitz, we must consider Jew and non-Jew, victim and victimizer. Shortly before the publication of *Sophie's Choice*, Styron said: "We shall perhaps never even begin to understand the Holocaust until we are able to discern the shadows of the enormity looming beyond the enormity we already know."

Styron says that he is amazed that he is as political as he is since he began as a writer who was ivory-tower oriented. Over the years, he says, "I have almost unconsciously let my work be connected with politics, with politics insofar as they govern history and human affairs." It was being recalled into active duty during the Korean War that wrenched him out of his rarefied world, that taught him how the authoritarian mind works. Styron dissects not only military authority but any form of human domination. Styron claims that his fiction does not have a strong sense of place (except for *Lie Down in Darkness*), that this lack of a milieu forced him to cast around for themes. As demonstrated, he, like Melville, goes after big fish. He attributes his attraction to big themes to his conviction that history is a "marvelous and clear mirror of human behavior." His work harks back to the nineteenth century, when story and character were preeminent. It is no wonder, then, that he criticizes postmodernists who are obsessed with language and technique almost to the exclusion of story and character, traditionally considered the heart and soul of literature. Styron contends that "great literature, great in the sense that it endures, is the art of creating characters whom people do not want to consign to oblivion."

There have been eminent American literary critics who have asserted that America and its fictional characters have escaped history, critics like R. W. B. Lewis in *The American Adam*, Richard Chase in *The American Novel and Its Traditions*, and Richard Poirier in *A World Elsewhere*. Actually, however, our literary texts do present a response to history and social reality. In the mid-nineteenth century, American authors had to come to terms with a rising capitalist society and its resulting alienation. Melville and Styron, in particular, dramatize that alienation is the dominant social condition in modern history. Some American authors and fictional characters, however, have not been able to reconcile themselves to being alienated. Certainly we see this in Melville, Faulkner, and Styron, writers who insist that the novel be a powerful ideological form positioning itself against alienation, loneliness, and industrialization, against all the dehumanizing symptoms of modern life. These writers know that novelists are speakers, not just alienated spectators, that a writer cannot hide behind subjectivist idealism or objectivist materialism.

Sophie's story, therefore, reveals the inadequacies of Emerson's projection of self-reliance, exposing the consequences of Emerson's denial of the flesh, the family, and the social relatedness of every individual in the human community. The rope which binds all of us permits no mastership, only mutual dependence. Ahab and Nathan, although grand and sympathetic defiers, ultimately, because of their deep wounds, deny the human family, and, of course, the Holocaust represents the total breakdown of any notion of the human family. It is important, then, that Ishmael and Stingo are not merely spectators but observing participants in the action, albeit Stingo much more so than Ishmael, whose role is more that of an ironic expositor. Modern novelists and their fictional alter egos must be active participants, not merely alienated spectators who refuse to see their own implications in social history. Melville, Camus, and Styron, then, share an important similarity in the way they view the role of the artist in modern society: they take their characters seriously, endowing them with tragic freedom, allowing them to work on their fates under narrow limits, forcing them to confront the full tragic condition of life. There may be no religious redemption, but fiction can compensate humanity for the inadequacy of the religious vision.

How much more alienated can an individual be than Styron's portrait of the Commandant of Auschwitz, Rudolph Höss, who is unable to feel remorse or have any sympathy for his victims? Evil is shown as the inability to feel guilt for one's actions. Any Nazis who were a bit squeamish drank to ease their discomfort or blamed the Jews for making them feel uncomfortable. In contrast, Styron provides us with a portrait of Jozef, the young Resistance worker, who vomited and nearly went insane when he had to kill an informer. This also helps to explain Styron's characterization of Dr. Jemand von Niemand, the doctor from nowhere, who, by forcing Sophie to choose which child would live and which would die, wants to experience guilt to become human again. Since the Nazis had no identification with their victims, they focused not on what horrible things they did to people but on what horrible things they had to watch in pursuance of their duties.

Sophie's Choice suggests that unless we can put ourselves in the victim's shoes, we are doomed to commit evil acts. Stingo's father understands this very well. He makes the young Stingo stay in a freezing shed to show him what it was like for his mother to be left with inadequate coal heating; Stingo's punishment fits the crime exactly. One of Styron's unique contributions in *Sophie's Choice*, then, is the double vision of the victim and victimizer. *Sophie's Choice* forces us to confront the fact that victims can also become victimizers. Nathan is part Jewish victim, part Rudolph Höss. The fact that Sophie can have moments of virulent anti-Semitism is an index of the degree of horror which the camps and crematoria represent. This victim/victimizer syndrome is thus not limited to the sane or insane, not in a world that has seen the Final Solution. Stingo comes to understand this duality, this tragic compulsion, through Sophie and Nathan, and his understanding enables him to write his first novel, *Inheritance of Night*, about the South's duality. Styron, as critic Frederick Stern says,

> lets the horror be seen not from the center of the charnel house
> but from those who can share the motivations of the perpetrators

of evil, even though they are also its victims. . . . Styron's choice is to try to understand the Holocaust, its perpetrators, and its awesome dead millions, by pointing out that victims can be victimizers and victimizers victims, in a complex interaction which is human and which we must understand if we are to have any hope of avoiding another such horror. What writer can be better equipped to undertake this task than a southerner who has left the South behind?

Stingo is able to identify with the victim; an American can feel European, can feel his own hollowness. When sweeping Sophie away from the crazed Nathan to a supposed southern love nest, Stingo says this about Washington, D. C.: "Washington suddenly appeared paradigmatically American, sterile, geometrical, unreal. I had identified so completely with Sophie that I felt Polish, with Europe's putrid blood rushing through my arteries and veins. Auschwitz still stalked my soul as well as hers. Was there no end to this? No end?" To complement this feeling, Stingo notices the "hollow, Protestant ring" of church bells outside their Washington hotel.

The consequences of not being able to identify with victims are dramatized in profound ways in the novel, the most obvious of which is the Holocaust itself. There are also subtler evils evidenced by this lack of identification, scapegoating in general being one of them. Styron demonstrates how easy it is to blame others for one's misfortunes. While Hitler certainly did this on a large scale, Stingo and Sophie do this on a smaller scale. When Stingo's apartment is robbed, leaving him virtually penniless, he puts the blame on Morris Fink, a Jewish scapegoat for Stingo's misfortune. It is important, therefore, that it is Jewish Nathan who impulsively and generously gives Stingo two-hundred dollars to be repaid only if Stingo becomes a famous author. In weak moments, particularly after a violent fight with Nathan, Sophie blames the Jews for all her troubles. On a larger scale, Stingo concludes that Poland and the American South are similar in that their pride and their recollections of past glories are bulwarks against the humiliation of defeat. Poland blamed the Jews, and the South blamed the blacks for their troubles.

Related to the scapegoating tendency is stereotyping people or places to avoid thought. Nathan assumes Stingo is a cracker because he is from the South. Later, Nathan realizes: "How can I really have hated a place I have never seen or known?" An identification with the entire human community would prevent stereotyping and scapegoating, would have prevented the black edifice of Auschwitz.

Styron insists that it is we who are cruel, not Fortune. We commit evil when we try to control Fortune. This "fortune-forcing" is what critic John

Kenny Crane focuses on in his book entitled *The Root of All Evil: The Thematic Unity of William Styron's Fiction*, published in 1984. Crane contends that the solitary pursuit of Fortune has repressed our natural instincts of empathy and identification. The remedy is the ability to turn away from the "lonely quest of Fortune's rewards" towards a fellowship with our fellow human beings, against the atrocities Fortune offers. It is not enough to know simply that evil and misery are going on while we are happy; we must experience the evil in order to squeeze evil into our hearts and souls—clearly the opposite of Emersonian compensation. The older Stingo is aware of this: "What had old Stingo been up to while Jozef and Sophie and Wanda had been writhing in Warsaw's unspeakable Gehenna? Listening to Glenn Miller, swilling beer, horsing around in bars, whacking off! God, what an iniquitous world."

Styron insists on Manichean dualism, demonstrating that human evil begins with the misuse of the less fortunate by Fortune's darlings. The young Stingo is one of Fortune's darlings, a potential misuser of the less fortunate; by extension, America is seen as Fortune's darling, a potential abuser. What saves Stingo from being an abuser, besides his ability to empathize with the sorrows of others, is having a father whose strong, coherent, moral sense provides a model Stingo can emulate. Stingo's father urges Stingo to cling to a stable moral center, to retain his humanity. But most of the fathers in Styron's fiction play God, and, attempting to force Fortune, are locked into self-destructive behavior. Stingo knows he is fortunate to have a father whom he can respect if not always agree with. Stingo's father demonstrates that it is possible to maintain a decent, loving sympathy in a selfish age. Nathan's brother, Larry, is another decent, loving individual, as are the young Resistance fighters, Wanda and Jozef. That they are all minor characters is the bitter point.

While some evils are curable, we are not meant to think that Stingo's vision of potential human goodness at the end of *Sophie's Choice* is absolute. The post-Holocaust years, the 1940s through the 1970s, according to the older Stingo, were "wretched unending years of madness, illusion, error, dreams, and strife." Stingo, however, looks forward with information that Nathan and Sophie lacked when they made their critical mistakes and choices. Stingo, the lone survivor, may be less grand than Nathan, but like Ishmael he is courageous in his pro-life choice, given what he has learned during his voyage of discovery.

The good person, then, is the one who finds goodness within and develops it towards others. Ahab, Sophie's father, and Rudolph Höss cannot do this, with obvious catastrophic results. Wanda and Jozef, however, the two young Resistance fighters, are able to find this goodness, this ability to identify with those suffering. Sophie thinks that while the Nazis are rounding up Jews she and her children will be safe. Wanda knows that no one is safe or free when human beings tyrannize the less fortunate, which meant in Europe in the 1940s not only Jews but Poles, Slavs, Gypsies, homosexuals, and the mentally and physically handicapped—all enemies of the Third Reich. Wanda, a non-Jew, forces Sophie to look at pictures of the bodies of all the innocent children gassed, to see that the concentration camps were not just labor camps but extermination camps. The final irony is that the daughter and two grandchildren of one of the masterminds of the Final Solution, Sophie's father, experience firsthand the charnel house designed for Jews. Her father, Biegański, "failed to foresee how such sublime hatred could only gather into its destroying core, like metal splinters sucked toward some almighty magnet, countless thousands of victims who did not wear the yellow badge." When we contrast Stingo's father with Sophie's we can see that the "progenitors of each new generation" must be held accountable for "the continued evolution of human evil." Most young people who populate Styron's fictions have no decent parental figure to suggest a better direction than crass materialism, ugliness, and immorality. Sophie knows instinctively that all of her problems began with her father. What did the fathers of the SS officers teach them? Many officers admitted to being battered children. It is not surprising, then, that some would become butchers.

Why *Sophie's Choice* is so artistically successful, for Crane, is that it is Styron's most full-fledged plot in the narrative present with a more developed transcendent present since the narrator has researched his topic and shares his opinions on the findings and meaning of his 1947 experiences. The major flashbacks are actually a search for instructive memories. Because the novel is told as a reminiscence, the narrator must be able to shift time frames easily. Crane contends that Styron was able to make the narrative present as dramatic as the major flashbacks, so the past is given an active meaning in the present, enabling the narrator and the reader to redirect it. This narrative strategy reveals an ability to view the world from many perspectives, a view that is liberating. Consequently, Styron merges theme and action into a satisfying, unified whole.

Styron urges that we see ourselves as part of a life force—a force which compels us toward good, toward the preservation of the species, toward the "birthright . . . to try to free people into the condition of love." Self-destruction, the wish for death, is the primary moral sin. The single good is the respect for the force of life. If evil is anything which is antilife, then, Styron makes it clear that the Holocaust was not just anti-Semitic but antilife; therefore, German and other historical revisionists who claim that the Holocaust never existed are evil because they, too, are antilife. That the Holocaust occurred at all is horrific beyond literal description; that some historians and others continue to try to rewrite history to obliterate the existence of the Holocaust is fortune-forcing of such frightening proportions that we are all at risk.

Both Melville and Styron demonstrate the dangers of mythmaking, the dangers of not being able to see things as they really are. For different reasons, Nathan and Sophie lie, rewriting their painful pasts. We are reminded, too, of *Billy Budd*, the novella which Stingo was reading at the beginning of his journey, particularly the penultimate chapter which provides a British newspaper account of what happened on board the *Bellipotent*, a clear attempt to rewrite history; the newspaper report contends that Billy was not an Englishman but some alien adopting an English cognomen who stabbed Claggart, the master-at-arms, to the heart. The evil revealed in this revisionist account is chilling.

Sophie's Choice is a novel which expresses outrage at the violence of authority and the submission of those who subscribe to it, as well as the pressure that its victims exert on the next generation to repeat the same mistakes. To revolt, as Camus said, is to refuse to lie, to refuse to be passive about suffering and evil; to revolt is to be fully engaged in history, in social reality. It is the liars who try to transcend, escape, or rewrite history.

We should be grateful, then, to our truthseekers—those artists who dive down into the blackest gorges and, like Melville's Catskill eagle, rise renewed from the ashes to soar higher than those who do not dive deeply. Styron agrees with Hardy that if a "way to the Better there be, it exacts a full look at the worst." This is what the early naturalistic novelists of the late nineteenth and early twentieth centuries did—delve deeply into the sordid in the hopes of finding remedies. Naturalism, then, had an idealistic, reformist strain which is all but dead today; Styron's dark picture of human waste is in effect, therefore, a beacon for progress. Grief has been conquered; so we are left not with bitterness but with an insistence that we assume freedom and responsibility as basic conditions of life, accept defeat and suffering—the full tragic conditions of life. Still we must try to create a purpose to offset the empty malice of a Moby Dick or the black edifice of Auschwitz. Otherwise, life would be neither bearable nor significant.

In his inaugural address, delivered in January 1989, President Bush discussed the final legacy of the Vietnam War, declaring, "No great nation can afford to be sundered by a memory." In effect, Bush urged national amnesia to encourage optimism and unity, rejecting the wisdom that is woe, thereby denying the possibility of awareness, repair, action, and personal meaning. Is this so very different from the German revisionist historians who claim that the Holocaust never happened, or from the Chinese government's attempt to deny its massacre of students in Tiananmen Square, claiming, while resodding the Square, that it merely "calmed" a "counterrevolutionary disturbance"? Bush's declaration is potentially as dangerous as Morris Fink's 1947 question, "What's Oswitch?" Clearly, there is still a need for Emersonian optimism in the America of the 1980s which betrays an unawareness of evil and ignorance of history similar to the America Melville confronted in the 1840s when he began his own exploration into our heart of darkness.

Sophie's Choice reminds us, however, that absolute evil will remain forever mysterious and inextinguishable and that Americans are not exempt from evil's lure; that is the meaning of Stingo's spiritual voyage. While it is obviously too late for Nathan and Sophie, Styron dramatizes through Stingo that the only way to confront Nazi inhumanity in retrospect is to show that it failed to dehumanize the judgment of its survivors.

FREDERIK N. SMITH

Bach vs *Brooklyn's Clamorous Yawp:*
Sound in Sophie's Choice

Ever since Robinson Crusoe reported his observations of distant shores,
the novel in English has been primarily, although not solely, a visual genre.
Poetry may have welcomed other types of sensory imagery, but the novel,
anxious to create for its reader a palpable world, has relied consistently on
the visual in constructing that world. Of course there are exceptions. Karl
Zender, in a recent article on "Faulkner and the Power of Sound," has
demonstrated the increasing frequency with which at least one novelist uses
images of sound. Without broaching the question of whether Styron might
have been influenced here by *"Weel-yam* Faulkner" (as Sophie calls him), I
want to stress the importance of sound in *Sophie's Choice*, which depends
heavily on the aural both in calling up a world outside the novel and in
bearing much of the weight of its meaning. Although his previous fiction
likewise makes much use of sound, Styron developed for his most recent
book an exceptionally subtle contest between music and noise.

When I first read *Sophie's Choice*, I became increasingly aware of the
significance of sound in the novel and its relationship to the meaning Styron
seemingly wanted to convey. Not that sound is obvious near the beginning. On
the contrary, in the first pages of the novel there is little or no use of aural
imagery, and if anything what prevails is a kind of austere silence. ⟨D⟩escribing
his senior editor at McGraw-Hill, Stingo says that he "had long before fallen

From *Papers on Language and Literature* 23, no. 4. © 1987 by the Board of Trustees Southern Illinois University.

victim to the ambitionless, dronelike quietude into which, as if some mammoth beehive, the company eventually numbed its employees, even the ambitious ones." Stingo himself escapes this numbing quietude when he is fired for blowing bubbles into the "wild breezes [that] whooshed around the McGraw-Hill parapets." Like those childish bubbles, Stingo runs headlong into the loud, chaotic reality of Manhattan. From this point on, he becomes a different sort of narrator, not one who reports what he *sees*, like Crusoe, but one who reports what he hears. Stingo refers at one point to his "inexhaustible ear" and elsewhere laments for "Stingo, the hapless eavesdropper." While these self-deprecations may be typically hyperbolic, they underscore the nature of this particular narrator's role in his novel.

Stingo soon finds himself in Yetta Zimmerman's Pink Palace, attempting to write a novel amid the noise of Brooklyn. Looking out his window, he describes what he sees, and it is interesting how the conventional visual image gives way to the aural:

> Old sycamore trees and maples shaded the sidewalks at the edge of the park, and the dappled sunlight aglow on the gently sloping meadow of the Parade Grounds gave the setting a serene, almost pastoral quality. It presented a striking contrast to remoter parts of the neighborhood. Only short blocks away traffic flowed turbulently on Flatbush Avenue, a place intensely urban, cacophonous, cluttered, swarming with jangled souls and nerves.

Much to Stingo's chagrin, however, this cacophony all too soon enters the Pink Palace as he is distracted by the noise of Sophie and Nathan's sexual jamboree immediately overhead: through the flimsy ceiling he hears voices, groans, shrill advice, huzzahs, the sound of splashing water, Beethoven's Fourth Symphony, and then angry feet and shouting. Much of the sound imagery in the novel does precisely this sort of thing, documenting the all-too-real worlds of Brooklyn and Auschwitz:

> Nathan had turned and pounded down the steps to the sidewalk, where his hard leather heels made a demonic *clack-clack-clack* as the sound receded, then faded out beneath the darkening trees, in the direction of the subway.

> She finished the letter without a mistake, appending an exclamation point to the salute to the Fuhrer with such vigorous precision that it brought forth from the machine a faintly echoing tintinnabulation.

He loitered for a moment at the edge of the park, watching the playing fields of the Parade Grounds where the young men and boys kicked and passed footballs and tackled each other, and flung happy obscenities in the familiar flat clamorous yawp of Brooklyn.

Styron's descriptions of the tones and rhythms of his characters' voices are similar but more original. Although the English language is far more fully equipped to deal with sights than sounds (or tastes, for that matter), this author has throughout his novel supplied us with an awareness of voice we ordinarily experience only in the theater.

On and on the voice went, a gentle monologue, lulling, soothing, murmurously infusing her with a sense of repose.

Startled, I recognized that Nathan's gifted voice was in perfect mockery of my own—pedantic, pompous, insufferable.

Höss's delivery tended to run in quick spurts separated by nearly interminable pauses—pauses in which there was almost audible a thudding tread of thought.

But the whiskey transformed her speech into a spillway notable for its precise, unhurried cadences.

His voice seems to be an amorous melodic murmur, cajoling, politely but outrageously flirtatious, irresistible and (to her utter distress now) wickedly exciting.

Perhaps more interesting to the idea being explored here is the frequency with which musical metaphors are used to describe someone's voice. These metaphors go well beyond the clichés of our language, such as "Sophie chimed in," or "I sensed a note of pleading in my voice," Styron speaks of tones of voices as "falsetto," "fortissimo," "mezza voce," "loutish vibrato," "sotto voce," and refers to certain talk as like an "aria." Moreover, on occasion these descriptions get extremely delicate, as Styron utilizes music to help him catch the tone and rhythm of speech. "There was something plaintive, childlike in her voice, which was light in timbre, almost fragile, breaking a little in the upper register and of a faint huskiness lower down." This reads like an excerpt from an opera review.

The chief struggle of Styron's novel is neither between Sophie and Nathan nor between Stingo and Sophie, but within Sophie herself. By focusing on Sophie, however, Styron hopes to come to terms with his broader topic; he believes, he says at one point, that it is worth "making a stab at understanding Auschwitz by trying to understand Sophie, who to say the least was a cluster of contradictions." These contradictions he describes in large measure through the clash of music and noise, which weave through the novel, sometimes appearing alone, sometimes set against one another, but almost always serving as objective correlatives, as audible opposites struggling for dominance within Sophie.

Sophie's first encounter with the Nazis was through her father; from her mother she inherited her passion for music. Sophie and Wanda (who had gone to Warsaw to study at the Conservatory) had been drawn together by "their mutual bewitchment with music." And to Sophie and Nathan, as to Stingo himself, "music was more than simple meat and drink, it was an essential opiate and something resembling the divine breath." Indeed the three principals of the story are pulled fatefully together as a result of their intense love of music, which cuts across their wide ethnic differences. Bach, Beethoven, Mozart, Purcell, Haydn, Handel, Scarlatti, Chopin, Mahler, and Brahms are all mentioned in *Sophie's Choice*, sometimes by allusion to specific compositions. And classical music, by virtue of the frequency of its appearance and also the way it is described in the novel, begins to assume special importance. When Nathan and Sophie quarrel, Nathan wants his records back; he knows how to get to Sophie, for music touches her more than anything else can, apparently because she was for so long deprived of it. "Providentially, though, it was music that helped save her, as it had in the past," says Stingo, and he goes on to describe Sophie, ill and alone in New York City, one day habitually turning on her radio and hearing Mozart's *Sinfonia Concertante* in E-flat major. The music is "mysteriously therapeutic" and causes her "to shiver all over with uncomplicated delight":

> Suddenly she knew why this was so. . . . Sitting in the concert hall [in Cracow], she had listened to the fresh new work as in a trance, and let the casements and doors of her mind swing wide to admit the luxuriant, enlaced and fretted harmonies, and those wild dissonances, inexhaustibly inspired. . . . Yet she never heard the piece again, for like everything else, the *Sinfonia Concertante* and Mozart, and the plaintive sweet dialogue between violin and viola, and the flutes, the strings, the dark-throated horns were all blown away on the war's wind in a Poland so barren, so smothered with evil and destruction that the very notion of music was a ludicrous excrescence.

In war-torn Poland, music is shouted down by noise; "So in those years of cacophony" begins the next paragraph.

Whatever it is to Nathan and Stingo, music, like sex and alcohol, becomes for Sophie an escape from the torments of the present: "Music for Sophie," John Lang has argued, "attests both to transcendent beauty and to an order and harmony recoverable within time." Moreover, music in *Sophie's Choice* assumes meaning beyond Sophie herself; its persistence through the novel—in Cracow before the war, in Auchswitz, on Sophie's small Zenith radio in Brooklyn—suggests the human will to survive, like Brahms's *Alto Rhapsody*, Marian Anderson exulting over "triumph wrested from eons of despair," like the sound of a Chopin polonaise, suggesting "the closest thing to a restoration of life," or like Bach's Cantata 147, *Jesu, Joy of Man's Desiring*. Connected to the past, having itself survived, classical music in Styron's novel suggests the strength of memory, human continuance, and our ability to construct order out of seemingly unconquerable chaos.

The music of the masters is opposed to the ersatz music of the welcoming band at Auschwitz, "hopelessly off-key and disorganized," the tiresome Tyrolean polka on the Commandant's phonograph, "a cackling barnyard of voices," and the Muzak Stingo hears on the train. It is likewise opposed to the sheer noise of Auschwitz and Brooklyn. Sophie's threadbare life in Auschwitz is punctuated not only by the relentless polka, but also by the clack of her own typewriter, the thudding of boots, the jangle of telephones, the shrieking of the camp whistle, and the rumble of boxcars. And these noises pursue Sophie after the war. Hurtling through Connecticut with Nathan, drugged, at the wheel, Sophie hears a siren, sees a flashing light, tries to talk but can't—"It is like the sound track of a movie pieced together by a chimpanzee," she thinks to herself, "in parts coherent but creating no design, making no final sense." During his father's visit to Brooklyn, Stingo, half asleep and dreaming of Virginia, is tormented by a police siren. His reaction is much the same as Sophie's:

> It grew louder, uglier, demented. I listened to it with the faint anxiety which that shrill alarm always provoked; the sound faded away, a dim demonic warble, at last disappeared up into the warrens of Hell's Kitchen. My God, my God, I thought, how could it be possible that the South and that urban shriek coexisted in this century? It was beyond comprehension.

Elsewhere Stingo complains when the tentative mood of trust he has nurtured in Sophie is shattered by a pandemonium of sirens: "City sirens even at a distance generate a hateful noise, almost always set loose in a soul-damaging, unnecessary frenzy." Whereas classical music in the novel is representative of hope and positive memories, the city siren, reminiscent of the camp whistle, suggests the discord of so-called civilization, chaos rather than order, the aggressive isolation of man from man. In either case, however, sound has the awful power of healing or destroying one's innermost, fragile identity.

Once Styron has gotten his reader to pay attention to sound in the book, as well as to sense the positive and negative associations with music and noise, he can begin to orchestrate these sounds in ways which can only be called symphonic. "Sophie's typewriter went clickety-clack in the stillness of the attic while Höss brooded over his cesspool diagrams and the flies droned and twitched, and the movement of distant boxcars kept up a blurred incessant rumble like summer thunder." In the seven pages prior to this sentence, each of these sounds has been introduced, in isolation; here they are simply combined, and the effect is powerful. Sophie's typewriter and the flies seem in this context to be almost ironic intrusions (like Dickinson's "I Heard a Fly Buzz When I Died"), but not so much on Höss's convenient silence as on the awful machinery of death operating in the distance. The sound of summer thunder only intensifies the impact of this well-wrought sentence which effectively combines close-up noise, distant noise (there is a kind of audial three-dimensionality in this and other passages), and metaphorical noise.

Later in the novel, however, sound is used in an even more complex way, as multiple noises are intertwined. A good example is the following slapstick paragraph:

> I had not meant to be cruel, but my words caused Sophie to drop a silk slip to the floor and then raise her hands to her face, and bawl loudly, and shed helpless, glistening tears. Morris looked on morosely as I held her for a moment and uttered futile soothing sounds. It was dark outside and the roar of a truck horn along a nearby street made me jump, shredding my nerve endings like some evil hacksaw. To the general hubbub was added now the monstrous jangle of the telephone in the hallway, and I think I must have stifled a groan, or perhaps a scream. I became even further unstrung when Morris, having silenced the Gorgon by answering it, bellowed out the news that the call was for me.

This reads like Laurel and Hardy with sound. Although the paragraph begins with the presumably inaudible dropping of a silk slip to the floor, there are five separate sounds here, one of which is described in terms of an additional sound metaphor ("shredding my nerve endings like some evil hacksaw") and another which is described by reference to two sounds instead of one ("I must have stifled a groan, or perhaps a scream"). And Styron's irony of a seeming silencing of noise followed by Morris's concluding shout reveals a marvelous comic timing.

Elsewhere, in a scene in which Sophie's daughter Eva gets her flute lesson, Styron explores the serious possibilities of his symphonic technique with great subtlety. Wanda is attempting to convince Sophie that she should play a more active part in the resistance. The music teacher fingers "some soundless arpeggio" before demonstrating several notes for his young student. Overhead a squadron of Luftwaffe bombers "droned deafeningly eastward toward Russia," obliterating Wanda's voice. And Sophie tries to listen to Eva practice:

> The music was familiar but unnameable—Handel, Pergolesi, Gluck?—an intricate sweet trill of piercing nostalgia and miraculous symmetry. A dozen notes in all, no more, they struck antiphonal bells deep within Sophie's soul. They spoke of all she had been, of all she longed to be—and all she wished for her children, in whatever future God willed.

The teacher praises Eva. Eva's brother pulls her pigtails and she yells for him to stop. Wanda demands a decision.

> For a time Sophie was silent. At last, with the sound of the children's tumbling, ascending footsteps in her ears, she replied softly, "I have already made my choice, as I told you. *I will not get involved.* I mean this! *Schluss!*" Her voice rose on this word and she found herself wondering why she had spoken it in German. "*Schluss—aus!* That's final!"

Here the intermingling of sounds conveys the complexity of the literal situation. Moreover, the clash of noise, both negative (the drones of the planes) and positive (the sounds of the children playing), with the strains of some unidentified piece of classical music, actually influences the outcome of the situation. Those few notes from Eva's flute contradict the droning of the Nazi bombers and cause Sophie to underscore for Wanda her previous decision not to get involved.

The confusion of sounds in *Sophie's Choice* becomes increasingly intense as the novel goes along. Stingo cannot sleep: "My brain swam with images, sounds, voices, the past and the future trading places, sometimes commingled." What follows is a surrealistic list of many of the significant images in the novel, with Mozart relegated here to the place of a mere item in that list, like "Nathan's howl of rage," "my father's voice on the telephone," or "that hideous gunshot swarming in my ear." Then in the concluding pages the classical music returns, serving as a signature to the suicide pact of Sophie and Nathan. Approaching the Pink Palace on his return to New York, Stingo imagines them as "two people who had willed themselves into an almost decorous ending, going off silently to sleep," and he is pleased to learn that they died in each others' arms, listening to *Jesu, Joy of Man's Desiring*. This is the Romeo-and-Juliet ending. But even this discovery is qualified by the presence of two white-jacketed morgue attendants who enter the room "with a rustle of plastic bags." And at Sophie and Nathan's funeral,

> No one bothered to consult about the music, and this was both an irony and a shame. As the mourners trouped into the vestibule to the popping of flashbulbs I could hear a whiny Hammond organ playing Gounod's "Ave Maria." Reflecting on Sophie's—and for that matter, Nathan's—loving and noble response to music, that peevish, vulgar utterance made my stomach turn over.

The final quotation from Emily Dickinson is a more fitting tribute to the pair: "Let no sunrise' yellow noise / Interrupt this ground." In the end, the beauty of Bach and Sophie is tragically shouted down by the chaotic clamor of Auschwitz as well as Brooklyn. Only death frees Sophie from the shriek of her memories.

Stingo and Styron are both writers, and together seem locked in battle with the language itself. "I was compelled to search, however inadequately, for the right word," observes Stingo, "and suffered over the rhythms and subtleties of our gorgeous but unbenevolent, unyielding tongue." *Sophie's Choice* is a novel which has as one of its subjects Styron's difficulty in writing *Lie Down in Darkness*, his first novel, and in this respect it belongs to a genre that stretches from *Tom Jones* and *Tristram Shandy* to *The French Lieutenant's Woman*; but this emphasis on writing is misleading. In the novel from Fielding on, it is the *written* word which is so often the narrator's nemesis, whereas in Styron's auditory novel the *spoken* word has become the focus of attention. The real subject of *Sophie's Choice* is the struggle among spoken languages (English, Polish, German) and dialects (broken English, Southern drawl, Brooklynese). And its real message is the excruciating difficulty of understanding—Sophie Auschwitz, Stingo Sophie—such profound experiences through the medium of any printed language. Paradoxically, noise in *Sophie's Choice* even belies Styron's own role as researcher, refusing as it does to let Sophie's story be kept at an historical distance; by means of sound, we are brought about as close to the realities of Auschwitz and Brooklyn as we want to get. We discover that a novel can be more than meets the eye. Styron has remembered his reader's ear.

JANET M. STANFORD

The Whisper of Violins in Styron's Sophie's Choice

William Styron's controversial approach to the subject of racism in *Sophie's Choice* has evoked a variety of commentary during the last decade. The nature of attack on Styron's subject—non-Jewish sufferers of the Holocaust—ranges from concentration camp-survivor Elie Wiesel's general sense of outrage to John Gardner's dissection of Styron's references to classical music. Gardner's comments, which assert that this type of music is a metaphor misused by the author, gives substance to Wiesel's, and the presence of music in *Sophie's Choice* does function as a literary device on several levels. However, these critics have misinterpreted that function, which is a facet of Styron's art worth careful analysis.

In an article entitled "Does the Holocaust Lie Beyond the Reach of Art?" Wiesel contends that "Between the dead and the rest of us is an abyss no talent can comprehend" and admits that it is his intent to "denounce" writing that attempts to convey such an understanding. He focuses on *Sophie's Choice* to illustrate this point as he asserts that characters such as concentration-camp manager Rudolph Höss are portrayed as outrageously ambiguous, that he is affronted by the portrayal of the Nazis as complex or dynamic characters. He claims that this novel echoes a genre of writing in which occurs the following transition: "All of a sudden, the emphasis has shifted from victims to their executioners. They are being analyzed,

From *The Southern Literary Journal* 25, no. 1. © 1992 by the Department of English of the University of North Carolina at Chapel Hill.

dissected, explained: they are being shown to be 'human,' sensitive to art and ideas; everything is being done to make us understand them."

The art to which they are "sensitive" is music, and Styron uses it as a technique through which he metaphorically probes the question of the potential for the existence and quality of good and evil within the soul of one human being. But through the use of music, Styron is making an objective statement regarding this potential; he is not excusing it or rationalizing the evil away. Furthermore, he layers the multifaceted significance of the aesthetic in a methodically subtle fashion, so that important aspects of that significance may be easily overlooked. A closer look at John Gardner's comments, which seem to sprout from the roots of Wiesel's protest, facilitates further understanding of those elements.

Gardner's vehement response to what he sees as "Styron's . . . setting down his occasional lapses into anti-Semitism" is, like Wiesel's, documented by the presence of classical music in *Sophie's Choice*. He claims that as a symbol of harmony and decency

> . . . classical music leads in exactly the wrong direction: it points
> to that ideal Edenic world that those master musicians, the Poles
> and Germans, thought in their insanity they might create here
> on earth by getting rid of a few million 'defectives.' I'm not . . .
> against Bach and Beethoven; but they do need to be taken with a
> grain of salt, expressing, as they do, a set of standards unobtain-
> able (except in music) for . . . humanity; they point . . . toward an
> inevitable failure that may lead us to murder. . . .

Although the point that German Romantic musicians strove to rid their music of "imperfect" strains is a valid one, the presumption following this point, that Styron's sole purpose is to use music to symbolize all that is decent and "good" in humanity, is a conclusion born of faulty logic. And although Frederik Smith, yet another critic, effectively links the "Clamorous Yawp" of arbitrary non-harmonious sounds in the novel with disorder and "discord" (*i.e.*, fascism) in the universe and the organic concord of (classical) music with all that is "hope(ful) and positive," the latter connection becomes too simplified, its significance too flatly interpreted, in light of all evidence to the contrary. So do the central characters take on added dimension with close inspection of the music to which they listen, the aforementioned Höss among them, but also Sophie and Nathan themselves.

A careful combining of interpretive theories best encapsulates Styron's purpose in using music as a metaphor. The complexity of these three important personae brings the gray area of overlap between two polar concepts—

good and evil—to light. Sophie and the rest are not always what they seem, and neither is the apparently "perfect"-ly benign use of the aesthetic in *Sophie's Choice*. A curious blend of opposites resides within the individual; this same blending exists within the metaphor of music as it works in accordance with Styron's purposes.

As Gardner suggests, within the origins of classical Romantic music lies a concept that was extended into the roots of the Nazi mentality. Historians have used the term "aggressive nationalism" to classify an element significant to the German Romantics as a type of nationalism striving to "impose a cultural identity on others." This aspect of Romanticism held tremendous appeal for Richard Wagner, who derived his quests for perfection in music from his philosophies of racial perfection. Wagner, who wrote extensively on the subject, said in an 1850 essay that Jews could never make good musicians, that "Our whole European art and civilization . . . have remained to the Jew a foreign tongue . . . in this speech, this art, the Jew can only after-speak and after-patch." He later refers to Judaism as "the evil conscience of our modern civilization."

Styron's heroine makes her first allusion to Richard Wagner as she is beginning to lead Stingo through the enigmatic maze of her past. She mentions this fascist composer in connection with her father's writing on the subject of the Jews. It is true that on the surface (of his characterization) Sophie's father is, according to her, "everything that music cannot be." But in relaying the fact of her father's racism she tells of work she once did for him: after she has incorrectly typed his anti-Semitic article, he asks her, "*Who is this Neville Chamberlain who so loves the work of Richard Wagner?*" It appears that an article used by her father in supporting his own theses was written by a much different "Neville"; this article is, says Sophie, "filled with love of Germany and worship of Richard Wagner and this very bitter hatred of Jews, saying that they contaminate the culture of Europe and such as that."

Through this allusion and others, Styron reveals a subtle mix of fascism and aesthetics. Music as product of an embryonic Nazi rationale such as Wagner's reveals, in Styron's own words, that "crucial region of the soul where absolute evil opposes brotherhood." Again, this region is exposed to the reader of Styron's work through the characterization of several important personalities. Of Sophie herself, Styron adds,

> I . . . realized that in order to make Sophie really complicated and give her other dimensions, I couldn't make her just a victim. That was very essential to the dynamism of the story. If she was just a pathetic victim she wouldn't be very interesting; but to put her in juxtaposition with the commandant—not really as a collaborator

. . . but as a person who in desperation is acting in an unconventional way vis-a-vis the Nazis, trying to masquerade as a
collaborator—this would give her a larger dimension.

The character of Rudolph Höss also reveals this element of dimension,
as Sophie's narrative continues. After she has produced her father's article as
proof of her sympathies with the Reich's cause in hopes of gaining freedom
for herself or for her son, Höss cruelly rebukes and disappoints her. Later,
however, claiming not to be the "monster" he appears, he makes promises of
a meeting with her son, breaks the promise, and then makes another to the
effect that her son will be removed from the camp. Then he dismisses her
from his presence. As this chapter draws to a close, she emphasizes to Stingo
a comment made by Höss as music is heard playing in a distant room of the
Nazi's house. He stops and bids her listen: Franz Lehar is his favorite
composer, it seems.

At this point, Styron deftly shifts his tone an ominous octave lower.
After Höss's exit, Sophie is drawn towards the room where the radio is
playing, and half-heartedly toys with the idea of stealing it for the Resistance.
But then she is distracted by the music and becomes incredulous: "Can you
imagine what it was that the radio was playing? Guess what, Stingo?" This is
followed by Stingo's own detailed observations:

> There comes a point in a narrative like this one when a certain
> injection of irony seems inappropriate . . . because of the manner
> in which irony tends so easily towards leadenness, thus taxing the
> reader's patience along with his or her credulity. But since Sophie
> was my . . . witness, supplying the irony herself . . . I must set her
> final observation down . . . adding only . . . that . . . these words
> were delivered in exhausted emotional pandemonium . . . which
> I had never heard before in Sophie . . .
> "What was it playing?" I said.
> "It was the overture to this operetta of Franz Lehar," she
> gasped, "*Das Land des Lachelns—The Land of Smiles.*"

This "injection of irony" has significance relevant to Styron's message
that people, like that which people produce, whether a twisted philosophy, a
piece of music, or children, are made up of a variety of conflicting and nebulous emotions and motivations. The story within *The Land of Smiles* is indeed
ironic as it pertains to Sophie's situation. However, as parallel to the predicament in which she finds herself, the degree of ironic coincidence found in the
events of Franz Lehar's own life is noteworthy indeed.

Lehar, not Jewish himself, had a Jewish wife, as did William Styron. This wife (named, coincidentally, Sophie) narrowly avoided a fate similar to that escaped by Sophie Zawistowska: death in a concentration camp. Lehar was living in Austria and enjoying great success in the opera houses of Vienna when Hitler invaded that country in 1938. In his account of Lehar's life, Bernard Grun tells us that the composer's friends begged him to emigrate to England, but he refused, feeling that at his age (sixty-eight) emigration was "no joke." For a well-known artist married to a Jew, any feasible alternative to fleeing the country was hard to fathom; but still Lehar remained. Inevitably, he attracted unwanted attention, and in giving details regarding the Reich's interest in him, Grun points out:

> In the view of Goebbel's propaganda Ministry Lehar represented a "debatable problem for the cultural policy of the Third Reich." The foreign currency his work brought in ran to millions of marks, and the Fuhrer, astonishingly enough, showed an ever-increasing predilection for (one of Lehar's most famous operettas). On the other hand, the composer's librettists were without exception Jews, he himself moved in Vienna's "exclusively Jewish circles," and wasted his talents on "culturally regrettable subjects."

The presence of a Jewish wife could only make matters worse, but the composer finally saw a solution to his problem: he sought to avoid scrutiny or harassment by the Nazis through the same type of "collaborative" measures used by Styron's character as she attempts to influence Höss. Grun heightens our sense of drama by further informing us that ultimately Franz Lehar was confronted by several accusations, which "filled his friends with horrified sadness, his enemies with vindictive fury." First he officially dedicated a waltz to Adolf Hitler, in the form of a program that he had bound in leather and to which he added a silver swastika. These last two additions were made at the Fuhrer's request. Within the leather binding he then included the manuscript "Lips are silent, violins whisper," along with his signature.

Another incident involved his good friend Fritz Lohner, a composer of lyric poetry who went to the gas chamber "after four and a half years of tortures and humiliations in the concentration camps. . . ." As a result, Lehar underwent a period of "tormenting self-accusation" because he ". . . was oppressed by the thought of whether anyone in the Nazi hierarchy approachable by him could have saved his friend . . . 'questions (one who heard them declares) full of endless pangs of conscience'." This particular incident was also referred to as a "sin of omission" and brings to mind the same type of guilt pangs plaguing Sophie as she recounts her conflicts with Wanda and the Polish

Resistance and, later, the agony endured as Nathan's uncanny accusations erode the barriers of her self-defense.

Inevitably, the Gestapo came for Sophie Lehar. In a panic, the composer made a call to a Nazi official, and orders were given over the telephone for the policemen to leave. Meanwhile, Lehar's wife had fainted. Grun tells us through the voice of Lehar himself: "If I hadn't happened to be at home, I should never have seen my wife again."

Styron's awareness of the details surrounding this chapter of Lehar's life may not have been a factor pertinent to his presence in the novel as Rudolph Höss's favorite composer. But the parallels between Sophie Zawistowska and Franz Lehar—their fears, their conflicts, their "betrayals" of self and loved ones (Lehar's of his wife and friends, Sophie's of Nathan, of the Resistance, and, ultimately, of her own child)—seem organic rather than arbitrary. The fact that Lehar is Höss's favorite composer ties the ambiguous Nazi, with whom Sophie has linked herself by claiming to be a sympathizer, to aesthetics. Sophie, in turn, reflects the ambiguous nature of the music itself, which is an offspring of its erring composer. Thus, all three elements, the two characters and the music to which each is drawn, become braided into the discordant evil of the Third Reich. In addressing his portrayal of Höss, Styron reacts to a most pertinent point made by Gordon Telpaz during a 1983 interview, published later in *Partisan Review*. Telpaz cites an incident in which a survivor of Auschwitz who testified at the Eichmann trial fainted during testimony, "because all of a sudden I realized that Eichmann can be me and I can be Eichmann." Styron agrees and responds:

> When I portrayed Rudolph Höss, I did not try to mitigate the evils of the man or make him look more or less human. The point is: he was human . . . it's of utmost importance to find out what made Eichmann tick, and what made Rudolph Höss tick.

As Sophie's character functions to a great extent as a mirror of Höss's, what makes Höss tick may reflect elements of what makes her serve as a blend of truthsayer/liar and victim/collaborator. A final look at her reference to Lehar's operetta should clarify this point.

The Land of Smiles has a title that is ironic in light of Sophie's predicament. However, the intense irony she experiences as she listens to its strains pertains to the narrative of the operetta itself, not to the title alone. The salon of the Austrian Count of Lichtenfels is the opening scene, where the count's daughter, Lisa, falls in love with a Chinese diplomat, Prince Sov-Chong (herein may lie the "culturally regrettable subjects" to which the German Ministry made reference). The two are married, but Lisa's life is not a happy one: her husband has four other wives with whom she must compete for his affections. Gustav von Pattenstein, an Austrian military attache who has always loved Lisa, arrives at Sov-Chong's house for a business conference, and Lisa's love for von Pattenstein is ignited.

Lisa tells Sov-Chong a partial truth: that she misses Vienna terribly and wants to return. This request is denied, however, and she attempts escape. She is caught, and in a climactic scene toward the end of the operetta confesses that she loves von Pattenstein and wishes to be with him. Rather than executing her, which would be in accordance with the laws of the land, the Prince sets her free along with her Austrian lover, while Sov Chong must remain in Peking to nurse a broken heart.

Unfortunately for Sophie, the man she tries to persuade is not deceived either, and, while perhaps not the "monster" he denies himself to be, refuses her request for freedom, a response unlike the Prince Sov Chong's. Nor is she ever convinced that anything has been done for her son. It is in this context that she is overwhelmed by the similarities in theme and difference in outcome between her own situation and Lisa's.

The references to Richard Wagner, Franz Lehar, and *The Land of Smiles* are but a few of many allusions to music throughout Styron's epic. There is one other in particular, however, which should not be overlooked as significant to the problem of Styron's approach to the interdependent relationship between character, music as symbol, and thematic complexity of good-vs-evil within character.

Shortly before reaching the horrifying climax of her story, that point at which she must choose between her children, Sophie refers to a memory of a dream, a memory which seems crucial to unity of theme via metaphorical use of music. She describes her dream to Stingo as they are traveling South, where they will presumably find refuge from the past. It involves Sophie's father and the Princess Czartoryska, to whom Sophie refers as an "old Polish Jew-hater with [a] love for music." Sophie has vivid memories of listening to the princess's phonograph upon which is played

> . . . Madame Schmann-Heink singing Brahms *Lieder*. On one side there was 'Der Schmied,' . . . and on the other was 'Von ewige Liebe,' and when I first heard it I sat . . . thinking that it was the most gorgeous singing I had ever heard, that it was an angel come down to earth . . . So in the dream . . . my father is standing next to the Princess and he is looking directly at me and he says "please don't play that music for the child . . . she is much too stupid to understand" . . . only this time . . . he seemed to be talking . . . about my death. He wanted me to die, I think.

Although her father is, again, "everything that music cannot be," he is once again woven into the musical contexts in Styron's novel. In the minds of people like her father, Sophie is perhaps "too stupid to understand" that even the seemingly untainted beauty of Brahms' *Lieder* may evolve adjacent to the flawed and fascist philosophy of aggressive nationalism. (Even Brahms wrote his *Triumphlied* to celebrate the German victory over the French in the Franco-Prussian war of 1871, a "watershed date in western Europe for the change from defending to aggressive nationalism.")

Sophie speaks of death as an element as pervasive in her dream as the music she hears. Indeed, the language used in the poignant lines of 'Von ewige Liebe' seems to prophesy, in an ironic sense, the very death to which, at Nathan's beckoning, she finally comes.

Von ewige Liebe (Eternal Love)
Josef Wentzig

Darkness has fallen on valley and hill,
Evening has come and the world is all still.
Nowhere a light, and the windows are dark,
Hushed is the song of the thrush and the lark.

Out from the village a lad and a maid
Walk to her home in the neighboring glade;
Onward he leads her by willow and fir,
Solemn the words that he says to her:

"Are you ashamed when they name you with me?
Shamed when they say: 'Her lover is he'?
For if you are then our love will not last,
Swift as it came it will swifter have passed,
Pass like the wind and dissolve like the dew,
Swifter than ever it came to us two."

But she said to him, answered him true:
"Nay, but our love will not pass like the dew,
Strong as is iron, and firm as is steel,
Our love is firmer, for woe and for weal.

Iron and steel are easy to mould,
Our love is changeless, as changeless as gold.
Iron and steel will rust all away,
Our love, eternal, our love, eternal,

Forever, ever and aye." (Drinker)

Many aspects of the Sophie-Nathan love story can be seen in this passage. However, the complex and interwoven personality of each as expressed through the lyric of music is most pertinent to questions raised by critics looking at Styron and his method of using that lyric as literary device. In an interview with Stephen Lewis, Styron tells us that:

> As a metaphor, death and love have always been entwined in literature. The death wish and the procreative wish have often been so closely connected you can't separate them. That was always essential to me, and to the relationship between Sophie and Nathan.

The "entwined" relationships of Sophie and Nathan and between death and love certainly seem reflected in the passages of this lyric. Nathan's complex function as character and as persona is evident in the second and third stanzas. As he walks the "maid" "to her home" ("home" to death, perhaps), echoes of his frenzied accusations toward her, that she is an anti-Semite herself if not a Nazi sympathizer, come to mind when he asks her if she is not "shamed when they say: 'Her lover is he.'" She is "shamed," of course, but her shame is ambiguous in that it is born of her guilt rather than of his Judaism. Again, Sophie's character and paradoxical nature are brought to light through his, as with Rudolph Höss. She replies that their love, "strong as . . . iron," will prevail "forever," and this line as parallel to the novel's conclusion sounds another ironic chord, another echo of plot, character, and theme within lieder.

In using 'Der Schmied,' a shorter piece, Styron effects the blend once again, but this time the nature of death changes. Chilling undertones of allusions to the ovens of Auschwitz take shape within previously innocent lines as Styron's purpose in including this touch becomes clear, and the translation chosen is quite different stylistically, as is Styron's tone in this context.

Der Schmied (The Blacksmith)
Ludvig Uhland

I hear the sound of
my sweetheart's hammer;
it clangs as he swings

It, and like a peal
of bells, it echoes away
in the alleys and
square.

There sits my
love by his black

chimney. As I pass by,
the bellows roar, and
flames flare up and

Glow all around him. (Phillips)

Here are those very flames escaped by Sophie but denied a sadistic—
yet at times tender—Nathan, who feels not only deprived, but extremely
bitter and envious as well. The pathos Sophie's character evokes throughout
the novel emerges through her point of view in this lyric; it is as if she were
the sole, wistful speaker here, whereas Nathan's voice is in a strange sort of
harmony with hers (although in opposition to hers as well) in "Von ewige
Liebe." Her insight into his demonic side seems to surface here, and the lines
convey the compulsive forgiveness so characteristic of Sophie. On the other
hand, Nathan's compulsive tendencies to sever their relationship during his
accusatory rages offset her masochistic acceptance of his abuse: "For if you
are [shamed], then our love will not last" in "Von ewige Liebe." Both vital
aspects of characterization are literally set to music in the lines of Brahms'
lieder. The fact that Styron veils intricate components of each character
within a musical allusion makes those characters all the more compelling.
Sophie's dream exposes the blend of truths and lies buried in her past and
foreshadows her future, and it is interesting, in the context of Frederik
Smith's article, that she precedes her narration of this dream with a stray
remark: "That fire engine just now—that siren—it was awful but it had a
strange musical sound." In this simple "Off-the-subject" comment as much
as in any other resides the strange immersion of one polar concept
completely within another.

Ever since Shakespeare tricked his audiences with Macbeth, writers
through the ages have fooled their readers into a false sense of security about
one hero or another. Styron tricks us with Sophie this way and skillfully
reveals her potential for deceit along with Höss's for decency in an unpeeling
of character Faulkner might have respected. Most critics, even those such as
John Gardner, who initially find *Sophie's Choice* a "Novel of Evil," have also
admitted to being profoundly moved by the experience of reading Styron's
epic. They admire his courage, perhaps, his remarkable eye for detail and his
approach to irony. As Frederik Smith has observed, he deftly uses the
metaphor of music to enhance his theme. It is his use of music to symbolize
the paradoxical fabric of human nature that is particularly compelling, and
this fabric as theme has effected considerable controversy. Styron himself
predicted this controversy. A literary subject as inflammatory as the Holocaust will spark controversy regardless of technique used to depict that

theme. The necessity of clarifying response to past critical commentary of the technique remains, however, if readers are to understand the author's treatment of a controversial theme. This understanding is crucial in turn to an awareness that as he incidentally uses music as an indirect expose of the best and worst within us, William Styron also gives powerful address to complex issues never ceasing to haunt us.

GIDEON TELPAZ

An Interview with William Styron

On April 17, 1983, after seeing the film "Sophie's Choice," Elie Wiesel published an article in the Sunday Arts and Leisure section of *The New York Times*, entitled "Does the Holocaust Lie Beyond the Reach of Art?" in which he challenged William Styron's capability of "imagining the unimaginable." A survivor of the concentration camps, Wiesel maintained: "Between the dead and the rest of us there exists an abyss that no talent can comprehend." Asserting that "the Holocaust has turned out to be the latest attraction; it is 'in' as far as show business is concerned," Wiesel denounced any tendency to portray the "executioners" as "humans," or "to make us understand them." My conversation with William Styron, in which the author of the novel *Sophie's Choice* responded to accusations made in Wiesel's article, took place several weeks later in New York City.

GT: What was your initial reaction to Wiesel's article?
WS: I read it with some irritation, and I had an urge to respond, but I took my own counsel about that and said, "No, I'm not going to do that." I did have it, though, in the back of my mind. I did feel it was saying things which muddied rather than clarified.
GT: Did you take it as a personal affront?
WS: Only at one point, where he used the word "honesty," or "total honesty," implying the lack of it on my part.

From *Partisan Review* 52, no. 3. © 1985 by P.R., Inc.

GT: Wiesel argues, "Only survivors of Auschwitz know what it meant to be in Auschwitz."

WS: It is simply not true. We've got to get rid of this idea that there is something sacrosanct about the Holocaust. Somehow, Wiesel has given the impression, and it's the wrong impression, that it's something so out of the bounds of mortal comprehension that we mustn't deal with it. He said in that piece something about his silence, and of course that's what George Steiner said. Well, I don't believe that.

GT: The point Wiesel is trying to make is that no words can convey the horrors of Auschwitz. He says, "Auschwitz defies imagination and perception; it submits only to memory. It can be communicated by testimony, not by fiction." He also says, "What we really wish to say, what we feel we must say, cannot be said."

WS: The contradiction lies in his own work. He counsels silence but he's been writing incessantly about it. How can a man, who has spent his life writing about something, deny to other people the right to deal with it? Especially, I might add, when it can never be proven that just because a person has experienced something it makes him a better artistic witness. On the crudest level of recapitulation of art and experience, I'm talking about writing novels based on real events. The best novel about combat and the horror, the bloody horror, of the American Civil War, was *The Red Badge of Courage*, written by a young man who never saw a war. It remains, to my mind, the single greatest fictional work about the Civil War. It was a totally imagined, or almost totally imagined, recreation of the horror of war.

GT: What Wiesel claims is that there's nothing that can be compared to the Holocaust. It's the greatest mystery of all times.

WS: Given my understanding of it, as a most appalling and truly desolating cataclysm, what still prevents someone who has not experienced it from trying to deal with it on his own terms? That brings me to the second point I felt Wiesel was making. He said or implied, to universalize the Holocaust is to trivialize it, because it was a singularly Jewish experience which no one else had any right to be drawn into.

GT: Should *Sophie's Choice* be regarded at all as a book about the Holocaust?

WS: It may not be about the Holocaust in the traditional sense as Elie Wiesel comprehends it. I can't accept his contention that to universalize it is to trivialize or to falsify it; I think he also used the word "dejudify." My book is, I believe, one long testimony to the agony of Jewish suffering. There is no place in the story where I try to minimize it.

GT: You make a point of telling the reader through Wanda, a member of the Polish underground, that everyone was a victim, and that the Jews, although "the victims of victims," as she referred to them, were not the only ones to suffer.

WS: That was not in the movie, it was in the book certainly, and I would, on a purely pragmatic level, say that. Maybe this is worth "dejudifying." We do know that a large number of non-Jews perished at Auschwitz. This is indisputable.

GT: He says not all victims were Jewish but all Jews were victims.

WS: Well, that's true—up to a point. Many Jews were victims. All Jews were potential victims. All European Jews were potential victims. All Jews were not victims because many were more victimized than others, including those who weren't sent to Auschwitz.

GT: If *Sophie's Choice* is not a book about the Holocaust à la Wiesel, how then should we understand the role the Holocaust plays in it?

WS: I think it is a book in which the Holocaust is overwhelmingly present, but which is more than that—a metaphor for something else. The metaphor lay in the title of the book—choice, Sophie's choice. The metaphor lay in the epigraph I use in the book from Malraux: "I seek that essential region of the soul where absolute evil confronts brotherhood." What is absolute evil? Absolute evil, to my mind, as a metaphor, is, or can be, or must be, an act in which a woman is forced to murder her own child, whether she be Jewish, Gypsy, Pole, Russian, French, or whatever. This seized me as being a metaphor for absolute evil as represented by Nazism. That is what impelled me more than anything else to write about the Holocaust. Not, God forbid, to write it from the vantage point of Elie Wiesel, the point of view of the barracks, the tortures, the beatings, the terrible deprivation.

GT: Why not?

WS: Because I didn't feel confident enough to write about it this way. I don't claim, I never claimed and would never claim to be an authority on Auschwitz or on the Holocaust. This only Elie Wiesel can be in a sense because he was there. He can tell me things that I am sure I have heard about; he can sear it on my memory in a way that perhaps no one else can, but I'm not claiming in my view of the Holocaust to have his vision of it. I have another vision, another metaphor, and I'm offended by the idea that somehow the metaphor of Sophie being forced to choose to murder one of her children is not a perfectly valid use of the Holocaust.

GT: You also describe some of the horrors of the Holocaust and not just the fact that she had to choose.

WS: I do that too, but as you know I'm very, very careful never to get too close to the thing. Aside from the feeling that I might have been inauthentic, I didn't want to deal in what might be construed as the pornography of violence; describing some Nazi thug taking a club and beating some wretched poor Jewish woman to the ground or something like that. It was not in my scheme.

GT: You are haunted by the phenomenon of slavery. In the book, you say: "I knew that in the fever of my mind and in the most unquiet regions of my heart I would be shackled by slavery as long as I remained a writer."

WS: I'm always concerned with themes that have to do with human domination. Slavery in its active form is probably the most powerful example of that.

GT: Could this be one of the reasons which made you write about Auschwitz?

WS: It may have been. First was the metaphor. I'll be quite frank. The thing that drove me to write the book was the image of a woman being forced to choose: it dominated me from the beginning to the end.

GT: How did you come upon this image? Was it something that you witnessed?

WS: It was something I'd heard very soon after World War II, when I was in college and I was reading about the Holocaust. There were one or two witness accounts. There was a book by Olga Lengyel. It was called *Five Chimneys*. She was a Rumanian doctor. She arrived at the camp with her children. She didn't have to make a choice, an active choice, like Sophie did. She had two children, and she sensed something was going haywire during the selection process and by guessing wrong, trying to shelter her child, in some way making him seem smaller or bigger, she realized later she had inadvertently sent him to the gas chamber. She described that very graphically in the very first pages of her book, which was not a terribly good book, but very, very honest and, as I say, very graphic.

GT: Was this the first time you had read about the Holocaust?

WS: Yes. I was just a kid in college. Then, while I was reading *Eichmann in Jerusalem* by Hannah Arendt, at some place in that book I had a sense of déjà vu. Arendt gave the example of the Gypsy woman who was forced to choose between her two children. This is what the Nazis were up to. And that all of a sudden reestablished my contact with the Holocaust and my desire to do something about it. This was way back in the sixties, long before I began to write the book.

GT: Talking about evil, in *Sophie's Choice*, you say, "Real evil is gloomy, monotonous, barren, boring." I believe you were quoting Simone Weil.

WS: Yes. I read Simone Weil. Her meditations on that kind of institutionalized evil struck me as being extraordinarily insightful.

GT: Did you travel to Auschwitz? Did you talk to survivors?

WS: I went to Auschwitz in 1974, and I saw quite a few survivors in
       Warsaw. I was incredibly moved by all of it. Especially Birkenau; the
       vastness of it. It was so huge, the total sterilized area for that camp.
       Birkenau and Auschwitz plus the outlying places which were
       completely stripped of Polish inhabitants. It was a devastating sight.
       It was horrendous. And you want to get out of there certainly by
       nightfall. To stay in Auschwitz after nightfall would be unthinkable.
       So I went back to Cracow.

GT: When you wrote about the camp you often made a juxtaposition
       between smoke which came out of the chimneys, and the pasture
       and the cows and the healthy people who were also part of the
       picture—the nonvictims. In a way, you do something which Wiesel
       is arguing against—spotlighting, in the chapter on Rudolf Höss, the
       executioner, while the victims, the Jewish victims, recede into the
       background. I'll read you the exact quotation from Wiesel. He
       claims, "The Holocaust has turned out to be the latest attraction; it
       is 'in,' as far as show business is concerned. There are now docud-
       ramas, plays, musicals; Adolf Eichmann? An inoffensive officer with
       courteous manners. Hitler? Crazy. The butcher of Rome, Herbert
       Kapler, is to be pitied: a man with a keen sense of duty. . . . All of a
       sudden, the emphasis has shifted from victims to their executioners.
       They are being analyzed, dissected, explained: They are being
       shown to be 'human,' sensitive to art and ideas; everything is done
       to make us understand them."

WS: I read all that. I find that there is nothing wrong with that. Yet I
       don't know what his point is. This is what Hannah Arendt was
       consistently trying to impress on people—that they were human.
       She hated them too, but her point, unlike what I assume was
       Wiesel's, is that unless we are intensely aware that they were human
       and often indeed responsive to art and so on, we tend to put them in
       the category of monsters or something called the supernatural. The
       danger is precisely that, being human like you and me, they were
       capable of these horrors. This to me is where Wiesel misses the
       point.

GT: Are you familiar with the author Katzatnik? He is a survivor of
       Auschwitz who lives in Israel. He wrote several books on Auschwitz.

WS: Yes, I have heard of him.

GT: As you recall, he appeared in the Eichmann trial. He was the one
       who fainted on the witness stand. When he was asked recently, I
       think by Mike Wallace of "60 Minutes," why he had fainted, he
       replied—and I paraphrase—"Not because I saw Eichmann, not
       because of all the horrors, but because all of a sudden I realized that
       Eichmann can be me and I can be Eichmann."

WS: In a nutshell that's what Wiesel seems to be ignorant about, or doesn't want to face. When I portrayed Rudolf Höss I did not try to mitigate the evils of the man or make him look less or more human than he was. The point is: he was human. He wasn't particularly nice, but he wasn't particularly un-nice. He certainly was not a monster. I'm sure the Nazis employed dyed-in-the-wool sadists, psychopathic monsters, to really do the worst work around the crematoriums. They have psychopaths like that in American prisons who are happy to do those sorts of things. But someone like Rudolf Höss had to be a bureaucrat, had to be very human, and if Wiesel doesn't recognize that, he's dealing in dangerous insights rather than in anything else.

GT: Is it feasible to expect a survivor to attain the epic distance necessary to write objectively about this horrible experience?

WS: It is important, it seems to me, to deal with the oppressors and not only with the victims. It's of utmost importance to find out what made Eichmann tick, and what made Rudolph Höss tick. Because these were the ones who were in the eye of the storm. To ignore them is to ignore a very important part of the whole story.

GT: Did writing about Auschwitz have any therapeutic relevance to you as a man and an artist?

WS: I suppose it had a certain kind of cathartic effect, surely. I mean, I wanted to cough this up out of my system, and to do it in some way that would have a meaningful effect on myself. Whether it was therapeutic, I don't know. I know I felt awfully good when the book was finished, and I'd realized I'd done as well as I could, given the material I had.

GT: While the book was in progress, in addition to the classical struggle with the material itself—did you have to struggle with the theme?

WS: I had certain struggles, yes. You know, it's very hard to recapitulate— you must as a writer realize this—to recapitulate your own motives at certain times, when you're off away from what you've done several years. You lose sight of the moments of determination. It's all lost in a kind of gestalt. But certain things I remember. For instance, when I started out having Sophie tell about her "humane" father— what a wonderful man he was, how he hid Jews in Poland—I knew that this was all right, but I really knew that deep down inside there was something wrong with it. I suddenly realized Sophie was lying. I discovered this intuitively, and that's where I broke through to a very significant area in the book. I realized that this is the place where I'd be able to explore Polish anti-Semitism by making her father an anti-Semite whom she was trying to cover up. So those moments were critical moments for the making of the book.

GT: And then you felt you had a grip on it?

WS: Yes, I realized that I was getting into the complexity of the thing, and that I wasn't trying to simplify it, and that I was really trying, in the best sense, to complicate the book for the sake of reality.

GT: You didn't set out to erect a monument to the Jews who perished in the Holocaust. Wiesel did, when he wrote his books. He wished to commemorate the Jews of his hometown, his relatives, the people he knew in his childhood, who met their death in the concentration camps. This is a basic difference between the two of you.

WS: I wasn't trying to establish any kind of monument. As a matter of fact, had I made Sophie Jewish, I think it would have become a banal story.

GT: Did you try to describe her, at one place, as sharing the Jewish fate by having her arm tattooed?

WS: I certainly didn't intend that. As a matter of fact, as you might recall, there's a very explicit passage where I try to describe why so many non-Jews are tattooed. Because the Jews were going right to the gas chambers they didn't need to be tattooed. That was the reason why today all over Poland many of the non-Jewish survivors you see are tattooed. Often they will admit it: "The Jews were going to the gas chambers, we had to be tattooed because they wanted to keep track of us." You don't tattoo someone you're sending to the gas chambers. Some Jews were tattooed because at one time the Germans wanted slave labor so badly, that they couldn't afford to send people to the gas chambers. That's when both Poles and Jews were being tattooed.

GT: As a Jew, I am forever opinionated about the Holocaust. I might never be able to view it adequately through a "universal" perspective. We touched on it before; still I would like to hear you more on it. Would you accept that the war was a war against the Jews?

WS: Yes, I would. I've said this over and over again, and I think I've said it several times in the book.

GT: Could Sophie's fate have been a Jewish fate?

WS: In a sense.

GT: She survives, though, and you bring her to Brooklyn, where she meets Stingo, the narrator. What was your purpose in bringing her to Brooklyn?

WS: That was the strategy of the story, to bring it into the American grain. I'm an American. I'm descended from a long line of American storytellers. What I had tried to do was to imbed the story of this Polish woman in some recognizable American matrix, where the reader could begin to see the story unfold through peculiarly American eyes, namely the narrator Stingo.

GT: Who was the reader you had in mind?

WS: Because I am an American, I probably think in terms of an American reader, and was talking about the story in a kind of American way and locating it in my own home ground, my own territory.

GT: Your territory? Yetta Zimmerman's Jewish rooming house and the Yiddish spoken there?

WS: Yiddish is not foreign to me. I know a lot of it. I've been around Jews all my life. If you have as many friends as I do who were brought up in families where Yiddish was spoken as a mother tongue by either the parents or grandparents, you get exposed to it too. Ever since I lived in New York, practically more than half of my friends have had this background. They liberally sprinkle their own conversation with Yiddishisms. I've been growing up with a knowledge of a kind of 'pidgin Yiddish,' if you want to call it that.

GT: Your use of Yiddishisms in the book appears to be precise and accurate. Every Yiddishism you use, not only do you not repeat it twice in the book, it's always in the right place.

WS: I struggled very hard to get that tone, and I also had a very good book to rely on, Leo Rosten's *The Joys of Yiddish*. That was a great help. I don't actually speak Yiddish myself, but I know the idioms.

GT: In the book, when Stingo recalls his growing up in the small Southern town, he betrays his fascination with the local Jewish community. His fascination comes out in his descriptions of the synagogue and the way he speculates about what the Jews did inside, and the mysterious way in which they disappeared into the Jewish fold after the regular business hours.

WS: In the South, a town like the one I lived in had a very distinct Jewish community, a visible one. Small towns in America—South and North—have had a merchant class of Jews. There was a very strong Jewish consciousness among Jews in the South. I've always felt there's some connection between the Jewish consciousness and the racial problem in the South. There was very little real anti-Semitism of the virulent sort that you get elsewhere, or have gotten else-where—not so much in America but in Europe. The South was a fairly placid place for Jews. Partly, it's due to the fact that the Negro problem siphoned off a lot of ugly energy. If you had a scapegoat, in the form of blacks, you didn't have to hate Jews. My father was a real Southerner to his fingertips. He was born in 1889, not too long after the Civil War, during a time of extreme racism, and had however a kind of liberal attitude toward people in general. He was a humane person. Well advanced, in terms of his humaneness, for that era. He would always tell me—he didn't realize he was patronizing—things like, "Now we'll go to this little gift shop run by Mr. Morgenstern." That was a Levantine Jew, a very good looking man, and very expansive. He had a very nice gift shop—china, silver, and so on.

GT: Where was that?

WS: In this town in Virginia, Newport News, a small city, large industry, big shipbuilding. My father would talk to Mr. Morgenstern, about families and so on. My father would leave, and he would say—I was about eleven or twelve—"Billy, you must never forget the Jews are the salt of the earth. They're like our people; they have a good tradition; they're decent people; they care about traditions." This was his attitude. It was always sort of self-conscious, but with lots of respect. And that would extend to practically all the Jews my father would encounter, and there were quite a few, because both he and they were involved in community work. I mean, there was a crossover. My father would say, "Mr. Cahn is one of the finest men I've ever known. An outstanding man!"

GT: This was in the early stage of innocence. In time you, or your protagonist Stingo, came to know Leslie Lapidus, the phoney sexpot, and the perspective changed.

WS: Yes, indeed. But that's an invention. Leslie is a total invention.

GT: Yet she reflects a certain concept of the Jewish American Princess.

WS: I just recreated it more or less out of whole cloth, without really ever having encountered a true Jewish Princess like her.

GT: Do you think you might have in any way been influenced by Jewish fellow writers who describe Jewish Princesses?

WS: To some extent. Yes, Philip Roth. My friend Philip Roth.

GT: In contrast to the sardonic tone you use toward Leslie, your empathy for Sophie, who lives under the shadow of the death camps, is conspicuous. In talking about the tragic love of Sophie and Nathan, Wiesel comments, "She loved him and he loved her and yet—it's complicated, I know: people such as Sophie and Nathan, they can be found everywhere in the rubble of history."

WS: I don't know what he's trying to get at there. I read that but I don't know what his point is.

GT: Later on he says, "Far from Birkenau, long after the war, Styron seems to be saying, one still dies there."

WS: Well, that was true. Certainly that was an ancillary part of the book. I certainly did not wish to disguise the fact that the power and evil of Auschwitz was sufficient to reach out and kill Sophie long after her departure. I always felt Nathan was simply an instrument.

GT: A most powerful one.

WS: One had to be, in order to destroy Sophie.

GT: Did you form him after somebody you knew?

WS: He's sort of an amalgam, drawn in exaggerated terms, of a lot of Jewish friends I've had. People I've known ever since I came North. I had a roommate who was a bit like Nathan, not nearly as self-destructive, who was Jewish, when I first lived in New York. A sculptor.

GT: Is it correct to assume that once Sophie finds herself in America, she has no choice but to gravitate to a place where Jews were heavily concentrated, such as Brooklyn, and to an affair with a Jew, in order to complete a tragic cycle of destiny?

WS: That may be. There's some atonement she was making in her relationship with Nathan.

GT: They needed one another to destroy each other?

WS: They were both seeking destruction.

GT: Why was she seeking destruction? She had survived. She came to a new world, started a new life. Was it the guilt of the survivor?

WS: Partly, I think.

GT: You brought her from, as you call it in one place, "her sojourn in the bowels of hell," and in another place you call it "society of the walking dead," to Brooklyn, to Mrs. Zimmerman's "Pink Palace," which, as it turned out, was just the final station on her way to the gas chamber. Do you think all survivors are irredeemably haunted by the burden of a death they had managed to escape?

WS: I really don't know. I can't answer that.

GT: Were you asked to appear before the gathering of survivors that took place recently in Washington?

WS: No, I wasn't.

GT: Would you have talked to them had you been invited? Would you have anything to say?

WS: If they had wished to solicit me, my feelings, I don't think I would have had anything to say.

GT: You had so much to say in your book.

WS: But that's the difference. That's the difference between life and art—if I may so dignify the book by calling it art. There is a difference, and I think Elie Wiesel seems not to perceive certain aspects of the part that's art.

GT: According to the captions *The New York Times* gave Wiesel's article, the questions are: "Does the Holocaust defeat the artist? Does the Holocaust lie beyond the reach of art?" According to Elie Wiesel it does. According to you—it does not. Is it basically a question of the quality of the artist?

WS: I think of course, ultimately, it always comes down to the quality of the artist. I would say that's what the artist is for, on his mission, if he has a mission. To be able to take almost anything and deal with it.

GT: The book, in spite of the fact that it is dealing with tragic people and their tragic end, ends on an optimistic note. When Stingo wakes up in the morning on the last page, he is ready for a new beginning. One cycle is over, another is about to begin. He is looking forward to the new day.

WS: Yes, I think so. The only other way for Stingo to end it would be on a scream of despair. But I always perceived him going to that beach and seeing the morning star and realizing that tomorrow is another day, "excellent and fair."

GT: Mainly Stingo's coming of age?

WS: The book has been called bildungsroman. It may be. Among other things it meant to show the rite of passage of a young man from relative innocence into manhood.

GT: Initiation ceremonies, especially as demonstrated by primitive rites, are associated with intimations of death, whether real or symbolic. Could the deaths of the two lovers, Sophie and Nathan, be seen as symbols of Stingo's initiation?

WS: *Sophie's Choice* is Stingo's tale. This is why Stingo is so utterly essential to the whole story. If I had told it any other way the book would not have made any ripples at all. It had to be told through the eyes of this young man—this young American—and this is what I think Wiesel totally ignores, or chooses to ignore. Perhaps it's a story not so much of Auschwitz but of discovering evil. It's a time-honored technique to have the young man revealed through a reminiscence by the older man of his youthful experience. This was a measure of my distance from Auschwitz. Had I gotten any closer, even if I had tried to tell it totally from Sophie's point of view, it would have lacked resonance and would have had no conviction whatsoever.

GT: One last question. Why should Auschwitz figure at all in Stingo's rite of passage?

WS: Because Stingo the elder, I, the alter ego, felt an absolute fascination with Auschwitz. When I conceived the book, it was without knowing exactly where I was headed, but I wanted desperately to deal with Auschwitz, and I realized the only way I could do it was to take this dewy-eyed young boy and expose him to the mysteries as revealed through Sophie.

GT: When you look back at it, do you think there is a mystery left untold about Auschwitz?

WS: I did not in any sense claim to have resolved the mystery. In fact, at the end of the book, I say that point-blank: no one will ever understand Auschwitz. But I also said that what I hoped to demonstrate through Sophie's life and her death was how absolute evil has never, will never, vanish from the world.

DAWN TROUARD

Styron's Historical Pre-Text: Nat Turner, Sophie, and the Beginnings of a Postmodern Career

William Styron is generally viewed in literary circles as an inheritor of the modern tradition—following in the footsteps of Faulkner and Robert Penn Warren. A kind of graceful dinosaur (because he is a careful stylist), Styron, according to this view, remains concerned with verities and traditional notions of plot—not to mention guilt, suffering, and truth—while his contemporaries have long since decamped to postmodernism. This makes the nature of his celebrity curious. For, unlike showboaters like Mailer and elitist *provocateurs* like Nabokov, Styron's literary performances are assumed not to be calculatingly self-conscious; he is not the kind of artist Richard Poirier has characterized as postmodern: "furiously self-consultive so . . . narcissistic and later so eager for publicity, love, and historical dimension."

It will be the aim of this paper to examine Styron's appropriation of history through his two latest novels, works employing "historical meditation" as controlling principle. In fact, when Styron enters into these confrontations with the historical record as in *The Confessions of Nat Turner*, and as in the holocaust of *Sophie's Choice*, he is attempting a postmodern fiction that struggles, as Poirier has noted, to make "the reality of history as a force physically as well as imaginatively felt." Fictional energy becomes peculiarly available to Styron with these particular forays into the historical past. In short, as a white Southerner, Styron carries the implied burden of

From *Papers on Language and Literature* 23, no. 4. © 1987 by the Board of Trustees Southern Illinois University.

racism (racism possibly overcome, but still a regional onus) into historically sensitive, even volatile historical junctures. To enter the mind of a slave revolutionist, to create the holocaust experience through the meeting of a Polish Catholic survivor's romance with a horny Southern autobiographical projection, is not only to dare hostility and notoriety; it guarantees a begrudging recognition—as in "that Bill Styron has got his nerve." While I do not believe Styron has abandoned his commitment to larger meanings as a responsibility of literature, or has embraced Mailer's "Hollywood or bust" ethos, I do believe that he has been misunderstood and misread, and that the central misreading is the failure to see his postmodern qualities. Specifically, Styron came out from under the shadow of Faulkner and regionalism and into his own when he took up the subject of history as a basis for "new" fiction with *Nat Turner*.

In the "Author's Note" Styron disclaims his intentions to write an "'historical novel'"; instead he favors a generic designation called "a meditation on history." This reclassifying allows him "the utmost freedom of imagination in reconstructing events . . . [while] remaining within the bounds of what meager enlightenment history has left us about the institution of slavery." In the interviews that surrounded the publication of *Nat Turner*, Styron was at pains to point out that he was not attempting to capitalize on the civil rights problems of the 1960s. But the ten black writers who responded to the book felt that Styron played fast and loose with historical facts and perpetuated a racist stereotype. In what they feel are deliberate manipulations by an "avowed liberal," the ten black authors contend that "the meaning of [Nat Turner's] life" was stolen and "illicitly appropriated for a dubious literary adventure." While not all the response was so negative, and the novel has subsequently been reassessed more sympathetically, many readers still patronize Styron and his fictional appropriations of history. Even in largely favorable discussions of *Nat Turner*, like Melvin J. Friedman's, the critics tend to find Styron's use of "meditation on history" a ruse since history is a "respectably solid word." But when vindication was offered by scholars who had investigated Styron's sources for historical detail in *Nat Turner* and found him scrupulous, "faithful to the historical record," there nonetheless remained a lingering sense of reservation: "Styron may still be guilty of distorting 'history' in the larger sense."

That Styron "can't win for losing" is best illustrated in Poirier's charges that *Nat Turner* fails most because it is "too historical": "[Styron] was in a sense too historical. Aside from the quite proper refusal to be bound by details in a historical record which is itself of questionable authenticity the larger design of his book allowed history to do the work of imagination. It is as if Styron felt that the historical fact of Nat's having led a rebellion sufficiently disguised the

literary fact that Styron in the novel has shown him incapable of doing so."
This indictment misses two of Styron's main aims in the book and points to the
general critical neglect of Styron's own directive to view the book as a "meditation on history." In the first place, as a meditation, the novel attempts to
present Styron's speculations on what motivated Nat Turner to rebellion. The
"hows" of successful insurrection that Poirier finds the book deficient in are
more properly the domain of a "historical" novel—a type of narrative from
which Styron is at pains to dissociate his meditation. In the second place,
Styron is exploring the limits of genre here. In electing a controversial subject
and a genre that could be effectively re-visioned, Styron satisfied his own
professional aesthetic. In a 1965 interview he admitted that a writer attempts
"to make his story as difficult to write as possible, to see if he can leap over
these obstacles with grace. I've always felt that I had to do this with everything
I've written to give the work a sort of tension." At that point in his career,
Styron usually found the artistic "challenge" in the rendering of time. In *Nat
Turner*, "meditation" compounds the difficulty of mere time. The postmodern
strategies used to resolve the difficulties in the novel result in the replenishment
of the "historical novel" and alter the way Stryon should be examined. History
as trap becomes theme and the very problem of the narrative reverberates into
the historical/political debate engendered by its publication and reception.

Because critics automatically evaluate Styron as merely a traditional
novelist, they have trapped themselves as readers in a psychological *cul de
sac*. Readers must grant Styron his biographical *données* because the book
aims ultimately at acsthetic self-sufficiency. So, as Jonathan Morse aptly
theorizes, the reader collaborates in a kind of illusion as he "invests"
himself in "the act of thinking about a life"; the reader's role reproduces the
author's so that the success of *Nat Turner* "derives its ordering control over
history from the power of text over context." In this collusion of reader and
author entering history to achieve the biographical truth of Nat Turner,
Styron threads the book with signposts about the book's premise. It is more
than a "presumptive" biography; it is, in fact, a self-reflexive document
which should lead readers to a subtle recognition of the intricate failure of
history, language, and truth. The book springs from a real document—a
confession, to the hypothesized construction of that document, to Nat's
own meditation on the glory and the cheat of history.

The sequence of quotations below will underscore the design of the
"meditation" as Styron employs it in Nat Turner:

> 1) Early in the novel, as Gray reads the document Nat is to sign
> he says: "'Of course, Nat, this ain't supposed to represent your
> exact words as you said them to me. Naturally, in a court

confession there's got to be a kind of, uh, dignity of style, so this here's more or less a reconstitution and *recomposition* of the relative crudity of manner. . . . [later] I'm glad you feel I've done justice to your own narrative, Nat.'"

2) Later, Styron has Nat wonder "just how much of the truth I was telling him might find its way into those confessions of mine that he would eventually publish, I assumed not much, but it no longer mattered to me."

3) Finally, at an apex of historical self-consciousness and cynicism, Nat contemplates his own significance to the rebellion: "surely they could not have gotten far without my knowledge of a strategic route, and my mission would have been set down as a 'localized disturbance' involving 'a few disgruntled darkies' rather than the earthquake it truly became."

In each case, Styron foregrounds the character's awareness of his participation in history, especially as it moves inexorably towards literate and literary document. Clearly, the self-consciousness of the frame story of Nat Turner, the flawed construction of a confession of a black revolutionist by "a white racist," and each man's view of his role in history satisfy the reflexive demands of postmodern fiction. Styron found in the choice of subject and point of view a chance to examine the fictional aesthetics of historical composition as process and product: "The beauty of the story to me—of the subject as a takeoff point of history—is the fact that so little really is known about this event. The outlines are there. . . . It seems to me that when you have a historical event which is documented almost to the point of boredom its validity as a subject for fiction is reduced . . . the beauty for me of Nat as a subject is the fact that I can use whatever responsible imagination I have trying to create my own myth."

The indignant and offended readers of *Nat Turner* provided Styron with a lesson in the hazards of authorship. It is worth noting that he adopted an anticipatory and guarded tone in interviews with his next "meditation on history." *Sophie's Choice* has brashness and risk as its subject. Styron, justifying his controversial choice of subject, claimed, "'I wanted to explore what Auschwitz represents in history. . . . I wanted a new way of looking at it, a new perspective. . . . It's a mistake to think that only the survivors have a right to write about it . . . its victims were not all Jews.'" When asked specifically if these decisions wouldn't "invite a barrage of criticism," Styron dodged, "'I've been scrupulous about the facts and used the historical record. It has a lot about the workings of the camp. But it is a novel, a novelist is not a scholar, and the book is not buried in footnotes.'" In other interviews, Styron assumes a wary but consciously adversarial posture when he defends his approach. He admits that if the critics had found errors in his handling of Auschwitz they wouldn't have "missed the opportunity to corner me"; or "Rabbis, Poles, ex-Nazis—they'll all be after my hide."

Yet, all the prepublication caution in the world was not sufficient to defuse an attack quite similar to that of the Ten Black Writers. This time it was Alvin H. Rosenfeld in *A Double Dying*. Rosenfeld indicts Styron, fearful that such powers of fiction may "achieve more immediate and pervasive impact than history. For this very reason, fictional representations of the Holocaust need to be judged against a particularly careful standard of truth." Rosenfeld proceeds to fault Styron for his fictionalizations, his naive use of sources (Höss's autobiography), Styron's charitable focus on murderers as abstractions of evil, and his perverted dedication to creating an "Erotics of Auschwitz." At his most generous, Rosenfeld deems Styron's folly an "unwitting spoof" on the Holocaust.

Even more insidious than critics who simply object to the fictionalization of the Holocaust are the critics who find in *Sophie's Choice* still another occasion to question Styron's ability as a Southerner—and thus presumably too morally deficient an observer—to address the Holocaust. John Gardner, who made a career of moral issues in literature, serves as a sterling case of a critic who missed Styron's transition into postmodernism. In fact, it is my contention that Styron's fictional strategies in the appropriation of history place him front and center, preempting not just his text, but virtually placing him in a postmodern showdown over the role of *auteur*. Gardner took the occasion of his review to foam about the novel as an occasion for all manifestations of bigotry: "the worst that can be said of humanity Styron claims for himself, wringing his hands, tearing his hair, wailing to all the congregation, *Mea culpa*!"

Gardner commends Styron for his "absurd" goal in *Sophie* of "*understanding Auschwitz*," but predictably waters the compliment: "Styron's justice and compassion . . . are impressive, almost awesome . . . precisely because we know by his slips that they [justice and compassion] are not natural to him but earned." Gardner succumbs to the temptation of what Styron views as either analytic "self-righteousness, or a suffocating and provincial innocence." And as if this condescension were not already sufficient, Gardner remarks further on what he considers Styron's practice of the Southern Gothic tradition, a literary tradition which has "always made Yankees squirm." Speaking as Every Yankee, Gardner concludes by judging that the South (I assume as embodied by Styron, typed by Gardner here as failed, earnest, and curious) "by its literary tradition . . . has always been an intensely emotional and in a queer way, idealistic place . . . [and consequently, Yankees] wince at novels in which the characters are always groaning, always listening in painful joy to classical music . . . and we blush at passages like [Styron's romantic and meditative "Oh, my God" sections]." In short, though Gardner pretends to objective literary criticism, what has happened is an artful sting. Gardner has become involved with the man he believes Styron to be and not the construction of the persona *Sophie's Choice* offers.

Cushing Strout has speculated on the nature of "border country" fiction, neither history nor fiction, and found Styron guilty of wasting the benefits and tolerance of both worlds. But judging *Nat Turner* and *Sophie's Choice* by generic standards does not account for very much of the merit demonstrated in both books. The generic problem becomes a kind of devious ruse by which Styron has managed to deflect attention from the real issue of timeliness and authorial presence. The heart of both novels is their language—the rich overvoice that recreates Styron's version of *Nat Turner*, and the nearly pedantic overvoice of William Styron, the Ishmaelic survivor or a young author named Stingo or formerly Stinky. In the emerging tradition of postmoderism, these versions and personae compete with the facts of history for a privileged position in the reading experience. Such rivalry may seem vain, inappropriate, a pretext to "meditate" on history, but such intimate responses to the past have become the literary order of the day: Vidal creates Burr; Mailer, Gary Gilmore. Styron is simply stepping into the mainstream of an emerging tradition. Because it is the narrator's voice—the non-eyewitness to history—that Styron ulti-mately wants us to attend, he can end the action of both novels with grue-some finales: Sophie and Nathan commit suicide; Nat is hung and made into grease and his remaining hide sold. But because Styron has left the despair behind, both novels conclude with renewal: "This was not judg-ment day—only morning. Morning: excellent and fair" in *Sophie's Choice*, and in *Nat Turner*, a prayer that ends "and I will be his God and he shall be my son." With postmodernism history becomes a pre-text for readings of the self that create historical event and document.

The creation and consequent preservation of Nat Turner and Sophie out of the shards of fact, history, and fiction lead us to the final question: Styron's motive for giving up traditional modernism and its attendant "truths of the human heart," in favor of the avowedly narcissistic emphasis on self characteristic of the postmodern tradition. Postmodernism as prac-ticed by Barth and Mailer has been faulted for self-indulgence and superfi-ciality—more game than serious exercise. But Styron has selected and refined the features of postmodernism in order to examine the nature of art and artist in the waning twentieth century. For Styron, the art of fiction and the art of history are co-extensive occupations which achieve meaning only when they are imaginatively realized and personally felt. The author forces himself into an interstice between event and recreation, thereby making meaning personal, even though mediated by the author's self-conscious presence. Through this risky juncture Styron offers aesthetic redemption for historical tragedy. There is no longer the universal panacea of "modernism"; instead, there is a personal, postmodern transcendence, and it is only available through aesthetics acting on memory. And in the literal center of *Sophie's Choice* Styron offers us a microcosm of his new position. It explains what the relationship of an individual is to time and memory; it illuminates what the relationship is between the artist and history as a subject:

> I had attempted more or less successfully to pinpoint my own activities on the first day of April, 1943, the day when Sophie, entering Auschwitz, fell into the "slow hands of the living damnation." At some point late in 1947—only a relatively brief number of years removed from the beginning of Sophie's ordeal—I rummaged through my memory in an attempt to locate myself in time on the same day that Sophie walked through the gates of hell. The first day of April, 1943—April Fools' Day—had a mnemonic urgency. . . . I was able to come up with the absurd fact that on that platform in Auschwitz, it was a lovely spring morning in Raleigh, North Carolina, where I was gorging myself on bananas.

> And what, I have asked myself . . . were the activities of old Stingo, buck private in the United States Marine Corps, at the moment when the terrible last dust—in a translucent curtain of powdery siftings so thick that, in Sophie's words, "you could taste it on the lips like sand"—of some 2,100 Jews from Athens and the Greek islands billowed across the vista upon which she had earlier fixed her gaze. . . . The answer is remarkably simple. I was writing a letter of birthday felicitations—the letter itself easily obtainable not so long ago from a father who has cherished my most vapid jottings (even when I was very young) in the assurance that I was destined for some future literary luminosity. I extract here the central paragraph, which followed an affectionate expression of greetings. I am profoundly appalled now by its collegiate silliness, but I think it worth quoting in order to further emphasize the glaring and even, perhaps, terrifying incongruity.

In recreating history by way of the artist's personal conception of it, the author offers the survivors of Holocaust, revolt, and sundry atrocities in a nightmarish world, their only chance for meaningful forgiveness. Styron sees his intrusive authorial self not as "trivial" or "impertinent." He confronts "the jaded reader surfeited with our century's perdurable feast of atrocities" a chance to offer a kind of repair through art, events which lacerate memory. Having resisted the notion that "the Holocaust was some sort of sacrosanct area that could not be treated," Styron struggles to find language sufficient for this historical place. It is a place he regards as "most unyielding to meaning or definition." In his hands, the tradition of postmodernism creates an opportunity for a new kind of meditation, a meditation that becomes medium, method and hope. Stingo/Styron makes his own appeal: "If one is historically minded enough, one can be charitable."

RALPH TUTT

Stingo's Complaint: Styron and the Politics of Self-Parody

William Styron's position as an American writer rests on four full-length novels and a novella published over a period of nearly thirty years. The dozen or so short stories he has published represent apprentice work for the most part or work extracted from novels-in-progress. He has shown no particular talent or predilection for the form. His occasional prose has been only a sideline, he admits (*Quiet Dust*), but several essays and review essays—those on Nat Turner, Lieutenant Calley, the prison letters of James Blake, Philip Caputo's *A Rumor of War*, Richard L. Rubenstein's *The Cunning of History*, and the case of eighteen-year old Peter Reilly charged in 1973 with the murder of his mother in Canaan, Connecticut—do command attention not only because they reflect the nagging moral anxiety of his fiction but also because they obviate the image foisted on him by Norman Mailer in the Sixties, that of a reconstructed Virginia Gentleman and literary opportunist with the mind of a virgin oyster. Gentleman he is—nowhere has this been more evident than in his public response to Mailer's vendetta—a gentleman driven by ancient moral imperatives in confronting Old- and New-World barbarisms like the Southampton insurrection, the My Lai Massacre, Auschwitz, and (to juxtapose the egotistical with the historical sublime) Mailer himself.

In addition to his fiction and occasional prose, Styron has collaborated on an unproduced film script, *Dead!*, based on the Snyder-Gray murder of

From *Modern Fiction Studies* 34, no. 4. © 1989 by the Purdue Research Foundation.

1927. *In the Clap Shack*, a play based on an episode both amusing and grue-some in his Marine Corps experience during World War Two, was produced by the Yale Repertory Theatre in 1973 and published the same year. Putting it gently, the play and screenplay served primarily as reminders that the gifts that had made Styron famous were not those of a playwright. It had been a good five years since he won the Pulitzer Prize for *The Confessions of Nat Turner*. Had all the racist fuss following it done him in?

Few novelists of Styron's generation have remained so long in the lime-light with such long hauls between books and without benefit of the celebrity grubbed by talk-show veterans, Norman Mailer, Gore Vidal, Truman Capote, Tennessee Williams, and Mary McCarthy in the Seventies. His last two novels, *The Confessions of Nat Turner* and *Sophie's Choice*, received more than a fair share of media hype, but he has always scorned the television spar-ring ring and during the Johnson administration grew wary of literary awards and White House invitations. Since a skirmish with student militants at Harvard in 1968, his appearances on college campuses have been rare. It was not until 1973 that his work was included in a major college anthology of American literature.

After his success with *Lie Down in Darkness* in 1951, Styron was widely considered the Southern writer most worthy of comparison with Faulkner and most likely to revitalize the "Southern School" for post-World War Two readers. In a *Paris Review* interview of this year, however, he declared his independence of the Southern School and all other Schools, berating those critics whose existence depends upon the invention and inventory of "Schools" and discouraging any thoughts of his becoming spokesman for a new generation. "What the hell is a spokesman, anyway? I hate the idea of spokesmen . . . so-called spokesmen trumpeting around, elbowing one another out of the way to see who'll be the first to give a new and original name to twenty-five million people: the Beat Generation, or the Silent Generation, and God knows what-all."

The following year *The Long March* was published. In thematic complexity, economy of means, and stylistic finesse, this novella is his most flawless performance to date. It deserves its place with Melville's *Bartleby the Scrivener*, Crane's *The Blue Hotel*, Faulkner's *Red Leaves*, and Flannery O'Connor's *Wise Blood* in Philip Rahv's collection, *Eight Great American Short Novels*. In its allegorical leaning as in its theme, *The Long March* resembles *Billy Budd*; in its spare prose and compact structure, it is unlike most of Faulkner's work or anything Styron himself has written since.

Eight years passed before the appearance of his second novel, *Set This House on Fire*. Fusty with operatic prose and existential hand-wringing, *Set This House on Fire* was nonetheless prophetic in what it had to say about the rocky road ahead for art in the Sixties: the dominance of science and the onslaught of drugs and pornography in what one of its characters calls "the age of the slob." *Set This House on Fire* is as close as Styron has come to writing a big novel of contemporary social analysis, the kind of novel Mailer was trying to write in the Fifties. The international movie colony setting of *Set This House on Fire* in Sambuco was, in fact, something of a second to Mailer's Deer Park in Desert D'Or, Southern California. Mailer had been working hard to rid himself of the image of a nice Jewish boy from Brooklyn; in the neoteric gleam of the Sixties, Styron seemed to be working just as hard to evade the parochialism of the "Southern School." Although critics have continued to make the Faulkner Connection—on the basis of Styron's mythological state, Port Warwick, Virginia, and what has been vaguely regarded as his Faulknerian brooding on the omnipresence of the historical past—he abandoned the hinterland for the anomic state of America in *Set This House on Fire*, tracking from Greenwich Village to Italy the road to excess and moral degeneration of his main characters. Both of them are Southerners: Cass Kinsolving, like Stingo in *Sophie's Choice*, is a blocked artist; King of the Slobs in Greenwich Village and Sambuco is Cass's tormentor, the sadistic Mason Flagg. Byronic victim of early satiety, Flagg is also a windy intellectual spokesman for the age. Like Nathan Landau, the big bully of *Sophie's Choice*, he bears close comparison with the Village Voice of the Fifties, Norman Mailer. "The Age of the Slob" did not become a catch phrase of the Sixties as "Beat Generation" and "Silent Generation" had in the Fifties. Styron's analysts, however, have frequently taken it as an indication of his outlook on the times; as such, it represents an author who, having shunned the role of "spokesman for a generation" in 1951, seemed to do a turnabout trying to fulfill it nine years later.

"I will try to be fair about his talent, but I do not know if I can, because I must speak against the bias of finding him not nearly as big as he ought to be." This is Norman Mailer writing at the tag end of the Fifties on the eve of Styron's long-awaited second novel. According to Mailer, Styron had written "the prettiest novel of [their] generation." At its best *Lie Down in Darkness* had beauty, he said; it was seldom sentimental and even had "whispers of near-genius as the work of a twenty-three-year old." (Styron was twenty-six in 1951 when *Lie Down in Darkness* was first published, and Mailer was twenty-eight.) "It would have been the best novel of our generation," Mailer went on, "if it had not lacked three qualities: Styron was not near to creating a man who could move on his feet, his mind was uncorrupted by a new idea, and his book was without evil. There was only Styron's sense of the tragic: misunderstanding—and that is too small a window to look upon the world we have known."

Mailer predicted that if Styron's long-awaited second novel was any good at all, his reception would be "a study in the art of literary advancement. For Styron has spent years oiling every literary lever and power which could help him on his way, and there are medals waiting for him in the mass-media." As luck would have it, *Set This House on Fire* drew critical fire as heavy as that which had greeted Mailer's *Barbary Shore* (1951) and *The Deer Park* (1955). Johnny-on-the-spot Mailer contributed gleefully to the barrage. "A bad maggoty novel," he called it. "Four or five half-great short stories were buried like pullulating organs in a corpse of fecal matter, overblown unconceived philosophy. . . ."

When Styron emerged six years later with *The Confessions of Nat Turner*, it was, as John Aldridge has pointed out, at a most propitious moment. The fashion for existential angst popularized by Sartre and Camus was passé in 1960 when *Set This House on Fire* appeared, but just as *Lie Down in Darkness* had come in 1951, a time when it could be regarded as the last flowering of the Southern novel after Faulkner, so too did the appearance of *The Confessions of Nat Turner* (1967) nicely coincide with the furor of the civil rights movement, and in the spring of 1979 when *Sophie's Choice* was published, controversy over the Holocaust as represented in fiction, drama, and film was still making headlines.

The fortuitous timing of *The Confessions of Nat Turner*, as everyone knows, brought mixed blessings for Styron. I will not resurrect here the tedious racial and historical controversy that followed its success. Nor will I contribute to the forlorn debate over a novelist's prerogatives in the appropriation of historical data for fictional purposes. "We must grant the artist his subject, his idea, his *donnée:* our criticism is applied only to what he makes of it" ("The Art of Fiction"). On this advice of Henry James, I will bow out by the front door, mentioning only, as others have, that social controversy attending initial publication of *The Confessions of Nat Turner* tended to subvert the question of its intrinsic literary merit.

No backslash comparable to that of William Styron's *Nat Turner: Ten Black Writers Respond*, the protest anthology edited by John Henrik Clarke in 1968, has yet sullied the initial popular and critical success of *Sophie's Choice*, but Styron's quasi-autobiographical narrator, Stingo, accounts so thoroughly for the research he has undertaken in tackling the Holocaust that it seems Styron was shoring himself up against further charges of historical inaccuracy, getting combat ready for the entire community of contemporary Jewish intellectuals: George Steiner, Elie Wiesel, and Bruno Bettelheim, all the way down to Norman Mailer. In this respect, as in others, the book is markedly similar to Philip Roth's *The Ghost Writer*, published the same year.

By my count, *The Ghost Writer* is Roth's sixth *Bildungsroman*. To be precise, it is a *Künstlerroman* like *Sophie's Choice*. If we take the artist-personae in these two books as close to gospel, they give us the most reliable news we have yet received of their creators' struggles with life and art.

Lustful snoop, Nathan (Dedalus) Zuckerman, the narrator-protagonist of *The Ghost Writer*, discovers in Henry James's short story, "The Middle Years," a new source of strength. Standing on a volume of James's short stories in the study of his current literary mentor, Emanuel Isidore Lonoff, Zuckerman listens in on a lovers' quarrel upstairs between Lonoff and his young mistress, Amy Bellette, whom Zuckerman subsequently fantasizes as an erotic Anne Frank.

Like Stingo's Sophie, Zuckerman's Anne has escaped the ovens and immigrated to America. Zuckerman imagines a scene in which he presents her to his family:

> I kept seeing myself coming back to New Jersey and saying to my family, "I met a marvelous young woman while I was up in New England. I love her and she loves me. We are going to be married." "Married? But so fast? Nathan, is she Jewish?" "Yes, she is." "But who is she?" "Anne Frank."

In this outrage against a revered Jewish martyr—and in his most refined comic manner yet—Roth presents the same frustrations with bourgeois Jewish culture that we find in his other fictional counterparts, Neil Klugman, Alexander Portnoy, David Kepesh, and Peter Tarnopol, all of whom find the Jewish community of their youth stifling and inimical to a writer's growth.

Styron's Stingo, on the other hand, expresses at much greater length a strong sense of kinship with the Jews, thereby trying to eliminate—or so it would seem—the possibility of objections to a Southern WASP poaching on sacred ground. "An unconscious urge to be among Jews was at least part of the reason for my migration to Brooklyn," he tells us.

> Like numerous Southerners of a certain background, learning and sensibility, I have from the very beginning responded warmly to Jews, my first love having been Miriam Bookbinder, the daughter of a local ship chandler, who even at the age of six wore in her lovely hooded eyes the vaguely disconsolate, largely inscrutable mystery of her race; and then later I experienced a grander empathy with Jewish folk which, I am persuaded, is chiefly available to those Southerners shattered for years and years by rock-hard encounter with the anguish of Abraham and Moses' stupendous quest and the Psalmist's troubled hosannas and the abyssal vision of Daniel and all the other revelations, bittersweet

confections, tall tales and beguiling horrors of the Protestant/Jewish Bible. In addition, it is a platitude by now that the Jew has found considerable fellowship among white Southerners because Southerners have possessed another darker, sacrificial lamb.

If the platitude referred to here is lost on the reader, Styron makes abundantly clear in discursive passages elsewhere his analogy between slavery in the South and Nazi concentration camps and the fact that no race and no time or place has a corner on virtue, crucifixion rights, or guilt.

Stingo identifies himself at the beginning of the novel as an Ishmael figure, "a lonesome young Southerner wandering amid the Kingdom of the Jews," jobless, with very little money, and suffering writer's block. "Call me Stingo," he says, and, sure enough, just as the lone survivor of the Pequod stumbles upon a sea of trouble, Stingo at sea in Brooklyn comes headlong into a rooming-house full of the same. Out of the BMT station with his suitcase and Marine Corps seabag, the twenty-two-year-old veteran emerges in Flatbush, summer of '47, heading for the rooming house of Mrs. Yetta Zimmerman. ("Yetta's Liberty Hall" is the owner's name for the place; because its monochromatic pink exteriors and interiors remind him of a back-lot set from *The Wizard of Oz*, Stingo dubs Mrs. Zimmerman's house the Pink Palace.) Armed with two dozen pencils, ten legal pads, and a new pencil sharpener, he sits at his desk unable to make any progress beyond the prologue of his novel, which he has compulsively reread nearly a hundred times. He tries to read Marlow; he performs his Seymour Glass ritual, inventorying the contents of his medicine cabinet; gazing out his window at the park across the street, he wonders what he, "an ineffective and horny Calvinist," is doing here in Brooklyn among all these Jews. As he is relishing the names of the six other tenants—Nathan Landau, Lillian Grossman, Morris Fink, Sophie Zawistowska, Astrid Weinstein, Moishe Muskatblit—that he has scribbled on a piece of paper, he is alarmed by a disturbance in his paper thin ceiling. The lamp fixture wobbles; plaster dust sifts down; he half expects the bed, on which two people are obviously fornicating like "crazed wild animals," to come plunging through the ceiling.

Thus, in an overblown passage reminiscent of Nathan Dedalus' ascent, with a boost from Henry James, to the ceiling of Maestro Lonoff's ceiling in *The Ghost Writer*, we are introduced, offstage, to Nathan and Sophie, who will become Stingo's chief cohorts in the Land of Oz. Their frenzied lovemaking is followed by music, Beethoven's Fourth Symphony, and a quarrel that reaches volcanic proportions, all but drowning out Beethoven.

In the calm following the storm overhead, Stingo, still hanging fire with his novel, opens a letter from his father with a newspaper clipping on the suicide of a girl named Maria (rhymes with pariah), who was his first serious love interest. Unknown to him at the time, Maria had lived around the corner from him on Sixth Avenue in his Village days. "It was a sign of the city's inhuman vastness that we had both dwelt for months in an area as compact as Greenwich Village without ever having encountered each other." The irony of such proximate distance between him and his first love and the question, "Could I have saved her?" haunt his imagination and provide inspiration to continue his novel. He broods on Maria all afternoon. In his dreams that night, he experiences "the most ferociously erotic hallucination" of his life. Wanton nymph, Maria, "in some sunlit and serene pasture of the Tidewater, a secluded place hemmed around by undulant oak trees," croons to him as lasciviously as ever did a sex-crazed nymph from the pages of Philip Roth.

When Stingo wakes up, his nursery-pink ceiling is stained with oncoming night shadows. He lets out a howl from the depths of his soul, only to find more nails in his crucifix—Nathan and Sophie at it again!

In this opening stage of the novel, what seems especially significant insofar as the portrait of a young artist is concerned—Stingo's adolescent rebellion, his desire for freedom through art—is that his artistic longings for the sublime are persistently undermined by his obstructed, broncobuster libido, inducing a mild state of hypochondria. Prolonged celibacy does indeed appear to take precedence over his novel as the chief cause of his anxiety. After he receives news of Maria's suicide, his sexual fantasies take a distinct turn toward the morbid and moribund, and the novel begins to take shape in his mind.

Like the news of Maria's death, Stingo's first sight of Sophie Zawistowska revives his creative urge as it stimulates sexual desire. His very existence is reclaimed by Sophie, who has "a distant but real resemblance to Maria Hunt. What is still ineffaceable about my first glimpse of her is not simply the lovely simulacrum she seemed to me of the dead girl but the despair on her grieving shadows of someone hurtling toward death."

Coming to know the Negro was Styron's moral imperative for every white Southerner in 1968. The case of Stingo in 1979 suggested that the new moral imperative of every Southern WASP was to know the Jew and the Nazi Holocaust. Nat Turner dreams persistently of the supernal; just as persistent is Stingo's desire for carnal knowledge and experience of the ghastly. He wants to *know* Sophie; he's as enthralled by her concentration camp tattoo as he is by her dentures, her madcap clothes, and Sally Bowles/Holly Golightly airs. He also wants to know ghastly Nathan.

Depending upon his appetite or mood, Nathan alternately praises Stingo's novel-in-progress and needles him about his Southern cracker background, pointing the finger at Senator Bilbo and the lynching of Bobby Weed. The Southern Renaissance is over, he proclaims; it has succumbed to the Jewish Renaissance under the leadership of the author of *Dangling Man*. Southern fiction died with Faulkner's best. A new day is dawning with Saul Bellow. In his more sadistic moods, Nathan is as hard on Stingo as he is on Sophie. He tries to make as much a fool of Stingo as Mason Flagg makes of blocked artist, Cass Kinsolving, in *Set This House on Fire*.

Crammed as it is with allusions to persons, places, and things, real and imagined, *Sophie's Choice* needs an index. Part autobiography, part fictionalized history, part *roman à clef*, it has interest on one level as a parlor game—like Truman Capote's unfinished gossip novel, *Answered Prayers*. Just as we are meant to guess at the identity of literary lions, Lonoff and Abravanel in the literary egosphere of *The Ghost Writer*, we are meant to guess at the identities of Sophie, Nathan, and others converging in Stingo's memories of the Pink Palace.

The stodgy man who fires Stingo from his first bona fide civilian job is lately-appointed editor-in-chief of McGraw-Hill in the heyday of Thor Heyerdahl. He was Maxwell Perkins' heir to the rampant manuscripts of Thomas Wolfe. Secretly this man is called by Stingo "the weasel." He further reveals Weasel to be a near-anagram of the Chief's actual surname. Like Brett Ashley and Sally Bowles, Sophie, by Styron's account, was an actual person whom he met at the same time and under the same circumstances described in the novel. Nathan Landau? With his murderous rages, Harvard degree, and delusion of winning the Nobel Prize for a breakthrough in cancer research, late Forties Nathan takes us at least as far back as Mailer's egosphere of the Fifties and Sixties. There was that nasty business about the stabbing (we all forget which wife it was), commitment to Belleview, and his New York mayoral candidacy. Then there was the campus lecture circuit, all that bullying and baiting: D.C., 1967, the Ambassador Theatre, and urination rites prior to his march on the Pentagon with a personal cameraman in tow. Woody Allen probably capped the legendary Aquarius for all time in his line about Mailer willing his ego to the Harvard Medical School; it's still getting laughs at revival houses in Cambridge.

Styron's takeoff on Mailer may be one of the more cunning characterizations of *Sophie's Choice*. It's also confusing, the way much of the novel is confusing, because of an imbalance between the high tragic sense Styron claims as his métier and a comic inclination, sometimes impish, more often sophomorically bawdy, that wants out. He can satirize the folly of Nathan and Mason Flagg pushing the limits of absurdity through sex and drugs—

until death and carnage become the result. Then, as if the star performer is stricken between acts, the curtain that closed on Megalomania in Toyland opens on *Götterdämmerung*. Like Holden Caulfield nostalgic for jerks like old Stradlater and Ackley, Peter Leverett and Stingo start thinking how much they're going to miss old Mason and Nathan.

Stingo may come to know Sophie a lot better than Nathan, but he's as fascinated by Nathan's sadism as he is by Sophie's suffering. On discovering that the "sweet siren of Cracow" is a *shiksa*, he is surprised, almost staggered. The revelation, he says, didn't matter one way or another at the time; in fact, "there was something vaguely negative and self-preoccupied in my reaction. Like Gulliver among the Houyhnhnms, I had rather thought myself a unique figure in this huge Semitic arrondissement." It becomes evident, however, that he takes great pleasure in finding he is not the only Gentile in Brooklyn. Under (or "over" as the case may be) his roof in the Pink Palace is another who is proof that Jews were not the exclusive victims of Nazi atrocities. Sophie becomes not only a macabre love object but a fellow exile in the Kingdom of the Jews—and an ally against the Wizard, Landau, who seems to know everything.

Soon after they meet, the trio is preparing to depart on an excursion to Coney Island. Nathan, in his sinister, kidding way, starts accusing Sophie of being a cheater and a tease. Here he is, pushing thirty, crazy in love with a Polish *shiksa* who withholds her favors as determinedly as a Jewish girl he'd spent five years trying to seduce. "What do you think of that?" He gives Stingo a sly wink, whereupon "Cracker" (Nathan sometimes calls Stingo "Cracker," much to Stingo's chagrin) does a shuffle step.

> "Bad news," I improvised in a jocular tone. "It's a form of sadism." Although I'm certain I kept my composure, I was really vastly surprised at this revelation: Sophie was not Jewish!
> . . . So Sophie was a *shiksa*. Well, hush my mouth, I thought in mild wonder.

Spaced-out Nathan treats Sophie and Stingo worse than house niggers; they are collaborators who can never know the agony of true-blue Jews.

On the autobiographical level, *Sophie's Choice* can't decide whether it wants to be picaresque sex comedy or a serious *Künstlerroman* relating Stingo's sexual blockage to his writer's block. That a libidinous young man pursuing voluptuous teases, Leslie Lapidus and Mary Alice Grimball, would also lust after an emaciated older woman with dentures and imagine her as his bride, the father of his children, and grand dame of his goober plantation is a curious incongruity that undermines the novel's tragic aspect and confounds our response to Stingo's characterization of himself as a "serious" writer of an incurably morbid and didactic disposition. His melancholy insularity, offset by periodic streaks of ribaldry, is further compounded of Satanic sexual appetites and a Faustian desire for ultimate knowledge. He's a Byronic hybrid with strong features of Manfred, Childe Harold, and Don Juan, and as he pictures Sophie, the chief object of his desire, she too is a hybrid, part siren, part hag.

When, on their flight south from crazy Nathan, Stingo's passion is finally—abundantly—gratified by Sophie in a seedy Washington hotel (Hotel Congress), we are greatly relieved—and somewhat embarrassed by the strenuous effort that has gone into making the scene "real." In this fagged-out era of sexual liberation, Stingo's adolescent trials on the borders of sexual initiation and his big breakthrough in Washington seem at best a quaint echo of Mary McCarthy, James Baldwin, Mailer, and Roth, at worst an uncensored Neil Simon concoction without the oneliners. Although Styron himself has confessed a certain discomfort in trying to write explicitly of sex, he pursues the task doggedly throughout *Sophie's Choice*. In Stingo, he gives us a dual portrait of himself as the fledgling artist struggling with his first novel and as a mature novelist struggling with his fourth. If *Sophie's Choice* is preeminently about the trials of a survivor, it is no less about the trials of a concentration camp survivor than it is about the trials of survival as an artist in post-World War Two America. Like *The Ghost Writer* and Kurt Vonnegut's *Slaughterhouse-Five*, it is partly about the art-making process in itself, power struggles within the American literary establishment and the overpowering task of a writer confronting events of great historical magnitude.

As a die-hard conventional novelist, Styron became an anomaly in the avant-garde of the Seventies, riding somewhere to the rear of a fox hunt in the *Esquire* cartoon accompanying Tom Wolfe's article on the supercession of the nineteenth-century novel by the New Journalism and the nonfiction novel. Kurt Vonnegut in *Slaughterhouse-Five*, a novel partly concerned with the impossibility of writing realistically about the one earth-shaking event he witnessed at first hand, resorted to his usual politics of parody and got comic mileage out of banal talk about the death of the novel. On one of his time-trips, Billy Pilgrim of the *Ilium Gazette* stumbles onto a New York City talk show where literary critics are discussing this issue. One of the discussants says it's "a nice time to bury the novel, now that a Virginian, one hundred years after Appomattox, had written *Uncle Tom's Cabin*." Another says people don't read well anymore. They can't translate print into exciting situations, so authors have had to do what Norman Mailer did, performing in public what he had written. In 1981 Mailer, 58, and considerably mellowed since his scurrilous attacks on Styron in their salad days, paid him a backhanded compliment:

> If I had no economic necessity I would have written about one and a half as many pages as Bill Styron and that's because I'm about one and a half times more energetic than old Bill. . . . I would have written books that are more like Styron's too, in the sense that they would have been more literary and more well-rubbed, and I would have spent more time on them and I would have polished them and I would have lived with them and would have sighed over them and I would have taken them more seriously than I take my books, although I do take them very seriously. But I mean I would have been truly solemn about them.

Thus Mailer expressed regret that his books had lacked the seriousness, solemnity, and polish of arch-rival Styron, while Styron had bounced back with a novel of huge popular success and modest critical approval.

Just how serious and solemn is William Styron in *Sophie's Choice*? Most reviewers and critics have assessed the novel almost entirely in terms of its newsworthy treatment of the Holocaust, giving only scant attention to its autobiographical framework. In an interview on the appearance of *Sophie's Choice*, Styron spoke of a dearth of material in the ordinariness of his life. "Vast areas of it," he said, "are just not dramatic or interesting enough to write about. I have never found in the quotidian much that was worthy of exploration. Updike can find his material there, but I require a larger canvas." Tacked on the wall of his study is Flaubert's advice to the writer: "Be regular and original in your life like a bourgeoise so that you may be violent and original in your work." Why, then, did he adopt a quasiautobiographical stance in writing and publicizing *Sophie's Choice*? Its larger canvas is *l'univers concentrationnaire*, a world of concentration camps that, he said, "altered forever our consciousness of evil." Its smaller canvas is the circumscribed world of Virginia, the Marine Corps, McGraw-Hill, and the Pink Palace, Stingo's domain, that gives every indication of self-advertisement, if not self-parody, recalling Mailer in the Sixties.

Robert Towers, puzzled by Styron's intentions as I was, suggested the problem that critics now face in evaluating Styron's work: "*Sophie's Choice* is a highly self-conscious performance full of autobiographical references, and it is narrated by a man called Stingo whose career parallels Styron's in many particulars. . . . Fact? Fiction? Self-parody? Stingo's claim to have also written *Sophie's Choice*, as well as a book closely resembling *Lie Down in Darkness*, makes it difficult to unravel author from narrator, Styron from Stingo."

Self-defense rather than self-parody seemed to me the predominant authorial mood of *Sophie's Choice* when I first read it. Rereading it in the light of *The Ghost Writer,* I thought of Towers' suggestion. The flight South; Stingo's fantasizing the presentation of Sophie as his fiancée to father and friends; Stingo and Sophie establishing a home on the order of Faulkner's "Rowan Oak" and trying to decide on a name: "Goober Haven"? "Five Elms"? "Rosewood"? "Sophie"? Can all this be serious? Or is it a case of the dish running away with the spoon? Is the entire novel an elaborate joke on the reader like the Anne Frank hoax in *The Ghost Writer*? (Remember it was April Fool's Day that Sophie entered Auschwitz and Stingo entered the Marines.) In the freewheeling references to his Southern past, his literary career, his sexual frustration, it seems clear that, twenty years after *Advertisements for Myself,* Styron was following the lead of Mailer (and Roth as well), armoring himself with personality as a guard against critical disparagement for having written another old-fashioned novel in an era of accelerating experimentation with language, form, and the idea of history.

Chronology

1925   William Styron born on June 11 in Newport News, Virginia to William Clark Styron, an engineer at the Newport News shipyard and Pauline Margaret Abraham Styron.

1931   Styron enters first grade at John W. Daniel Grammar School in the Fall, where he and the other children are put to work on the *Bay Ray* texts—forerunners of the *Dick and Jane* readers of the 1950s. After his parents move, Styron begins the second grade at Hilton Village Elementary School where he thrived, taking part in many of the numerous artistic and historical pageants which were an important part of the curriculum.

1938   Styron begins his freshman year at Morrison High School. Having skipped a grade in elementary school, Styron encounters difficulty adjusting. Being too small and light for athletics, Styron was oppressed by his schoolmates. However, as an antidote to this abuse, Styron began writing fiction for the Morrison High School newspaper, *The Sponge*.

1939   Styron's mother, Pauline, dies of advanced cancer, a long and protracted illness which caused her young son to feel distant and powerless to help. Nevertheless, Styron is off to a good start in the Fall, having been elected president of his class and winning the title of "Wittiest" in another class election. This promising beginning, however, is not sustained, with Billy earning mostly C's and D's for his classwork and becoming disobedient in school.

1940   Styron's father, W. C. Styron, decides that his son Billy should go to Christchurch in the autumn, a small Episcopal boys' prep school not far from Newport News, located on a magnificent broad, wooded hill overlooking the Rappahannock River. Basically a relaxed and happy environment, the curriculum was standard for the time: English, Latin, French, history, science, and mathematics with sports and activities in the afternoon, followed by chapel (with coat and tie required), supper and study hall. While at Christchurch, Styron worked for the *Stingaree*, the school newspaper, co-edited with Vincent Canby, who later became the lead movie critic for *The New York Times*. While at Christchurch, Billy also excelled in the dramatic arts.

Before entering Christchurch, Billy travels to New York City to see the 1939 World's Fair in Flushing Meadows, and takes in such exhibits as the Westinghouse pavilion where he appeared on a gadget called television and the fair's twin symbols, the Trylon and Perisphere.

1941   Styron's father, W. C., is remarried to Elizabeth Buxton on October 14, during Billy's second year at Christchurch. Billy was uneasy about this new alliance, as Elizabeth had previously criticized him for not working up to his capacity while at Christchurch, for his carousing and beer drinking, and often mentioned the financial sacrifice his father was undergoing in order to send him to prep school.

1941–42   During his second year at Christchurch, Billy tries his hand at fiction, writing a short story, set in wartime Germany, entitled "A Chance in a Million." The story is dated December 8, 1941, and was probably put in final draft the evening before, only a few hours after the news of the Japanese attack on Pearl Harbor.

1942   Styron graduates from Christchurch. He will turn seventeen that June, the same month in which he arrived at Davidson College in Charlotte, North Carolina. Davidson is a Presbyterian college. Here he receives a traditional education grounded in the classics. However, life at Davidson is almost entirely monastic, and it is unusual to see females on campus during the week. Nevertheless, the war has is impact on the population at Davidson when some two hundred Army Air Corps cadets, mainly comprised of men from the North (of Irish, Jewish, Italian and East European extraction), are brought to the campus for temporary training. Styron stays at Davidson for one year only.

1943   Styron enters Duke University near the end of the year, which at the time was known as a good private university catering to affluent northerners unable to get into Ivy League colleges. Unlike Davidson at that time, Duke had no compulsory chapel and Bible class and, moreover, was a large and diverse mixture of undergraduate, graduate and professional schools. Styron was also a V-12 trainee in the Marine Corps and, as such, was enrolled in their officer-training program.

While at Duke University, Styron takes writing classes with Professor William Blackburn, a demanding professor of creative writing, for whom Styron would work very hard at pleasing. Styron would soon embark upon a "rampage" of reading poetry and prose of various styles and periods, a passion for which would soon be seen as rebellious in those classes required for the V-12 program. It is here, at Duke, that Styron meets Barbara Taeusch, known as Bobbie, a lovely young woman who shares Styron's adoration for Professor Blackburn.

1944   In October, Styron is called up and ordered to report to boot camp at the Marine Corps base on Parris Island, South Carolina.

1945   Styron chooses an assignment in October at the Naval Disciplinary Barracks on Harts Island in Long Island Sound, a naval prison in which he was commander of the First Guard Platoon. It is Styron's first experience with imprisonment and helps him to better understand American Negro slavery and the Nazi concentration camps. His choice to work near New York City also enables him to be near Bobbie Taeusch as well as the many artistic and cultural attractions of the city. Styron completes his stint at Harts Island in November.

1946   Styron returns to Duke in the Spring, but is not happy there. His overwhelming desire is to become a writer. He applies to the

Bread Loaf writers' conference in Vermont, the best-known writing program in the country, and is accepted for a two week course in August. In the interim, Styron spends time in Italy, helping with the recovery from the war and gathering background material for *Set This House on Fire*.

1947   Styron returns to Duke, graduates, and moves to New York City, where he spends a brief and unhappy stint as a copy editor and book-jacket blurb writer for McGraw-Hill Publishers. Styron enrolls at the New School for Social Research, an institution which in 1935 became affiliated with the University in Exile, a group of European scholars who fled Hitler and Mussolini, to study writing with Hiram Haydn, the leader of their fiction-writing seminar. Here he begins *Lie Down in Darkness*, a novel which concerns a girl from Virginia who commits suicide in New York City.

1951   In late January, Styron is contacted by the Marine Corps and ordered to report to Camp Lejeune. With Haydn's assistance, Styron receives a deferment until May. To divert his attention from the military life, Styron pores over the galley proofs of *Lie Down in Darkness*. He is enormously popular in France with *Lie Down in Darkness* being named for the Agrégation, the reading list for French Universities, for 1973–1974.

1951   Publishes *Lie Down in Darkness* (Indianapolis: Bobbs-Merrill, 1951; London: Hamish Hamilton, 1952).

1952   Styron meets Rose Burgunder at Johns Hopkins University following a speaking engagement in which he read some passages from *Lie Down in Darkness*. At that time, Rose is working on her Masters Degree at Johns Hopkins and writes a thesis on Wallace Stevens. A poet herself, she also had a great passion for modern poets among them Yeats, Auden, Eliot and Stevens as well as such contemporary critics as I. A. Richards, William Empson, R. P. Blackmur and Alan Tate.

1952   Styron books passage for England on March 5. By April he is in Paris with plans to visit Rome in the Fall. Shortly thereafter, Rose leaves a note for Styron telling him that she is there. They spend a great deal of time together and in early December he asks Rose to marry him.

1953   Although there is opposition from both their families, the couple are wed on May 4, 1953, at the Campidoglio. Many guests were invited to the reception by their friends, Irwin and Marian Shaw, among them Lillian Hellman, whom neither William nor Rose had ever met before.

1955   The Styrons' first child, Susanna Margaret is born at Mount Sinai Hospital in New York City on February 25.

1956   Publishes *The Long March* (New York: Random House; London: Hamish Hamilton, 1962).

1958   The Styrons' second child, Paola Clark, is born at Mount Sinai Hospital in New York City on March 13.

1959   The Styrons' third child, Thomas Haydn Styron, is born while the family is vacationing on Martha's Vineyard on August 4, 1959.

1960   Publishes *Set This House on Fire* (New York: Random House, 1960; London: Hamish Hamilton, 1961).

1961   Styron becomes involved in prison reform through the case of Benjamin Reid, a black man who faced the death sentence until Styron led a crusade to have his sentence commuted to life imprisonment.

1963   Named to the board of directors of the Inter-American Foundation of the Arts.

1964   Styron named a fellow of Silliman College at Yale. His ties to the university are particularly strong given his close friendship with Robert Penn Warren.

        Lie Down in Darkness is a candidate for the Pulitzer Prize. Styron wins the Prix de Rome of the American Academy of Arts and Letters.

1966   The Styrons' fourth child, Alexandra, is born on October 28.

1967   Publishes *The Confessions of Nat Turner* (New York: Random House, 1967; London: Cape, 1968). Awarded Pulitzer Prize for

The Confessions of Nat Turner, a work which evoked strong reviews, both positive and negative, from the academic community.

1968   Never shy of declaring his firm stance for human rights, Styron testifies in court that he witnessed Chicago police beat demonstrators in Lincoln Park during the 1968 Democratic Convention.

1969   Creates waves by commenting on the defection of Anatoly Kuznetsov from the Soviet Union, stating that the author's defection could endanger other dissidents remaining in that country.

1970   Named to the editorial board of the *American Scholar*.

1972   Yale Repertory Theatre stages his play, *In the Clap Shack*. Styron again becomes involved in the cause of other Soviet writers when he joins Bellow, Mailer, Herbert Mitgagn, Malcolm Cowley, Bernard Malamud, Louis Auchincloss, Lionel Trilling and Rex Stout in sending a letter to Soviet leader Nikolay Podgorny, urging the restoration of fundamental human rights to Soviet Jews.

1973   Publishes *In the Clap Shack* (New York: Random House, 1973). During the summer with his family at Martha's Vineyard, Styron has several dreams about Sophie, the Polish Catholic survivor of Auschwitz whom he had known briefly in Brooklyn during the summer of 1949.

1975   Styron joins Arthur Miller and director Mike Nichols in establishing a defense fund for an eighteen-year-old convicted in 1973 for the manslaughter of his mother in Canaan, Connecticut, near Styron's home. Joan Barthel's *A Death in Canaan* (1976) details the case, a book for which Styron wrote the introduction.

1976   Receives the University Union Award for Distinction in Literature from the University of South Carolina, an award previously given to Robert Penn Warren, Robert Lowell and Archibald MacLeish.

1979   Publishes *Sophie's Choice* (New York: Random House, 1979; London: Panthera, 1979).

1982   Publishes *This Quiet Dust and Other Writings* (New York: Random House, 1982), a collection of some of his non-fictional prose, on such subjects as racial tension, prisons, capital punishment, other writers, the craft of writing, the South, military service, and adolescence.

1990   Publishes *Darkness Visible: A Memoir of Madness* (New York: Random House, 1990; London: Cape, 1991).

1993   Publishes *A Tidewater Morning: Three Tales from Youth* (New York: Random House)

            Alarmed by the suppression of freedom of expression and information through the deaths of more than a dozen Turkish journalists in 1992 1993, writes letter to *New York Review of Books* (May 13), along with his wife Rose and such writers as Edward Albee, E. L. Doctorow, Toni Morrison, Harold Pinter and Kurt Vonnegut, to the Turkish government to "demonstrate its commitment" to human rights.

            President Bill Clinton awards Styron the National Medal of the Arts at the White House for "outstanding contributions to the cultural life of the nation."

Contributors

HAROLD BLOOM is Sterling Professor of the Humanities at Yale University and Henry W. and Albert A. Berg Professor of English at the New York University Graduate School. He is the author of over 20 books, including *Shelley's Mythmaking* (1959), *The Visionary Company* (1961), *Blake's Apocalypse* (1963), *Yeats* (1970), *A Map of Misreading* (1975), *Kabbalah and Criticism* (1975), *Agon: Toward a Theory of Revisionism* (1982), *The American Religion* (1992), *The Western Canon* (1994), and *Omens of Millennium: The Gnosis of Angels, Dreams, and Resurrection* (1996). *The Anxiety of Influence* (1973) sets forth Professor Bloom's provocative theory of the literary relationships between the great writers and their predecessors. His most recent books include *Shakespeare: The Invention of the Human*, a 1998 National Book Award finalist, and *How to Read and Why*, which was published in 2000. In 1999, Professor Bloom received the prestigious American Academy of Arts and Letters Gold Medal for Criticism.

NANCY CHINN teaches in the English Department at Baylor University, Waco, Texas. She is the author of "'The Ring of Singing Metal on Wood': Zora Neale Hurston's Artistry in 'The Gilded Six-Bits'" (1996) and "Like Love 'A Moving Thing': Janie's Search for Self and God in *Their Eyes Were Watching God*" (1995).

SAMUEL COALE teaches in the English Department at Wheaton College, Norton, Massachusetts. He is the author of *The Mystery of Mysteries: Cultural Differences and Designs* (2000) and *Mesmerism and Hawthorne: Mediums of American Romance* (1998).

GAVIN COLOGNE-BROOKES is the author of "Disclosing the Closure: Endings in the Recent Novels of Joyce Carol Oates" (1995) and "Discord Toward Harmony: 'Set This House on Fire' and Peter's 'Part in the Matter'" (1987).

CAROLYN A. DURHAM teaches in the French Department at the College of Wooster, Wooster, Ohio. She is the author of *The Contexture of Feminism: Marie Cardinal and Multicultural Literacy* (1992) and *Double Takes: Culture and Gender in French Films and Their American Remakes* (1998).

WILLIAM HEATH, a Professor of English at Mount Saint Mary's College in Maryland, is the author of a prize-winning novel about the civil rights movement, *The Children Bob Moses Led* (Milkweed Editions, 1995) and a book of poems, *The Walking Man*.

ELISABETH HERION-SARAFIDIS teaches in the Department of English, Uppsala University, Uppsala, Sweden. She is an editor of *American Literary Scholarship*, a journal published by Duke University Press.

MICHAEL KREYLING teaches in the English Department at Vanderbilt University, Nashville, Tennessee. He is the author of *Inventing Southern Literature* (1998) and *Understanding Eudora Welty* (1999).

RICHARD G. LAW has taught in the Department of English, Washington State University, Pullman, Washington. He is the author of "Warren's World Enough and Time: 'Et in Arcadia Ego'" (1986) and "'Doom Is Always Domestic': Familial Betrayal in Brother to Dragons" (1983).

LARS OLE SAUERBERG teaches at Odense University. He is the author of *Versions of the Past—Visions of the Future: The Canonical in the Criticism of T. S. Eliot, F. R. Leavis, Northrop Frye and Harold Bloom* (1997).

RHODA SIRLIN is the author of "William Styron's Uncollected Essays: History Collides with Literature" (1998) and "William Styron's 'A Tidewater Morning': Disorder and Early Sorrow" (1995).

FREDERIK N. SMITH is the author of "Beckett and Berkeley: A Reconsideration" (1998) and "The Dangers of Reading Swift: The Double Binds of *Gulliver's Travels*" (1992).

JANET M. STANFORD is the author of "The Whisper of Violins in Styron's *Sophie's Choice*" (1992).

GIDEON TELPAZ is a contributor to *Partisan Review*. He is the author of *Israeli Childhood Stories of the Sixties*.

DAWN TROUARD teaches in the English Department at the University of Central Florida. She is the author of "Welty's Anti-Ode to Nightingales: Gabriella's Southern Passage" (1997) and "X Marks the Spot: Faulkner's Garden" (1997).

RALPH TUTT is the author of "Realism and Artifice in Jean Renoir's *The Southerner*"(1989) and "Seven Beauties and the Beast: Bettelheim, Wertmuller and the Uses of Enchantment" (1989).

Bibliography

Bakker, J. and D. R. M. Wilkinson, eds. From *Cooper to Philip Roth: Essays on American Literature* Presented to J. G. Riewald on the Occasion of his Seventieth Birthday. Amsterdam: Rodopi, 1980.

Bell, Pearl K. "Evil and William Styron" in *The Critical Response to William Styron*. Daniel W. Ross, editor. Westport, Connecticut: Greenwood (1995): 181–85.

Berger, Alan L. *Crisis and Covenant: The Holocaust in American Jewish Fiction*. Albany: State University of New York Press, 1985.

Bryer, Jackson R. and Mary Beth Hatem. *William Styron: A Reference Guide*. Boston: G.K. Hall, 1978.

Casciato, Arthur D. and James L. W. West III, eds. *Critical Essays on William Styron*. Boston: Hall, 1982.

Chametzky, Jules. "Styron's *Sophie's Choice*: Jews and Other Marginals." *Our Decentralized Literature: Cultural Mediations in Selected Jewish and Southern Writers*. Amherst: University of Massachusetts Press, 1986: 137–46.

Coale, Samuel Chase. *William Styron Revisited*. Boston: Twayne Publishers, 1991.

Cologne-Brookes, Gavin. *The Novels of William Styron: From Harmony to History*. Baton Rouge: Louisiana State University Press, 1994.

Colville, Georgiana M. M. "Killing the Dead Mother: Women in *Sophie's Choice*." *Delta* 23, 1986: 111–35.

Crane, John Kenny. *The Root of All Evil: The Thematic Unity of William Styron's Fiction*. Columbia: University of South Carolina Press, 1984.

Friedman, Melvin J. *William Styron*. Bowling Green, Ohio: Bowling Green University Popular Press, 1974.

Gardner, John. "A Novel of Evil" in *The Critical Response to William Styron*. Daniel W. Ross, editor. Westport, Connecticut: Greenwood (1995): 175–80.

Galloway, David D. "Holocaust as Metaphor: William Styron and *Sophie's Choice*. *Anglistik & Englischunterricht* (April 1981): 57–69.

Hadaller, David. *Women in the Novels of William Styron*. Madison, New Jersey: Fairleigh Dickinson University Press, 1995.

Insdorf, Annette. *Indelible Shadows: Film and the Holocaust*, 2nd ed. Cambridge, New York: Cambridge University Press, 1989.

Janssens, G. A. M. "Styron's Case and *Sophie's Choice.* Presented to J. G. Riewald on the Occasion of His 70th Birthday." From *Cooper to Philip Roth: Essays on American Literature.* Ed. J. Bakker and D. R. M. Wilkinson. Amsterdam: Rodopi (1980): 79–92.

Leon, Philip W. *William Styron: An Annotated Bibliography of Criticism.* Westport, Connecticut: Greenwood Press, 1978.

Morris, Robert K. and Irving Malin, eds. *The Achievement of William Styron,* rev. ed. Athens, Georgia: University of Georgia Press, 1981.

Nolan, Richard. "Psychological Themes in *Sophie's Choice.*" *Delta* 23 (1986): 91–110.

Ratner, Marc L. *William Styron.* New York: Twayne Publishers, 1972.

Rosenthal, Regine. "Defying Taboos: The Sense of Place in William Styron's *Sophie's Choice.*" *Dolphin* 20 (1991): 76–88.

Rubenstein, Richard L. "The South Encounters the Holocaust: William Styron's *Sophie's Choice.*" *Michigan Quarterly Review* 20 (Fall 1981): 425–42.

———. *The Cunning History: Mass Death and the American Future.* New York: Harper, 1975.

Ruderman, Judith. *William Styron.* New York: Ungar, 1987.

Schwarz, Daniel R. *Imagining the Holocaust.* New York: St. Martin's Press, 1999.

Seeskin, Kenneth. "Coming to Terms with Failure: A Philosopohical Dilemma." In *Writing and the Holocaust.* Ed. Berel Lang. New York: Holmes and Meier, 1988.

Shepherd, Allen. "The Psychopath as Moral Agent in William Styron's *Sophie's Choice.*" *Modern Fiction Studies* 28 (1982–83): 604–11.

Steiner, George. *Language and Silence: Essays on Language, Literature and the Inhuman.* New York: Atheneum, 1972.

Stern, Frederick C. "Styron's Choice." *South Atlantic Quarterly* 82 (Winter 1983): 19–27.

Vice, Sue. *Holocaust Fiction.* London; New York: Routledge, 2000.

West, James L. W., III, ed. *Conversations with William Styron.* Jackson: University Press of Mississippi, 1985.

Acknowledgments

"Games and Tragedy: Unidentified Quotations in William Styron's *Sophie's Choice*" by Nancy Chinn from *English Language Notes* vol. 33, no. 3 (March 1996): 51–61. Reprinted by permission.

"Styron's Disguises: A Provisional Rebel in Christian Masquerade" by Samuel Coale from *Critique: Studies in Modern Fiction* 26, no. 2 (Winter 1995): 57–66. Reprinted by permission.

"Dialogic Worlds: *Sophie's Choice*" by Gavin Cologne-Brookes from *The Novels of William Styron: From Harmony to History*. Baton Rouge: Louisiana State University Press, 1995: 156–201. Reprinted by permission.

"William Styron's *Sophie's Choice:* The Structure of Oppression" by Carolyn A. Durham from *Twentieth Century Literature* 30, no. 4 (1984): 448–64. Reprinted by permission.

"I, Stingo: The Problem of Egotism in *Sophie's Choice*" by William Heath from *Southern Review* 20, no. 3 (1984): 528–45. Reprinted by permission.

"*Sophie's Choice:* In the Realm of the Unspeakable" by Elisabeth Herion-Sarafidis from *A Mode of Melancholy: A Study of William Styron's Novels* (Doctoral Thesis, Uppsala University, 1995): 139–165. Reprinted by permission.

"Speakable and Unspeakable in Styron's *Sophie's Choice*" by Michael Kreyling from *Southern Review* 20, no. 3 (1984): 546–61. Reprinted by permission.

"The Reach of Fiction: Narrative Technique in Styron's *Sophie's Choice*" by Richard G. Law from *Southern Literary Journal* 23, no. 1 (1990): 45–64. Reprinted by permission.

"Fact-Flirting Fiction: Historiographical Potential or Involuntary Parody?" by Lars Ole Sauerberg from *European Journal of English Studies* 3, no. 2 (August 1999): 190–205. Reprinted by permission.

"*Sophie's Choice:* An American Voyage into the Mystery of Iniquity" by Rhoda Sirlin from *William Styron's* Sophie's Choice: *Crime and Self-Punishment.* Ann Arbor, Michigan: UMI Research Press, 1990: 55–96. Reprinted by permission.

"Bach *vs* Brooklyn's Clamorous Yawp: Sound in *Sophie's Choice*" by Frederik N. Smith from *Papers on Language and Literature* 23, no. 4 (Fall 1987): 523–30. Reprinted by permission.

"The Whisper of Violins in Styron's *Sophie's Choice*" by Janet M. Stanford from *The Southern Literary Journal* 25, no. 1 (Fall 1992): 106–117. Reprinted by permission.

"A Conversation with William Styron" by Gideon Telpaz from *Partisan Review* 52, no. 3 (1985): 252–63. Reprinted by permission.

"Styron's Historical Pre-Text: Nat Turner, Sophie, and the Beginnings of a Postmodern Career" by Dawn Trouard from *Papers on Language and Literature* 23, no. 4 (Fall 1987): 489–97. Reprinted by permission.

"Stingo's Complaint: Styron and the Politics of Self-Parody" by Ralph Tutt from *Modern Fiction Studies* 34, no. 4 (Winter 1988): 575–86. Reprinted by permission.

Index